Politics in

edited by
Rodney Smith
and Lex Watson

ALLEN & UNWIN
Sydney Wellington London Boston

First published in 1989
Fourth impression 1992
Allen & Unwin Australia Pty Ltd
8 Napier St. North Sydney, NSW 2059, Australia

National Library of Australia
Cataloguing-in-Publication entry:
Politics in Australia.

ISBN 0 04 364027 3.

I. Australia–Politics and government. I. Smith. Rodncy. II. Watson, Lex.

994.04

Library of Congress Catalog Card Number: 89-80238

Set in 10/11½pt Caledonia by Graphicraft Typesetters Ltd, Hong Kong
Printed by Chong Moh Offset Printing in Singapore

Contents

Tables

Figures

Acronyms

AAT	Administrative Appeals Tribunals Act
ABC	Australian Broadcasting Corporation
ABS	Australian Bureau of Statistics
ABT	Australian Broadcasting Tribunal
ACOA	Administrative and Clerical Officers' Association
ACP	Australian Consolidated Press
ACTU	Australian Council of Trade Unions
ADJR	Administrative Decisions (Judicial Review) Act
ADs	Australian Democrats
AGPS	Australian Government Publishing Service
ALP	Australian Labor Party
APSA	Australian Public Service Association
AWU	Australian Workers' Union
BCA	Business Council of Australia
CAI	Confederation of Australian Industry
CP	Country Party
CPI	Consumer Price Index
DLP	Democratic Labor Party
ExCo	Federal Executive Council
GDP	Gross Domestic Product
HWT	Herald & Weekly Times
IAC	Industries Assistance Commission
LPA	Liberal Party of Australia
NAL	New Administrative Law
NCP	National Country Party
NCSC	National Companies and Securities Commission
NDP	Nuclear Disarmament Party
NFF	National Farmers' Federation
NPA	National Party of Australia
PMC	Prime Minister and Cabinet
PND	People for Nuclear Disarmament
PR	Proportional Representation
PSA	Prices Surveillance Authority
RIA	Radioimmunoassay
RTLA	Right to Life Association

SBS	Special Broadcasting Service
SDA	Shop, Distributive and Allied Employees' Association
THC	Trades Hall Councils
TLC	Trades and Labour Councils
UAP	United Australia Party

Contributors

Ernie Chaples is a Senior Lecturer in the Department of Government, University of Sydney.
Christopher Hood is Professor of Political Science in the Department of Government, University of Sydney.
Michael Hogan is an Associate Professor in the Department of Government, University of Sydney.
Michael Jackson is an Associate Professor in the Department of Government, University of Sydney.
Martin Laffin is a Lecturer in the Department of Government, University of Sydney.
Trevor Matthews is an Associate Professor in the Department of Government, University of Sydney.
Helen Nelson is a Senior Lecturer in the Department of Government, University of Sydney.
Sue Outhwaite is a Tutor in the Department of Government, University of Sydney.
Barbara Page is a Lecturer in the Department of Government, University of Sydney.
Martin Painter is a Senior Lecturer in the Department of Government, University of Sydney.
John Ravenhill is an Associate Professor in the Department of Government, University of Sydney.
Marian Simms is a Senior Lecturer in the Department of Political Science, Australian National University.
Rodney Smith is a Lecturer in the School of Political Science, University of New South Wales.
Ken Turner is an Associate Professor in the Department of Government, University of Sydney.
Lex Watson is a Lecturer in the Department of Government, University of Sydney.
Karen Wilcox is a Tutor in the Department of Government, University of Sydney.

Introduction

Most debate about Australian politics—whether it takes place in pubs, universities, the media or Parliament—revolves around three themes, each of which can be expressed as a pair of questions. The first theme is power, and the pair of questions is 'Who exercises political power?' and 'Who *should* exercise political power?' The second theme is political values, and the pair of questions is 'Which values underpin the institutions and processes that make up the political system?' and 'Which values *should* underpin these institutions and processes?' The third theme is public policy, and the questions here are 'What factors shape public policy?' and 'What factors *should* shape public policy?'

People engaged in debate about these political questions often lack the factual, conceptual and analytical tools to resolve their debates satisfactorily or even to present their own position clearly and coherently. This book is an attempt to provide people with some of these tools. It focusses primarily on the first question in each of the pairs outlined above, in the belief that it is only through a better understanding of politics as it is that people can properly decide how it should be in the future. Clearly, there are some areas where Australia's political system falls short of its ideals. However, while several chapters in this book touch on these (see, for example, chapters 4, 5 and 15), any comprehensive attempt to deal with reforming the Australian political system falls outside the present book's scope.

This book has three inter-related parts. Part I lays out the theoretical groundwork for the rest of the book. It begins with a chapter that attempts to define the scope of politics, political behaviour and political institutions. Chapter 2 teases out some of the key issues involved in the deceptively simple question: Who has political power in Australia? Chapter 3 begins the book's discussion of the values underpinning Australian politics. Since Australian political institutions are most commonly summed up by academics and others as 'democratic', this chapter examines what democracy entails. Chapter 4 discusses competing general explanations of Australian public policy making.

In Part 2, the formal institutions of Australian politics are analysed using the questions raised in Part 1. Chapter 5 asks what patterns of power were established by the Australian constitution. To what extent are these relations democratic? What impact do they have on public policy? The other eight chapters in Part 2 focus on particular Australian political institutions. What power relations exist *within* institutions such as political parties (chapter 9), elections (chapter 10) and local government (chapter 13)? What power relations exist *between* political institutions like the states in the Australian federation (chapters 11 and 12), or the Parliament, Cabinet and the public service (chapters 6–8)? To what extent are these power relations democratic? How do they interact in the making of public policy?

Part 3 deals with broad socio-political forces and informal political institutions. These are as important to the understanding of power, political values and policy making in Australia as are formal institutions (for example, if the theorists arguing for the existence of a ruling class are correct, then democratic parliaments are largely a sham). Chapter 14 outlines some major contemporary western theories of social structure and—using Australian examples—discusses the difficulties of finding evidence for each of them. Chapter 15 examines theories of gender politics and relates these to the practice of gender politics in Australia. Chapters 16–18 canvass the role of interest groups in Australia, focussing on two interests—those of business and unions—whose power is sometimes seen as a threat to Australian democracy. Chapter 19 examines the power relations within the news media and the power of the news media vis-à-vis other political actors. Finally, chapter 20 looks at the role of the citizenry: how is the power that it exercises through participation and voting shaped by social forces such as class and gender?

Most of the people reading this book will be students formally engaged in introductory politics courses at tertiary level. This book is written primarily for this audience, by university teachers engaged in running introductory politics courses. Each chapter was specially commissioned for this book. All the authors wrote their chapters with the three themes in mind, in order to give the book much greater coherence than could be hoped for in an introductory reader containing chapters previously published elsewhere. Every attempt was made to incorporate recent developments in Australian politics. The twenty chapters were chosen to provide students with reading material about core issues and topics covered by almost all lecturers in introductory Australian politics courses. They were also designed to raise questions and problems around which tutorial discussions could be structured. To the extent that teachers of Australian politics can use the book in these ways, and students can deepen their political thought and debate by grasping the tools it offers, the book will have been successful.

Books cannot be produced without the help of many people. The editors and contributors would like to thank Lyn Fisher for indexing work, Lynne Thomson, Liz Kirby and Lyn Fisher for their research work, as well as Sandra Donnelly, Sonja Waikawa, Maria Robertson and Shareen Matthews for putting parts of the manuscript on to word processor disks.

Part One

THEORIES

1 The nature of politics

Christopher Hood

What does the word 'politics' convey to your mind? Do you think of politics narrowly, as a particular set of specialised organisations remote from the everyday experience of most of us—parties, parliaments, government? Or do you think of it broadly, as a type of behaviour running through all social life, including relationships in families, sport teams, religious orders, etc? Do you have a 'high' vision of politics as a method of solving social problems and arriving at common decisions in a way that reflects the wishes of the people? Or do you have a 'low' vision of politics as a trivial, vain, hypocritical, talk-centred world, involving back-stabbing, power-struggles, the unprincipled in pursuit of the impracticable?

Each of these visions gives us a perspective on politics, because the word has a great many shades of meaning in the English language. To open up some of these dimensions I will here explore politics as: a special type of *situation* involving jointness, choice and conflict; a special type of *behaviour* involving strategy, power and uncertainty; and a specialised set of *institutions*.

Political situations: jointness, choice and conflict

When you are in a situation in which

- some issue(s) affect you *jointly* with one or more other people; or
- there is more than one possible way of handling the issue(s); or
- there is some underlying *conflict*—in terms of interests, beliefs, opinions—over the way the issue(s) should be handled,

you are in a *political* situation (see, for example, Miller, 1965: 14–23).

You have had a strangely sheltered background if you have never found yourself in such a situation. Real-life examples are easy to give. But I will start instead with two semi-fictional examples. The first is a parable of primordial politics: two farmers, A and B, in an arid area draw water from the same groundwater basin. Each farmer can increase his or her income by pumping out more water. But the capacity of the basin is limited, so that it will run dry if more than a fixed amount of water is taken out. How do they decide how much each can pump?

The second is a parable of modern high-tech politics. A community of 1 800 000 people is divided over the issue of whether or not medical treatment and research by RIA (radioimmunoassay) should be continued in the area. RIA is commonly used for the detection and treatment of diabetes, thyroid and heart disease. It can, for example, be used to detect underactive thyroid glands in newborn babies, a condition that causes irreversable mental retardation unless treated shortly after birth. But RIA also increases the exposure of the population at large to low doses of radiation. There is good evidence that chronic exposure to moderate doses of radiation can result in cancer and early death, but there is no conclusive evidence on exactly what is the danger level. For example, experiments conducted in parts of the world where the natural level of radiation is well above average have concluded that there is no clear evidence that exposure to radiation levels at three or even ten times the average background level affects aggregate health adversely (see Douglas, 1987: 2–4). But such evidence does not convince the sceptics. How does such a community decide what to do about RIA treatment and research?

You will, I hope, agree that both of these cases involve rather serious matters. Water is fundamental to human life, as no Australian needs to be reminded. The RIA issue is also a matter of life and death—more precisely, a matter of *who* lives and who dies. Both of the cases are political situations in that they contain the basic ingredients of jointness, choice and conflict.

The water case illustrates a fundamental problem in politics, the paradox of cooperation (see Brams, 1976: 79ff). Both A and B would be better off if they cooperate in limiting water consumption than if there is no cooperation. But either would be *even* better off (in the short term, at least) if he or she cheats or 'holds out' on the other one, increasing water consumption while the other acts cooperatively in limiting consumption. You can see that a tragic dynamic can easily occur in a situation like this. If both A and B *individually* try to get into the 'best off' position for themselves, by acting uncooperatively in the hope that the other person will act cooperatively, their *collective* behaviour will drive them *both* towards the worst possible outcome—another dry hole in the desert.

The cooperation problem is both fundamental and pervasive in Australia. For example, it is central to the physical management of the country, with its fragile, easily-degraded environment. Problems of soil erosion, water and air pollution, lowering of groundwater levels in artesian basins, degradation of grasslands by scrub, are larger-scale versions of the sort of problems faced by A and B in this simple example. The unintended collective result of activities by individuals each trying to improve his or her personal position can, paradoxically, result in everyone being worse off in the longer term.

This cooperation problem can occur at all levels of social aggregation, from the small-group level to the level of international action. Where only two persons or organisations are involved in such a case, it is often referred to as a 'Prisoner's dilemma', after a well-known example used to illustrate the structure of such situations (see Rapoport and Chammah, 1965). A case with the same basic logic, but involving more than two persons or organisations, is

Table 1.1 Ordering of preferences on a hypothetical political issue

	Group intensity of feelings	Order of preference
A	Strong	1 keep RIA treatment and research 2 keep RIA treatment but ban further research 3 ban RIA treatment but keep research 4 ban RIA treatment and research
B	Weak	1 keep RIA treatment but ban further research 2 ban RIA treatment and research 3 keep RIA treatment and research 4 ban RIA treatment but keep research
C	Weak	1 ban RIA treatment but keep research 2 ban RIA treatment and research 3 keep RIA treatment and research 4 keep RIA treatment but ban research

often referred to as a 'tragedy of the commons' problem, after an example used by Hardin (1968).

The RIA case is more complex. Since both research and treatment are in question, there is more than one issue at stake, and the number of people affected is almost a million times bigger than in the water case. Arriving at a collective view may be difficult, even if no one tries to cheat or hold out, because of the varied patterns of preference that can arise in such a case. For example, suppose that the 1 800 000 people divide on the two issues (ban or keep research, ban or keep treatment) into three different groups, A, B, and C. Suppose that each group consists of 600 000 people and has a clear ordering of preferences on the issues at stake. Suppose further that each group's order of preferences is as illustrated in Table 1.1.

Consider this ordering of preferences for a moment. Is there some way of arriving at a collective view of the group in a situation like this? Is there a majority view? Should the majority view be followed, even if there was one?

If all political situations share the ingredients of jointness, choice and conflict, they can vary widely in other ways, as these two examples demonstrate. The size of the affected group is important, because ways of handling political situations in small groups are often not applicable to large groups. The number of issues at stake is important, because the outcome may depend on the way that the issues are grouped together, as we will see later. The distribution and intensity of feelings is important: outcomes often depend on this. For example, in the RIA case above, the distribution of preferences is such that a majority (groups B and C) weakly prefers the banning of RIA treatment and research to keeping RIA treatment and research, but a minority (group A) has a strong preference for keeping RIA treatment and research over banning RIA treatment and research. Intense minorities pose a pervasive and classic problem in politics, because the application of majority-rule decision procedures in such situations always causes friction and sometimes leads to violence.

More generally, the nature of the conflict is important, because it affects the scope for manoeuvre in the situation. Some political situations are such that whatever one person or group wins can only be gained at the expense of a corresponding loss by another person or group (this is known as a 'zero-sum' situation in game theory). In the RIA case, benefits from RIA treatment for those currently sick have to be at the expense of (possibly) reduced risks from exposure to lower radiation levels for those who are currently healthy, and vice-versa. But not all political situations are like this: in the water case, as we have seen, both A and B would be better off if both cooperate than if neither cooperates. Some political situations have the possibility of offering something for everyone, or a mixture of good and bad for all of the key players in the game—for example, if the situation lends itself to package deals or other compensatory arrangements.

Political behaviour: strategy, power, uncertainty

When you approach a collective-choice situation

- by acting *strategically*: that is, your behaviour relates to and depends on the moves made by others;
- by trying to bring *power* and *influence* to bear on the outcome;
- by a mixture of *cooperation and conflict* with others; or
- by argument over matters that are *uncertain or disputed*,

you are acting *politically*.

Again, you have had an oddly sheltered background if you have not encountered and practised behaviour of this kind since your early childhood. When we speak of 'a good political move' or of 'playing politics', it is behaviour of this kind that we are referring to.

Aspects of political behaviour

Strategic action (action which is contingent on the moves of others) is fundamental to political behaviour. Perhaps that is why politics is so often likened to a game (Brams, 1975). Strategic action includes using information selectively: that is, deciding on what information to give or receive, to and from whom, when, in what order. To put over a message politically is to find the available means of persuasion appropriate to a particular audience; to adapt 'the facts' by emphasising or stressing some pieces of information while holding back others; to respond effectively to what others have said or may say (see Aristotle's [1932] classic treatise on political rhetoric).

Strategic action also includes having preferences that are complementary: that is, having preferences on one issue that depend on what is happening, or is expected to happen, in relation to other issues. This is a very distinctive aspect of political behaviour (Black, 1958: 125). In the RIA case, for example, your preference on what happens to RIA research would probably depend on what happens to RIA treatment, and perhaps to other nuclear-related issues too.

Packaging issues, that is, attempting to link some issues together, and dividing others into separate parts, is also strategic action. When we speak of 'making a political issue out of...' something, it is usually issue-packaging behaviour that we are referring to. Issue packaging can be very important for outcomes. For example, if the two issues at stake in the RIA case (treatment and research) are voted on together, the outcome will be quite different from what it would be if the two issues were taken separately. If you look back at the order of preferences of the three groups in this case, you will see that a majority vote would result in the combination of banning RIA research and banning RIA treatment defeating the combination of retaining RIA treatment and research. But if the two issues were voted on *separately*, a majority vote would result in just the *opposite* outcome (cf. Brams 1976: 30–1). That is, keeping RIA treatment would defeat banning RIA treatment, and keeping RIA research would defeat banning RIA research. In other words, what counts as the majority view and what as the minority one depends in this case on how the issues are packaged.

The use of *power* and *influence* is also fundamental to political behaviour. Political behaviour is about the use of power, to which the next chapter in this book is devoted. Suffice it to say here that power in politics is to people what electrical or mechanical power is to objects: something that enables its possessor(s) to maintain or change relationships that would otherwise change or stay the same. Often, to exert power in politics is to employ the property of servomechanisms in engineering—that is, the ability to intervene in a pent-up balance of forces in such a way that a small change at a critical point can bring about a larger change at another point. Central to power is leadership and followership (cf. Bailey, 1969), and access to the resources that count in social influence, notably sanctions, rewards, the ability to shape opinion and define the agenda. Political power is not always easily visible. Often the most effective kind of power is that which is invisible.

Mixing *cooperation and conflict* is also fundamental to political behaviour (cf. Laver, 1983: 5). Conflict, as noted earlier, is inherent in political situations, even if it is not always visible or consciously felt. Political behaviour is essentially about the generation and management of conflict—including war and its diminutives. But politics is also about co-operation: about forming coalitions, about thinking alike and sharing visions of the world, about papering over cracks and smoothing differences, about persuasion, negotiation and bargaining. A world in which no one ever cooperated would give no more scope for what is here conceived as political behaviour than a world in which no conflict ever existed.

A fourth feature of political behaviour is that it relates to matters that are *uncertain or disputed* (de Jouvenel, 1963). Sometimes those disputes concern basic values; just as commonly, the dispute and uncertainty concerns the likelihood of some future event(s) occurring or the relationship between cause and effect. For example, in the water example given above, the exact capacity of the groundwater basin is not likely to be known with certainty. In the RIA case, we can expect dispute both over the facts (what precisely is the effect of RIA on the health of the population at large?) and over the values according to which the matter should be decided, even if the facts are fully known and agreed upon (what is an acceptable level of risk, how conservative should we be, how do we weigh the lives of newborn babies against the lives of healthy adults, etc?). Political behaviour begins where certainty and unambiguous scientific proof leaves off, or where such proof as there is arouses distrust, as in the RIA case. Political argument differs from scientific proof in that it is essentially conducted by a cumulation of persuasive examples and analogies, not by long chains of syllogistic reasoning (Aristotle, 1932) or laboratory experiments.

Political behaviour in this sense is not generally regarded with much reverence and respect. Commonly, the word 'politics' is used: with rather negative connotations: unprincipled craftiness, dishonesty, low cunning, mudslinging, bickering, petty point-scoring, the exploitation of social problems for the pursuit of individual power or narrowly partisan ends, rather than facing up to those problems squarely (Dunsire, 1984: 85–6). We tend to use the term politics for what other people do rather than what we do ourselves. The rather sleazy image of politics is reflected in the frequent comparison between politics and dealing in used cars, and in political jokes (for example, 'How do you know when politicians are lying? When their lips are moving . . .' etc.). (See Larsen, 1980.)

Political behaviour may have its unattractive side. But some or other form of it is simply unavoidable, for at least two reasons. First, the only other way to resolve political situations as defined above is by the use of force. 'Politicking' may be bad, but the alternative is usually worse. Second, most areas of social management cannot be reduced to genuinely technical decision-making because, as in the RIA case, the contingencies are not fully known and the cause-effect relationships are uncertain, even if the community in question were completely agreed on its basic values. In fact, simply deprecating the existence of politics is not likely to be of much value, except for rhetorical purposes. You need to understand and demystify it. That is what political science—the academic study of politics—tries to do.

Emergent properties of political behaviour

Political behaviour sometimes puzzles the outside observer because it often appears to lead to bizarre outcomes and because the decisions of political bodies frequently seem impossible to square with what we might expect a sane and rational individual to decide. What we are observing in such cases are *emergent* properties of political behaviour—that is, results that nobody intended, or characteristics of a group that do not belong to any one of its individual members.

Both of the cases described earlier are examples of this. In the water case, both A and B may end up worse off as a result of actions intended to make themselves better off. In the RIA case, each of the 1 800 000 people has a

Table 1.2 Voting on hypothetical political issue

	Group A	Group B	Group C	
Motion				Result
1	yes	no	yes	carried
2	no	yes	yes	carried
3	yes	yes	no	carried

clear, stable and consistent set of preferences, but the same does not necessarily go for the group. Suppose, for instance, that the community tries to settle the RIA issue by voting. Say it is agreed that all the possible courses of action will be carefully voted on in pairs, in order to find exactly how the group ranks the various options. What would then emerge in this case is what is known as the paradox of voting, probably the most famous paradox in political science (see Black, 1958: 46–51 and 214–34). The group as a whole turns out to have no clear or stable set of preferences. If each possible course of action is taken as a motion and the motions are taken in pairs, there is no motion that can defeat all the other motions once and for all.

Consider the following three motions:

- Motion 1: prefer banning RIA treatment but keeping research to banning both treatment and research;
- Motion 2: prefer banning both treatment and research to keeping treatment and research;
- Motion 3: prefer keeping treatment and research to banning treatment but keeping research.

Given the distribution of preferences that was described earlier, voting on these three motions would go as indicated in Table 1.2.

What would happen in this case, as you can see, is that the order of preferences established by motion 3 would conflict with the order of preferences with which the community starts in passing motion 1. In effect, the community would decide that it preferred x to y, then that it preferred y to z, and then that it preferred z to x.

What this case shows is that puzzling things can happen when we try to translate the preferences of a set of individuals into a group preference. In politics, groups have properties that individuals do not have. Groups can agree on means while being deeply divided about goals. It can be impossible to arrive at a clear 'group preference', even when every single individual in the group has a clear order of preferences. This is what happens in our RIA example. The larger the group and the greater the number of possible options or motions, the more likely this is to happen. In other words, political processes may lead to group decisions that have qualities that would be considered completely 'irrational' in an individual—i.e. apparent arbitrariness and inconsistency and a lack of congruence between means and ends.

Political institutions

So far, politics has been discussed without bringing institutions into the centre of the stage. This is quite unrealistic. Almost all politics takes place within institutional settings.

Institutions are sets of conventions, rules, formal classifications, ceremonies, traditions and habits, organisation and formal authority. Marriage is an institution; the law is an institution; universities are institutions.

When you are in an institution

- that specialises in arriving at or influencing decisions on political situations;
- that mainly operates as a forum for political behaviour; or
- that operates mainly through some means of making decisions other than by violence or by spontaneous coordination,

you are in a *political* institution.

All institutions in society are political institutions in so far as they relate to political situations and contain political behaviour, because there is a political dimension running through all social life. We can talk of the family, the school, the office as political institutions in that sense. But the term 'political institutions' is usually applied to institutions that specialise in dealing with political situations through political behaviour. This is the sense in which people speak of 'going in to politics' or 'a week is a long time in politics'.

Any institutional structure can be described as a set of prevailing assumptions or patterns of thought and a set of decision rules. Elinor Ostrom (in Kaumann, Majone and Ostrom, 1986: 468–70) has identified six basic kinds of rule as the 'DNA' of any political institution:

- *boundary rules*—rules that determine who is eligible to participate in the decision, or to be formally recognised as players in the game. For example, in the RIA case, should the decision be taken by health professionals only, or by the wider community?
- *position rules*—rules that determine what the different kinds of players are, and the circumstances in which they hold their positions. For example, in the RIA case, should the sick minority be recognised as having some special interests as against the healthy majority?
- *scope rules*—rules that lay out the scope of the action that each type of player can take. For instance, the scope of law courts to decide the water case will depend on how the law conceives property rights in water (for example, whether the law takes historical patterns of use as the key to property rights in water, or whether it takes 'reasonable use' without regard to historical patterns).

- *authority and procedural rules*—rules that determine what procedures are to be followed in making decisions. For instance, the outcome of majority voting on the RIA case would differ according to whether the community used the normal committee procedure as a decision rule (i.e., that a motion disappears once it has been defeated) or the alternative rule that a motion must not only defeat the status quo, but also all other motions being proposed in order to change that status quo.
- *information rules*—rules that determine who is entitled to what kind of information and when. For example, the outcome in the RIA case might be different if voting was by an open show of hands than if it were conducted by secret ballot.
- *aggregation rules*—rules that determine how the decisions of each player are to be aggregated into a single decision. For example, in the RIA case, should a simple majority be sufficient to ban RIA research and treatment—or does that stack the odds too heavily in favour of the healthy majority and against the sick minority, meaning that unanimity or some special majority should be used to decide the question?

Formal rules are important. They help to determine who gets what. For example, in the RIA case, the cyclical nature of the 'majority' view means that on majority voting the winning motion will simply be whatever motion is taken last, however preposterous that might seem to be for a supposedly democratic decision making procedure (see Black, 1958: 217). That means that the rules about the order in which motions are taken are all-important to the outcome. So are the rules that determine whether the two issues at stake (research and treatment) are to be taken separately or together, since as we saw earlier, the outcome on a majority vote will depend on whether the two issues are taken separately or together.

Rules are also important because they are *artificial*. They are designed. They can be changed. They are levers of social management. This does not apply to the social nature of the community, which is usually fixed (or changing only fairly slowly), and it often does not apply to the nature of the decision situation. That is why argument about the rules of the game is a central part of politics, and why the analysis of institutions will always be central to the study of politics.

Government

The most important specialised political institution is government. Government is that unit in society that has the ultimate legal right to forbid, permit, require and punish (known collectively as 'the public power' in Roman law). The distinctive characteristic of government is its capacity to make and enforce law. The politics of government is ultimately about the use of force. By no means all political situations or political behaviour involve government —in particular, international politics is distinctive in that there is no overall 'government'. However, most government activity involves politics, because the use of the public power by definition creates a political situation in the sense described earlier.

Government's public power—its powers to compel, forbid, punish and permit—is very special. Not everyone can wield it; and those who do wield it have a large measure of power over the rest of us. What if they use those powers to tyrannise over others, to vote themselves ever-larger salaries and perquisites, to appoint their toadies to high office? Such cases are hardly unknown, and they are not confined to a few of the more notorious Latin American police chiefs.

When we start to argue about who should wield the public power, subject to what restraints, we are discussing a special kind of politics, namely *constitutional* politics. Constitutional politics is about the rules that lay down who can exercise what powers in government, through what procedures, subject to what limits. A constitution is a set of rules concerning the ordering of the offices of authority, following Aristotle's (1962: 154) classic definition. Constitutional rules are important. About half of those who have died in war over the past 150 years or so have died in civil wars—wars concerning who should rule, or under what set of rules.

Any set of constitutional rules embodies a basic choice between risk, deadlock and inconvenience. If you are one of those sceptical people who believe that those in authority will abuse their powers if they get half a chance, you will want a constitutional rule structure which minimises this risk. You could avoid the risk altogether if you required unanimous approval before public power could be wielded. Less drastically, you could reduce the risk by dividing the public power among institutions set up in such a way that it is unlikely that all of them will always be controlled by the same group. But such 'failsafe' rules for protecting citizens against the abuse of power carry a certain price. That is, the more that you require a broad basis of consent before government's powers are used, the greater is the likelihood of deadlock, of paralysis or delay in the face of pressing problems, of widely approved action hampered by a few hold-outs, or of heavy and inconvenient demands for constant participation by the public at large (see Buchanan and Tullock, 1962). Accordingly, conflicts in constitutional politics often turn on different assessments of the likelihood of 'worst-case' risk of abuse of power, as against paralysis. Certainly, this is a strong underlying theme in Australian constitutional politics, given that the Australian institutional structure contains a variety of procedural rules requiring that political action be grounded in a broad basis of consent—for example, the constitutional prescription of a short term between federal elections and a strong upper chamber of Parliament, and the statutory adoption of compulsory voting and the alternative vote system.

Summary and conclusion

Politics in these senses is both a phenomenon and a field of study. The academic study of politics—usually termed political science—is to some degree distinct from the practice of politics, although the two things intersect. When you try to generalise about political situations, behaviour or institutions systematically, you are doing political science. It is the systematic study of cases that separates academic analysis of politics from ordinary or everyday talk about politics.

References

Aristotle (1932) *Rhetoric* New York: Appleton-Century
—— (1962) *Politics* Harmondsworth: Penguin
Bailey, F.G. (1969) *Stratagems and Spoils* Oxford: Basil Blackwell
Black, D. (1958) *The Theory of Committees and Elections* London: Cambridge University Press
Brams, S.J. (1975) *Game Theory and Politics* New York: Free Press
—— (1976) *Paradoxes in Politics* New York: Free Press
Buchanan, J.M. and Tullock, G. (1962) *The Calculus of Consent* Ann Arbor: University of Michigan Press
Douglas, M. (1987) *How Institutions Think* London: Routledge and Kegan Paul
Dunsire, A. (1984) 'The Levels of Politics' Ch 5, in A. Leftwich and A. Callinicos (eds) *What is Politics?* Oxford: Blackwell, pp. 85–105
Hardin, G. (1968) 'The Tragedy of the Commons' *Science* 162 December, pp. 1243–9
de Jouvenel, B. (1963) *The Pure Theory of Politics* Cambridge: Cambridge University Press
Kaufmann, G. Majone, V. Ostrom (eds) *Guidance Control and Evaluation in the Public Sector* Berlin: de Gruyter, pp. 458–75
Laver, M. (1983) *Invitation to Politics* Oxford: Martin Robertson
Larsen, E. (1980) *Wit as a Weapon: The Political Joke in History* London: Frederick Muller
Miller, J.D.B. (1965) *The Nature of Politics* Harmondsworth: Penguin
Mueller, D. (1979) *Public Choice* London: Cambridge University Press
Ostrom, E. (1986) 'A Method of Institutional Analysis', Ch. 22 in F–X
Rapoport, A. and Chammah, A.M. (1965) *Prisoner's Dilemma: A Study in Conflict and Co-operation* Ann Arbor: University of Michigan Press

2 Power

Rodney Smith

Power relationships pervade society. In coming to read this chapter, you almost certainly had power exercised over you, and yourself exercised power over others. You probably would not be reading these words unless your lecturer had instructed you to do so. In order to read them, you possibly had to ask your sister to wash up instead of you, or to tell your friends to go home, or to get your children to turn down the television. The common element in these examples is that they involve relationships in which some people get others to act in a certain way. As a first approximation, then, power can be defined as the American political scientist Robert Dahl has done: 'A exercises power over B to the extent that he (or she) changes B's actions or predispositions in some way' (1976: 29).

If you keep this definition—sometimes called the one-dimensional view of power (Lukes, 1974: 11–15)—in mind, and think back over the things you have done in the past few days, you will see that many of your day to day activities involve power.

Several points are worth making here. First, Dahl defines power in terms of changing someone's actions or dispositions, but this definition could be usefully extended to include instances in which someone deliberately *prevents* an individual's actions or dispositions from changing. Consider, as an example, a government wishing to pull down a historic building. The government knows that if it announces its decision to do this, conservationists will embark on a series of disruptive protests. So it keeps the decision a secret, and in the dead of night, while the conservationists snore on, the building is demolished. The government has exercised power, not by changing the conservationists' immediate actions (sleeping), but by ensuring that those immediate actions do not change. Power exercised in this way to exclude certain views or people from a decision-making process is sometimes called the second dimension of power (Lukes, 1974: 16–20).

Second, the relationships described above as power relationships are often described in other ways. When people think about relationships within their families, they probably think of them in terms of love, or caring, or getting jobs done. This is perfectly valid, but it is equally valid to think about these relationships as power relationships. To do the latter is simply to take a different perspective—the perspective of the political scientist.

Third, power may be exercised in mundane environments such as families, or in very significant ones such as the Prime Minister's office. Political scientists generally concentrate their attention on the more significant power relationships in a society. Nonetheless, a Prime Minister ordering the government to pursue a policy and a mother sending her daughter to bed early are both doing the same thing—exercising power.

Fourth, power as it is defined above describes relationships between people; for example, between a parent and child, or a Prime Minister and his or her ministers. Power of this sort does not exist outside relationships between people. When students of politics write about the power of Bob Hawke, they have in mind the Prime Minister's power *over* other people. Power is not something like money or property that people can possess. It is a relationship, which only exists in interactions between people. If Bob Hawke were the sole undiscovered survivor of a plane crash on a desert island, he might be able to retrieve food, clothes and other property from the wrecked plane, but there is no way that he could retrieve his power. To describe someone as 'powerful' is to summarise their relationships with other people.

Fifth, power is not intrinsically bad or good. The exercise of power may result from good or bad motives, and it may result in good or bad consequences, but power itself is morally neutral. Although powerful people are often seen as real–life versions of Darth Vader, the power they wield can be used for good or bad purposes. Whatever you value in Australian society, you can be sure that it exists because some people got other people to change their actions in order to create and maintain it.

A sixth point is that not all power is the same. A parent getting a child to turn the television down by persuading her to do so and a parent threatening to hit the child if she does not do so have both exercised power, but it is power of a quite different sort. Similarly, a government that gets people to pay extra taxes because the people elected the government to spend more money on health programmes exercises quite different power from a government that raises revenue by sending out soldiers to forcibly confiscate citizens' money and property.

Quite ancient disputes exist about how to characterise different types of power. Almost everyone writing about power has a different list of types of power and different names for the types of power on the list. With this in mind, the following list of types of power should be treated as introductory and somewhat arbitrary.

Authority—Authority is a form of power in which one political actor obeys another without question. Political actor A expresses a wish, instruction or command, and political actor B acts in accord with it without need for further stimulus, because B accepts A's right to command him or her. Wrong (1979: 35) writes: 'In authority, it is not the content of a communication but its *source*, that is, the perceived status, resources or personal attributes of the communicator, which induces compliance.'

Coercion—This refers to power in which a political actor secures change in another's actions or dispositions by threatening that other actor with force. This may be force against the individual ('Either you come quietly or we'll beat you up') or against persons or things valued by the individual ('Come quietly or we'll hurt your children, shoot your dog, and burn down your house'). Coercion is not the same as force, although the two are closely linked. Coercion is the threat of force, not the exercise of force. People submit to coercion to avoid the use of force against them.

Force—Force is direct physical intervention to change a political actor's actions or dispositions. In its most extreme form, force means eliminating actors altogether, a practice found in assassinations, wars, and genocide. In a less extreme form, force involves direct physical manipulation of individuals, such as occurs when police remove demonstrators from the steps of Parliament House.

Inducement—Inducement occurs when one political actor gets another to change his or her actions or dispositions by offering a reward. This reward may be material (for example, money), status oriented (a knighthood), or even spiritual (a passage to heaven).

Persuasion—This form of power exists when a political actor changes another's actions or dispositions solely by communicating the virtues of, or reasons for, such a change. The first actor convinces the second to change by appealing to the second actor's intellect or emotions. Thus, for example, someone may convince a friend who normally supports Labor to vote for the Australian Democrats in an election, by arguing that the ALP had sold out on its policies and thus no longer deserved support.

Manipulation—Manipulation is any exercise of power in which a political actor conceals his or her intentions or identity from the individual whose actions or dispositions are changed. Consider, as an example, a spy who befriends a government official in order to gain access to secret information.

In situations where power is exercised, it is often difficult to work out exactly what form of power is involved. If a voter decides to vote Liberal following a speech by John Howard, has she changed her disposition because she was persuaded by Howard's arguments, or because she was induced by Howard's promise of tax cuts? Forms of political power are rarely found in their pure types, and students of politics have to exercise careful judgement in deciding which types are present in specific political situations.

A temptation that sometimes befalls students of politics is to ascribe to these different types of power positive or negative moral overtones. Force, coercion, manipulation and sometimes inducement are seen as bad; persuasion and authority are seen as good. The problem with these moral overtones is that they cannot be applied consistently. In some circumstances, force may be bad; in others—such as the apprehension of violent criminals—it may be very good. Likewise, someone may persuade another to commit bad as well as good acts.

The main feature distinguishing types of power is not morality at all. Rather, each is distinguished by the reason for which one political actor responds to another in the exercise of power. In inducement, it is for reward; in coercion, it is to avoid force; in persuasion, it is by conviction; in authority, the status of the power wielder; in force, through lack of choice; and in manipulation, through unwitting cooperation.

Each of these responses depends on the would be power wielder possessing appropriate 'power resources'. Thus the police can only exercise coercive power if they are physically fit and possess batons, handcuffs and guns. A Prime Minister can only persuade electors if he or she has a good research staff and speechwriter, and possesses oratorical skills. Power resources can be defined as individual or collective assets necessary to provide their controllers with the potential to exercise power (see Wrong, 1979: 124–126). A list of such assets in contemporary political systems would include resources of economics, status, knowledge, solidarity and physical coercion.

Economic resources—Attempting to exercise power almost always requires economic resources. Parties need money to pay organisers; pressure groups need money to publicise their causes; it even costs a few cents to post a letter to a parliamentarian. At a more basic level, control of substantial amounts of capital or labour brings with it the potential for significant power. When mining companies threatened to reduce gold mining in Australia because of a gold tax proposed by the Hawke Government in 1986, the government abandoned the tax. Similarly, when the Miners' Federation threatened a long strike to stop New South Wales coal miners being sacked in 1987, the government stepped in and subsidised the mines to postpone the sackings. According to Marxist theorists, economic resources are fundamental in explaining the patterns of power in a society (see chapter 14).

Status resources—Status resources derive from the fact that all societies are divided according to social rank. The bases for these divisions are culturally determined, depending on which qualities are valued by the people within a society. Race, religion, gender, intellect, accent, caste, sporting ability, beauty, noble birth, occupation, mastery of certain arts and wealth are some attributes which, singly or in combination, determine a person's status. These attributes may be used to exercise power over others. Australian anti-nuclear groups, for example, have used rock singer Peter Garrett to promote their cause, because they believe that he has the status to change a number of young people's actions and dispositions.

Knowledge resources—Control over knowledge forms a basis for power in a number of ways. Those with information about what actions have or have not worked in the past, or about current factors that need to be taken into consideration, can suggest plausible courses of action for the future. This is the basis for much public service power (see chapter 8). Information about how the political system works is essential for citizens who want to change or affect government decisions. This is the basis for the power of professional political lobbyists.

Control of the dissemination of information can cause people to change their actions or dispositions, as the power of the media indicates (ee chapter 19). Possession of information about another individual's past behaviour may give its possessor power over that individual. Examples of this can be found in the forced resignations of Australian Cabinet ministers who are found to have misused their ministerial positions (see chapter 7).

Solidarity resources—Solidarity exists whenever two or more individuals identify characteristics, goals, enemies, sympathies or interests that unite them. Solidarity enables individuals to combine their other power resources to achieve goals they could not have achieved on their own. Trade union power, as the very name 'union' suggests, is ultimately based on the solidarity of workers. Unless all the relevant workers refuse to work during a strike, the strike will fail. Similarly, while one vote is not a powerful political resource, the combined vote of several hundred thousand people who recognise that they have common interests is, as the continued existence of Australia's rural party—the National Party—indicates.

Physical coercion resources—These include physical strength and weapons or other instruments with the capacity to '. . . damage a person or to damage what (s)he values' (Sederberg, 1977: 39). Chinese leader Mao Tse-tung once said, 'Political power grows out of the barrel of a gun'. If this is true, the coercive basis of power remains largely hidden in Australian society. It emerges in the politics of some families, where husbands use their physical strength to exercise power over their wives and children. Physical coercion resources are also sometimes used by individuals wanting to exercise power in local branches of the Australian Labor Party (ALP). Nonetheless, coercion is used openly and routinely as a power resource only by government agencies such as the police. Even for governments, physical coercion is the resource of the last resort, used only when all other resources have failed.

This is only a partial list of power resources, which could easily be extended (see Dahl, 1961: 223–67). Rather than do this, it might be more appropriate to develop some propositions about power resources and power.

First, while power resources help to explain why one political actor exercises power over another, this does not mean that the other actor had no power resources to draw upon. *All actors have some resources.* When Bob Hawke forced Bill Hayden to resign the federal parliamentary leadership of the ALP on 3 February 1983, Hawke did so because he held a number of power resources: his personal attractiveness and immense popular support; his experience as ACTU President and ALP President; his self-confidence; his record as a negotiator; his communication skills; and the support of the right-wing and some of the centre-left faction of the ALP. But Hayden also had resources: his wide parliamentary and frontbench experience; his knowledge of the ALP Caucus; his proven economic ability; and the support of the Party's left-wing and part of the centre-left (Kelly, 1984). All actors have at least some power resources. The ease with which power is exercised is in part a measure of the size of the disparity between the power resources of the actors involved.

Second, while some power resources such as intelligence and physical strength are properties of *individuals*, others such as solidarity are irreducibly collective resources; that is, they are properties of *groups* (Wrong, 1979: 130–42). These collective resources can only be used by individuals to the extent that the group that possesses them allows individuals to use them. Thus Bill Hayden's power within the parliamentary ALP weakened from December 1982 with the crumbling of his centre-left support, and the centre-left's growing solidarity behind Bob Hawke (Kelly, 1984: 335–47, 373–75).

Third, all power resources are more or less *socially defined*. In the case of some resources—for example, social status—this point is fairly obvious.

It may be less obvious in the case of 'individual' qualities such as speaking ability, strength or intelligence; however, even these resources are defined by the social context of the actor attempting to use them. Bob Hawke was able to exercise power in the ACTU partly because his oratory was superior to that of other union officials. In the different context of Parliament, Hawke's oratorical skills were no better than those of many of his fellows, and therefore became a much weaker power resource (Kelly, 1984: 148, 149).

Fourth, power resources gain or lose effectiveness depending on the *aims and outlook* of the organisation or group within which an attempt to exercise power is made. While Bob Hawke had a number of power resources at his disposal in his ALP leadership challenge, he relied primarily on his electoral appeal. Kelly (1984: 212, 213) writes:

> Hawke himself brought clarity to the choice [of ALP leader] when he said that what he offered Labor was popularity. He never actually campaigned for the leadership on grounds of superior judgement, policy grasp, parliamentary ability. That is, he never campaigned as a better Prime Minister. Hawke's appeal was totally pragmatic: he promised to be a winner. . . Winning. This was Hawke's slogan.

Hawke could not have used his popularity as an effective power resource had the ALP not been a parliamentary party aiming to contest popular elections. Because the ALP was such a party, and because it was so desperate to win after losses at the 1977 and 1980 elections, Hawke's popularity became the key power resource, and Hayden's superior parliamentary and policy skills became ineffective.

Fifth, one type of power resource may be *exchanged* with other types of power resources, or used to generate other resources (Sederberg, 1977: 42–5). Businesspeople may use their capital (economic resource) to gain ownership of newspapers or television stations (knowledge resource). Lobbyists may exchange their knowledge of a political party's workings (knowledge resource) for money (economic resource), and so on. The third and fourth points made above suggest why political actors attempt to diversify their resources. Since the usefulness of a particular power resource depends on the social context and the aims of the group in which the exercise of power is attempted, the greater the variety of resources held by a political actor, the greater will be the number of contexts in which that actor can exercise power.

The stories of powerful individuals and groups in Australia are all stories of exchanges of power resources, undertaken to maintain or increase their exercise of power. Australia's best-known political novel—Frank Hardy's *Power Without Glory* (1950)—focusses on one person's exchange and expansion of power resources. In the novel, John West begins with a very small economic resource, an illegal Melbourne betting shop. He uses this economic resource to buy physical coercion resources (thugs and crooked police), to buy status resources (good clothes, a car, a large house, sponsorship of sporting clubs, well-publicised donations to the Catholic Church), to buy knowledge resources (tame journalists and eventually ownership of newspapers), and uses these resources in turn to gain organisational resources (tame officials in the

ALP) and to expand his economic resources (more companies). By developing his power resources in this way, West becomes the most powerful person in Australia.

This leads to a sixth point, which is that a political actor's ability to exercise power is limited by the *skill* with which that actor conserves, increases and uses power resources. In the Hawke-Hayden leadership struggle, Hawke used his key resource of electoral popularity very skillfully, pointing Labor parliamentarians to opinion polls that showed his own popularity, and arguing that Hayden's relative unpopularity would lose the ALP the coming election (Kelly, 1984: 153, 171–75, 187, 205, 233–37).

A seventh and final point concerning power resources is that these resources *need not be directed towards the exercise of political power*. Money, intelligence, status and so on can be used for many ends other than the exercise of power, and many people who possess these resources have no thoughts of using them to exercise power. Even a political actor who generally uses resources to exercise power may decline to use these resources in this way on specific occasions. Bill Hayden took this path in February 1983 when he decided to resign rather than attempt to use the resources he had left to fight an imminent leadership challenge from Bob Hawke (Kelly, 1984: 375–86).

The general conclusion to be drawn from these seven points is that possession of power resources does not necessarily make a political agent powerful. As the discussion above shows, the barriers between control of power resources and the actual exercise of power can be quite extensive. This means that students of politics cannot discover the identity of powerful actors in a society simply by examining who possesses the most power resources. Such examination may give some indication of who *might* be expected to exercise power, but it cannot substitute for the examination of power relations themselves (Dahl, 1976: 27).

Further thoughts about power

The discussion of power in this chapter so far has focussed on individuals changing the behaviour or thinking of other individuals in a very direct way. Power is not always this straightforward, and students of politics have argued long and hard about how to understand it.

One controversial area concerns intentionality; that is, does political actor A have to *intend* to change the behaviour or dispositions of another actor B before it can be said that A has exercised power over B? If A *unintentionally* changes B's behaviour or dispositions, has A still exercised power? If not, what should A's unintentional action be called?

Wrong (1979: 4) argues that power must be restricted to mean only '. . . intentional and effective acts of influence by some persons on other persons' if it is to be usefully distinguished from more general and subtle 'social controls'. Wrong's aim here is to make the concept of power more useful by cutting down the number of situations that can properly be described as power relationships. He argues that if power is allowed to extend to unintended influence it will simply cover too many trivial interactions between people to be helpful in analysing politics and society (1979: 3–5).

Wrong is quite happy to accept that '. . . intentional efforts to influence others often produce unintended as well as intended effects on their behaviour . . .' (1979: 4), but he argues that the two can be distinguished from one another. When Treasurer Paul Keating intended to force companies to pay tax on executive lunches, and made them do so by introducing a fringe benefits tax in 1986, he exercised power over companies. On the other hand, Keating did not exercise power over owners of restaurants who were forced to sack staff because of declining trade following the introduction of the new tax, because Keating had not intended this consequence. Power only applies to situations where an intended effect is brought about.

Insisting that power be restricted to intentional influence also avoids the apparently absurd position of having to describe as instances of power occasions where political actors produce quite opposite effects to the ones they intended. Consider a group of aboriginal leaders in a country town who approach police during a riot to try to discuss how to develop harmony between blacks and the police. Instead of talking with the leaders, the police arrest them. The aboriginal leaders certainly have changed the behaviour of the police, but it seems strange to claim that they have exercised power over them.

These are credible reasons for restricting power to intentional influence, but restricting power in this way raises a range of problems for political scientists. These problems can be discussed usefully on three levels, namely, the power of individuals, institutional power and the power of groups.

The power of individuals

Although linking power to intentions is initially attractive, the distinction between intentional and unintentional effects does not do what Wrong claims; that is, distinguish between trivial and non-trivial influence. Intentional and unintentional influence can be equally trivial or important. Driver A forcing driver B to stop because A drove through a red light is trivial whether A did so intentionally or not, while the intended and unintended consequences of Paul Keating's fringe benefit tax are both important matters.

Further, since intentions can be hidden, restricting exercises of power to intentional acts makes it very difficult to investigate power (see Clegg, 1979: 20). Did Paul Keating really know that a fringe benefits tax would harm restaurant trade, and simply keep quiet about it? How, unless Keating makes a confession, will this ever be known? Political scientists can, of course, make judgements about what a reasonable and intelligent person in the position of Treasurer should have known, much in the way that juries make judgements about whether or not people intended to commit illegal acts. Even so, it is clearly much simpler to include intended and unintended consequences under the concept of power.

Restricting power to intentional acts also excludes the broad area of routinised power. Routinised power exists when an individual's actions or dispositions become changed over time in response to external factors, but without other individuals repeatedly and intentionally attempting to change those actions or dispositions. Routinised power develops between individuals, such as husbands and wives, but it is most commonly found in formal institutions.

Institutional power

The operations of institutions like the Australian public service reveal routinised power every day. Tax assessors processing tax refunds do not work in response to the specific intentions of any particular person. They process forms according to a routine developed by bureaucratic procedures and guidelines. This does not mean that assessors have no power exercised over them, as they would soon discover if they began to authorise tax refunds of a million dollars to every taxpayer. But who exercises this power? This example suggests that power does not have to be intentional and does not even have to be exercised by individuals, but is also exercised by institutions and their rules. How can institutional power be understood, if not in individualistic terms?

One way of understanding institutional power while still maintaining that power involves intentional influence is to argue, as Michel Foucault does, that institutions themselves have intentions that can be discovered in their formal and informal rules, charters, aims, goals, and objectives (see Smart, 1985: 85–8, 122, 123). In this way, it could be argued that the intention of the taxation office is to collect taxes, and that the intention of the tax refund assessment section within the tax office is to calculate tax refunds efficiently and fairly.

The aims, goals and rules of most institutions are not invented by anyone in particular. They emerge as a result of trial and error and the decisions and actions of many people and groups inside and outside the institution over a long period of time. Some aims, goals, rules and so on are formally recorded in writing, whereas other informal rules are maintained by social convention. Through this process the intentions of an institution develop and change (Smart, 1985: 122, 123). Thus tax assessors have power exercised over them not by any individual acting intentionally, but by the formal and informal rules (intentions) of the tax office.

This analysis explains the power exercised by a whole range of institutions, including political parties, government departments, courts, the military and media organisations. Some writers call this institutional power 'structure' (Lukes, 1977: 3–29) or 'domination' (Dearlove and Saunders, 1984: 431) to distinguish it from intentional power exercised by individuals, but their analysis of it is similar to the one given above.

Group power

This analysis can be extended to group power. It is perfectly sensible to talk about the power of formal pressure groups without reducing the discussion to the power of individuals. Pressure groups such as the Tasmanian Wilderness

Society or the Australian Farmers' Federation have aims, goals and rules that can be reasonably construed as intentions.

If the analysis of power can be extended to formal groups, can it be extended further still to informal social groupings such as men and women, or owners and workers? Feminists, for example, argue that patriarchy is not simply the power of individual men over individual women, but refers to the systemic power of men as a group over women as a group (see chapter 15). For Marxists, capitalism involves not simply the power of individual managers over workers, but the power of the capitalist class over the working class (see chapter 14). If power can only mean intentional acts of influence, then it is difficult to see how amorphous groups such as men or capitalists can properly be said to exercise power.

Again, an example might clarify this problem. A woman is brutally pack-raped and killed one night in an outer suburb of an Australian city. The men who committed these crimes are caught, tried and sentenced to long prison terms. Even after the men's imprisonment, women who were formerly happy to walk around after dark in the suburb complain that they can no longer do so, and in fact cease doing so.

Who or what is exercising power over these women? Not the men who committed the original crimes, because they are locked away in jail. Other men in the suburb? If power must be intentional, then the individual men who walk or drive around the suburb at night do not exercise power over the women, since their intentions are simply to get home or go out. Who then exercises power?

What this example indicates is the need to broaden further the concept of intentions to encompass all instances of power. Arguably, the women stay inside at night not because they fear the intentions of a particular man or particular men, but because among the intentions of *men as a whole* is violence towards women. The women anticipate this violent reaction, an anticipation heightened by the recent rape-murder, and stay indoors.

This sort of intention is perhaps not as clear or easy to investigate as the intentions of individuals, but the intentions of men as a group can be constructed by examining the statements and actions of men as a whole towards women as a whole (see Brownmiller, 1975).

The richest and most persuasive accounts of power always involve analysis of the three types of power outlined above—individual, institutional and group power. They may place different emphases on each of these types of power, but the best of these accounts will always acknowledge the importance of each type of power in the political process.

Power, freedom and constraints

Some writers argue that regardless of whether or not influence must be intentional to count as power, political agents must be free to choose actions before the actions they choose can be properly described as exercises of power. If a political agent is completely constrained and forced to take a course of action, then even if that action changes the actions or dispositions of others, it is not an exercise of power (Lukes, 1977: 4–7).

It is easy to think of examples of people who initially appear to exercise extensive power, but who are, in fact, constrained by circumstances around them to act in the way that they do. The tax assessors discussed above afford one example. John Steinbeck presents another good example in his novel *The Grapes of Wrath*. A desperate farmer, whose property is about to be bulldozed to force him to leave, confronts the bulldozer driver with a rifle. The driver pleads:

> 'It's not me. There's nothing I can do. . . You're not killing the right guy.'
> 'That's so,' the tenant said. 'Who gave you orders? I'll go after him. He's the one to kill.'
> 'You're wrong. He got his orders from the bank. The bank told him: "Clear those people out or it's your job".'
> 'Well, there's a president of the bank. There's a board of directors. I'll fill up the magazine of the rifle and go into the bank.'
> The driver said: 'Fellow was telling me the bank gets orders from the east. The orders were: "Make the land show profit or we'll close you up".'
> 'But where does it stop? Who can we shoot? I don't aim to starve to death before I kill the man that's starving me.'
> 'I don't know. Maybe there's nobody to shoot. Maybe the thing isn't men at all.' (Steinbeck, 1951: 36, 37)

Lukes calls these constraints on people's actions 'structure' (Lukes, 1977: chapter 1). In some cases, the relevant structure might be the dictates of the market, as in the case of the bankers in the Steinbeck quotation above. In other cases, it might be the rules of the institution within which individuals act, as in the case of the tax assessors. Other sorts of structural constraints, such as technological limitations or strong cultural traditions, are easy to imagine.

This distinction between power and structure may help to refine the concept of power further; however, as with intentionality, it involves making some difficult and contentious judgements about political actors. First, how free do political actors have to be before their actions can be described as exercises of power? All political actors are constrained to some degree by their circumstances, so how useful is it to attempt to divide constrained, 'unfree' influence from unconstrained, free exercise of power?

Second, even if these questions can be answered in theory, in practice doubt will always remain over the constraints on a political actor. Did the bulldozer driver really have to demolish the farmer's property, or could he have refused, and formed an alliance with the farmers to prevent the banks from carrying out evictions? Could the bank's directors have resisted the instructions they received from 'the east'?

These questions are difficult, and students of politics have divided on them (Lukes, 1977: 14–18). On the one hand, individualist theorists have argued that individuals face very few constraints, and are free to act as they choose. On the other hand, structuralists argue that political actors are caught in a web of constraints that make it impossible for them to act freely. Indeed, these constraints are so strong that it is often impossible for political actors to even conceive of any alternative actions outside those offered by the structural constraints. The bulldozer driver acted in the way that he did because no alternative was imaginable. Some theorists call this power to restrict the options envisaged by other political actors the third dimension of power (Lukes, 1974: 21–5).

In the face of the difficult questions surrounding freedom and power, it seems wise not to assume that either the individualists or the structuralists are correct in every case. Choosing between these alternative perspectives requires careful investigation of specific political situations.

Conclusion

The study of power is central to political analysis, just as power is central to politics. Disagreements about the concept of power are worth examining, and have generated shelves full of scholarly debate. At some point, however, the student of politics must abandon this debate and attempt to understand Australian politics with whatever conceptual tools he or she has. Despite its problems, the concept of power is one of the most useful tools to take to this task.

References

Brownmiller, S. (1975) *Against Our Will* Harmondsworth: Penguin
Clegg, S. (1979) *The Theory of Power and Organisation* London: Routledge and Kegan Paul
Dahl, R.A. (1961) *Who Governs?* New Haven: Yale University Press
—— (1976) *Modern Political Analysis* 3rd edn, Englewood Cliffs: Prentice-Hall
Dearlove, J. and Saunders, P. (1984) *Introduction to British Politics* Cambridge: Polity
Hardy, F. (1950) *Power Without Glory* Melbourne: F. Hardy
Kelly, P. (1984) *The Hawke Ascendancy* rev. edn, Sydney: Angus and Robertson
Lukes, S. (1974) *Power: A Radical View* London: Macmillan
—— (1977) *Essays in Social Theory* London: Macmillan
Sederberg, P.C. (1977) *Interpreting Politics* San Francisco: Chandler and Sharp
Smart, B. (1985) *Michel Foucault* London: Tavistock
Steinbeck, J. (1951) *The Grapes of Wrath* Harmondsworth: Penguin
Wrong, D.H. (1979) *Power* Oxford: Basil Blackwood

3 Democratic theory and practice

Michael Jackson

In William Golding's novel *The Lord of the Flies* even a confused group of young boys in a new and frightening situation know what voting is and how to do it. When conflict first occurs between Jack and Ralph, 'the dark boy, Roger, stirred at last and spoke up. Let's have a vote', he said (1957: 30). Voting is the all-purpose method of conflict resolution and decision making for many people. Within a few minutes of Roger's suggestion Ralph was elected chief. True, no votes were counted, but it seems pretty clear that Ralph was acclaimed by more than a majority of the boys. Moreover, most of his supporters were enthusiastic, while the choir gave its support to Jack dutifully. Ralph was the people's choice. So why does the democratically elected Ralph lose authority so quickly? What does the rise and fall of Ralph say about democracy?

Democracy and voting

The first thing Ralph's political career shows is that voting alone is not democracy. Why not? Because voting alone is not effective in establishing authority. For the boys the vote was, as Golding observes, simply a toy (1957: 30). It is not that Ralph had authority and then lost it. He never had it in the first place. At best, his election gave him the opportunity to establish his authority. Ralph did seem to think the vote gave him authority; he started making rules that he gradually discovered he could not enforce. But for the boys the vote was a game, and, of course, one can always change the rules of a game, or stop playing it altogether.

That voting and all that goes with it is not democracy can be seen in history. Which of these two politicians were democrats (whatever that term means for the time being): Winston Churchill or Adolf Hitler? The most overwhelming impression of Churchill is surely as the war time Prime Minister of embattled Britain. Britain was and still is a democracy. It would seem to follow that Churchill was a democrat, and he was. But was he the winner of a vote?

Churchill the heroic war leader had not won a single national election when he became Prime Minister. He was simply the elected representative of one constituency. He governed throughout the war years from 1940 to 1945 without an election, exercising the constitutional prerogative of a British

Prime Minister not to call an election in a national emergency and to prolong the existing Parliament. Britain, sole defender of western democracy for more than a year between the fall of France and the American entry into the war, went almost ten years without national elections, from 1935 to 1945. When the war was finally over Churchill did call an election and he was roundly defeated.

Churchill the war leader was not the people's choice, but the nominee of the executive committee of a desperate political party seeking a strong leader in a crisis. He was appointed by the King. Nevertheless, it is true to say that he was a democrat in his war Governments. Why? Hints are contained in the description of Churchill above. He maintained parliament, where he gave speeches and answered questions. He also worked within the established democratic constitution. There were established institutions within which Churchill worked, and these institutions together constituted a democratic political system. Equally important was the fact that Britain was a democratic political culture. Accordingly, the Parliament contained and gave vent to voices of opposition. Newspaper columns contained debates on policies, and so on. The constitution spelled out and limited government authority, even in a national emergency. Here then are two keys to a modern democratic political system: limited government and opposition.

It is true if an election had been held in 1942 Churchill would probably have won it, but this supposition is less important in conceding to Churchill the title democratic than either of the two reasons above. Insofar as calling the post-war election as soon as the emergency was past was in keeping with the British culture and constitution, it is a sign of Churchill's commitment to democracy. But the important point to note here is that he acted in keeping with the spirit of the constitution throughout the war. That is more important, for the moment, than the fact that elections were finally called. Had he abused Britain's democratic institutions and culture throughout the war, and then called elections in 1945, his claim to being a democrat would be substantially impaired.

The obvious contrast to Winston Churchill is his antagonist Adolf Hitler. Few, if any, reasonable people would have called Hitler a democrat during his time and none would do so in retrospect. Yet Hitler led his infamous Nazi Party in no less than five parliamentary elections. Under the Weimar constitution of Germany at that time the Government of the day was based on a parliamentary majority led by the Chancellor (in Australian terms, Prime Minister). In addition, the head of state was the President, who was elected separately (as though Australia's Governor General were to be elected). Hitler once contested this office as well. Finally, he also ran two plebiscites. A plebiscite is a direct vote of all electors on an important public question (a referendum to change the Australian constitution is a kind of plebiscite).

Before commenting further on Hitler's career as an electoral politician, his party's fortunes should be examined (see Table 3.1). Each of these elections, by the way, was marked by a high turnout of 70 percent or more. Voting was not compulsory. The total of voters was around 40 million each time (Eyck, 1964).

Table 3.1 Parliamentary elections 'Hitler for Chancellor'

Date	1928	1930	July 1932	November 1932	1933
% Nazi votes	3	18	37	33	44

A great deal of coercion was exercised by the Nazis in the 1933 election. It was less free than the other four shown, but it was nonetheless an election with competing, opposing candidates including communists and liberals. It is also worth noting that had Germany had the first-past-the-post electoral system (see chapter 10) that Britain had and has, the Nazis would have won a parliamentary majority in the November 1932 elections.

In the November 1932 election the Nazis won a plurality of votes in the majority of constituencies, just as Margaret Thatcher did in the 1987 British elections when she turned 44 percent of the vote into 52 percent of the seats in Parliament. Getting back to Germany, in addition to constituencies there was also in operation a system of proportional representation too complicated to describe here, except to say that it was rather like the Australian system of voting for the House of Representatives and Senate at the same time to form *one* legislative chamber, and not two. After the 1933 elections, Hitler made a coalition with the Nationalist Party to form a Government with 340 of the 647 parliamentary seats. Of the 340, 288 were Nazis. Hitler was then Chancellor. Throughout this period the Nazi Party also contested any number of elections in the seventeen states that made up the Weimar federal system.

In March of 1932 Hitler took part in the first of two votes for President. He won 30 percent of the popular vote. No candidate won a majority and the constitution required another vote so that the winner would have a majority. In this second round, Hitler's vote increased to 37 percent.

On the death of the President, von Hindenberg, in 1935, Hitler called a plebiscite asking the people to agree to merge the office of chancellor, which he held, with the presidency, which was now vacant. More than 88 percent of the 43 million who turned out voted 'yes'. Though it was not a free vote (by Australian standards), 5 million people did vote 'no'. In 1938 Hitler held a double plebiscite after the *Anschluss* of Austria to ratify this arrangement. By this time there were virtually no negative votes. Official returns gave the turnout at 99 percent and the 'yes' vote for the integration of Austria into Germany in both Austria and Germany was more than 99 percent. By this time it was suicide to oppose Hitler.

In assessing Hitler as a democrat it is also important to add a speculation to these facts. If Hitler had called free elections in 1940 or 1942 or even 1944 he would have won an overwhelming majority. He and his policies were popular, just as Churchill and his war policies were.

If democracy means only voting, then Hitler has more credentials than Churchill. On the other hand, he consistently and explicitly campaigned against the democratic institutions of the Weimar constitution. He advocated eliminating the checks and balances of different branches of government, and he did away with the restraints that limited government as when he merged the offices of Chancellor and President and he used the form of democracy—a plebiscite—to do so. Moreover, he encouraged criminal violence and coercion as means of intimidation in voting in the 1933 election. Then and later all who opposed him were labelled as disloyal traitors. All of the plebiscites were held in conditions where voting 'no' was difficult.

This historical comparison between Churchill and Hitler is important because democracy is complex: it is made up of a number of factors, one of which is voting. One might be inclined to say that voting is a necessary condition of democracy, but voting alone does not make for a democracy. That inclination would require two important qualifications. First, to be significant a vote must be a free vote. Second, on occasion a democracy may forego voting as Britain did under Churchill's wartime rule.

Defining democracy

This information alone is enough to make it clear that democracy would be a difficult concept to define. One way to see some of these difficulties is to consider six hypothetical examples concerning two political systems, Alpha and Beta (May, n.d.). Remember, each case is distinct.

- Which is the more democratic polity, Alpha or Beta? Alpha exceeds Beta in achieving government *for* the people. More of government actions in Alpha are for the benefit of the people than in Beta. However, Beta effects government by the people. More people in Beta participate in governance at all levels. Is Alpha more democratic than Beta? Why?
- Alpha surpasses Beta in responsive government, that is, those who govern Alpha meet more of the wishes of all of the governed. On the other hand, Beta leads Alpha in the extent to which its governors meet the wishes of the largest class of the governed. This class is the lowest class. Is Alpha more democratic or is Beta? Why?
- Beta has a more responsive government (as defined above), but Alpha's governors obtain office by means of free, competitive, regular, popular elections. Which is the more democratic and why?
- Those who govern in Alpha are chosen by lot every second year. Beta's governors are chosen by direct, popular election based on a one person, one vote, one value scheme. Which is more democratic? Why?
- Politics in Alpha and Beta involves conflicts between bare numerical majorities whose members feel lukewarm on each issue and large minorities whose members feel strongly on the issues. In Alpha the government heeds the wishes of the majorities on all occasions. Not so in Beta, where the government heeds the wishes of Beta's sizable, intensely committed minorities. Which is more democratic? Why?

To think about each case is to realise that there are no right answers to these five cases. That is the point. Alpha and Beta each represent part of the complex meaning of democracy. That much is clear. What is less clear is the relative importance of criteria, as when Alpha is responsive to the wishes of the people, but Beta has free democratic elections. To resolve these cases where different polities meet different criteria requires the criteria to be ranked, for example, to say that responsive rule is more important than free elections. It would then follow that, all other things being equal, the more responsive government would mean the more democratic polity. A comparison from *The Lord of the Flies* might help. Ralph won the election, but Jack gave the people (the boys) what they wanted.

Further examples of Alpha and Beta could be hypothesised to tap other criteria of democracy, because many other criteria have been used as the basis to claim that a polity is democratic. It is the most important sign of the power of the word 'democracy' that no one, above all no politician, admits to being anti-democratic and nearly every political system claims to be democratic. Thus the Soviet Union has always claimed to be democratic, citing several criteria, among them a variant of responsive rule according to which the Government does what is in the best interest of the people. This is what people should wish the Government to do. Other governments have claimed to be democratic because they meet the criteria of responsive rule, or because they favour the large, lower class, or because they have some kind of election. The Soviet Union, South East Asian military dictatorships, and the Government of South Africa all claim to be democratic (see Macpherson, 1965). These claims are salutory reminders of how complex democracy is.

Equally, the democratic character of polities like Australia has been challenged both from without and within. Critics have claimed that polities like Australia are not really democracies. The two most common themes in these criticisms are, firstly, that few citizens participate fully in the democratic process and, secondly, that the democratic process is a sham.

As to the first of these criticisms, it is certainly true that in some polities with free elections the only political participation of most citizens is voting. Most citizens never speak to a politician, write a letter to the editor of a newspaper about a political issue, contribute money to a political cause, attend a political meeting or the like. Most of the time most citizens are neither interested in nor informed about politics. In 1984 the Australian Electoral Commission tried to establish how readily electors distinguished between the Senate and the House of Representatives. In a national Morgan Gallup Poll the Commission asked a sample of electors to name the two Houses of the Commonwealth Parliament. More than 22 percent of the respondents were unable to name either house. This sample was also asked to name the House in which the Prime Minister and the leader of the Opposition sit. Only 60 percent correctly identified the House of Representatives. More than 17 percent incorrectly named the Senate (Hughes 1985: 10). These results are all the more surprising since voting is compulsory in Australia, so virtually every elector has seen a ballot paper and voted.

In the United States, where voting is not compulsory, the turnout at elections is often low. The highest turnout is for presidential elections. Despite the fact that these election campaigns run for more than a year as candidates jockey for position, the turnout now hovers at around 50 percent of eligible voters. The winning candidate may receive slightly more than half of that vote, representing a quarter of eligible voters. In other polities where voting is not compulsory the electoral turnout can also be low, though few are as low as in the United States. It was once argued that the failure of nearly half of the eligible voters to vote was proof of their confidence in the status quo. Critics, however, have taken the view that the indifference to voting of such a large part of the electorate, and, by analogy, the ignorance of the parliamentary system in Australia, means that a large proportion of the electorate see voting as insignificant. This point leads to the second criticism.

Some have argued that parliamentary democracy does not determine who rules or how rule is exercised. It has been claimed for example that there is little or no difference between competing parties. One American observer, C. Mills (1959), wrote of a power elite that exercises influence through the corporate and financial world. More recently in Australia writers like R.W. Connell (1977) have argued similarly that a ruling class controls public life. A number of remedies have been recommended. One suggestion that has enjoyed much attention has been participatory democracy (Pateman, 1970). The central thesis of participatory democracy is that all citizens should participate in determining the nature of those organisations that influence their lives. In this situation, participatory democracy might mean that university students should have a voice in determining what courses are given, how they are taught, or who is employed to teach. This movement was particularly strong in the 1970s and represented a translation into the modern industrial society of the idea of direct democracy.

Direct democracy

In a direct democracy all would take part in decision making. The illustration is a small, simple, and homogenous community. If such a community of, say, 100 people existed in isolation it would be an instance of direct democracy if all 100 people took part in making government decisions. But even having said as little as this, it is clear that the boundaries of direct democracy are far from obvious. For example, if that 100 included babies and children must they participate, too? If so, is their participation to have a value equal to everyone else's? The answers to such question about the *demos*, the people who comprise the citizenry of a democracy, have changed over time. Once women would have automatically been excluded. The constitution of the *demos* may also vary from one society to another. It is easy to imagine circumstances in which people of this or that race or religion are excluded. Consider a miniature version of South Africa with 60 blacks, 20 coloured, 5 mixed race, and 15 whites. The whites could rule the other 85 on the basis of direct democracy for whites only. Those who are subjected to such a government of direct democracy would hardly be likely to think of it as a democracy at all.

Getting back to the original example of a community of 100, if all assemble and make decisions as a whole, direct democracy is evident. If decisions are not unanimous, and it is not likely that many would be unanimous even in a small, homogenous community, then a rule must exist to determine when a decision has been made. Without commitment to a decision rule nothing would ever be decided. There would be politics without government.

If democracy is government by the people and each person counts the same as another, then the majority is one obvious decision rule, because, all other things being equal, the majority could by the weight of numbers enforce its will on the minority. No minority could ever do that, so a minority would make a poor democratic decision rule in practice, though in principle there is nothing wrong with saying that any proposal supported by, say, at least 33 percent of citizens should be implemented. Some democrats have been anxious to strengthen the influence of some minorities.

John Stuart Mill, the nineteenth-century English political economist, suggested that adults with a university education should have five votes (1910: 285). University graduates were few in Mill's day and he wanted both to give them an incentive to participate in political life and to have the community profit from their wisdom.

More recently, Robert Dahl, an American political scientist, suggested that some extremely technical and dangerous matters should not be left to the marketplace of ideas, but should be entrusted to carefully chosen experts (1985). Dahl had in mind nuclear energy and weapons. These subjects should never be decided upon in the give-and-take of politicians courting the electorate.

Though contemporary democratic practice does not favour minorities as Mill or Dahl recommended, an important part of it is the protection of minority rights. One crucial assumption of democracy is that majorities shift: the individuals who comprise a 50 percent plus one majority today on abortion are not the same individuals who constituted the 50 percent plus one majority on aboriginal land rights last year or the ALP majority of the next election. To ensure that majorities do shift, minority rights are necessary. In this way no majority, be it the bare majority of 50 percent plus one or 95 percent, can deprive a minority of its political rights to speak, gather, recruit, lobby, vote, and the like.

If the majority is the decision rule, it is necessary to decide between the two different kinds of majority rule. One is simple majority rule and the other is limited majority rule. Most polities combine the two. For a simple majority 50 percent plus one suffices. A simple majoritarian would argue that this criterion suffices in each and every case. In contrast, a limited majoritarian puts some decisions beyond the reach of the simple majority. For example, the creation and change of the constitution is left to an extraordinary majority. In some countries it requires a two-thirds majority, while in Australia it requires a majority of those who vote in a majority of states. Limited majoritarianism sometimes allows the minority a veto. A proposal for a constitutional change in Australia can be vetoed by a majority of states containing a minority of the country's population.

Among majoritarians there is another dispute. It concerns what the majority represents. Is it a majority of people, of adults, of sane adults, of registered voters, or of those that vote? In most democracies only sane adults who are not imprisoned may participate in politics, including voting. Now if it is necessary for the majority to represent all these who are eligible to vote, then some form of compulsory voting is required. Otherwise not even a 60 percent majority of those who voted would constitute a majority where 80 percent of the eligible voters abstain. An eligible majority system without compulsory voting would give active minorities a veto. Compulsory voting solves this problem, but it creates problems of its own because it ensures that the ill-informed and uninterested vote. Over the years it has created a network of safe seats for each party where virtually no campaigning is necessary. The real contest is confined to a few so-called marginal constituencies. The voters most likely to swing from one party to another are those who know and care least about politics. Campaigns aimed at marginal constituencies target these swinging voters, struggling to get their attention, courting their favour. Should such people be accorded such a disproportionate degree of influence over elections? Should the result in a few constituencies be decisive?

Most often democracies are satisfied to decide the outcome of elections on a majority of those who voted. The level of voter turnout in these polities is usually much less than that of Australia. Campaigns in these democracies are often much longer, more intense, and more expensive than in Australia because it is necessary to identify voters who can be motivated to go to the polls on election day.

Representative democracy

Because direct democracy is difficult in large communities and widespread direct citizen participation in politics is hard to achieve, what has evolved is representative democracy. Instead of an assembly of all of the people meeting to decide, in representative democracy the citizens vote for some of their number to represent them. Once elected these representatives meet in an assembly to make decisions.

Representatives can be one of two types. They can see themselves as the delegates of those who have elected them. Delegates have little scope for their own initiative. Instead they must follow the wishes of their voters. In this way the voice of the ordinary voter is heard. Politicians who are responsive to public opinion polls act like delegates.

The other main role type for representatives is the trustee. A trustee accepts the responsibility for conducting public affairs, preserving the public interest. Trustees are not the delegates of constituencies. Rather, the constituency entrusts the best available person to act on its behalf. Edmund Burke, a British politician of the eighteenth century, expressed this idea (Hill, 1979: 158).

One crucial aspect of the difference between the delegate and the trustee is that the delegate champions the local interest of the constituency while the trustee looks to the national interest. Most elected representatives try to compromise these two roles. This compromise role type has been called the politico.

Some years ago Hugh Emy (1974: 455–99) interviewed 75 parliamentary backbenchers in Canberra. A backbencher is a member of Parliament who is not a minister or a shadow minister. For these 75 members of Parliament Emy found that 35 percent classed themselves as trustees, 20 percent as delegates, and 46 percent as politicos. Interestingly, Emy found differences between the parties on this score. Those from the present National Party emphasised the politico (59 percent) and delegate (31 percent) roles. The Liberals emphasised the trustee (63 percent) and politico (37 percent) roles. The ALP was more divided, with 50 percent politico, 24 percent trustee and 26 percent delegate. In part what these findings indicate is that democracy—representative democracy—means different things to different people.

Is democracy good?

Democracy is something almost everyone is for and yet no one can agree on what it is. Even this brief account of some of the characteristics of democracy will have aroused some disagreements without diminishing enthusiasm for democracy. What is good about democracy? There are two chief arguments in its favour.

The first is the Churchillian argument: democracy is the worst form of government—except for all the others. This may be termed the fallibility argument. It admits the fallibility of democracy, but in the context of alternatives it sees democracy as less fallible than other kinds of government.

In part the fallibility argument contends that everyone is liable to error, including the democratic majority. Hence it is important to recognise and defend minority rights. In this view democracy is the best form of government because it recognises human fallibility.

A further refinement of the fallibility argument assumes that good government must give people what they want to some extent. Who knows better what I want than I do? Consequently, there must be some scope for me to participate in the political process to defend my interests.

The fallibility argument is a strong, but negative, justification for democracy. A more positive argument for democracy is excellence. According to the excellence argument, made by John Stuart Mill in his book *Considerations on Representative Government* (1910: 202–19), is that democracy brings out the best in people. The widespread participation in public debate characteristic of democracy promotes intellectual, practical, and moral growth in citizens. In permitting and promoting public participation in shaping its own future, representative democracy encourages citizens to understand social realities and constraints.

If nearly everyone, particularly politicians, claims to be a democrat, arguments against democracy are uncommon, and so perhaps all the more important to consider. If democracy is nearly universally favoured today, it has not always been so. Throughout human history prior to the past 200 years, the arguments against democracy prevailed. The outstanding exception to this generalisation was ancient Athens.

At the height of its golden age, Athenian freedom and democracy was celebrated by Pericles in his famous funeral oration for those Athenians killed in war. On that day, more than 2000 years ago, Pericles said:

> Our constitution is called a democracy because power is in the hands of the whole people. When it is a question of settling private disputes, everyone is equal before the law; when it is a question of putting one person before another in positions of public responsibility, what counts is not membership of a particular class, but the actual ability which the man possesses. No one . . . is kept in political obscurity because of poverty . . . We are free and tolerant in our private lives; but in public affairs we keep to the law. (Thucydides, 1954: 114)

The speech contains much else in praise of Athens, reknowned for its democracy. It paints a memorable picture of Athens in its prime that makes it seem almost utopian. So it may have seemed to many who heard the speech, for we know from other sources that Athenian politics in the time of Pericles was extremely bitter. There were plots and counter-plots galore. Bribery and corruption were common. War was the basis of foreign policy. Slaves were held. Women were not citizens. Socrates would be sentenced to death, democratically.

But if that were so, why does Pericles wax so enthusiastic about Athenian democratic politics? Pericles was, let us remember, a politician. Moreover, he was a democratic politician. Above all else that meant he owed his position to the *demos*, to the citizens. Is it any wonder then that on a ceremonial occasion he would praise the system—democracy—that raised him to leadership and, in addition, that he would praise those—the *demos*—who supported him? Hardly. Pericles was no fool. He used the occasion very astutely to flatter his supporters. This interpretation is much more realistic than those who idealise Pericles and democracy, using his statement as testimony to the excellence of Athenian democracy.

Other Athenians were less enthusiastic about both democracy and Pericles. One of these was Plato, whose teacher Socrates died at the hands of the *demos*. In *The Republic*, Plato (1974: 282, 283) characterised democracy in the allegory of the ship:

> Imagine this state of affairs on board a ship or number of ships. The master is bigger and burlier than any of the crew, but a little deaf and short-sighted and no less deficient in seamanship. The sailors are quarrelling over the control of the helm; each thinks he ought to be steering the vessel, though he has never learnt navigation and cannot point to any teacher under whom he has served his apprenticeship; but what is more, they assert that navigation is a thing that cannot be taught at all, and are ready to tear to pieces anyone who says it can. Meanwhile they besiege the master himself, begging him urgently to trust them with the helm; and sometimes, when others have been more successful in gaining his ear, they kill them or throw them overboard, and, after somehow stupefying the worthy master with strong drink or an opiate, take control of the ship, make free with its stores, and turn the voyage, as might be expected of such a crew, into a drunken carousel. Besides all this, they cry up as a skilled navigator and master of seamanship anyone clever enough to lend a hand in persuading or forcing

> the master to set them in command. Every other kind of man they condemn as useless. They do not understand that the genuine navigator can only make himself fit to command a ship by studying the seasons of the year, sky, stars, and winds, and all that belongs to his craft; and they have no idea that along with the science of navigation, it is possible for him to gain, by instruction or practice, the skill to keep control of the helm whether some of them like it or not. If a ship were managed in that way, would not those on board be likely to call the expert in navigation a mere stargazer, who spent his time in idle talk and was useless to them?

In this rich allegory the worthy master is the state. The sailors are the citizens or those among them who represent them in politics. The sailors or their representatives vie with each other unscrupulously, using every available means. They explicitly deny that anyone is intrinsically better suited to rule when they claim that 'navigation is a thing that cannot be taught'.

Plato thought the unscrupulous competition of unqualified people was inevitable in a democracy. His portrayal of the dark side of democracy certainly has echoes in contemporary democratic practice. Seldom does a politician dare to defy public opinion, no matter how ill-informed. Politicians are equally reluctant even to lead public opinion, cautiously preferring to wait to see what the majority opinion is. Corruption recurs.

Plato saw a similar phenomenon in Pericles. Admirable though Pericles was as a man, Plato thought him to be as much a slave to public opinion as any elected official today. Consequently, Plato (1960: 129–36) argued that Pericles had failed in the chief duty of a leader. What is that chief duty? To make citizens better. For Plato proof that Pericles failed lay in the fact that at the end of his life Athens entered into an imperial war that ended in a disastrous civil war (Thucydides, 1954).

Like John Stuart Mill, Plato thought a chief purpose of politics was to promote human excellence. If politics did not do that there was that much less reason to bother with it. However, he disagreed with Mill's view that democracy promotes excellence.

References

Connell, R. (1977) *Ruling Class, Ruling Culture* Melbourne: Cambridge University Press

Dahl, R. (1985) *Controlling Nuclear Weapons* Syracuse: Syracuse University Press

Emy, H. (1974) *The Politics of Australian Democracy* Melbourne: Macmillan

Eyck, E. (1964) *A History of the Weimar Republic* London: Oxford University Press

Golding, W. (1957) *Lord of the Flies* London: Faber

Hill, B. (ed.) (1979) *Edmund Burke on Government, Politics and Society* London: Collins

Hughes, C. (1985) *Election Administration* Brisbane: The Endowed Lecture of the Royal Institute of Public Administration, Queensland Division

Macpherson, C. (1965) *The Real World of Democracy* Toronto: Canadian Broadcasting Company

May, J. (no date) *Alpha and Beta* (mimeo) Department of Government, University of Queensland

Mill, J. (1910) *Considerations on Representative Government* London: Dent

Mills, C. Wright (1959) *The Power Elite* New York: Oxford University Press
Pateman, C. (1970) *Participation and Democratic Theory* Cambridge: Cambridge University Press
Plato (1960) *The Gorgias* Harmondsworth: Penguin
—— (1974) *The Republic* Harmondsworth: Penguin
Thucydides (1954) *The Pelopennesian War* Harmondsworth: Penguin

4 Public policy making

Martin Laffin

What government does and does not do is important to everyone. Government provides the roads along which you travel to universities and colleges, which are also provided by government. When you enter the employment market, government action or inaction has a major impact on whether or not you can find work and what sorts of work are available. When you look for somewhere to live, your search is affected by government through planning controls, the tax structure and interest rates. Meanwhile, in your leisure time you expect government to keep the beaches clean and prevent industrial companies from polluting the sea.

Government bodies have come to be involved in an enormously wide range of activities. In Australia, government expenditure constitutes over 40 percent of the gross domestic product, while the government sector includes by far the largest employers in the economy. Commonwealth, state and local governments employ about a third of the entire workforce, 1.7 million people out of a total workforce of 5.4 million.

Quite simply, the study of public policy is about how decisions and purposes are formed by government organisations. The aim of this chapter is to explain ways of setting about understanding these decisions and purposes. In so doing it breaks with the conventional approach to public policy in Australia, which has been predominantly descriptive. This chapter argues for a more analytical approach to the study of public policy and for the use of several different theoretical frameworks. Accordingly, the chapter outlines three theoretical approaches to the study of public policy—pluralism, corporatism and Marxism—and considers how each can contribute to an understanding of public policy.

Pluralist approaches to public policy

The dominant assumptions behind the study of public policy in Australia have been pluralist. The classical pluralist approach emphasises the role of parliaments and competitive party politics, which dominate a political marketplace where there are few obstacles preventing interest or pressure groups from stating their case and obtaining attention from policy makers. Ultimately, policies are determined through competition between the political parties for electoral support, the winning party bringing its own set of policies to government (see, for example, Emy, 1978). This conventional pluralist view is contained in media representations of policy debates, where the main event is seen to be the conflict between the two parties. Meanwhile, the governmental machine itself remains neutral and distant from the competing interest groups and political parties.

However, recent changes have emphasised the limitations of a purely pluralist analysis of the policy process in Australia. Party differences seem to be decreasing and there must be some question over the extent to which the electorate is presented with clear cut choices between two political programmes (see chapter 9). International economic pressures and entrenched domestic interests constrain the freedom of action of politicians once elected, often compelling them to abandon or modify policy stances taken up in the heat of opposition (see chapters 16–18). Moreover, many undoubtedly important decisions are made outside the context of parliament and cabinets at both Commonwealth and state levels. Major investment projects like the Snowy River Scheme and the Sydney Harbour Tunnel have their origins within government departments rather than in Parliament or Cabinet. Policy dynamics within departments also produce many policy continuities between governments that are largely unaffected by changes in the parliamentary and party arenas (see chapter 8).

Thus conventional pluralist ways of thinking about government policy can distort an understanding of how modern large-scale government works. To take account of the realities of policy-making in modern government, recent pluralists have modified the classical pluralist approach. They acknowledge that policies cannot be explained by reference just to the processes of parliamentary, party or even cabinet government. Instead they stress the wider range of influences and actors, such as senior public servants and professional experts, that have to be considered to understand fully the contemporary policy process.

One of the most interesting attempts to revise pluralism is that of Richardson and Jordan (1979). They argue that countries like Australia and Britain should be understood as 'post-parliamentary democracies' in which policy making is increasingly conducted within closed 'policy communities' that dominate specific policy fields. The basis for these policy communities is seen as lying in the growing specialisation of policy-making labour and as such they are composed of senior public servants, experts and professionals in the field and representatives of 'respectable' interest groups. Significantly, these interest groups are given special recognition by government, enjoying close, informal consultative relations on a continuing basis with public servants. So these days it is the bureaucrats, the professionals and the experts who increasingly define social problems (or at least adopt problems), who organise government response and whose survival and careers are bound up with the maintenance of problems.

In addition, the recent pluralists can point to an important finding of much public policy research—that in most policy fields it is virtually impossible to identify the dominant individual actors. For example, it seems quite impossible to identify any person or small group who is controlling those actions making up national policy on abortions, or on income distribution, or consumer protection or energy. Although the power of the elected politicians may have been eroded, the fragmented nature of power in the post-parliamentary democracy ensures that no one group or individual can become dominant. The free market for policy ideas has simply become more fragmented and less dominated by politicians; it is the experts rather than the politicians who refine the problems, debate the evidence, and work out the policy options.

Corporatist approaches

Corporatism has emerged more recently than pluralism as a theoretical approach, and in some ways is a development of pluralism. The corporatist approach argues that government has a more active role than that allowed for in pluralism in controlling and structuring the policy-making process, especially in the development of interest groups themselves. It stresses the imperfections of the policy-making marketplace and the barriers to entry by groups and individuals, according government an active role in creating these imperfections and maintaining barriers to entry. Government adopts such an active role to maintain social stability, the formation of close relationships being a means of containing conflict. Thus interest groups are seen not just as reflections of socio-economic interests within the wider society but as produced, at least in part, by the interventions of government. Accordingly, corporatist approaches assign government two main functions within the policy process: firstly, structuring interest groupings; and secondly, bargaining relationships with recognised interest groups (see Brugger and Jaensch, 1985; and Harrison, 1980).

Firstly, when governments make and implement policies they inevitably structure the ways in which interests are aggregated and organised. Those in government aim to build up relationships with key interest groups in order to prevent and resolve social conflicts threatening social stability. They try to structure interest groupings to create and strengthen interest organisations representative of an entire set of interests. The advantage to government of such interest organisations is that they provide a unified and stable interest group with whom government can bargain in a given policy field. Thus the corporatist view depicts government as bargaining with just a few key interest groups in key sectors, whereas the pluralist view depicts government as responding to pressures from many interest groups. Moreover, corporatists argue that these key groups are involved in governing insofar as they are taking authority and responsibility for carrying out policies agreed with government within a specific policy field, in particular controlling their membership in line with agreements reached with government. An important example of such corporatist arrangements is the relationship between the Commonwealth Government and the ACTU over recent years. The ACTU, on behalf of the other unions, has agreed to control the level of wage claims in return for increased involvement in macro-economic decision making. Meanwhile a major problem, highlighted by a corporatist analysis, is the increase in tensions between trade union leaders and their rank and file membership as the latter question whether their fall in real wages is adequate compensation for the deals made between their leaders and the government.

Marxist approaches to public policy

Marxist approaches to the study of public policy seek to explain public policies in the context of the continuing tensions between labour and capital. Public policies are seen as primarily directed at maintaining the process of class exploitation and as serving the interests of the economically and socially dominant class at the expense of the working class. In other words, the primary functions of public policies are seen to be the social control of the working class and the facilitation of capital accumulation (capital investment). Unlike the pluralists, Marxists do not see government or the state as neutral or independent of class interests; they see it as an instrument used by the capitalist class to perpetuate their domination.

More recent Marxist theorists have modified the simple view that state organisations always serve the interest of the dominant capitalist class in favour of a more sophisticated view. According to this view, governments can act independently of and even against the short-term interests of capital by improving social conditions and trying to resolve political conflicts. Of course, once public policies come to be seen by most people as serving the interests of the capitalist class, governments would rapidly lose support. Accordingly, recent Marxists stress that public policies serve wider aims relating to the maintenance of political consent and stability, in particular the deflection of potential working-class challenges, rather than simply the short-term interests of capital (for example, Offe, 1975; and Jessop, 1982).

The importance of the Marxist approach lies in its focus on the political significance of wider social forces, especially those of competing class interests. It forms an important corrective to the excessively individual-centred explanations adopted by the many pluralists who emphasise factors such as the role of individuals in promoting policies and the expressed values of these individuals. Marxist approaches also call into question the emphasis of many pluralists on the formal institutions of government. For example, a pluralist account of the drawing up of the Australian constitution would focus on the role of British parliamentarians, the representatives of the states and the clash of ideas among individual delegates over the allocation of functional responsibilities. In contrast, a Marxist account would focus on the socio-economic interests that underlay the process and the consequences of the constitution for class power—in particular stressing its role in perpetuating the existing distribution of power and wealth in Australia.

However, Marxist approaches tend towards blanket explanations. They portray all policy outcomes as determined by conflicting class interests and neglect other important interests and divisions within society. Class may constitute the most fundamental set of social interests, but policy outcomes and processes usually have to be explained by reference to other significant interests, such as the professions, the organised consumers of goods and services, ethnic groups and reforming pressure groups.

All three approaches have much to offer in unravelling the complexities of public policy outcomes and processes. The more recent pluralist writers have acknowledged that parliamentary politics and party competition are of only limited explanatory value in most policy fields. They emphasise the need also to take into account the wide range of possibly influential individuals and groups, particularly the bureaucrats and professionals. The corporatist approach goes further in emphasising the closed and exclusionary characteristics of the contemporary policy process. In particular, the corporatists point to how governments and interest groups seek close and structured relationships and the problems of such relationships. Finally, Marxist approaches take us beyond the immediate political system in stressing the need to understand government policies within the broad context of competing social and economic interests, especially in posing the question of how given policies contribute to the maintenance of the existing distribution of wealth and power.

All three approaches point to potentially significant factors in the understanding of policy processes and outcomes. Indeed the best public policy studies are written with some consciousness of all three perspectives on policy. Of course, there are important differences between policy fields, the policy process is structured quite differently and involves quite different people in the fields such as agriculture and multicultural affairs. Policy issues are also fluid and change over time; for example, cyclists no longer enjoy the influence they once enjoyed in the urban roads policy sector at the turn of the century. Some policy questions, such as child sexual abuse in recent years, suddenly become major public issues and the elected politicians have to take account of them. Yet other policy questions simply never surface as public issues but are resolved between recognised interest groups and bureaucrats outside competitive party politics. A full understanding of public policy requires an awareness that different explanations of particular policy outcomes are possible. What does this mean in practice? What sorts of questions should students of policy be posing?

The problem-centred approach

The problem-centred approach starts from the basic question 'What makes a social problem?' Usually when people think about government, they think of how a particular decision or policy was made and look for an explanation in terms of which actors were involved and their motivations. While these questions are important, it is equally important to ask the prior question: why do some problems become a focus for widespread social concern, while others are largely excluded from concern? In other words, students of public policy have to begin by asking about the ways in which political agendas are fixed and changed.

There are many social conditions that could be or are being recognised as social problems and arriving on the political agenda. For example, people may be concerned with the shrinking value of the dollar in their pocket, disturbed by reports of large numbers of aboriginal deaths in police custody or concerned that poor road conditions are damaging their car suspensions. Some of these concerns become social problems, while others do not. Moreover, there are many examples of social conditions that have always existed yet have not always been recognised as 'problems'; for example, child sexual abuse. For a condition to become a social problem requires that it move from being a matter of public indifference to being one of widespread social and political concern. How and why does a *condition* become recognised as a *problem*?

The recognition of a condition as a social problem is a political process of claim and counter-claim. Social problems are more than just objective conditions that can be checked out and measured. For example, the social problem of 'poverty' cannot be summed up simply in terms of income statistics, but requires some arguments about how many people are on incomes that can be defined as below the 'poverty level', why they are poor and what priority in resources terms should be given to eliminating their poverty.

For a condition to become a problem requires it to be widely seen as socially significant, usually as a threat to certain interests or values cherished by a group. Interest groups, then, create social problems through claiming that a condition is serious enough to require government action. A group or groups claim that a condition exists, define it as a problem and demand government action to resolve the problem. The aim of such groups is to push their concerns onto the political agenda as a first step towards getting government action. Claims can take a wide range of forms, such as a group of urban local municipalities demanding action over worsening housing conditions from state government, a petition from a residents' group calling on the council to close down a potentially dangerous chemical factory, or a campaign to increase child care provision (see chapter 16).

The corporatist approach opens up a further perspective on problem emergence. It points to how previous public policies affect the origins and forms of interest groupings. In a sense, yesterday's policy response is today's social problem, for example, high-rise public housing schemes were a 1970s response to the housing shortage but they have now themselves become a problem as people resist being housed in such schemes. Meanwhile the Marxist approach adds another perspective in seeing social problems as protests by the disadvantaged against their experience of a repressive social order. The dominant class interests within society give in to these protests only in so far as such concessions are necessary to prevent serious challenges to their position.

How problems are adopted

When it comes to explaining how and why problems are adopted by policy makers, the pluralist approach concentrates on the selection of problems by government policy makers and the organising activities of interest groups. Government policy has to be selective as those in government cannot take on all possible public problems. They are careful to manage the political agenda, that is they try to control the numbers of problems adopted and the ways in which they are defined. They are more likely to resist than welcome attempts by interest groups to get issues adopted onto the political agenda. Meanwhile interest groups have to win influence through organisation—gathering together sufficient numbers of people, acquiring sufficient funds to mount a campaign, and lobbying parliamentarians. In addition, interest groups have to legitimate their stance through documenting their problem and generalising from their experience to demonstrate that they have a *public* and not simply a *private* problem or grievance.

To counter interest group pressures, policy makers often question the legitimacy of interest group claims. They usually find it easier to resist new claims on the grounds of the proper or legitimate scope of government than of the substantive merits of a group's case. So they deny that a problem is of proper government concern or question the 'respectability' of the group. Alternatively, they may define a 'problem' as essentially a matter of individual pathology and failed individual responsibility rather than as a matter of collective failure and therefore of governmental responsibility. The problem of unemployment, for example, is often presented by ministers as a question of individual unwillingness to work or to retrain rather than one of government decision to hold down demand in the economy (Harding, 1985). Another response to group pressure is simple indifference, a powerful weapon often overlooked in policy making studies. Indifference is a powerful weapon because new groups, especially of the poor and powerless, can quickly lose their impetus and enthusiasm when government fails even to acknowledge their existence.

Even if ministers and senior bureaucrats accept that a problem is a matter of public concern, they may still reject a problem on the grounds that a policy response is simply not feasible. Financial cost is one obvious objection to any policy change, for example, cost has been the main objection to universal childcare provision in Australia. Another is the amount of organisational change that any policy change is thought to involve. If such change is seen as too great, policy makers are likely to be deterred from seriously considering the problem. Any claim-making group has to respond by arguing that some policy response could be made without too much organisational disruption.

However, policy makers may whisk a problem onto the political agenda when events produce an upsurge in popular concern. For example, after the Melbourne Hoddle Street massacre and other incidents in 1987 involving gunmen, strengthened gun laws suddenly became a major political issue at state level, especially during the New South Wales elections in the following year. Problems can also receive rapid attention when the activity of a group is consonant with political priorities or bureaucratic interests (in terms of expansion or inter-departmental competition).

The corporatist approach adds a further dimension to this pluralist account of policy adoption. Problem selectivity and adoption should be seen within the context of government's need to limit conflict by containing potentially disruptive interests, especially from the trade unions and investment capital. The formation of close and institutionalised government-interest group alliances can be used to choke off new and potentially disruptive problems. The 'private' interest groups involved in such alliances themselves acquire an interest in excluding competing groups. For example, farming interest groups often collude with the bureaucrats in excluding environmental groups from policy discussions on agricultural affairs.

An awareness of the wider social and economic interests is also vital in understanding why a problem is adopted. The Marxist approach stresses the material interests underlying a process of apparently political reform, though this approach tends to oversimplify in assuming that class interests are easily translated into political reforms. For instance, a balanced account of the welfare state should include an analysis of how social and economic pressures relate to the political process of change. Marxist accounts stress that governments are forced to consider welfare reforms to buy off growing working class militancy, overlooking the role of reformers and of humanitarian reactions to widespread poverty emphasised by pluralists.

How problems compete with each other

Policy makers face a daily problem of overload. At all levels of government, politicians and bureaucrats are confronted by a multitude of problems all apparently worthy of their attention and of government action. The barriers to problem adoption just mentioned are one check on the overcrowding of the political agenda. Another response, suggested by the corporatists, is that of delegating powers to non-governmental bodies or interest groups, for example professional associations, such as the Australian Medical Assocation, regulate the training and work practices of vital occupations with legal powers given them by the state.

The pressure of these competing problems means that policy makers have to allocate priorities among adopted problems. Governments typically have mechanisms for determining priorities among problems and policies. Cabinets and annual budgets are good examples of such mechanisms. Although, as was argued earlier, many major decisions have effectively been removed from cabinets at commonwealth and state levels, the pluralist emphasis on cabinet government should not be entirely forgotten. Cabinets still retain a significant role in decisions and in the implementation of major switches in priorities, or resources, between departments. Many research studies indicate that major policy switches require the full political force of cabinet commitment for their implementation in the face of the conservative forces of policy maintenance (see, for example, Laffin, 1986).

Budgets also have a vital role in policy competition so it is no accident that the study of the budgetary process has become a major part of public policy studies. The budget of the Commonwealth or a state government can be seen as a measure of the balance of advantage between the various beneficaries of government spending. As such, it is the closest there is to an objective statement of the policy priorities of government and so offers an important measure of the direction of changes in policy priorities. The main lesson of these studies is that policy change is a matter of political bargaining that tends to produce only incremental or gradual policy change.

There have been numerous attempts to escape from incrementalism and improve budgeting as a decision-making tool. Techniques have been introduced such as programme budgeting, which encourage decision makers to review every spending programme and assess its relevance to their broad policy goals. These attempts to imposed greater managerial 'rationality' on the process have had only limited success. It would seem that the politicians and even many bureaucrats prefer political horse trading rather than the 'rational' approach of trying to reach mutually agreed goals and apply them to budgetary decisions (Wildavsky, 1984).

How problems are maintained

Once a social problem is recognised, adopted and acted upon by those within government, the problem and the response become institutionalised. In other words, problems become officially defined, with a group of officials or even a department committed to that definition and a particular policy response, often also accompanied by a corporatist arrangement between the associated interest group and government. It is this tendency towards problem institutionalisation and political closure that the corporatists stress and the pluralists underestimate. The political system is not as open and as responsive to outside forces as the pluralist analysis implies. Any individuals or groups—whether from inside or outside government—pressing for a new problem to be adopted or a redefinition of an existing problem, have to overcome powerful interests concerned to maintain existing policies. In addition, as the Marxists argue, these interests may be allied with wider class and social interests.

Within government, problem adoption produces organisational interests with a strong investment in problem maintenance and resistance to change. Government departments become committed to certain problems and their definition as senior officials come to see their career prospects and departmental loyalties being tied up with the existing set of problems (see chapter 8). In Australia, the professions and organised occupational groups within departments are important examples of such organisational interests. The professions are most evident at state level, where many departments, at least until recently, have been dominated by particular professional groups—engineers in road construction departments, surveyors in lands departments, doctors in health, teachers in education, and so on. These professionally dominated organisations tend to throw up problems and solutions that reflect professional policy definitions and interests—roads departments usually favour engineering solutions to problems of traffic congestion rather than traffic diversion or increased use of public transport. Policy fields come to be dominated by one set of interests that excludes alternative problem definitions and policy responses. Such appropriation of public problems does raise complex problems of control and accountability outside parliament and cabinet, which the corporatist approach highlights.

Another important set of organisational interests, often overlooked, is that of government employees. They have a general employment interest in terms of pay and conditions and an interest in their particular policy field. Their employment interests are expressed through union membership, which is considerably higher in the public than in the private sector. Traditionally, governments have sought to contain this source of potential disruption by co-opting union leaders onto consultative committees (a corporatist type strategy). However, this strategy of co-option is coming under increasing strain as public servants are expected to bear the brunt of public expenditure cutbacks and public sector unionists are growing more scepticial of the value of 'consultation'.

Finally, problems and policies are maintained through the pressure of interests formally outside government. As the coporatists stress, government action creates and shapes interest groups, the establishment of new services typically creating a set of people in society with a strong interest in seeing that service continue. Where the links between government and interest groups are institutionalised in the ways highlighted by the corporatist approaches, the forces for problem maintenance are likely to be especially strong. Such combinations of internal organisational commitment and outside support raise important questions over the capacity of government to achieve policy changes.

How problems are depleted and deleted

Despite the forces of problem maintenance public policies do sometimes change as old problems disappear and new ones emerge. Indeed, there is a continuing process of problem depletion and deletion whereby problems slip off or are removed from the political agenda and policies modified or terminated. Consequently, government organisations may see the problem to which they owe their origin disappear or change. For instance, the Metric Conversion Board was abolished once metrification was achieved and the Australian Bicentennial Authority was similarly dissolved after 1988.

Those affected by problem depletion will usually try to maintain problems and resist the forces of problem depletion. Public servants employed in affected agencies and outside beneficaries of these agencies usually try to survive, particularly where corporatist relationships have developed. They may seek to maintain the existing political agenda by suppressing attempts by others to challenge existing problem definitions and to push new problems to the fore. Of course, they are far from helpless in the face of these challenges as they have the considerable resources of government at their disposal—access to the media, control of information and of financial resources.

Even so, changes in the social and economic environment of government often undermine the case for maintaining a problem and compel policy makers to adopt new or redefined problems. Problems are depleted as social and economic changes cast doubt on established definitions. For example, recent demographic changes involving the 'greying of Australia' are inclining policy makers to pay more attention to the problems of the elderly; and population movements and falling birth rates lead to falling school rolls in the inner cities, so that existing school provision is seen to be uneconomic and schools are closed.

Another reason for problem depletion is changed social attitudes towards affected groups. For example, the problem of caring for the mentally ill has recently been redefined away from the nineteenth-century view that they should be removed from the community and placed in special hospitals and towards the view that they should be de-institutionalised and placed in community hostels. While this change also reflects a concern to reduce the high costs of caring for the mentally ill in hospitals, the shift in medical and social attitudes is at least as significant.

Public expenditure cutbacks are also of increasing significance in the depletion and deletion of problems. Over recent years governments have responded to growing international and domestic economic pressures by trying to reduce public expenditure. These questions of problem depletion and deletion are moving towards the centre stage of public policy as the years of public sector growth are being overtaken by public sector financial constraint.

Conclusion

Public policy is the study of the processes whereby social problems are recognised or overlooked, defined, adopted or rejected by policy makers, maintained by them, and depleted and deleted. Pluralism, corporatism and Marxism can be used to build up a full understanding of the policy process by focussing on a 'problem-oriented' approach to public policy.

References

Brugger, B. and Jaensch, J. (1985) *Australian Politics: Theory and Practice* Sydney: George Allen and Unwin

Emy, H. (1978) *The Politics of Australian Democracy* Melbourne: Macmillan, 2nd edn

Harding, Anne (1985) 'Unemployment Policy: A Case Study in Agenda Management' *Australian Journal of Public Administration*, 44, September

Laffin, M. (1986) 'No Permanent Head: Minister-Bureaucrat Relationships in Victoria' *Australian Journal of Public Administration* 66, March

Offe C. (1975) 'The Theory of the Capitalist State and the Problem of Policy Formation', in L. Lindberg, R. Alford, C. Crouch and C. Offe (eds) *Stress and Contradiction in Modern Capitalism* Lexington: D.C. Heath

Richardson J.J. and Jordan A.G. (1979) *Governing Under Pressure: The Policy Process in a Post-Parliamentary Democracy* Oxford: Martin Robertson

Wildavsky A. (1984) *The Politics of the Budgetary Process* Boston: Little, Brown, 4th edn

Part Two

INSTITUTIONS

5 The constitution

Lex Watson

Constitutions are the laws that govern the governors. They are a set of rules that differs from other laws and policies in that they are supposed to be superior to the laws and decisions made from day to day by governments. Many organisations in society as well as nations have constitutions, and they serve similar purposes.

Though not all constitutions have all of them, there are a number of elements commonly found in constitutions, and a number of purposes are served by them. The first is often a rhetorical flourish at the start, declaring such things as belief in a certain deity, or a monarch, perhaps a patriotic statement about the unity of the nation, and often a commitment to certain ideals such as democracy, justice, and the like. The statements, however, usually have no force or meaning in law.

The second, a major element of all constitutions, is a statement of the formal institutions and offices that will exist—parliaments, presidents, etc., their powers and functions, how they relate to one another, in the case of conflict who or which is to override the other or how conflicts are to be resolved, and often some rules about the relationship between these various institutions and the electorate as a whole.

A third element of many though not all constitutions is some sort of bill of rights, some statements of human rights and civil liberties. Typically these are rights of the citizens versus the state, the government. They are statements about things government may not do, areas into which it may not intrude. Very occasionally they may also impose obligations on governments. In liberal democracies they are very much part of the rules of the political game.

Fourth, in countries that have a federal system of government, the constitution will specify the powers of the two levels of government, central and regional, commonwealth and state, and perhaps some mechanisms through which they can formally interact.

Fifth, constitutions will contain rules about the way in which they can be amended or changed. Often, though not always, this will be a more difficult process than making and amending ordinary law, and may be taken out of the hands of government and legislature and reserved for the people as a whole.

Last, constitutions will frequently establish an arbiter of the meaning of the constitution, to rule in cases where there is dispute as to who has a particular power, what a section might mean, and so on. Normally this will be a court, the highest court in the country.

Australia's constitutions

In Australia there are seven constitutions: one for each of the six states, one for the Commonwealth. The state constitutions have not attracted great political interest in recent years. Only two areas have aroused controversy—provisions for fair electoral arrangements, essentially for one person, one vote, one value; and the powers of upper houses. While there is potential for future conflict in state constitutions, they are not discussed further here.

The Australian constitution, however, has had a much more controversial existence. When it was being drafted in the 1890s, it drew its inspiration from two different models—the British or Westminster model for much of its institutional arrangements, and the United States for some of its federalism provisions. It is possible to see many of the subsequent problems with the constitution as originating from this hybrid set of arrangements.

Federalism requires a very formal and rigid constitution to ensure the sovereign powers of the two levels of government. In part this is achieved by provisions such as section 51 of the Australian constitution, which specifies many of the powers—the areas of policy—that are given to the Commonwealth, leaving the others to the states. There have been very extensive disputes and problems with the federalism arrangements in Australia, covering not only section 51 but also other sections such as 92 and 96 (see chapter 11).

The demands of the states, or colonies as they were at the time, which they set as a price for federating, went beyond preserving their sovereignty, their exclusive right to legislate in certain areas of policy. They also insisted on preserving and writing into the constitution provisions for state intervention in the operation and institutional arrangements of the Commonwealth Government. Specifically, this meant detailed provision about the allocation of seats to each state in the House of Representatives or Lower House of the new Parliament, the creation of an Upper House (the Senate) as a states' house with equal representation for each state, the provision of great power to the Senate to allow it to protect 'States' Rights', and a form of state veto in section 128 of the constitution, which is the provision for amending the constitution.

More generally, the dictates of federalism resulted in a set of provisions in the constitution that were explicit, exact, and intended to be observed, as they have been, quite literally. These related to institutional arrangements of the Commonwealth Parliament.

On the other hand, the British Westminster tradition—unlike those of most countries in the world—had been one of an 'unwritten constitution'. The system had evolved over centuries through a series of ordinary laws, through documents without the supreme force of constitutional law, and through the development of a number of 'constitutional conventions'. Colonial governments established in the nineteenth century had adopted these conventions and operated in accord with them. It was automatically assumed that they would apply and operate in the new Commonwealth Government.

Writing such a political system into a necessarily rigid document, as required by federalism, posed problems. The system was a constitutional monarchy. How far could or should the document go in limiting or denying ultimate power to the Monarch or her vice-regal representative, the Governor-General? What were the consequences of making legally rigid a system that was flexible and based on convention?

Australia's answer to these questions was to produce a thoroughly schizophrenic constitutional document. Provisions for the relationship between the electorate and the elected representatives and for the establishment of the legislature, the Parliament, and federal sections are to be taken literally. But from there on the sections dealing with the executive level of government and the role of the Governor-General were intended to be—and largely are—pure fiction.

Thus such notions as cabinet government, majority rule and party government, as well as the office of the Prime Minister, were left to constitutional convention. Instead of specifying those principles and bodies, the document has written in an almost all-powerful office of Governor-General and a Federal Executive Council (ExCo) with a feeble advisory role only.

Governor-General

The ambiguity of the Governor-General's role is illustrated by the contrast between his or her formal powers and the public face of the daily activities of the office. Formally the Governor-General decides when Parliament meets, when it shall be dissolved and go to election, who shall be ministers (provided only that they are or become elected), and what laws may be vetoed. The Governor-General also commands the armed forces, and in some cases is obliged to consult with the Federal Executive Council. The only major formal constraint is that a Governor-General cannot raise or spend money without parliamentary approval (section 83).

Publicly, this immensely powerful figure is reduced to endless rounds of trivia and social events. Vice-regal columns in the newspapers report nothing but dinners with people, theatre evenings, opening non-controversial events and edifices and having people staying at Government House, along with the usually weekly ExCo meeting.

In practice, the role of the Governor-General lies somewhere between the two extremes suggested above. Constitutional convention, at least until the sacking of the Whitlam Government in 1975, referred to the powers in the written constitution as 'reserve powers'. This, as with all conventions, was not entirely clear. Were these reserve powers to be exercised only under rare and extreme circumstances, and if so what were they? Or were they, as some democrats thought, never to be used?

Certainly convention said, in accordance with the evolving role of the British Monarch over the last 150 years or more, that the office was to be 'above politics', non-partisan, impartial, and as the titular head of state to embody non-controversial national aspirations as expressed in Australia Day addresses to the nation. Publicly that has largely been the case in Australia.

The animosity toward the office caused by Sir John Kerr's actions in 1975 is in stark contrast to the normal view of the office, and his successors as Governor-General have recognised the need to restore the impression of impartiality.

The events of 1975 and the sacking by New South Wales Governor Sir Phillip Game of the Premier, Jack Lang, in 1932 are rare public examples of the exercise of vice-regal reserve powers. Because of the convention of apolitical Monarchs and their representatives, communications between governments and Governors-General, including the interaction in ExCo, are confidential. Prime Ministers will announce that they have advised the Governor-General to call an election, but little more than that is public.

Yet it is known that there is more intervention than that. In Britain occasionally it is reported, from 'informed sources', that the British Monarch is concerned about certain policies, though subsequently 'the Palace' will always strongly deny any such leak. In Australia, a rare glimpse was given by Sir Paul Hasluck, Governor-General from 1969 to 1974, when he wrote about aspects of the function and operation of his office (Hasluck, 1979).

Hasluck makes it clear that ExCo meetings were more than just rubber stamping of government decisions. He wrote (1979: 38–41):

> In my own study of Executive Council papers, I tried to satisfy myself first that the Council had the power under the Constitution or statute to make the decision recommended, that the recommendation was made by competent authority and that any preliminary enquiry or other steps required by law had taken place. . . On matters which might be more controversial I would seek to satisfy myself that there was no conflict between the actions recommended and any agreements, commitments or decisions of the government, and that respect had been paid to the conventions of the Constitution and the established procedures. . . I was also concerned with ensuring that there was no conflict among my advisers. . .
>
> Broadly speaking my experience was that in the course of five years under three different Prime Ministers there were four or five occasions on which a major issue arose in Executive Council and, as a result of discussion in the Council, a government eventually acted more wisely than was at first proposed. In the usual routine of business dealing with a variety of matters I found that possibly two or three items out of every hundred were deferred for reconsideration on one point or another.

Hasluck (1979: 39) added that 'The Governor-General-in-Council is the executive instrumentality and is not the policy-making instrumentality of government', an important distinction, and one which, at least in theory, may moderate the concerns of those democratically minded people who object to such extensive powers being exercised by unelected people in secret. The secrecy of ExCo business means that those concerns cannot be completely satisfied, and the accountability of government, the executive government, remains inadequate.

In discussing the working of ExCo in his time as Governor General, Hasluck suggests that it may not always have always exercised the same level of scrutiny as he demanded. Different incumbents will have different styles of working, but the sort of expertise brought to the position is important. Early colonial governors were largely military men who ruled directly and exercised power through their command of the British armed forces stationed here. At least since 1901 Governors-General and state governors have been essentially formal figureheads, most commonly retired military personnel, often imported from England, and minor members of the English royal family. More recently, particularly at the Commonwealth level, the tradition has been to appoint Australians; the last six Governors-General have all been ex-politicians or ex-judges from Australia.

Appointing Australians with political or legal experience has both advantages and disadvantages. The advantage is that the person in the office will have much greater experience and expertise to bring to the tasks Hasluck outlines, and so will be better able to fulfil those tasks. The potential disadvantage is that they are, as a consequence, more likely to exercise some of the powers of the office on their own discretion rather than acting on the advice of the elected Government, as the constitutional convention expects.

Some, though not all, of the Governor-General's powers are to be exercised by the 'Governor-General in Council', that is the 'Governor-General acting with the advice of the Federal Executive Council' (section 63). Here convention dictates that he will take his government's advice, sometimes after some questioning. Other powers are, in the written document, his alone, including appointing and dismissing ministers and calling elections.

One issue faced by Governors-General is that, if they do not take their Government's advice, to whom can they turn? They can rely on such expertise as they have. They have a personal staff, but that is domestic, not political or legal. ExCo has a secretary, a public servant seconded from the Prime Minister's Department, whose role is essentially to give administrative advice, not advice on more sensitive matters. This can pose major problems for a Governor-General, given the ambiguity of parts of the constitution.

Constitutional Ambiguity

No legal document will be without its ambiguities. No such document will allow for all possible contingencies, especially those arising decades after its drafting. In its division of powers between Commonwealth and state levels this has proved to be particularly true in Australia (see chapter 11). It has also proved true in addressing the institutional arrangements in Australia, a problem exacerbated by the deliberate vagueness and fiction written into the description of the executive levels of government. For some of these ambiguities, notably the federal jurisdiction areas, the High Court is the authority charged with resolving these conflicts and making a ruling. But in others the task falls to the Governor-General and has had the potential to draw that office into areas of political controversy.

One such is the power of the Senate, and in particular the controversy that arose in 1975. The constitution makes it clear that the Senate's powers over money bills (raising taxes and spending money) is less than that of the House of Representatives. Under section 53, money bills must originate in the House of Representatives, a recognition that the government which raises and spends money will be based in, and have majority support from, that House. Further, they cannot be amended by the Senate, though Senate requests can be made to the House of Representatives for amendments. Since neither House can unilaterally amend bills, one reading of this section is that the Senate cannot reject such a bill either. Certainly some Senators in 1975 took the view that they should not defeat the Budget and so it was deferred, not defeated.

The mechanisms provided for breaking deadlocks between the two Houses (section 57) could not be used to solve a dispute over the Budget because the Government would run out of money long before they could be implemented. The ambiguity might have been resolved by a High Court case, but again time would not allow that. Thus the situation inevitably put the Governor General in the position where he had to decide whether or not to intervene. Either way, the result would have been seen as partisan by one side of politics. The constitution had failed to provide a satisfactory solution.

Choosing the Government may also cause problems. Since 1910 the Commonwealth Parliament has usually contained a clear distinction between a majority or government party (or coalition) and a minority or opposition party (or coalition). Even in such cases a Governor-General will exercise a well founded discretion, based on advice from the outgoing prime minister, about which Member of Parliament the Governor-General will ask to form a Government. Following an election this is done well before the first meeting of the new Parliament and so before any formal test of the numbers in the parliament.

None the less, situations can arise when discretion has to be exercised by Governor-General, when the party complexion of the parliament is not clear cut. He or she may have to make a decision whether to grant an election to a Prime Minister who has lost control of the Parliament or whether to give a commission to someone else. Take the result of the 1940 election, which was conservative coalition 37 seats, Labor 37 seats, and two independents in the House of Representatives. The coalition, with general support of the independents, was asked to form a Government. In 1941 the independents decided to give their support to Labor in the course of the Budget debates. Had it not been wartime, the coalition Prime Minister, Fadden, might have asked for an election rather than giving government to Labor without a fight. In such circumstances, should a Governor-General refuse a prime minister's request? Westminster tradition says there is a regal, or in this case vice-regal, discretion to refuse.

Another problem which almost arose in 1977, concerns the double dissolution power (section 57). The constitution sets out the circumstances under which a governor-general 'may' grant a double dissolution of the two Houses of Parliament. Convention says that the bill or bills rejected by the Senate, which are the grounds for the election, must be major bills, preferably important parts of the Government's previous election manifesto, for which they can claim a mandate from the electorate. Did the grounds on which the

Prime Minster, Fraser, seek a double dissolution satisfy those convention criteria? Would a Governor General be justified in exercising a discretion in accord with convention and reject the request? In the event, the election was granted.

Most recently the proposed 'Australia Card', a national ID card system, threatened to raise a constitutional issue. The Senate's rejection of the legislation on two occasions was the ground for the 1987 double dissolution election. Following that election the parties opposed to the ID card still had the numbers to defeat the legislation in the Senate but announced that when the 'Australia Card Bill' came before the Senate again it would be referred to a committee, in the first instance, and that it would be a considerable time before it was formally debated and defeated in the Senate.

Section 57, the double dissolution provision, provides that the Governor-General may convene a joint sitting of the two Houses after such an election if the Senate 'rejects or fails to pass' the original legislation. How long a delay is needed to satisfy the requirement of a failure to pass a bill? Does it require the Senate formally to defer acceptance, is referral to a Senate select committee sufficient, or where and on what criteria is a line to be drawn? In such a case it can be assumed that at some stage the Government will formally request the Governor-General to convene a joint sitting of the Houses of Parliament and he or she would have to decide whether the constitutional conditions had been fulfilled.

In the specific case of the 'Australia Card' the Government had to drop the legislation for separate reasons, the potential constitutional crisis was averted and the interpretation of that aspect of section 57 was left untested and unresolved. Had the legislation gone ahead, however, highly controversial legislation as it was, inevitably the Governor-General would have been drawn into making a decision with partisan consequences, whichever way he decided. The constitution would have again been found wanting in its failure to provide clear guidelines for conflict resolution.

It is not an accident that many of the relatively recent examples of constitutional ambiguity and potential politicisation of the office of Governor-General focus on the powers of the Senate and the resolution of deadlocks between it and the House of Representatives. The electoral system used in the Senate since 1949 (see chapter 10) and an apparent shift toward minor party voting (see chapter 20) have meant that the Senate is now posing strains on the written constitution. It is not and never has been a states' house, it is neither the docile servant of the Government (i.e., the majority party in the House of Representatives), nor can it be dismissed as opposition obstruction, as it was for the first 50 or more years of federation. The contrast between what was and what is can be easily made—in the first 70 years of Commonwealth Government there were two (Senate caused) double dissolutions, in 1914 and 1951. In the last fifteen years, there have been four double dissolutions and several other potential constitutional brawls. Furthermore, two of the latest cases, in 1974 and 1975, have been forced on the Government because they threatened its very ability to govern by denying it money, that life blood of government.

This ambiguity in the written constitution, and the lack of real force of constitutional conventions as some thought them to exist, highlights the inadequacy of that document. Furthermore, it has and may continue to threaten the political neutrality and essentially titular status of the Governor-General as head of state, and it exposes the problems that any Governor-General might face in dealing with crises.

An 'Australian' constitution?

Technically the written constitution, while drafted by Australians in Australia, started life as an Act of the British Parliament in 1900, namely the Commonwealth of Australia Constitution Act. Some of its provisions also suggested continuing subservience to Britain.

In theory the constitution could have been changed by Act of the British Parliament, the final court of appeal remained the 'Privy Council' (officially Her Majesty in Council), and some state constitutions left some limited powers over state matters in the hands of the ex-imperial Parliament. These links have now been broken, starting with the conventional view that Australia was in fact fully independent from 1901, and formally with the Statute of Westminster in 1931. The last links were broken by the Australia Act of 1986, except for the formal power of the Monarch to appoint Governors-General and governors.

In the debate about the role of the Governor-General, particularly since 1975, a number of issues concerning Australia's independence have arisen. The Governor-General is the vice-regal representative of the Monarch. That Monarch is also head of state of another country, and some maintain this is anomalous, even though since the Whitlam Government she has held the separate title of Queen of Australia. For some this symbolises a continuing deference to the ex-imperial power. For others it offends the many Australians whose origins are not Anglo-Saxon or British. Others uphold the status quo. But there remains the issue of nationalism.

A second issue is egalitarianism. Monarchies and aristocracies enshrine inherited power and authority. When linked with the right to hold unelected office and exercise political power this offends many democracts. Republicanism is concerned with opposing such inherited power.

Third is the presidential issue. A solution, for some, of the problems inherent in the position of the Governor-General is to adopt a rather different system of government, such as one of the presidential models, thus eliminating the unelected head of state. At its simplest, the Governor-General could be elected (Solomon, 1976), or more drastically, Australia's present 'responsible' government system could be replaced with the United States' 'separation of powers' system. Direct election of the chief executive is not unknown at local government level in Australia; some lord mayors are directly elected.

Despite some people's concerns and periodic public debate, such drastic reforms are unlikely in the immediate future.

A bill of rights?

Bills of rights have become common features of many constitutions. As a part of the laws that govern the governors, such bills traditionally incorporate at least two elements—political rights and legal process rights.

Political rights include rights such as freedom of speech and the media, the right to vote and to a free and fair electoral system, freedom of association and assembly. They are the rules within which political debate and elections should be conducted in a liberal democratic system. Governments are constrained in that there are areas of activity they may not restrict, the rights of the governed versus the Government.

Legal process rights deal with the operation of the law, its implementation, enforcement and administration. Citizens are to be protected from arbitrary, unjust and discriminatory action by governments and their officials.

Australia does not have a bill of rights. The constitution's Founding Fathers rejected the suggestion in the 1890s, including only a few elements on a piecemeal basis. 'One person, one vote' is guaranteed (sections 8, 30), the right to property (section 51 [xxxi]), to trial by jury in certain cases (section 80), and to freedom of religion (section 116) get some protection. All are of limited application, having been given narrow interpretations by the High Court (Hogan, 1981). None of these sections applies to state governments. In some respects the constitution specifically violates political rights—for example, Senate electoral provisions defy the concept of one vote, one value.

Interest in a bill of rights and human rights protection generally has increased in the last twenty years, partly for domestic reasons, but also because of the increasing international pressure on all countries to ratify and observe the growing number of international human rights treaties and conventions.

Australian attempts to implement human rights, specifically political and legal process rights, started in 1973 with the introduction of a Human Rights Bill into the Commonwealth Parliament. It was not passed, though subsequent measures in 1981 and 1986 have passed. These measures remain ordinary or statute law, not in the constitution. They, along with the unsuccessful Australian Bill of Rights Bill of 1985 and several other measures, have attracted strong political opposition as well as support. Given the controversy, no government has been tempted to propose a referendum for their constitutional adoption as it would almost certainly fail.

Constitutionally, human rights have had an impact in a way not predicted by the Founding Fathers. Only the Commonwealth Government has the power to ratify international treaties and conventions, state governments may not do so. International human rights conventions were unknown in 1901 but have become common since 1945, typically including an obligation by the ratifying government to act to achieve the objects and rights in the document. Many of the areas covered by those international conventions, however, constitutionally fall to the Australian states.

This situation has raised tensions within the federal system, with the

Commonwealth using its 'external affairs' power (section 51 [xxix]) to pursue its international obligations. In effect the Commonwealth can now impose a range of human rights observance on state governments.

The High Court

The Australian High Court has two major functions. As the highest court in the land it is the final court of appeal on matters of law involving criminal or civil cases (section 73) and it is the arbiter of all cases where the interpretation of the Australian constitution is involved (sections 75 and 76).

Generally in Australia courts are held in high esteem and none more so than the High Court. It has attracted some political interest, though rather less than its United States counterpart, the Supreme Court. It is perhaps surprising that even its establishment was surrounded by controversy, with some being opposed to it being set up at all (Galligan, 1987, chapter 3).

Much of the High Court's work is as the final appellate court on matters of interpretation of statute law. While important, the constitutional concern lay primarily in the abolition of appeals to an English court. Now the High Court is truly the final court of appeal for Australia.

It is as interpreter of the constitution that the High Court firmly enters the political arena. Overwhelmingly the Court has been faced, in its constitutional work, with the question of jurisdiction—does the Commonwealth Government have the power to legislate in a given area or is it reserved for the state governments? Inevitably its decisions, whether favouring the central or the provincial level, will be seen as political, as favouring one or other philosophy of what the 'federal balance' is or ought to be, as well as having an impact on what laws are likely to be passed or blocked. It has become common to chart the periods of High Court decisions in terms of which side of that debate it leant toward.

There can be no doubt that the Court has been called on to resolve questions about the meaning of the constitution in circumstances that were not envisaged by the Founding Fathers. The most recent and arguably most dramatic of these cases have been those arising out of human rights treaty obligations and the interpretation of the 'external affairs' power (section 51 [xxix]).

Such cases raise two related but separate issues, seen most clearly in the 'Franklin Dam case'. Objection to the decision to uphold the Commonwealth Government's power to block the Tasmanian decision to build that dam was made first because it infringed on state powers, and second because it blocked an action (building the dam) that some supported. In addition, some worried that the decision was by a 4:3 majority of judges, which was seen as lacking sufficient certainty.

Certainly judges disagree, not only on points of law but on their whole legal and sometimes political philosophies. The controversy over Mr. Justice Lionel Murphy is the clearest example of this, though there are many. While Australia has not experienced a high level of public scrutiny of the qualifications for High Court office, there has been interest. Ex-politicians have been targetted for most interest due to the fear that their political experience will prejudice their judgement on constitutional cases, especially those where issues of federal powers are at stake. Of the 34 Justices of the High Court between its founding in 1903 and 1984, about 30 percent were also politicians at some stage, though all were also distinguished lawyers.

Judges are appointed by the Governor-General in Council, in practice on a decision by the Prime Minister and the Attorney-General. As such they are political appointments, and some consultation is held with the states, though they serve until they are 70 years old if they so choose and are free of further political pressure.

Amending the Constitution

The point has already been made that the Australian constitution is a written document and therefore relatively inflexible. By their nature constitutions should be relatively hard to change compared to ordinary statute law, making them resistant to the day to day whims and interests of the government. This is especially so in a federal system where the constitution lays down the powers and boundaries of the two levels of government.

Constitutions can, do and must change over time. They can change in a number of ways. These include:

- formal amendment of individual clauses by changing the wording or inserting new provisions;
- change in circumstances, especially economic resources in federal systems so that the power at the disposal of different parts of the system changes;
- interpretation of sections by some higher court so that the meaning of particular sections or powers effectively alters the original drafters' intentions, whether in the light of new circumstances or for other reasons;
- recognition of conventions that either flesh out or override specific provisions of the written document, or in some cases allow provisions to fall into disuse; and
- by total repeal and replacement of the document or less dramatically by a thoroughgoing and extensive review and amendment of the original document.

Formal amendment has proved difficult in Australia (see Table 5.1). Of 42 proposals only eight have passed, four giving greater power to the Commonwealth Government, four dealing with institutional matters at Commonwealth level. A further five, however, attracted a majority of the total vote but failed because they did not gain a majority in four or more states, as required by the constitution's section 128. While this low record of amendment might suggest electoral conservatism, party and state government attitudes are more important. In general, for a referendum proposal to pass it needs support not only

Table 5.1 History of Referendums

Year	Subject	Government submitting	States where voters in favour of proposal	Percentage of voters in favour of proposal
1906	*Senate elections*	*Protectionist	6	82.7
1910	Finance	*Fusion	3 (Qld,WA,Tas.)	49.0
	State debts	*Fusion	5 (all exc.NSW)	55.0
1911	Legislative powers	Labor	1 (WA)	39.4
	Monopolies	Labor	1 (WA)	39.9
1913	Trade and commerce	*Labor	3 (Qld,SA,WA)	49.4
	Corporations	*Labor	3 (Qld,SA,WA)	49.3
	Industrial matters	*Labor	3 (Qld,SA,WA)	49.3
	Railway disputes	*Labor	3 (Qld,SA,WA)	49.1
	Trusts	*Labor	3 (Qld,SA,WA)	49.8
	Monopolies	*Labor	3 (Qld,SA,WA)	49.3
1919	Legislative powers	*Nationalist	3 (Vic.,Qld,WA)	49.7
	Monopolies	*Nationalist	3 (Vic.,Qld,WA)	48.6
1926	Legislative powers	Nat.CP	2 (NSW,Qld)	43.5
	Essential services	Nat.CP	2 (NSW,Qld)	42.8
1928	*State debts*	*Nat.CP	6	74.3
1936	Aviation	U.A.P.	2 (Vic.,Qld)	53.6
	Marketing	U.A.P.	0	36.3
1944	Post-war powers	Labor	2 (SA,WA)	46.0
1946	*Social Services*	*Labor	6	54.4
	Marketing	*Labor	3 (NSW,Vic.,WA)	50.6
	Industrial employment	*Labor	3 (NSW,Vic.,WA)	50.3
1948	Rents, prices	Labor	0	40.7
1951	Communists	Liberal/CP	3 (Qld,WA,Tas.)	49.4
1967	Nexus	Liberal/CP	1 (NSW)	40.3
	Aboriginals	Liberal/CP	6	90.8
1973	Prices	Labor	0	43.8
	Incomes	Labor	0	34.4
1974	Simultaneous elections	*Labor	1 (NSW)	48.3
	Amendment	*Labor	1 (NSW)	48.0
	Democratic elections	*Labor	1 (NSW)	47.2
	Local government	*Labor	1 (NSW)	46.9
1977	Simultaneous elections	Liberal/NCP	3 (NSW,Vic.,SA)	62.2
	Casual vacancies	Liberal/NCP	6	73.3
	Territorial votes	Liberal/NCP	6	77.7
	Retirement of judges	Liberal/NCP	6	80.1
1984	Simultaneous elections	*Labor	2 (NSW,Vic.)	50.6
	Interchange of Powers	*Labor	0	47.1
1988†	4–Year terms	Labor	0	32.9
	Democratic elections	Labor	0	37.6
	Local government	Labor	0	33.6
	Rights and freedoms	Labor	0	30.8

Note: * Referendum held at same time as a federal election.
Italicised subjects achieved sufficient majorities for change to Constitution
† 1988 figures are not final

from the major parties at Commonwealth level but also their counterparts at state level, and the two have by no means always gone together.

Changing circumstances and judicial interpretation have produced rather more changes and in some respects has allowed the constitution to be quite a flexible document. Overwhelmingly this evolution has been in the division of power between the Commonwealth and state governments, fairly consistently favouring the former (see chapter 11). While 'states' righters' bemoan these developments, the rigidity of the written document meant that other ways had to be found to allow Government to respond to the vast changes in economic demands on Government, to domestic and international economic circumstances and to technological developments. Economic management has become increasingly complex and important, necessitating greater centralised control of matters such as taxation levels and monetary policy, while, to take just the obvious cases, the Constitution was drafted before the advent of air transport or electronic communications media.

Conventions have played a rather small role in the evolution of the constitution. As noted earlier, the inherited Westminster conventions have ossified in the Antipodes and failed to show the flexibility that might avoid crises. Evolution has been greater in the federalism area, where the Commonwealth has stretched its powers with little opposition in areas such as education, health and scientific research (CSIRO) responsibilities that the states either do not want or cannot afford.

Wholesale amendment or rewriting of the constitution has been debated, on and off, over many years. Three major studies have been made. The first in the 1950s by a Senate committee was promptly shelved. The second was instituted by the Whitlam Government. It took the form of a series of constitutional conventions comprising delegates from the various parliaments. Politically this exercise was doomed from the start by the hostility of conservative state governments to the Labor Commonwealth Government and vice versa. The events of 1975 ensured that partisan views on the constitutional issues would preclude almost any rational debate, though the referendum proposals of 1977 owed their origins in part to agreement on those points.

In 1985 the Attorney General, Lionel Bowen, decided to tackle the issue of the constitution anew and in a different way. He established a 'people's' Constitutional Commission comprised not of serving politicans but of prominent people from a range of walks of life. The Commission had five advisory committees dividing the issues into the Australian judicial system, the distribution of powers, the executive government, individual and democratic rights and trade and national economic management. Their task was to report by 30 June 1988 with the prospect of a referendum proposing extensive changes in each area as a bicentennial affirmation of contemporary nationhood (Constitutional Commission, 1988).

The Commission sought to educate the public about the issues raised in reform debates, to canvass public views, and to take the debate out of the arena of party politics. Perhaps, it was thought, in this way a greater consensus in favour of reform would be achieved than in the past. As Table 5.1 shows, however, the four 1988 referendums were defeated by greater percentages than any in the past.

It may seem extraordinary that in 1988 Australia was not prepared to vote for the principle of one vote, one value, nor was it prepared to vote for freedom of religion in the states, nor even to protect the right to property against state governments. The opportunity in 1988 to revise, even partially,

Australia's constitution, has been lost. Rightly or wrongly the prospects for change in the near future are bleak.

As always, views on the constitution will be significantly governed by the political views and party self-interest of the major actors—the politicians.

References

Constitutional Commission (1988) *First Report of the Constitutional Commission: Summary* Canberra: AGPS

Galligan, B. (1987) *Politics of the High Court* Brisbane: University of Queensland Press

Hasluck, P. (1979) *The Office of Governor-General* Melbourne: Melbourne University Press

Hogan, M. (1981) 'Separation of Church and State: Section 116 of the Australian Constitution', in *Australian Quarterly* 53:2

Solomon, D. (1976) *Elect the Governor-General!* Melbourne: Thomas Nelson

6 Parliament

Ken Turner

> Instead of the function of governing, for which it is radically unfit, the proper office of a representative assembly is to watch and control the government...to compel a full exposition and justification...to censure them if found condemnable, and, if the men who compose the government abuse their trust, or fulfil it in a manner which conflicts with the deliberate sense of the nation, to expel them from office, and either expressly or virtually appoint their successors...In addition to this, the Parliament has an office, not inferior to this in importance; to be at once the nation's Committee of Grievances, and its Congress of Opinions...(Mill, 1910: 239)

Most traditional statements about the functions of Westminster-model parliaments are nostalgic rhetoric about what they are believed once to have done or what the writer would like to think they should be able to do. Because the reality falls well short of this, parliaments and especially parliamentarians are often summarily dismissed as sadly deteriorated and ineffective.

What can realistically be expected of parliaments? The conventional expectations of the Australian Parliament are that it ought to represent the people; debate public policy and make the laws; and provide and control the Government. All three need qualification in practice.

Representation

Participatory democrats prefer to maximise direct personal participation in the formulation of the rules that shape our lives, but liberal democrats settle for the likelihood that freely and fairly elected representatives will perform in reasonable conformity with the wishes of those represented. Parliamentarians have legitimacy because the process of electoral choice is publicly approved and seen as a practical sanction keeping them in line.

There is a common sense feeling that parliaments should include representatives of a wide cross section of the community. In selecting candidates, political parties consider the need for 'balanced tickets' and seek 'horses for courses', so that voters will feel that their parliament includes people with a feel for the problems of 'people like us'. Yet the Australian Parliament is far from being a representative sample or microcosm of the electorate.

In her study of Australian national parliamentarians from 1901 to 1980, Joan Rydon demonstrated that farmers (especially graziers) had constituted about one-fifth of all members, while merchants, shopkeepers and most professional groups (especially journalists and lawyers) had also been over-represented. By contrast, tradesmen, workers, and union and party officials together had constituted only one-fifth of the total. Similarly, she showed that parliamentary politics in Canberra had remained 'very much a middle aged occupation'. Roman Catholics had been under-represented, Presbyterians over-represented. Those not of Anglo-Celtic origins hardly appeared at all: only four of 1033 members had not had English-speaking parents, while only two members had been non-white. Not surprisingly, members were better educated than the general community. To 1980, 22.1 percent of members had been university graduates; in the 1980 Parliament, the figure was 40.9 percent. Those educated in private schools were much over-represented (Rydon, 1986: chapters 3, 9–12).

Politics in the Australian Parliament has been man's business. Until 1982 New South Wales had never sent a woman to either house of the national parliament. To 1977 only 62 women had ever been elected to any parliament in Australia, including twelve to the Senate and four to the House of Representatives. In that year women constituted 27 (3.7 percent) of 735 members in all Australian parliaments, mostly to be found in upper houses. Despite recent efforts to reduce this gross under-representation, by 1983 women still constituted only 8.5 percent of all members. The 1987 Australian Parliament included seventeen women in the Senate (22.4 percent) and nine in the House of Representatives (6.1 percent).

The legitimacy of Australian parliamentarians, then, is not based upon their being 'typical' of the population. They need only be authorised by free and fair elections—but authorised to do what? Political styles may differ, members seeing themselves as delegates (following instructions), trustees (independently deciding issues as they see fit), or politicos (varying according to the issue involved). Similarly members may differ as to the constituency they see themselves primarily serving (for example, the nation, the party, or the individual electorate). In Emy's study of the 1974 Australian Parliament, only 19 percent of his sample identified themselves as delegates, including no Liberals and only 26 percent of Labor members, while 63 percent of Liberals and 24 percent of Labor members identified as trustees (Emy, 1974: chapter 16).

That most saw themselves as politicos or trustees is no surprise, since a parliament cannot simply mirror 'the deliberate sense of the nation'. Members cannot be a phonograph, playing the community's recorded message. Apart from the fact that representatives have their own priorities, they can sense only vaguely what their clientele want. There is rarely anything clear to be reflected: on most public policy questions the public lacks information and interest; its preferences may be unformed, or unexpressed, or not capable of being easily translated into action. So parliamentarians may be partly vehicles for demands, but they must also be shapers and mediators of demands. The community needs them to be 'fixers', while often criticising their 'lack of principle' when they are.

As a group, Australian representatives face a bundle of expected roles. They are public figures, attending ceremonies, speaking to the media, or perhaps representing their country overseas. They have parliamentary duties, for example, to attend and vote regularly, to take part in debates and committee work, to provide opportunities for the less heavyweight interests to have their views aired in parliament, and to present petitions from their electorate. (This last task has recently become more considerable. To 1960 the average number of petitions received per year had never exceeded 100. In 1985 there were 2955 presented.) For their parties they are expected to organise and sustain branches, raise money, campaign, and help formulate policy through party committees. They are permitted little privacy, being expected to devote a large amount of their personal time and energy to constituency duties, interviewing locals, dealing with grievances, and guiding bewildered constituents past bureaucratic barriers. Naturally, not all individually play all these roles. Some see themselves primarily as policy specialists, legislative critics, party consciences, committee contributors, 'good local members', or brokers resolving conflicts (Emy, 1974: chapter 16). But it is appropriate to stress the overriding importance of party focus in shaping what Australian parliamentarians will be and do. Party discipline is remarkably strong in Australian parliaments, especially lower houses. 'The party line is the bottom line' (Jaensch, 1986: 474).

Debating public policy and making the laws

Few would see the Australian Parliament as a 'Congress of Opinions' genuinely formulating public policy. Indeed critics of liberal democracy, like Lonie and Playford, depict parliament as a sham, 'in part a facade to disguise the dictatorship of the bourgeoisie, in part a safety valve, in part a danger signal for capitalism.' Since basic property relations in society are not challenged by parliament, it is portrayed as incapable of altering the realities of power. 'Reformists' who see through a 'parliamentary haze' can at best attain office and not power. They serve only to subdue workers' class interests, since capitalists make the decisions elsewhere behind the parliamentary screen. To believe otherwise is 'parliamentary cretinism' (Lonie and Playford, 1973: 167–8).

Certainly it is important to stress that crucial points of power exist outside the parliamentary arena and that the importance of Parliament is often exaggerated in public discussion because of lack of attention to the strong constraints upon what can be achieved by the mere possession of office. Nevertheless, those who adopt parliamentary methods are not necessarily 'cretins'; they may be aware of limits but see no workable alternative. What strategies do their critics offer that have any credibility? Furthermore, parliament remains a significant arena: office bestows some power, as does the opportunity to write and rewrite the rules or to supervise their administration.

Yet it remains somewhat misleading to talk of the Australian Parliament as 'making the laws'. Courts may have a final say on whether its Acts are valid.

Table 6.1 Amendments to proposed laws, 1924 and 1974

	No. of amendments	Moved by minister:		Moved by government backbencher		Moved by Opposition	
		Accepted	Not	Accepted	Not	Accepted	Not
1924							
House of Reps	294	160	2	18	28	13	73
Senate	240	95	16	41	32	1	55
1974							
House of Reps	205	113	—	1	—	7	84
Senate	281	130	—	5	1	78	67

Nor does it make all the laws. Apart from judge-made case law, it only perfunctorily supervises a vast volume of delegated legislation. In 1978 the Attorney-General's Department was about five years behind in the compilation of accurate statistics on the number of Acts in operation and their associated regulations. By 1986, federal departments and instrumentalities had produced a total of some 18 000 sets of regulations; in 1985 alone 387 statutory rules (totalling 1440 pages) were made under Acts of the Commonwealth Parliament (Statutory Rules, 1986. See also chapter 8).

The most significant qualification to Parliament's law-making role is that it rarely plays an initiating role in the legislative process. It 'makes' law largely in the sense that its imprimatur is necessary for the Government's legislative programme to be formally processed. In the period 1978–82, 1025 Government bills were introduced (only 77 of them in the Senate); of these 917 were passed. Meanwhile, only two were passed of the 46 bills introduced by 'private members' (this term may denote all members other than ministers, speaker, leader or deputy-leader of the Opposition, or leader of a recognised party; but it may also be used more widely, as in Figure 6.1, to mean non-ministers). For comparison, the British Government in the same period had an even higher success rate with its own bills (472 passed of 497 introduced in the two Houses), but it did not monopolise legislation to the same extent (with 122 of the 632 private members' bills passing) (IPU, 1986: 912).

Similarly, over time the Executive has tightened its control over amendment of legislation in the House. Table 6.1 indicates that Government backbenchers became readier to leave it to their ministers, while opposition attempts in the House were even more unsuccessful than they had been 50 years before. However, Table 6.1 also indicates that the Government may have to accept unwanted amendments by a hostile Senate, as in 1974 (Reid, 1980: 128–9). The Senate of 1974 was uniquely hostile, but analysis of Senate amendments for 1986 shows that the Government had to accept many amendments. Amendments were moved to 65 bills, of which 33 were amended. Of 522 proposed amendments, all 150 Government amendments were accepted, along with 24 of 179 Opposition proposals, 35 of 185 Australian Democrat proposals, and one of two from independents. (Department of the Senate, 1986: 2).

Parliament has the formal power to amend or defeat Government bills and to initiate private members' bills, but a more appropriate description of what it is doing might be not law-making but the scrutiny and near-automatic registration of proposals fed in by the Ministry.

Provide and control the Government?

The Ministry comes from within Parliament. The House of Representatives has apparent power to make and break governments, usually at the cost of its own dissolution. In 1975 the Senate also asserted its power to break governments. Yet in Australia the selection of the Government is normally by the voters, who determine clearly which party or coalition has a majority in the House of Representatives. Party discipline has long been so strong that even criticism from within the majority party will be regarded as disloyalty.

By convention, the Government resigns if it no longer has the confidence of the lower House. A motion accepted as a want of confidence or censure motion takes precedence over all other business until disposed of. To 1980 there had been 87 such motions or amendments moved. Despite their potential, increased use may have weakened their dramatic impact, for example, nineteen censure motions being moved in the period 1971–80 (Pettifer, 1981: 418). Since federation there have only been eight defeats on the floor leading a government to resign or to have Parliament dissolved; of these, five were before 1910 (Pettifer, 1981). The only cases since the early 1940s where the selection of government has been taken out of the hands of the voters have been Labor's assumption of office in 1941 without new elections, when the transfer of support of two independents gave it a majority, and the Governor-General's appointment of a 'caretaker' government in 1975.

So Parliament does not normally make and unmake governments. Yet it does play an important role in the development of ministers. Coming from within Parliament, they have been trained in the expected roles, although Australian ministers have generally served much less lengthy apprenticeships than their British counterparts.

Similarly, Parliament has important apparent powers in checking public expenditure and supervising public administration, by asking questions, demanding answers, and holding ministers accountable. Yet the size, remoteness, and complexity of government are so great that backbenchers may not know what questions to ask (see chapter 7). Parliament cannot be said to exercise control, yet it may contribute some supervision and redress of grievances, especially with the improvement of its committee system.

Clearly, 'parliamentary government' is not government by parliament or even government controlled by parliament. Parliament establishes expected roles including conventions of 'ministerial responsiblity', and trains and influences ministers, whose actions it publicly attempts to scrutinise (see chapter 7). Indeed most contemporary observers of its procedures are more likely to conclude that the Executive controls the Parliament, rather than the reverse.

Executive dominance

Gordon Reid has commented that: 'In hobbling their rank and file party leaders on both sides have attitudes in common' (1969: 505). Even without Opposition front bench connivance, the Government front bench appears to run Parliament, more especially the House of Representatives, to suit its convenience. A *Herald* editorial summed it up thus:

> MPs undoubtedly work hard. But how useful is the work?... Backbench MPs have little chance of introducing or amending legislation. Debates are a foregone conclusion. The whips crack their orders and MPs toe the party line. It is true that Parliament remains a useful forum for the Government to publicise what it is doing and for the Opposition to dramatise mistakes of the administration. Yet essentially the House of Representatives is a chamber of implementation, not of persuasion. The real debate takes place in the party. Even here, however, there is a tendency for the executive to clamp down on independence or outspokenness. (*SMH*, 17 August 1979)

As suggested, front bench control rests upon the centrality of party. Government leaders have great prestige as newsworthy public figures, needed for the party's continued success. Usually appeals to loyalty are enough, but both Labor and the coalition, if necessary, effectively enforce solidarity, although the Coalition lacks Labor's officially binding machinery of pledge, platform and caucus. The media reinforce this by reporting even minor disagreements as party 'splits'. Parliamentary leaders also have other inducements at their disposal, for example influence over backbenchers' chances of renewed preselection or preferment; jobs and other favours; and perhaps support for favoured policies.

With the support of its loyal majority, the Government has institutionalised advantages in the very procedures of Parliament. It controls the process of electing the Speaker and Chairman of Committees; usually determines times of sitting; appoints chairmen of enquiries and decides their terms of reference and resources; amends Standing Orders (frontbenchers in the House dominating the membership of the Standing Orders Committee); curtails debate; timetables legislation and arranges the drafting of bills, effectively monopolising the initiation of legislation (not only of finance measures where its monopoly is constitutional). Within their departments, ministers will subsequently enjoy wide discretion in the detailed implementation of the statutes so created.

The consequences of these procedural advantages are notorious. Largely for the benefit of ministers who thus have more time for their departments and less risk of awkward inquiries, the Australian Parliament is a 'part-time legislature'. The actual sitting hours of Parliament, not counting meetings of its committees, have not declined consistently. Indeed the average from 1901 to 1985 of 472 hours per year is a little less than the average for the period 1981 to 1985. Yet the total is very low. From 1901 to 1985 the House of Representatives averaged only 68 sitting days per year. For most of that period the Senate average was much lower. (Recently, however, the Australian Parliament has been unusual in that the upper house has frequently sat more often

Table 6.2 House of Representatives sitting times

Period	Sitting days per year	Average sitting hours per year	Acts passed per year	Hours per act
1901–10	95	577	23	25.1
1911–20	71	449	40	11.2
1921–30	67	425	47	9
1931–40	58	382	75	5.1
1941–50	70	452	73	6.2
1951–60	63	461	96	4.8
1961–70	62	483	120	4
1971–80	69	543	173	3.1
1981–85	56	480	173	2.8

Source: From House of Representatives Standing Committee on Procedure (1986) *Days and Hours of Sitting Time and the Effective Use of the Time of the House* Canberra: AGPS, p. 64

than the lower. From 1981 to 1986 the Senate sat for an average of almost 72 days a year, while the House sat for an average of a little over 60 days.) An International Parliamentary Union comparison of average sitting days per year estimated that for a recent four- or five-year period Australia's House of Representatives averaged 66 sitting days per year, while the Canadian House of Commons averaged 148. This can overstate the contrast since the Canadian sitting day is usually about 5.5 hours, compared with 8.5 hours of the Australian House in 1986. Yet the British House of Commons, sitting generally about nine hours a day, averaged 170 sitting days per year and the House of Lords 140, while the United States House of Representatives averaged 144 and its Senate 152 (IPU, 1986: Table 8; and Nethercote, 1987: 6).

Australia's part-time legislature has had to cope with a greatly increased legislative load. From 1901 to 1910 the average number of Acts per year was 23, with an average of 25.1 hours afforded to each Act. In the period 1981–85, 173 Acts per year were passed, with an average of only 2.8 hours each.

This overload is increased by the regular use of 'legislation by exhaustion'. In the early weeks of a session whips try to get members to fill up time, the House being left to consider a flood of legislation and annual reports in the last weeks of session. For example, in the 1985 autumn session 51 percent of legislation was introduced in the last three of a nine week session (House of Representatives Standing Committee on Procedure, 1986: 7). This reduces the time available to the Opposition to prepare its critique and often necessitates late night sittings, as on 4 April 1971, three days before the winter recess, when Standing Orders were suspended to permit the passage of seventeen bills (including some dealing with such matters as Papua New Guinea, restrictive trade practices, the wool industry and rural reconstruction). The House sat from 2 pm on Wednesday until 6.22 am Thursday, resuming at 10 am the same day and continuing until 3.45 am Friday.

Clearly this effectively short circuits parliamentary scrutiny. It also means that other opportunities for backbench participation are sacrificed to the urgency of government business. Debates on whether to adjourn (during which private members can raise any matters they wish) have been the particular victim of this end of session rush. In the period 1983–85 no adjournment debate was permitted on 34 percent of sitting days and many more were severely limited (House of Representatives Standing Committee on Procedure, 1986: 22).

In addition, the Government's numbers give it the opportunity to use closure devices. Since 1905 the 'gag' has been available to silence a member or end debate on an issue. From 1918 the 'guillotine' could be used to set in advance a time schedule for the termination of each stage of a bill. Such procedures are not indefensible. Their historic origins in Britain were as safeguards against Irish minorities determined to delay the business of government. For that matter, an opposition is not necessarily defenceless against them. It can sometimes make political capital out of the query 'what have they got to hide?' Or it can inconvenience the Government by playing to the rules, for example, by forcing repeated divisions, forcing Government members to keep up a quorum in the House, or refusing 'pairs'. (Pairing is a convenient arrangement by which a member covers for an absence from the chamber by getting a member of the opposing party to agree not to vote in divisions during that absence.)

Nevertheless, the use of closure has recently expanded. To 1950 the House resolved 'the question be now put' on an average eleven times a year, but from 1951 to 1980 the average was over 60. Similarly until 1974 the House resolved on only 22 occasions in all that a member 'be no longer heard', while it averaged 24.7 such votes per year between 1975 and 1980 (Pettifer, 1981: 776–7).

One of the strongest recent complaints about the dominance of the Executive is the growth of 'questions without answers'. Besides complaints about slowness in answering questions on notice, backbenchers seem especially irritated by the erosion of question time. In question time, the Speaker invites questions without notice, usually addressed to a particular minister about the portfolio for which he is responsible. Generally the leader of the Opposition gets to ask the first question, after which questions alternate between Government and Opposition. The period permitted for this is not prescribed by Standing Orders, but it is generally between 45 and 50 minutes per sitting day. Its theatre often gets media attention. It is supposedly an opportunity for guerrilla action, the probing and unpredictability of which have a salutary effect, making ministers keep on top of departmental affairs. However, it has recently earned the tag of 'questionable time'. There has been a decline in the number of questions asked, from an average of 25.2 per sitting day in 1946 to 12 in 1985—and some of these would be 'Dorothy Dixers' (friendly questions arranged in advance to make the minister look good). Since there is a tendency for the opposition leader and deputy leader to be the most frequent questioners, the opportunities for backbenchers are few. Even in the early 1970s, when the number of questions answered was usually about sixteen per day, the average backbencher could hope for about one question a month, while waiting two to three months to place a question on notice. Senate backbenchers are less dissatisfied with their opportunities, since the number of questions without notice (excluding frequent supplementary questions) in 1986 still averaged 19.4 per sitting day (Business of the Senate, 1986: 4) and there are fewer Senators.

There are more rules about what questions may be asked (concerning relevance, etc.) than about the proper form of answers. Indeed ministers do not have to answer at all. Of course they normally do, but often with long, rambling and vacuous responses. Although supplementary questions may be asked on the discretion of the Speaker, they are rarely available in the House. Parliamentary reformers frequently suggest this as one of the areas where Speakers should be more active and independent, to ensure relevance and economy in answers, to reduce evasion of questions, and hence to provide more opportunities for backbench scrutiny.

Constraints on Executive dominance

Concentrating thus on the parliamentary arena greatly exaggerates the Executive's power. In the context of the wider society, liberal democracies may have more to fear from 'ungovernability' than from Executive dominance. Indeed, even within the parliamentary arena there are important counter forces to Executive power. Although private members' opportunities are restricted by such devices as those mentioned above, 'Her Majesty's Opposition' has a vested interest in effective scrutiny. Australia's 'two-sided' party contest and its electoral system guarantee that there will be an Opposition. Parliamentary procedures offer it a legitimate public role. As the alternative government, its probing helps keep existing office holders responsive. It seeks to express and focus grievances. Government policies have to run the gauntlet, as the Opposition seeks support in the audience outside by pointing out implications of Government policies and suggesting alternatives.

However, oppositions often are ineffective. In the 1960s many Australian governments seemed unshakeable (for example, the Coalition governing nationally from 1949 to 1972 and New South Wales Labor governing from 1941 to 1965). It then seemed natural to stress the advantages of incumbency (for example, the prestige and resources of office, the opportunity to choose the timing of elections, and the capacity to manage the economy in such a way as to provide a favourable economic climate for an election). More recently, the task of oppositions has seemed less formidable as governments wrestle with intransigent economic problems.

Parliamentary performance certainly affects the morale of the rival parties. At times it is also seen as newsworthy, so that it may also affect public images of the parties and the public mood. While the Government limits the Opposition's opportunities, parliamentary procedures still afford an effective Opposition a substantial role.

Figure 6.1 illustrates that the House of Representatives from 1970 to 1980 afforded very little of its time to consideration of legislation or motions sponsored by private members. 'Other opportunities for private members' were also restricted, so that the total for private member initiatives ranged between 15.2 percent in 1975 and 25.3 percent in 1978. Clearly the role of

Figure 6.1 House time spent on various types of business

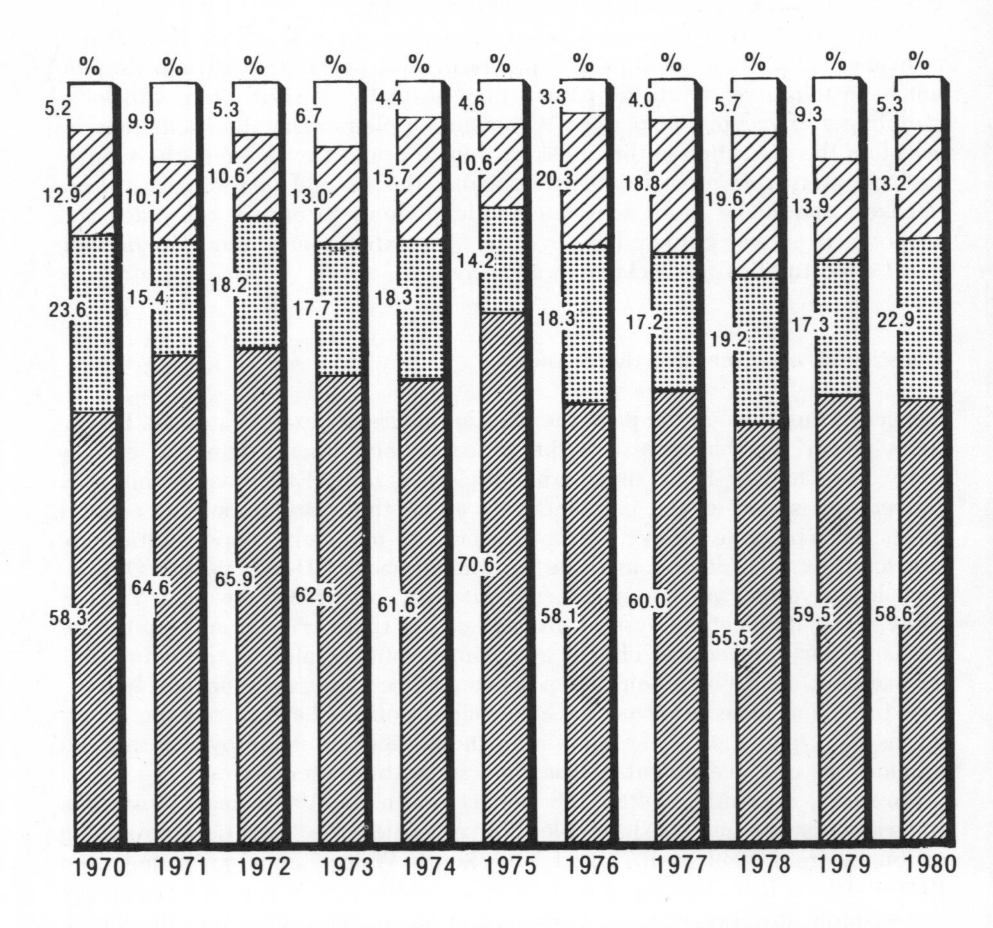

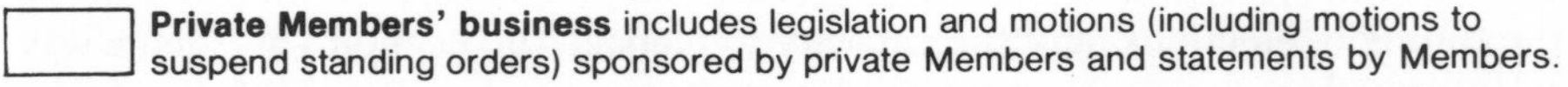
Private Members' business includes legislation and motions (including motions to suspend standing orders) sponsored by private Members and statements by Members.

Other opportunities for private Members includes adjournment and grievance debates, discussion of matters of public importance, and debates on the Address in Reply (1970, 1973, 1974, 1976, 1977, 1978 and 1980).

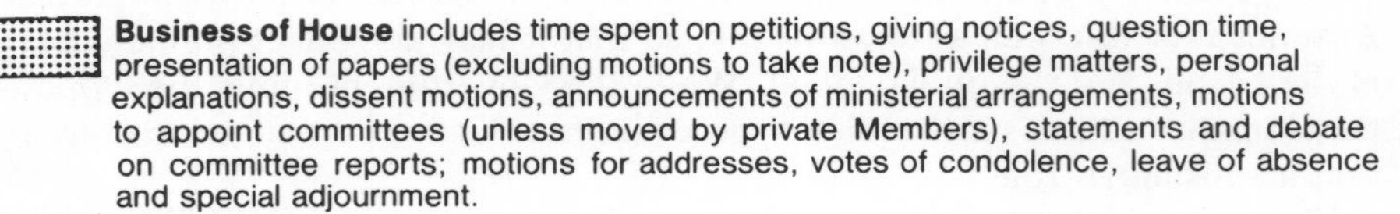
Business of House includes time spent on petitions, giving notices, question time, presentation of papers (excluding motions to take note), privilege matters, personal explanations, dissent motions, announcements of ministerial arrangements, motions to appoint committees (unless moved by private Members), statements and debate on committee reports; motions for addresses, votes of condolence, leave of absence and special adjournment.

Government business includes government sponsored legislation and motions (including motions to suspend standing orders) and ministerial statements.

Source: J.A. Pettifer (ed.) (1981) *House of Representatives Practice* Canberra: AGPS, p. 783

the House is to consider the Government's programme. Yet that process involves guaranteed opportunities for the Opposition. Figure 6.2 illustrates the stages through which all bills pass, and the opportunities for debate. Despite the Executive's ruthless use of its procedural advantages during the substantial time allotted for debate, Opposition members will alternate with Government members, and thus have the opportunity to present their critique.

The Opposition's main problems are usually not procedural, but rather its difficulties in presenting itself as a viable alternative in the voters' eyes; its leader may not be credible, it may not seem a united team capable of running things, its policies might not seem 'with it'. This seems especially likely after a long period in Opposition, without access to public service information. Australian parties at least until recently have been run 'on a shoestring', often lacking professionalism in their own administration and in research. Unless an Opposition has something to say and is able to get media and public attention, its parliamentary opportunities will not matter. Communication is its particular problem. The Government is more newsworthy since it is doing things, while the Opposition follows events. Nevertheless, political news flows best when Parliament is in session and the Opposition is usually then more visible. It is clearly to the disadvantage of the Opposition if Parliament as a forum is devalued by press conferences, ministerial handouts or attempts by Government information units to manipulate the media.

Parliamentary committees

Those who hope to improve parliamentary performance, especially its supervision of the Executive, generally base their main hopes upon the system of parliamentary committees. These are portrayed as ways to train backbenchers and improve parliamentary morale by giving greater job satisfaction; to provide better, more objective scrutiny; to provide greater access for community groups, which will also benefit by the research information committees provide; and to provide supplementary administrative supervision.

The committee system of the Australian Parliament before 1970 did little to meet these rosy expectations. Disregarding such internal committees as Standing Orders, Privileges, House, Library, and Publications, the House of Representatives before 1970 had appointed a total of only 40 committees including joint committees (with members from both Houses) (Pettifer, 1981: Appendix 31). The 1976 Report on Committees pointed out that 38 percent of the 146 committees appointed to 1975 had been appointed between 1969 and 1975, these producing 108 reports compared with a total of 103 for the whole earlier period.

A step forward began in 1970 when the Senate, not then under Government control, experimented with a set of estimates committees to examine department expenditures and a range of legislative standing committees intended to cover all areas of government activity.

Certainly there was a need for such expansion. Gordon Reid has shown that

Figure 6.2 The legislative process

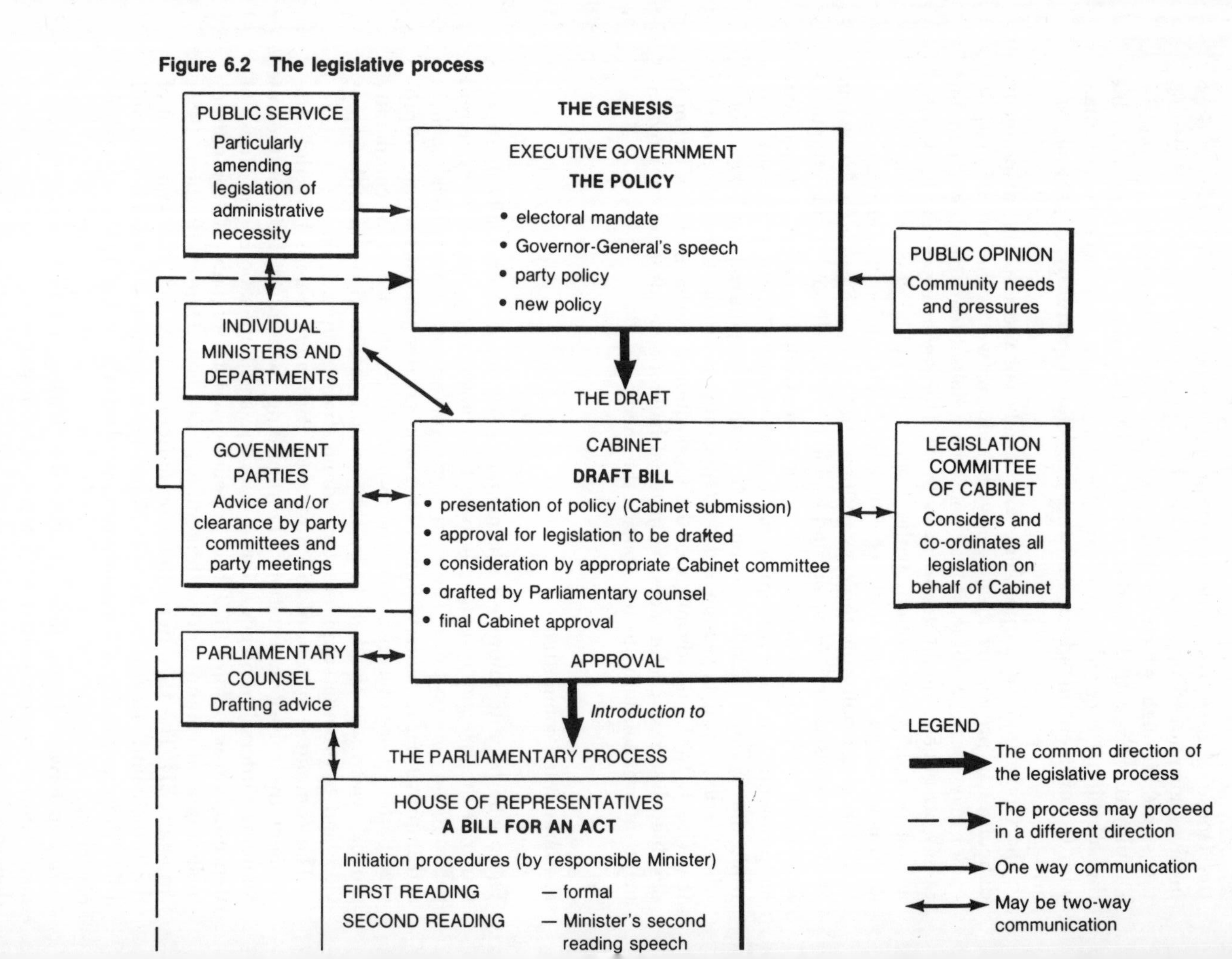

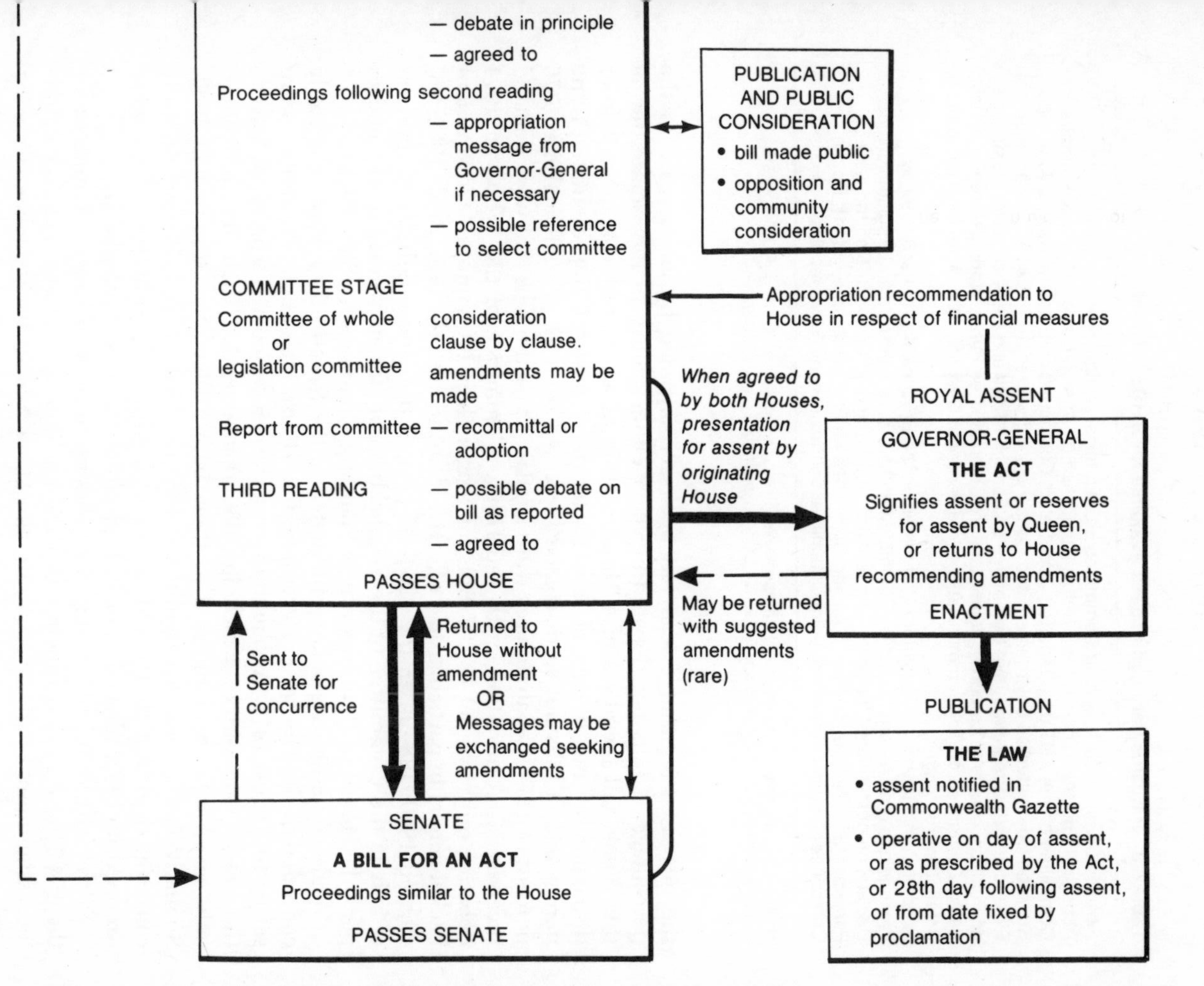

Source: J.A. Pettifer (ed.) (1981) *House of Representatives Practice* Canberra: AGPS, pp. 312–13

Table 6.3 Parliamentary committees available for MHRs 1985–86

Scrutiny Committees: Standing Committee on Aboriginal Affairs; Select Committee on Aboriginal Education (one report); Select Committee on Aircraft Noise (one report); Joint Committee on the ACT (four reports); Joint Select Committee on Electoral Reform (one report); Standing Committee on Environment and Conservation (two reports); Standing Committee on Expenditure (five reports); Joint Committee on Foreign Affairs and Defence; Joint Committee on Public Accounts (21 reports); Joint Statutory Committee on Public Works (16 reports); Joint Select Committee on Telecommunications Interceptions; Standing Committee on Transport Safety (two reports).
Internal Committees: Joint Statutory Committee on the Broadcasting of Parliamentary Proceedings (one report); Standing Committee on Members' Interests and Registration and Declaration of Members' Interests (two reports); Joint Standing Committee on the New Parliament House (five reports); Standing Committee on Procedure (one report); House Committee; Library Committee; Joint Committee on Publications (eight reports).

Source: Department of the House of Representatives *Annual Report 1985–6* pp. 7–12, 15–24 and Appendix 1

the increased legislative load has been accompanied by an increase in the percentage of bills not debated at all in either House in the Committee of the Whole (all members of a House sitting as a committee to permit freer discussion of the details of a bill). In the House of Representatives the percentage of bills not so discussed increased from 21 percent in 1924 to 76 percent in 1974. Senate figures were similar. Even the bills that were debated received scant attention, with the House Committee of the Whole in 1974 debating only five out of 207 Bills for longer than 100 minutes. Government backbenchers in particular had effectively abandoned the task (Reid, 1982: 48, 49; and 1980: 128–9). In the 1984–85 period, the House debated 27 percent of bills in the Committee of the Whole, but only for an average of 41 minutes per bill (House of Representatives Standing Committee, 1986: 29).

While committees quickly proliferated in the Senate, they were reluctantly conceded in the House. For example, two House legislation committees were set up in August 1978. Although their performance seemed worthy, at least to the Select Committee, which in 1986 recommended their reintroduction, only seven bills were referred to them before they were dropped in 1980. Similarly two estimates committees were established in 1979, but carefully constrained so that they could not vary proposed expenditures. These were dropped in 1982, allegedly for lack of interest amongst members.

In the late 1970s, there were 83 positions on parliamentary committees for the 104 House of Representatives backbenchers; almost half had no committee assignment at all. By contrast almost all Senate backbenchers were on such committees, averaging over two each. In addition, House backbenchers averaged about three positions each on party committees, Senate backbenchers a little less (Solomon, 1978: 118). Tables 6.3 and 6.4 indicate the contrast in the mid 1980s. The 38 parliamentary committees available to Senators in 1986 had produced 128 reports, while the nineteen committees available to MHRs had produced 70 reports in the year ending 30 June 1986. Moreover, the range of House committees was much narrower, with two committees (Public Accounts and Public Works) totalling 70 percent of the

Table 6.4 Parliamentary committees available for senators 1986

Standing Committees: Appropriations and Staffing; Disputed Returns and Qualifications; Library, Privileges; Publications; Standing Orders. (Total of 18 reports.)
Legislative Scrutiny Standing Committees: Regulations and Ordinances; Scrutiny of Bills. (Total of 26 reports.)
Legislative and General Purpose Standing Committees: Constitutional and Legal Affairs; Education and the Arts; Finance and Government Operations; Foreign Affairs and Defence; Industry and Trade; National Resources; Science, Technology and the Environment; Social Welfare. (Total of 23 reports.)
Estimates Committees: A–F. (Total of 12 reports.)
Select Committees: Animal Welfare; Human Embryo Experimentation Bill; Private Hospitals and Nursing Homes; Television Equalisation; Volatile Substances Fumes (one report).
Joint Committees Joint Statutory: Broadcasting of Parliamentary Proceedings; National Crime Authority; Public Accounts; Public Works. (Total of 35 reports.)
Joint: Australian Capital Territory; Foreign Affairs and Defence; New Parliament House. (Total of ten reports.)
Joint Select: Australia Card; Electoral Reform; Telecommunications Interceptions; Video Material. (Total of three reports.)

Source: Department of the Senate (1986) *Business of the Senate*, p. 4, 78–105

reports of its scrutiny committees. These two and Foreign Affairs and Defence accounted for 60 percent of the meetings of all its committees to scrutinise the work of the Executive and its administration (House of Representatives Annual Report, 1985–86: 15).

'Statutory' committees are appointed by an Act of Parliament, which requires their appointment at the commencement of each Parliament and specifies their terms of reference, powers and procedures. 'Internal' or 'domestic' standing committees are appointed under the Standing Orders of the House concerned at the commencement of each Parliament. Other standing committees and select committees may be appointed by a resolution of either House. (The differences are that a standing committee has more general terms of reference and continues until the end of the Parliament, while a select committee is ad hoc, with its term prescribed in the resolution of appointment, and generally ends upon production of the final report upon its specified topic.)

The 1976 report of the committee inquiring into a possible new parliamentary committee system was critical of the ad hoc way in which the committee system had evolved. There was duplication of effort and overload of some committees, notably those supervising administration. Backbenchers seemed more interested in examining policy issues, but here too there was incomplete coverage, with little provision for big spending areas like education, health, and social security, or for hot areas like tax policy or economic management. Effective scrutiny of legislation was still inadequate.

Such gaps must be expected. Advances in the committee system will come not just because of a dominating desire to be thought 'good politicians', but will only occur when two conditions are met:

- There must backbenchers of sufficient quality, with the incentive to make their time and energy available. Conscious of the workload implied, many may not see this as the best way to achieve their career aspirations. Will their constituents allow them the time or value their efforts? Will party leaders' judgements about preferments be influenced more by these sorts of activities? It seems likely that Senators who are less concerned with constituents' claims and have fewer ministerial posts to aspire to may continue to see committee work as more central to their parliamentary role.

- The Executive must cooperate. Governments like a quiet life and hence will wish the House of Representatives in particular to remain safely under party control. Yet they also desire good government; they may find committees useful to 'fly a kite' or to share the blame or even to help supervise administration, when that is seen as not threatening.

Pursuing a quiet life, the Executive may refuse to set up parliamentary committees, perhaps allowing their own backbenchers to be 'put into the picture' in party committees, safe from the public gaze. They may inhibit committees by restricting the terms of reference, hand picking their chairs, refusing to refer matters to them, or providing insufficient staff to support the committees. (In fact, after 1969 committee secretariats increased dramatically. The Senate committee secretariat, including clerical administrative and keyboard staff, rose from three in August 1968 to 47 in June 1975. Despite a decline from a peak of 72 in June 1982, it remained at 61 in June 1986. The comparable House increase was from four in 1969 to 61 in 1986 (information kindly provided by John Uhr and the committee officers of each House). Between 1969 and 1975 library legislative reference staff increased from 27 to 69, legislative research staff from 11 to 48 (Solomon, 1978: 134). The library staff of 133 at the end of 1978 had risen to 202 by mid-1987. However, Executive control over the finances of the Parliamentary Department remains a highly contentious issue, with the Senate in particular asserting that it is improper for the Executive to treat it as just another department, without control over its own finances and priorities.

An uncooperative Executive could also frustrate committees by retreating behind the cloak of ministerial responsibility, restricting access to public service documents or refusing to permit senior officials to testify before committees. However, in a context of freer information, the public service has gradually evolved more workable guidelines for dealing with such matters. Senator Rae commented in 1982, 'Now we are getting automatically what we spent the past ten years dragging out of the Government' (*Weekend Australian*, 8 May 1982).

A more difficult problem to overcome has been persuading governments to respond to the recommendations of committee reports. Mountains of information have been produced but reports are treated cavalierly. Although perhaps 60 percent of recommendations had been accepted at least in part by the mid 1970s, only about 20 percent of reports were debated, usually with many members absent, including the Minister (Emy, 1978, p. 415). Some reports are accepted readily, like the 1978 Galbally Report on immigrant services and the 1979 reports on water resources and refugee policy. Others are ignored,

Table 6.5 The Senate: party composition 1949–87

Total	Coalition	Labor	Democratic Labour Party	Australian Democrats	Others	
1949	26	34				6
0						
1951 (1)	32	28				
1953 (2)	31	29				
1955	30	28	2			
1958	32	26	2			
1961	30	28	1	1	1	
1964 (2)	30	27	2		1	
1967 (2)	28	27	4		1	
1970 (2)	26	26	5		3	
1974 (1)	29	29			2	
1975 (1)	35	27			2	6
4						
1977	35	26		2	1	
1980	31	27		5	1	
1983 (1)	28	30		5	1	
1984	33	34		7	2	7
6						
1987 (1)	34	32		7	3	

Note: In all cases, the figures reflect the position after the newly-elected Senators had taken their seats.
(1) Double dissolution elections
(2) Senate elections alone

like the 1976 report on parliamentary committees, or delayed, like the 1979 report on freedom of information, which finally led to watered-down legislation in December 1982.

In 1978 the Fraser Government committed itself to respond to committee reports within six months. Subsequently the President of the Senate drew attention to its failure to meet this commitment. In 1984 the Hawke Government promised response within three months, though not to reports presented to a previous parliament. Nevertheless, a 1986 House report indicated that only two of 26 reports had been responded to within three months, with a further ten late responses (House of Representatives Report, 1985–86: Appendix 2).

Here too procedures are apparently evolving. Clearly the committee system is strengthening and already useful. Nevertheless, the above list of Executive manoeuvres should raise few hopes about the capacities of committees to be above party or a considerable restraint upon the Executive, especially in the House, where the Government by definition has the numbers.

The Senate check

In the Senate, as Table 6.5 indicates, the Executive has not the same control as it has in the House: the Senate does sometimes aggressively assert its role as check upon the Executive. In its first 70 years the Senate initiated less than 10 percent of bills, rejected less than 2 percent and amended about 12 percent. By contrast, in the period 1973–75 the Senate systematically obstructed the Whitlam Government's programme, rejecting or deferring more bills than in its whole previous history combined (Emy, 1978 p. 216). Between July 1974 and November 1975 it defeated outright 51 bills. Whitlam termed such 'checking' as 'government in exile'.

As the 'States' House', the Senate had to be strong. It was given equal legislative power except that it could not initiate or amend money bills, nor amend any other bill so as to increase proposed taxation. It could not be dissolved before the end of its term except by a double dissolution under the deadlock procedure in section 57 of the Australian constitution. By its deferral of supply in 1975, the Senate showed that it too could unmake a government. Since the deadlock procedure is too clumsy and slow to resolve a supply crisis, a hostile Senate may indeed hold up supply without having to undergo a new election.

The States' equal representation may have permitted small states a stronger say within party meetings. Somewhat unconvincingly, Odgers has argued that the mere existence of the Senate has prevented schemes unfavourable to state interests even from being proposed (Odgers, 1976: 45). Infrequently, senators have crossed party lines to protect a state interest; for example, in March 1977 four Liberals from Tasmania voted against the Coalition in favour of an apple and pear subsidy. Yet the Senate has long been another party House and only formally a 'States' House': the defence of state interests has occurred rather in such forums as loan councils and premiers' conferences.

Before 1949 the Senate suffered badly from the usual dilemma of strong upper houses. Being strong, they must be dominated and may not even be allowed to be useful. When the Government had the numbers, the Senate echoed the party line, sometimes in ridiculously one-sided contests, for example in 1946 when there were only three opposition senators out of 36. When there was a hangover majority from an earlier election, hostile Senates often tried unconvincingly to justify partisan blocking as review or 'safeguarding'. However, since the introduction of proportional representation in 1949, clear control of the Senate has been difficult to establish for either Government or opposition. Governments have had clear majorities only in the parliaments following the elections of 1951, 1953, 1958, 1975 and 1977. As Table 6.5 indicates, for the rest of the time after 1951 control was at best uncertain, especially because there were also some 'maverick' Liberal senators. Between 1965 and 1967 only ten Liberal senators never voted against their Government (Mackerras, 1968). Especially interesting were the 'hung' Senates between 1967 and 1974 and after 1980, when first the Democratic Labor Party then the Australian Democrats had the balance of power.

Clearly the emphasis upon 'Executive dominance' in Parliament needs to be heavily qualified by the Executive's current inability to keep a grip on the Senate. This is not due only to its different electoral basis. In 1987 the Ministry's eight senators together with seven 'shadows' constituted a much less overwhelming frontbench than that of the House. Indeed some leading senators, stressing its role as a check upon the Executive, describe senate ministers as 'trojan horses'. They advocate instead that the Senate should be managed not by ministers but by chairmen of key committees, with similar rewards to non-Cabinet ministers (Hamer, 1979). Senate backbenchers have longer tenure and fewer promotion prospects, so that sanctions for party consistency are not as strong. There is also some tradition of tolerance for mavericks, while greater opportunities for backbenchers are built into Senate procedures. For example, they may speak longer, are not often subjected to closure and get more opportunities to ask questions without notice.

In the last twenty years, the Senate's morale, will to act, prestige and performance have improved dramatically. 'Hung' Senates have helped by putting minor parties in the spotlight; results are negotiable, not cut and dried, and hence more newsworthy. But it is the continued development of the Senate's committee system that provides the solid basis for its new image. Its successes have included well-received reports on such matters as freedom of information and human rights. But other gains should be noted too, where committees have patiently stretched their room to manoeuvre and evolved operating procedures for improving cooperation with the administration. For example, the Scrutiny of Bills Committee was set up to examine proposed legislation in order to alert the Senate to possible infringements of rights or erosion of the legislative power of the Parliament. Its procedure is to issue Alert Digests commenting on bills introduced in the previous week. Ministers then have the opportunity to respond before a definitive report is made to the Senate. On average it has drawn attention to items in over one-third of all bills introduced; has received some response to three-quarters of its comments; and has seen desired amendments made to over one-tenth of the clauses to which it had drawn attention (Tate, 1985).

The Senate has the power to check the Executive in the sense of confrontation and even of unmaking governments. Yet that cure is as bad as the illness. The central role for Parliament, especially for an upper house, is review or scrutiny and improvement of government rather than just dramatic confrontation of the Government.

References

Department of the Senate (1986) *Business of the Senate, 1 January—31 December 1986* Canberra: Procedure Office

Emy, H.V. (1974) *The Politics of Australian Democracy* Melbourne: Macmillan

—— (1978) *The Politics of Australian Democracy* Melbourne: Macmillan 2nd edn

Hamer, D.J. (1979) 'Some Proposals for Senate Reform', in G. Hawker et al. (eds) *Working Papers on Parliament* Canberra: Canberra CAE

House of Representatives Standing Committee on Procedure (1986) *Days and Hours of Sitting and the Effective Use of the Time of the House* Second Report, May 1986 Canberra: AGPS

International Parliamentary Union (IPU) (1986) *Parliaments of the World* Aldershot: Gower

Jaensch, D. (1986) *Getting our Houses in Order* Ringwood: Penguin

Lonie, J. and Playford J. (1973) 'Parliamentary Cretinism' in H. Mayer (ed.), *Labor to Power* Sydney: Angus and Robertson

Mackerras, M. (1968) *The Australian Senate 1965–1967: Who Held Control* Sydney: APSA Monograph No. 9

Mill, J.S. (1910) *Utilitarianism, On Liberty, Considerations on Representative Government* London: Everyman

Nethercote, J.R. (1987) 'The Senate, the House of Representatives and the Condition of the Commonwealth Parliament' *Legislative Studies* 2, 2, Spring

Odgers, J.R. (1976) *Australian Senate Practice* Canberra: AGPS

Pettifer, J.A. (ed.) (1981) *House of Representatives Practice* Canberra: AGPS

Reid, G. (1969) 'Parliamentary-Executive Relations: The Suppression of Politics', in H. Mayer (ed.) *Australian Politics: A Second Reader* Melbourne: Cheshire

—— (1980) 'The parliamentary contribution to law-making', in A.E.S. Tay and E. Kamenka (eds) *Law-Making in Australia* Melbourne: Edward Arnold

—— (1982) 'The Parliament in Theory and Practice', in M. James (ed.) *The Constitutional Challenge* Sydney: Centre for Independent Studies

Rydon, J. (1986) *A Federal Legislature. The Australian Commonwealth Parliament 1901–1980* Melbourne: Oxford University Press

Solomon, D. (1978) *Inside the Australian Parliament* Sydney: Allen and Unwin

Statutory Rules Made under Acts of the Parliament of the Commonwealth of Australia during the year 1985 Canberra: AGPS

Tate, M. (1985) 'The Operation of the Australian Senate Standing Committee for the Scrutiny of Bills 1981–1985', paper to the Conference of the Australasian Study of Parliament Group, Adelaide

7 Cabinet

Barbara Page

Cabinet is the committee of senior politicians responsible for directing the Government's policies. It is the centre of power, the repository of legitimate political authority and the top political prize in the Australian system of government. Cabinet is the political Executive—that part of the government system that is responsible for taking the initiative in government and controlling the administration. This Executive role is in contrast to the legislative role of Parliament in passing laws.

There is an executive branch in all forms of government. In some countries with presidential systems, like the United States, the executive is quite separate from the legislature and no person can be a member of both simultaneously. By contrast, in countries like Australia which have adopted the British model of responsible parliamentary government, the Executive and the legislature are fused. Here, members of Cabinet are drawn from the ranks of the parliamentary members of the governing party or coalition. After an election the party with the majority of seats in the Lower House forms the governing party, its leader becomes Prime Minister and its senior politicians become members of Cabinet.

It is the aim of every ambitious member of Parliament to make the transition to Cabinet minister because Cabinet is where the really important decisions are made. The decision to commit Australian troops to the Vietnam War—and to pull them out—was not made by Parliament, nor was it made by public servants; it was made by Cabinet. Decisions that can be taken without accompanying legislation—like entering a war, or floating the dollar—are the political Executive's prerogative. Other decisions—like introducing a new form of tax—require legislation that has to be passed through Parliament. This gives Parliament the chance to consider Cabinet's proposals. In some cases Parliament may stall or overturn them. Cabinet cannot make laws—only Parliament can do that (see chapter 6). But, given that almost all legislation that comes before Parliament is Government-sponsored, it is Cabinet that decides what laws should be passed. Party discipline in Parliament ensures that Cabinet is predominant. The political initiative lies with Cabinet; Parliament reacts to that initiative.

Cabinet is assisted by—and is dependent upon—the administrative arm of the Executive, the public service. Cabinet determines the general long-term direction of government policy (paying more or less heed to party policies in the process), but when it comes to initiating and coordinating specific policies it is heavily reliant on the knowledge, experience and expertise of the public service. Whether this reliance has reached the stage where public servants are usurping the power that rightfully belongs to the elected executive is a question considered in the next chapter.

This chapter is concerned with contemporary developments in the Australian Federal Cabinet. Recent developments in all Westminster based systems of government have raised some common concerns. Can Cabinets deal effectively with the workload and complexity of contemporary executive government? Has new machinery designed to deal with this complexity—like Cabinet committees—undermined Cabinet's collective responsibility? Have the traditional forms of Cabinet government been affected by the increasingly 'presidential' electoral campaigning and leadership styles of some Prime Ministers? Do Prime Ministers now exercise so much power that collective decision-making by Cabinet has been supplanted? Has the increased bureaucratic support provided to Prime Ministers and Cabinet put new power in the hands of officials? Finally, but perhaps most importantly, can ministers be held accountable by Parliament for their collective and individual actions? These concerns are reflected in the descriptions that follow of the workings of the Australian Cabinet and recent changes that have taken place within the Cabinet system.

The composition of Cabinet

The first Australian cabinet had nine members, reflecting the relatively limited responsibilities of the Commonwealth Government at federation. Since then the growth in Federal Government activities has been mirrored by the growth in the numbers of federal ministers to the present 30, seventeen of whom are in Cabinet (see Spann, 1979: 53ff; Hughes, 1984). The Prime Minister and the majority of ministers come from the House of Representatives, reflecting its importance as the decider of governments. Senators usually make up about one-quarter of the Ministry.

The manner in which Cabinet (and outer) ministers are appointed differs according to which party wins government. The parliamentary members of the Labor Party (the caucus) elect ministers from among their ranks (and in this election factions play a crucial role). In the Liberal and National Parties the leader chooses those to be ministers. In both cases the Prime Minister then allocates ministerial portfolios. Non-Labor Prime Ministers in Australia also have the power to dismiss ministers. Ministers in a Labor government were traditionally removable only by caucus. However, in 1975 Prime Minister Whitlam dismissed the Minister for the Environment and former Treasurer, Dr Cairns, without first seeking caucus approval. It is now agreed that the dismissal of federal Labor ministers is in the hands of the four ALP parliamentary leaders (the leader and deputy leader in the House of Representatives and the Senate).

While Labor Prime Ministers have more formal constraints on their power to appoint and dismiss ministers than do non-Labor Prime Ministers, there are still *informal* constraints on the latter. Liberal Prime Ministers for most of this century have headed coalition governments and have had to take account of the preferences of their coalition colleagues in making ministerial appointments. They must also, for practical political reasons, take into account factors such as Senate and regional representation, the standing of colleagues within the party, and, if they are wise, party factions. Prime Ministers of both parties have the power, through the allocation of portfolios, to promote or demote ministers.

The work of Cabinet

Cabinet ministers collectively have responsibility for directing all a government's activities. Cabinet ministers individually have responsibility for particular policy areas (portfolios) and related public service departments and government agencies. A great deal of Cabinet business is concerned with marrying these two responsibilities—with coordinating individual ministerial or departmental policies and weaving them into some unified overall plan (for instance, a party's broad objectives, or a government's strategy for a forthcoming election). Sometimes this coordination takes the form of adjudicating between ministers who are primarily intent on looking after their own portfolio interests. Often Cabinet is the place where potential conflicts or contradictions between separate departmental proposals are sorted out.

The most concrete manifestation of this coordination role is seen in the process of determining the annual budget. Here all ministers compete for resources to fund their department's programmes. Cabinet decides both its overall strategy for the coming year and the particular programmes and policies it will continue, abolish or introduce. Ideally, the determination of annual budget priorities—and other Cabinet decisions—would be made within a framework of a government's long-term plans. In practice, however, pressures of time, workloads and unanticipated events mean that for the most part Cabinets do not have time to indulge in long-term planning.

Cabinets authorise policies, as well as coordinate them. Any major new proposal or significant variation to an existing proposal will be considered by Cabinet. Cabinet will also monitor proposals for any significant impact they may have on relations with other governments, both foreign and Australian. Cabinet will be asked to approve certain government appointments, such as those to the boards of statutory authorities.

Cabinet meetings may be called at any time by the Prime Minister, but are generally held once a week through most of the year. Attendance at Cabinet meetings takes priority over all other ministerial commitments. Cabinet discussions and documents are kept strictly confidential and Cabinet decisions, once made, are binding on all Cabinet ministers who, under the doctrine of collective ministerial responsibility, must support them in public.

The secrecy surrounding Cabinet deliberations adds to its power and mystique, but also makes it difficult for outsiders to know what goes on. In recent years, however, the Government has made public the guidelines issued to all ministers and departments about Cabinet procedures (Cabinet Handbook, 1983) and has also published statistics of Cabinet business. While numbers cannot tell anything like the full story, they do give some indication of the size of Cabinet's task. For example, in 1985/86 Cabinet met 57 times and, in addition, there were eight meetings of the full Ministry and 156 Cabinet committee meetings. A total of 1040 papers were submitted to Cabinet (which ministers should read if they are to be fully informed) and Cabinet and its commmittees made a total of 1597 decisions—an average of 30 a week (Department of the Prime Minister & Cabinet, 1986: 47–8). With this sort of workload, with the many competing demands on ministers' time, and given the growth in the number of ministers and the scope of government activities, it is not surprising that ways have been sought to streamline Cabinet's procedures. Two tactics in particular have been adopted for this purpose—splitting the Ministry and the systematic use of Cabinet committees.

Inner and outer ministries

A large Cabinet may prove an unwieldy body for effective policy deliberation and decision making. By 1956 when Prime Minister Menzies decided to split his Ministry, the number of ministers needed to accommodate the increasing size and scope of Federal Government activities had risen to 22. Menzies kept twelve ministers in Cabinet and consigned ten to the outer Ministry. Apart from Whitlam's record Cabinet of 27 (which Whitlam had wanted to, but was unable to, split) (Walter, 1986: 49), Menzies' example has been followed by all succeeding Prime Ministers.

Non-Labor Prime Ministers have the authority to decide the total number of ministers and on how many and which of them will be in Cabinet. In a Labor government caucus approval is required in deciding on the number of ministers and whether all will be in Cabinet. When caucus was persuaded in 1983 that the Hawke Ministry should be divided into a Cabinet and outer Ministry, the four parliamentary leaders then decided which particular ministers should be in Cabinet (Weller, 1983: 305–15). However, once portfolios have been allocated, Cabinet ministers to a great extent pick themselves. Those who are treasurers, ministers for finance, defence, foreign affairs and other critical portfolios will almost always be in Cabinet, not in the outer Ministry.

Splitting a Ministry may enable Cabinet to work more efficiently and effectively but, depending on how they are treated, it may leave non-Cabinet ministers out in the cold. Non-Cabinet ministers can only attend Cabinet meetings if they are co-opted. This will normally happen if they are responsible for an item on the agenda, if matters concerning their portfolio are to be discussed, if they are assisting in a relevant portfolio or if they represent a portfolio whose minister sits in the other house. They may also ask the Prime Minister's permission to attend Cabinet meetings if they have a special interest in an item to be discussed. In the Fraser years, once outer ministers got into a Cabinet meeting they could stay there as long as they wished (Weller and Grattan, 1981: 113). Under Hawke they can attend only while their particular item is being discussed (Lucy, 1985: 134; Cabinet Handbook, 1983: 7).

However, following the 1987 federal election, the third Hawke Ministry of 30 members was divided into sixteen 'super' ministers, thirteen junior ministers and one minister (Susan Ryan) who fitted into neither of these categories. The sixteen super ministers and Senator Ryan formed the Cabinet. Between them, the sixteen super ministers had responsibility for all portfolios, assisted by junior ministers with responsibility for particular areas within those portfolios. Under this scheme, it seems possible that outer (junior) ministers may have less access to Cabinet than before because they no longer have sole responsibility for a particular department.

Another way in which outer ministers may have some direct input into Cabinet decisions is through their membership of Cabinet committees. All ministers will usually be members of at least one committee: some will gain wider exposure than others. However, some of the most important Cabinet committees—such as Expenditure Review and Security—are composed solely of Cabinet ministers (Department of the Prime Minister and Cabinet, 1986: 46). Given this, and the fact that meetings of the full Ministry (Cabinet and non-Cabinet ministers together) are relatively rare, some outer ministers may have very little say in Government decisions and very little knowledge of what is going on. This may not only cause low ministerial morale, it may also create extra coordination problems for the Government in trying to ensure that statements and actions by outer or junior ministers accord with Government policy.

Cabinet committees

A second technique adopted to help Cabinets cope with the increased volume and complexity of government business is the use of Cabinet committees to relieve the full Cabinet of some of its load of policy deliberation. Cabinet committees are not new; they have existed since before World War I and were used increasingly from World War II onwards (Crisp, 1983: 380–81; Weller, 1985a: 92–3). What is new is their *systematic* use to ease Cabinet's load. This started with the Whitlam Cabinet (Hawker, 1979: 76–87) and continued under the succeeding Fraser and Hawke Governments. In 1986 there was a system of nine Cabinet committees: three coordinating committees covering expenditure review, parliamentary business and legislation; and six functional committees for economic policy, industry, international and defence, social policy, legal and administrative and security. The Prime Minister, guided by the recommendations of his department, allocates ministerial Cabinet submissions to the appropriate committee for consideration. The decisions of the committee tend to be final, and matters can only be reopened for discussion in the full Cabinet with prime ministerial approval (Cabinet Handbook, 1983). In these circumstances, it is obvious that membership on Cabinet committees is at least a potential source of considerable influence on Cabinet decisions. Cabinet committee membership is generally determined on functional lines—according to the portfolios that ministers hold. However, Prime Ministers have the potential to stack committees, either to try to ensure that their decisions will accord with the Prime Minister's views or to isolate political rivals. It is also quite common for Prime Ministers to use an 'inner' Cabinet, a small informal group of senior or like-minded ministers to discuss and decide important issues.

It is inevitable that some Cabinet committees will have more clout than others, either because of the seniority of their membership or because of their function. In times of economic restraint, for example, expenditure review committees occupy a strategic position. This was the case in the Whitlam era (Hawker, 1979: 76–87), and again under Hawke the ERC is a formidable committee. Its members are all senior Cabinet ministers and some other ministers have complained that the ERC's priority of cost-cutting has supplanted the 'real business of government' (Cockburn, 1987).

Power in Cabinet

The delegation of Cabinet work to committees and the division of the Ministry into Cabinet and non-Cabinet ministers have been attempts to coordinate, expedite and facilitate policy deliberation and decision making in Cabinet in the face of an ever-increasing workload. A by-product of this has been the strengthening of the position of senior ministers and especially the chief minister, vis-a-vis other ministers.

Cabinet has traditionally been seen as a collegial body with ministers sharing equally in the powers and responsibilities of executive government, with the Prime Minister or Premier being, 'first among equals'. However, Prime Ministers have always had an ascendancy over their ministerial colleagues because of their power to appoint, dismiss and allocate portfolios to ministers, because of their control over the proceedings and structure of Cabinet and because it is they who have the greatest say in deciding when to call an election. These traditional levers of control have been supplemented by the development in the twentieth century of disciplined parties, which provide a Prime Minister with guaranteed support in Parliament, and by the dominant electoral role now given to the 'leader'.

Prime Ministers control the proceedings of Cabinet. They chair the meetings and set the agenda. They can, therefore, decide what will be discussed, in what order and for how long. They sum up the discussion and summarise decisions. They can also—and most do—take decisions that are binding on Cabinet without first obtaining Cabinet approval. The way Cabinet operates depends very much on the personal style of the Prime Minister. The Whitlam and Fraser Cabinets generally operated with very crowded agendas, which allowed both Prime Ministers to dominate proceedings because they were much better informed on almost all matters than their Cabinet colleagues. Fraser was said to have a 'presidential' style and usually got his own way

(Walter, 1986: 50–1; Schneider, 1980: chapters 1, 5). Hawke is said to have a very different style—to be much more 'first among equals'. His Cabinet is said to work usually 'with collective decision-making, established and predictable procedures, and [through] consensus' (Weller 1985b: 343).

Through their control over the processes and structures of Cabinet, Prime Ministers are in a better position than any other minister to appreciate the broad picture of government activities and to know what is going on in the various policy areas. Their ability to do this has been strengthened by the more recent development of the Department of Prime Minister and Cabinet (PMC) from a merely administrative support to a policy-formulating and coordinating body, and by the expansion of their ministerial staffs.

The Prime Minister's Department was first established in 1911 but up until the 1940s it operated as little more than a post-office (Crisp, 1967: 31). It then gradually developed a coordinating function through the department head's role as secretary to the Cabinet. But the greatest development in its capacity for policy coordination and control took place under Prime Minister Fraser:

> . . . where the prestige of the department has grown to the point where its authority and broad ranging coordinating responsibilities are accepted by other departments . . . (L)ike its prime minister, it exercises a dominating coordinating role in government activities. (Mediansky and Nockels, 1981: 396)

PMC had achieved this through its servicing of Cabinet and its committees, through the increasingly powerful role of its secretary (who, as a member of all the officials' committees supporting cabinet committees, and chairperson of all but one, had 'unparalleled access to, and role in, cabinet decision making' (Mediansky and Nockels, 1981: 403). As well, the rival power of Treasury was reduced when that department was split into two (Treasury and Finance Department) in 1976. But above all PMC had achieved this because of the support and direction given to it by a dominant Prime Minister, a support that has continued under Hawke.

The increased support provided to Prime Ministers by the upgrading of PMC has been supplemented by the expansion of their ministerial staffs. This expansion started in the Whitlam era. (Prime Ministers had had personal staffs before then—but they had been small and mostly concerned with administrative duties, rather than policy advice.) The Whitlam Government was sceptical of the public service's ability and willingness to support its reformist aims and the use of ministerial staff was one of the avenues explored to provide alternative sources of advice. (The total numbers of ministerial staff rose from 155 in April 1972 to 219 in November 1975, although it has been estimated that less than 20 percent of these could be classed as policy advisers) (Walter, 1986: 53–4). While the Fraser Government wound down or abolished many of the Whitlam initiatives in this area—including, initially, ministerial staff for other ministers—the Prime Minister's own ministerial office was maintained and its policy advising capacity upgraded. This was another factor that helped Fraser to dominate his ministerial colleagues. Hawke maintained this trend and, in addition, had the final say on staff appointments to other ministers' offices (see Walter, 1986: chapters 3 and 4). The dominance of chief ministers and the upgrading of their departments and advisory staff has not been confined to the federal sphere. Similar developments have occurred at the state level (see Steketee and Cockburn, 1986: chapter 7; Chaples, 1985: 43; Painter, 1982; Walter, 1987).

The changing balance of power

The net result, then, of the changes made to cope with the ever-increasing size and complexity of government business has been the development of a network of structures and procedures that have changed the collegial nature of Cabinet and the balance of forces operating in and around it. The 'collegiality' of Cabinet was in any case always a somewhat romantic notion. While some Cabinets doubtless work better as a team than others, all are, in one important respect, political battlegrounds. Ministers are there to 'fight for their corner', to see their projects and views prevail over others, to compete for resources with others during budget negotiations and to win advancement for themselves at the expense of their colleagues. The changes to the structure of Cabinet described above also reflect these political forces. The growth in size and scope of government business places on the centre not just a heavier load of decision making but also a heavier burden of managing conflict. The often acrimonious, exhausting and exhaustive process of budget reviews undertaken by the Hawke Government illustrates these burdens (Cockburn, 1987).

Measures such as inner/outer Ministries and Cabinet committees are ways of minimising conflict or facilitating its resolution. They embody procedures that exclude some participants from effective involvement, that give some ministers more status and power than others, and that allow officials and the Prime Minister to organise business and information in a way that will guide issues through the system. These procedures reduce the number of contestants, relegate some to the reserve benches, and strengthen the power of the referee to intervene in the game and even 'fix' its result.

It is now more accurate to speak of a 'Cabinet system' than 'Cabinet'. This system contains both a complex organisational structure and a delicately balanced tension between conflicting tendencies towards fragmentation and integration. In recent years integration has been in the ascendancy, with the chief minister in conjunction with his or her advisors and selected senior ministers holding new levers of strategic power over other participants.

Power and effectiveness in Cabinet do not depend solely on structural features. The abilities, energies and skills of individuals vary greatly and must be included in any analysis. Ministers have many competing claims on their time. As well as being members of Cabinet they have other roles to perform—as members of Parliament representing their constituents, as overseers of public service departments and as senior members of their party. Despite the structures and processes devised to ease Cabinet's load, some ministers still lack the time—or in some cases, the expertise—to read and understand all Cabinet submissions (Weller and Grattan, 1981: 110–12). Many ministers, therefore, are well informed only about their own portfolio, and this enhances the influence of those ministers who are more widely briefed through the nature of their portfolios and the expertise of their departments (for example, the Prime Minister, Treasurer and Finance Minister), especially when it comes to the planning of broader strategies and priorities (see, for example, Cockburn, 1987).

But while some ministers will inevitably have advantages over others in the power game of executive politics, it would be misleading to overstate the power of even the chief minister or the Cabinet system itself. When viewed in the context of the wider political system, there are various constraints within which they have to operate.

External constraints on Executive power

The Government does not operate in a political or economic vacuum. The constraints imposed on it by the wider economic context and by political parties are discussed in chapters 17 and 9 respectively. A third external constraint is that of Parliament.

Under the British model of responsible parliamentary government on which Australia's political institutions were largely based, popular control over the Executive depends on the concept of ministerial responsibility, which has two components. First, that ministers are individually responsible to the Parliament (the elected representatives of the people) for their own actions and those of their administrative departments. Secondly, that Cabinet ministers are collectively responsible to Parliament (and through Parliament to the people) for their conduct of government. If ministers are to be responsible to Parliament this implies that Parliament should be able to hold them accountable for their actions. Parliament should have enough information about government policies and actions to be able to question ministers effectively, to criticise and if necessary censure their actions, and, in the ultimate, force them to resign. If ministers are to be responsible for the actions of their departments, then ministers need to be aware of what goes on in those departments and be able to control them.

It has become almost a truism to say that ministerial responsibility can no longer be counted on to operate effectively as a means of control—if it ever could. Parliament is not sufficiently informed about government policies to be able to question the Government effectively and, in any case, party discipline will prevent a vote of censure being carried where a successful censure motion in the Lower House would mean the defeat of the Government. Furthermore, increased complexity of issues, the sheer size of the administration, and the lack of time that ministers have to devote to departmental matters, all make it impracticable if not impossible for ministers to have a detailed knowledge of and control over all the actions of their departments (see Parker, 1976).

While ministers may rely on this point to avoid censure over mistakes in their departments, their resignations are still routinely called for by the opposition and the media, suggesting that the principle of ministerial responsibility is not dead. And when it comes to *personal* misjudgement or impropriety a significant number of ministers have been forced to resign or have been suspended over the last decade or so. In the Fraser years from 1976 to 1982, for example, seven ministers resigned or were suspended pending charges of alleged personal impropriety ranging from bribery and forgery to the evasion of customs duty. (All but three were reinstated after being cleared of the charges.) It does seem that criticism of ministers in Parliament, aided and abetted by the media, can make life very uncomfortable for the minister, although whether or not a minister resigns will depend on the political circumstances of the time, on the minister's support within the party, and, in the final analysis, on the Prime Minister's judgement. Moreover, resignation may be the ultimate sanction but it is not a necessity as proof that ministerial responsibility still has some force.

> The great quality of the doctrine of ministerial responsibility is that it forces a minister to dig—or to get his (sic) officials to dig—down into his department, to explain his department's actions and to find remedies in case of demonstrated error. The sanction on his doing this is that his political reputation depends on it. (Butler, 1972)

If resignations were required as proof of responsibility, then *collective* ministerial responsibility in Australia would, with a few exceptions, be dead and long since buried. Collective ministerial responsibility is about Cabinet solidarity. (It also originally included the principle that Parliament can only enforce its power over the Executive if the latter can be brought down collectively—responsibility divided is not responsibility at all.) Once decisions have been taken in Cabinet all Cabinet ministers must, in theory, support those decisions in public. Ministers who cannot so defend the collective policy of government should, in theory, resign. However, Cabinet solidarity is, in practice, a tool for protecting Executive power, not for facilitating collective responsibility in Parliament. It strengthens Cabinet's hand against the opposition, its own backbench, the press and the public.

In Australia, however, collective ministerial responsibility is not strictly upheld. In periods of Liberal/National Party Coalition Government, National Party ministers maintain their right to express their Party's view, even when this may differ from that of Cabinet. Perennial disagreements of this sort have been over tariff policy, the value of the dollar and interest rates. In pre-Hawke Labor Governments ministers maintained the right to make statements (in their role as members of Parliament) before caucus, and ministerial disagreements were frequently made public. This made the Whitlam Cabinet, for example, appear 'divided and indecisive' (Weller, 1985b: 339). Whitlam himself was known to appeal to caucus in an attempt to have it overrule a cabinet decision (Walter, 1980: 53). Under Hawke, however, while all ministers are expected to support Government decisions in public, Cabinet ministers are also expected to support Cabinet decisions in caucus, as are any members of the outer Ministry who are in attendance in Cabinet when a particular decision is taken (Cabinet Handbook, 1983: 3). The effect of this distinction between the collective responsibility of Cabinet and outer Ministers has been that some outer Ministers have deliberately not attended Cabinet meetings and have refused to be co-opted so that they can later argue against a Cabinet decision in caucus. Stewart West, a Cabinet minister, resigned from Cabinet—but not from the Ministry—to enable him to oppose Cabinet's decision on uranium policy in caucus. In other words, there is partial collective responsibility (Weller, 1985b, 339; Lucy, 1985, 136–7).

Some ministers have resigned or been sacked from Cabinet because of breaches of collective ministerial responsibility (for example, Leslie Bury in 1962 under Menzies and again in 1971 under McMahon, John Gorton in 1971, and Glen Shiel in 1977, even before he was sworn in to the Fraser Ministry), but those instances have been far outnumbered by ministers who have publicly disagreed with Cabinet policies and have not resigned. Certainly it is unlikely that Lower Houses of Parliament, with their strongly disciplined parties, will force the resignation of entire Cabinets.

Conclusion

Cabinets, more than any other actor in the political system, have the power to initiate and control events. Within the cabinet system itself the balance of power in recent years has shifted further in favour of the chief minister, partly because of structural changes to cabinet and the upgrading of prime ministerial sources of support.

References

Butler, David (1972) 'Ministerial Responsibility: a doctrine still full of life' *Canberra Times* 19 October, p. 2

Cabinet Handbook (1983) Canberra: AGPS

Chaples, E. et al. (eds) (1985) *The Wran Model: Electoral Politics in New South Wales 1981 and 1984* Melbourne: Oxford University Press

Cockburn, M. (1987) 'An axe, not a razor, was wielded in Cabinet room' *Sydney Morning Herald* 13 May, p. 17

Crisp, L.F. (1967) 'Central Coordination of Commonwealth Policy-Making: Roles and Dilemmas of the Prime Minister's Department' *Public Administration* (Sydney) XXVI, 1, pp. 28–54

—— (1983) *Australian National Government* Melbourne: Longman Cheshire, 5th edn

Department of the Prime Minister and Cabinet (1986) *Annual Report 1985–86* Canberra: AGPS

Hawker, G. et al. (1979) *Politics and Policy in Australia* St Lucia: University of Queensland Press

Hughes, C.A. (1984) *'The Proliferation of Portfolios' Australian Journal of Public Administration XLIII 3*, pp. 257–74

Lucy, R. (1985) *The Australian Form of Government* Melbourne: Macmillan

Mediansky, F. and Nockels, J. (1981) 'Malcolm Fraser's Bureaucracy' *Australian Quarterly* 53, 4, pp. 394–418

Painter, M. (1982) 'Premier's Departments and Coordination' *Politics* 17, 1, pp. 8–21

Parker, R.S. (1976) 'The meaning of responsible government' *Politics* 11, 2, pp. 178–84
Schneider, R. (1980) *War Without Blood: Malcolm Fraser in Power* Sydney: Angus and Robertson
Spann, R.N. (1979) *Government Administration in Australia* Sydney: George Allen and Unwin
Steketee, M. and Cockburn, M. (1986) *Wran: an unauthorised biography* Sydney: Allen and Unwin
Walter, J. (1986) *The Ministers' Minders: Personal Advisers in National Government* Melbourne: Oxford University Press
—— (1987) 'Political Advisers: The Ministers' Minders' *Current Affairs Bulletin* 63, 9, pp. 4–13
Weller, P. (1983) 'Transition: Taking Over Power in 1983', *Australian Journal of Public Administration* XLII, 3, pp. 303–319
—— (1985a) 'Cabinet Committees in Australia and New Zealand', in Mackie, T.T. and Hogwood, B.W. (eds) *Unlocking the Cabinet: Cabinet Structures in Comparative Perspective* London: Sage
—— (1985b) 'The Hawke Cabinet: collective or responsible?' *Australian Quarterly* 57, 4, pp. 333–44
Weller, P. and Grattan, M. (1981) *Can Ministers Cope? Australian Federal Ministers at Work* Richmond: Hutchinson

8 The public service

Barbara Page and Martin Painter

The public service is an indispensable arm of government. In theory, in Australia it is subordinate to the elected arm of the executive, the Ministry. Its subordinate status is embodied in the rules and conventions drawn from the Westminster tradition of responsible, representative government. The characteristics of this tradition are that elected ministers, drawn from and responsible to the parliament, will exercise control over the government's administration; that officials will be appointed, promoted and removed by an authority independent of the party political process; that in the relationship between ministers and officials the minister will have the final say; and that 'the lines of accountability of the whole administration run from the lowliest official up through (the) minister to the cabinet, the parliament and ultimately...to the elector' (Parker, 1979: 353).

The control which ministers are expected to exercise over the government's administrative activities varies according to the type of agency chosen to perform a particular function. At the core of the machinery of government are ministerial departments. Ministers responsible for specific functions of government such as education, defence and so on have authority over their respective departments, formulating and overseeing the implementation of policies that are ultimately determined by Cabinet. Public servants in each department are organised in a hierarchy, at the apex of which is a departmental head, the minister's most important advisor and the channel through which the minister's commands are conveyed to the department.

Most public employees, however, work in 'non-departmental' bodies such as statutory authorities—bodies like Telecom and the ABC. In 1986, for example, of the 442 400 civilian Australian government employees, only 30 percent worked in ministerial departments. This division is even more pronounced at the state level. In the late 1970s Wilenski (Review of NSW Government Administration, 1977: 53) estimated that about three-quarters of all commonwealth and state government employees were employed in statutory authorities. Some functions are considered best administered by such bodies because they enjoy a degree of autonomy from immediate ministerial control. The ABC is in this category because of its politically sensitive opinion-forming role (see chapter 19); Telecom (like other government business enterprises) because it conducts commercial activities. Most government business enterprises have social as well as commercial obligations. For example, to ensure equality of access to communication, Telecom is asked to subsidise services to rural areas from its more profitable metropolitan services. Non-departmental bodies, therefore, are not entirely free from the demands of political accountability. Ministers often have specified powers over them and statutory authorities are often subject to some measure of budgetary control by departments responsible for government finance.

Even within the ministerial departments and agencies that form the public service proper there is an important element of independence from ministerial direction in staffing matters. During the nineteenth century, when the need for continuing, expert administration became evident, public service boards or commissions were set up to take over from politicians the roles of recruitment, setting terms and conditions of employment, training and promotion. These central personnel agencies came to have considerable autonomy, with jurisdiction over staffing in ministerial departments. The 'career public service' emerged, in which recruitment and promotion were based on merit rather than patronage. Permanence of tenure became a central feature of the career service, partly as a way of strengthening its 'apolitical' basis. Along with this came the ideal of the experienced, impartial and anonymous public servant who would faithfully pursue the aims and diligently implement the programmes of elected governments. Public servants were meant to be 'neutral'; not in the sense of being equally supportive of government and opposition, but in that they would loyally serve the government of the day, whichever part of the political spectrum it came from—and just as loyally support a succeeding goverment of a different colour.

Career public servants have a responsibility to support, advise and caution the government, but the buck does not stop with them. A dissatisfied electorate cannot sack them. The ultimate sanction of loss of office is borne by the government. For this reason, the final responsibility for—and the final say on—any decision rests with the minister. That is the theory.

This chapter will focus mainly on how accountable departmental public servants are, in practice, in their relations with their ministers. Do officials operate in the manner prescribed—as subordinate, loyal servants of the government of the day? This is partly a question of the respective power of ministers and public servants over policy making. The next section surveys various arguments that suggest that the public service wields undue power and that ministers and governments are often unable to exercise the control that is supposedly theirs. The chapter then returns to the issue of accountability in the light of this assessment of the nature and extent of bureaucratic power.

Bureaucratic power

Most arguments about the power of bureaucracy begin from the presumption that this power is illegitimate or irresponsible. But senior public servants are not meant to be mere ciphers. They are expected to contribute to policy formulation and manage its implementation. Thus, when top officials play prominent roles in policy formulation, and even argue vigorously against or point out difficulties in government proposals, so long as the minister's view finally prevails they are doing no more than is expected of them—offering 'frank and fearless advice'. However, there is cause for concern about the potential power of the bureaucracy if a minister is confronted with advice that portrays consistent biases, if public servants wilfully obstruct a government's or minister's stated aims, or if policies are deliberately not implemented as intended.

There are three different types of argument on the nature, extent and effects of bureaucratic power. First, it has been claimed that individual senior public servants can exercise power because of their crucial roles in framing advice and 'managing' their ministers and their departments. There are no better exponents of this view than the writers of the BBC series 'Yes Minister'; Sir Humphrey Appleby is the archetypical 'mandarin' manipulator (Lynn and Jay, 1984). Secondly, there is the view that a bureaucratic elite can collectively exercise undue and pernicious influence in a conscious attempt to preserve public servants' own interests or to promote shared political attitudes. Alternatively, the bureaucracy is seen not as a cohesive group but rather as a number of different groups more interested in competing among themselves for power and influence than in furthering government aims. A third view focusses on the bureaucratic nature of organisational structures in the public service, which can make it difficult for governments both to exert control and to effect changes.

The power of individual officials

Ministers have many demands on their time and may not have the necessary abilities or energy to master the work of their department in all its aspects. Some prefer the more glamorous arenas of Parliament or public appearances to the hard grind of departmental office work—mastering briefs, commenting on proposals from officials and so on. Even when this is not the case, permanent public servants will still generally have the advantage in technical expertise and knowlege of previous policy experience. This puts permanent, skilled public servants in a position of great potential power. However, rather than pressing their own interests or personal views, they are expected to take on the minister's goals and intentions in their work. If they do not, as Wilenski (1978: 30) argues is sometimes bound to be the case, the minister's authority to command and to have the 'last word' means little.

Crisp (1972: 294) has claimed that submerging their personal views is part of the normal, daily working life of public servants. An important part of their training is to take on the trappings of 'impartiality', to be able to write briefs from whatever perspective is asked of them and, sometimes, to present advice that strives to cover all angles. Aside from ministers' demands, an official's public service superior will often expect this, and the ability to subordinate personal opinions when that is demanded may be a requirement for promotion.

Even if officials do use their positions to advance their views, or if their prejudices and biases enter into their work unconsciously, the potential power of any one public servant can be over-emphasised. Astute ministers can make allowances for the biases of their senior officials. And in any case, the work of gathering information, sifting options and presenting advice is a collective effort involving many public servants. Checking and redrafting memos and submissions have a moderating, 'sanitising' effect on the final result.

The relationship between a minister and departmental head depends to a great extent on their respective personalities, energies and abilities. Where public servants dominate ministers this is often because the latter have abdicated their responsibilities, leaving a vacuum that officials may fill (Spann, 1979: 264–71). Nevertheless, a potential imbalance clearly exists in the minister/departmental head relationship, and measures have been taken in recent years (see page 104) to redress this and strengthen the minister's hand.

While the power of individual officials can be exaggerated, the potential for groups of like-minded public servants to exercise collective power through common or concerted actions may be a greater threat.

The collective power of public servants

Arguments under this heading come in a variety of forms.

Conspiracy theories

The first argument is also the crudest. This is that the public service elite is a cohesive group, self-consciously and clandestinely acting to preserve its interests. Senior public servants come from similar backgrounds, share common views about what constitutes 'good government', and are in continual contact, perhaps belonging to the same clubs, meeting regularly for lunch and so on. In Britain, they are often referred to as 'the establishment'. The isolated, close-knit world of Canberra provides the ideal breeding ground for bureaucratic conspiracy.

Informal social networks like clubs and lunching together are important means by which top officials exchange ideas and facilitate business. But this does not have to have sinister connotations. Senior officials may cultivate these networks to build bridges, overcome departmental differences and smooth out personal rivalries. The onus is on conspiracy theorists to prove that networks are used to develop common political positions and make sure they prevail.

To some extent, acceptance of a conspiracy theory is a leap of faith: either you believe or you do not. Outsiders cannot know for sure because conspiracies are by definition clandestine; and insiders who spill the beans probably have a self-inflated view of their importance.

Collective, uniform political bias

The question of a conspiracy would not need to arise if it could be shown that the administrative elite acted in unison not because of any organised, concerted effort but simply because its members all shared the same underlying beliefs. Suggestions that this might be the case are often made because of the upper/middle class status of senior public servants and because the bulk of them also come from privileged backgrounds. Boreham, Cass and McCallum (1979), in a 1975 survey, found that 74 percent of higher commonwealth public servants came from upper or middle class backgrounds, compared with only 29 percent of the total population. From this kind of data it is often claimed that senior public servants will share common values that will be inimical to the aims of other than conservative, right-wing governments (Miliband, 1973: 111).

Research into the attitudes and belief systems of top public servants and politicians in a number of western democracies (not including Australia) has shown that, whereas political elites are polarised and view social and political issues from ideological viewpoints, career public servants tend to adopt an apolitical, somewhat technocratic orientation to policy (Aberbach, Putnam and Rockwell, 1981). Public servants are political 'centrists' and adopt a consensus rather than a conflict approach to public issues. Possibly, this is due to their training and experience as public servants. In one sense, they seem to conform to the ideal of neutrality expected of them.

In their survey of Australian elites, Higley, Deacon and Smart (1979) also show that the views of public servants as a group do not cluster clearly along ideological lines. The administrative elite does not have either a clear right-wing or left-wing bias. If the public service does not share the political enthusiasms of either left or right, it might be a potential brake on all radical change, but it also suggests that the strain of adapting to governments within the 'normal' spectrum of left and right will not be great.

Claims of a politically conservative bias in the Australian public service gained credence from the experience of the Whitlam Labor Governments of 1972–5, which took office after 23 years of Liberal/Country Party rule and pursued a relatively radical, left-wing programme. The public service was accused of obstructionism at worst, and a lack of urgency and enthusiasm at best, in implementing the new Government's reforms. Hawker (1981: 11–22) and others have argued that this arose in part because the long years of conservative rule had produced a conservative, complacent public service.

But it would be a mistake to generalise from this instance and jump to the conclusion that the administrative elite is inherently politically conservative. It is not hard to understand that top officials who rise to the top under governments of one political flavour (whether left or right) and have never experienced any other would find it hard to adjust to the expectations of a radically different government. Moreover, in 1972 the new Labor Ministry lacked experience in handling and mastering the public service. There are always likely to be 'settling in' problems for a new government, particularly one that departs significantly from a prevailing policy spectrum.

Fragmentation and diversity in the administrative elite

Another argument about the exercise of collective power by the bureaucracy sees the administrative elite not as one group but as a number of groups, formed around departmental interests, shared professions, a common status in the hierarchy of jobs, shared responsibilities for particular programmes, and so on. Several studies have emphasised their competition for power in the policy process (Ball, 1979; Painter and Carey, 1979; Hawker, Smith and Weller, 1979). Allison (1971) has applied the expression 'bureaucratic politics' to this model of executive policy making. As Allison (1971: 176) puts it: 'where you stand depends on where you sit'. Different branches of the military, for instance, take somewhat predictable stands on conflicts over military strategy and compete fiercely with each other for new equipment. In turn, civilian elements in the defence administration take different positions (Ball, 1979). The Defence Department as a whole sometimes unites against Treasury or against Foreign Affairs. Crisp (1972) has called aspects of this 'the politics of the departmental line'—when a department stands up in defence of its predispositions, policies and interests against all comers, including ministers. When a department possesses a long-standing view on a matter it can be very hard for a minister to shake it.

Bureaucratic politics itself limits the power over a government of any one department, because its proposals will be subject to close scrutiny and challenge by other, competing departments. There are, nevertheless, grounds for arguing that bureaucratic power plays might be obstructive to a government's programmes. Many bureaucratic conflicts are worked out in interdepartmental committees. Because committee members (who are public servants) see themselves primarily as delegates for their departmental positions, their search for a common position to present to a government can produce a 'lowest common denominator' outcome, which is a product of bureaucratic compromises rather than a reflection of government intentions (Painter and Carey, 1979). Little gets through that any one significant power bloc strongly objects to and the bias is towards the status quo. This can be a source of great frustration to a government (Lloyd and Troy, 1981).

'Bureaucratic politics' provides a much more useful approach to understanding bureaucratic power than others so far considered. Senior administrators and ministers are participants in the one 'game': the struggle within the executive for influence over policy outcomes. The lines of conflict are much more complex than a simple separation between ministers and public servants. Ministers divide among themselves and groups of officials and departments form alliances with different ministers. Tactical decisions, like which departments to consult or what committees to set up, are part of the games that ministers must learn to play and win in order to be effective.

The bureaucrat as empire-builder

There is one other, recently influential strand in the analysis of bureaucratic power, based on 'public choice theory' (Downs, 1957; Niskanen, 1973). The assumption is that a bureau chief is motivated primarily by 'budget maximisation', that is, getting as big a share of resources as is possible for his or her agency, over and above or regardless of government policy.

However, Goodin (1982) shows that it is more likely that an agency chief will support his or her minister, resulting in allocations that reflect political priorities as well as bureaucratic ones. Goodin also questions the simple budget maximisation motivation, proposing that agency chiefs might actually care about the policies they administer rather than just the size of their budgets. Dunleavy (1985) has argued that agency chiefs may be quite willing to reduce the size of their agencies if, for instance, it resulted in more congenial work environments for them. In sum, public choice models do not generally allow for the variety of motives and inter-relations that exist among different senior officials or the many outcomes that can result from the power plays among them.

Bureaucracy as a constraint

The third type of argument about bureaucratic power claims that a bureaucracy will exert a conservative influence on policy and administration simply by virtue of its bureaucratic nature. Most discussions of bureaucracy start with Max Weber's famous analysis (Gerth and Mills, 1947). He argued that, among other things, bureaucratic organisations embody centralisation of authority and hierarchical chains of command; rigid allocation of tasks to specific offices; strict rules and procedures to govern officials' actions; and a norm of impersonality in the way officials approach their jobs.

The consequences for decision making include the likelihood of new problems being defined in terms of existing 'standard operating procedures'; a tendency for officials to follow the rules somewhat obsessively and to be inflexible and cautious; and a tendency for orders and information that pass up and down the hierarchy to be reinterpreted and distorted in policy implementation. In sum, bureaucratic organisations are rigid, insensitive in their dealings with the public, slow to adapt to change and bad at responding adequately to new outside ideas. Not every government department possesses all these bureaucratic traits, although most will exhibit many of them (Jordan, 1974). A government in charge of such organisations will have difficulties in controlling them and getting them to change. Managerial reforms aimed at eliminating bureaucratic structures might help to make government organisations more flexible and responsive to ministers' wishes (Hawker, 1981: 79–88). In the next section, some remedies for the problems of ministerial control and the lack of responsiveness of bureaucratic organisations are discussed.

Accountability and control

The previous section highlighted the potential power of public servants. While it questioned some of the more alarmist interpretations of the exercise of that power, effective checks and controls over the public service are still required. Controls can be subdivided into two main types—external and internal. The Westminster model emphasises external controls over the bureaucracy, originating in Parliament but exercised mainly through the political executive. Internal controls, on the other hand, rely on developing a sense of responsibility within the public service itself. In most cases, both external and internal controls operate together—the problem is to make them compatible.

External controls I—Ministerial

Two main remedies have been suggested to bolster the ability of ministers to exercise direct control: changes in the way senior staff are appointed and the increased use of ministerial advisors.

Public service staffing

The traditional picture of a senior public servant in a Westminster model career service was of an anonymous, highly experienced administrator who would serve loyally, impartially and objectively the government of the day, whatever its political complexion. But because they stayed while governments came and went, enthusiastic commitment to government policies was not part of the portrait of the quintessential public servant. To the suggestion that if it was his job to carry out government policies, then he should believe in them, that career public servant, Sir Humphrey Appleby, retorted that he had served eleven governments over 30 years and if he had believed in all their policies he would have been (among other things):

> . . . a Keynesian and a Friedmanite, a grammar school preserver and destroyer, a nationalisation freak and a privatisation maniac; but, above all, I would have been a stark, staring, raving schizophrenic. ('Yes Minister', BBC Televison series, 'The Whisky Priest')

As a result of the experiences of the Whitlam Government referred to earlier, many argued that the 'cool, detached, expert adviser' did not provide the kind of help that an active, modern government required. What ministers needed to ensure that the public service was responsive and accountable to them were senior public servants who were committed to the government's aims and policies.

A wave of outside inquiries and commissions into public services in Australia in the 1970s/80s stressed the need for increased ministerial control. Common recommendations included fixed terms for and greater mobility of department heads, the devolution of staffing responsibilities from independent public service boards to ministerial departments, and opening up recruitment at senior public service levels to outside (lateral) appointments. In line with these recommendations, Commonwealth ministers, through Cabinet, now select their department heads (which may mean a reshuffle of top officials with a new government or a change of ministers); the public service board has been abolished; and every senior appointment is now widely advertised.

These measures, in varying degrees, provide potential avenues for the appointment of public servants who are sympathetic to a particular government's or minister's policies. Some of the measures have been accompanied by cries of 'politicisation' from critics who claimed that increased involvement of politicians in the appointment, promotion or placement of public servants would lead to a decline in the quality and professionalism of the service and to political patronage—'jobs for the girls and boys'. Much of this opposition could be put down to fear of change. There is, after all, nothing sacred about the principle of a career service. In the United States, however, experience of presidential political appointees to top administrative jobs shows that they are often inexperienced and unsuitable. Would such people be able to exercise control over the permanent bureaucracy any more effectively than ministers?

In Australia, the career service has not yet been overturned to the extent that a whole layer of top officials comes and goes with a change of government, as happens in the United States. While lateral recruitment is on the increase, merit criteria are still applied; but, in addition, political criteria seem increasingly important. If politically appointed officials, committed to the aims of a particular government, are given tenure, then this does raise problems about their future and that of the service when that government loses office. This is now being seen in some Australian states, where ministers have exercised personal influence over senior appointments and where opposition parties are talking of the possibility of wholesale sackings or replacements.

Ministerial advisers

These people are appointed to a minister's personal staff rather than to senior departmental positions. They are responsible only to their minister and their tenure depends solely on the will and fate of that minister. Before 1972 their numbers were small and they were usually engaged only in fairly mundane support and housekeeping duties. Most of them were public servants seconded from the minister's department. The advent of the Whitlam Government changed all this. The numbers, pay and status of ministerial advisers increased, as did the proportion of appointments of non-public servants and the number engaged in offering alternative policy advice (see chapter 7). The succeeding Fraser and Hawke Governments appreciated the advantages that this additional resource offered ministers in negotiations over policy and they continued—and strengthened—ministerial staff structures. A similar development occurred at the state level (Walter, 1987).

External controls II—Cabinet and budgetary reforms

The attempts described in the last chapter to strengthen Cabinet's power and streamline its proceedings have also enhanced the ability of ministers collectively to control the public service. They have been accompanied by budgetary reforms designed to provide the Government with greater control over the resources available to it and a better means of ensuring that expenditure and revenue decisions actually reflect its policy priorities. With this aim, the Commonwealth (as have most state governments) has moved from the traditional 'control' budget focussed on inputs (salaries and services) and classified by 'line-items' (e.g., stationery, wages, travel) to a 'programme' budget format that focusses on outputs and is divided into programme categories. Whereas the traditional budget process was designed primarily as a financial auditing tool to control expenditure and ensure compliance with the conditions set out in the appropriations, programme budgeting is concerned, as well, with evaluating how effectively and efficiently government priorities are translated into budgetary outcomes. Because it sets out more clearly where and for what funds have been allocated, programme budgeting should enhance not only executive control over the use of public sector resources but also the ability of Parliament to scrutinise the activities of the Government and its administration. However, experience both overseas and in Australia with programme budgeting is mixed; some of the more optimistic forecasts of its advantages have not come to fruition (Wildavsky, 1975).

In addition to the controls exercised through the budgetary process, cabinet also initiates reviews of particular programmes or agencies. A recent initiative was the establishment in September 1986 of an Efficiency Scrutiny Unit (headed by businessman David Block), which worked in cooperation with the responsible minister and senior departmental officials and reported its findings and recommendations directly to the Prime Minister and through him to the Expenditure Review Committee of Cabinet. A number of the measures adopted have aimed to combat the bureaucratic character of some parts of the public service.

External controls III—non-executive controls

Parliament

Parliamentary scrutiny of executive government is another traditional Westminster control that has fallen into disrepute. However, Parliaments in Australia have taken some steps to try to improve their ability to secure the accountability of the executive, including the activities of the public service.

The traditional methods of parliamentary scrutiny—questions with and without notice, parliamentary debates, and representations to government departments by individual MPs on behalf of their constituents—have been supplemented at the Commonwealth level by a system of parliamentary committees (see chapter 6). At both Commonwealth and state levels public accounts, and in some cases other financial, committees have been strengthened or revamped. While parliamentary committees have their weaknesses —lack of time and resources, changing membership leading to loss of continuity and experience, lack of Executive cooperation, and dependence on the Executive for referral of topics in the first place and implementation of their recommendations in the last—they do offer perhaps the most effective weapon whereby Parliament can systematically examine the actions of the Executive.

Two types of committees of particular relevance to control of the public service are those that scrutinise delegated legislation and those that look at public accounts. The former oversee the discretionary power given to public servants to make regulations under acts passed by Parliament, although, generally speaking, the quantity and complexity of delegated legislation make effective scrutiny very difficult. Public accounts committees examine the reports of Auditors-General—officers who report directly to Parliament on their financial and, in some cases, performance or efficiency audits of government departments and agencies. Some audits have revealed large-scale waste and inefficiency. However, the ability to follow up recommendations for improvement remains a problem, as this rests with the Executive and, ultimately, the agency concerned.

'New administrative law'

The external controls over bureaucratic power discussed so far have been mainly concerned with achieving overall responsibility of the Government to the people through ministerial or parliamentary oversight. The final external control to be considered is one whose primary concern is to ensure justice for individual citizens in their dealings with the bureaucracy, as well as improved administrative procedures in the implementation of policy.

The perception that the avenues available—through Parliament and its members, through ministerial control of the bureaucracy, through the courts and internal departmental tribunals—did not offer effective recourse for all citizens against unsatisfactory administrative actions led in the mid 1970s to a package of reforms known as the 'new administrative law' (NAL). At the Commonwealth level these took the form of the Administrative Appeals Tribunal Act 1975 (AAT), the Ombudsman Act 1976, the Administrative Decisions (Judicial Review) Act 1977 (ADJR) and, after much delay, the Freedom of Information Act 1982. (There is an ombudsman in every state but only Victoria has followed the Commonwealth lead by introducing freedom of information legislation (1982) and an AAT Act in 1984.)

These acts give citizens the means to challenge administrative decisions. Decisions of officials (and in some cases, ministers) can be reviewed by the AAT and the ombudsman on their merits and by the Federal Court (under ADJR) on their legality. The AAT has the power to change decisions and the Federal Court to set them aside. Ombudsmen can only recommend and report following investigation of complaints, but they are nonetheless quite effective in obtaining redress in a large number of cases. The Freedom of Information Act, and provisions in both the AAT and ADJR Acts, are designed to provide citizens with information to enable them to challenge administrative decisions. Only a very small proportion of cases and decisions are directly reviewed by these mechanisms but their existence, and thus the possibility of review, probably acts as a spur to public servants to improve their decision-making procedures.

The reforms introduced by the NAL make the public service more accountable to those affected by its decisions. However, they also in some measure cut across the traditional lines of accountability to ministers and raise questions about the proper role and power of the judiciary in government policy and administration.

Internal controls

Whereas most external forms of control over the public service presume that appointed officials need to be watched closely in case they abrogate power or become indifferent to their obligations, internal controls rely on the responsibility of the administrator. Thus the Royal Commission on Australian Government Administration (1976) proposed that 'a new system of accountability should be built on a positive recognition that officialdom had a creative and, in some ways, an independent role to play in governing the modern state' (Emy, 1976: 61). Notions of ministerial responsibility should be supplemented by a system of 'accountable management' giving greater financial and managerial responsibilities to department heads, coupled with a system of efficiency audits.

Other methods of internal control include performance indicators to monitor efficiency and effectiveness, training programmes designed to foster 'professionalism' and the development of codes of ethics to regulate behaviour.

One recent initiative embodying the principle of a more professional approach to management in the Commonwealth public service is the Financial Management Improvement Program, which encourages departmental managers to apply more rigorous methods of planning, performance review and resource allocation. Behind such initiatives is a private–sector model of management, stressing managerial autonomy within policy guidelines set from above. However, this approach may downplay the political element in policy advising and decision making, and may in the long run result in a public service elite that only evaluates issues from a narrow, efficiency perspective. This could well work against aims to make the public service more flexible and responsive to changing values and new political directions originating in the wider political process. Indeed, one of the problems with relying on internal controls is that they may create a more independent, powerful public service, directed in its actions not by politicians but by internal, technical standards that are monitored by other public servants.

Conclusion

Modern governments have deliberately created a potentially powerful public service to take advantage of the experience and expertise it provides. The very professionalism of the public service may prove a greater threat to the supremacy of the political executive than any purported political biases or deliberate obstructionism within the service. Too much stress on managerial efficiency and technocratic values may obscure the more important political choices which governments have been elected to make.

References

Aberbach, J.D., Putnam, R.D., and Rockwell, B.A. (1981) *Bureaucrats and Politicians in Western Democracies* Cambridge: Harvard University Press

Allison, Graham T. (1971) *Essence of Decision* Boston: Little Brown and Company

Ball, Desmond (1979) 'Australian Defence Decision-Making: Actors and Processes' *Politics* 14, 2, pp. 183–97

Boreham, P., Cass, M. and McCallum, M. (1979) 'The Australian Bureaucratic Elite: The Importance of Social Backgrounds and Occupational Experience' *The Australian and New Zealand Journal of Sociology* 15, 2, pp. 45–55

Crisp, L.F. (1972) 'Politics and The Commonwealth Public Service' *Public Administration (Sydney)* 31, 4, pp. 287–309
Downs, A. (1957) *An Economic Theory of Democracy* New York: Harper and Row
Emy, Hugh V. (1976) *Public Policy: Problems and Paradoxes* Melbourne: Macmillan
Gerth, H.H. and Mills, C.W. (1947) *From Max Weber* London: Kegan, Trench, Trubner & Co. Ltd.
Goodin, R.E. (1982) 'Rational politicians and rational bureaucrats in Washington and Whitehall' *Public Administration* 60, 1, pp. 23–41
Hawker, G. (1981) *Who's Master, Who's Servant?* Sydney: George Allen and Unwin
Hawker, G., Smith, R.F.I. and Weller, P. (1979) *Politics and Policy Making in Australia* St Lucia: University of Queensland Press
Higley, J., Deacon, D. and Smart, D. (1979) *Elites in Australia* London: Routledge & Kegan Paul
Jordan, A. (1974) 'Living death in the social policy section', in Don Edgar (ed.) *Social Change in Australia* Melbourne: Cheshire
Lloyd, C.J. and Troy, P.N. (1981) *Innovation and Reaction: The Life and Death of the Department of Urban and Regional Development* Sydney: George Allen and Unwin
Lynn, J. and Jay, A. (1984) *The Complete Yes Minister* London: BBC Publications
Miliband, R. (1973) *The State in Capitalist Society* London: Quartet Books
Niskanen, W.A. (1973) *Bureaucracy and Representative Government* New York: Aldine-Atherton
Painter, M. and Carey, B. (1979) *Politics Between Departments* St Lucia: University of Queensland Press
Spann, R.N. (1979) *Government Administration in Australia* Sydney: George Allen and Unwin
Walter, J. (1987) 'The Ministers' Minders' *Current Affairs Bulletin* 63, 9, pp. 4–13
Wildavsky, A. (1975) *Budgeting* Boston: Little, Brown
Wilenski, P. (1978) 'Labor and the Bureaucracy', in Graeme Duncan (ed.) *Critical Essays in Australian Politics* Melbourne: Edward Arnold (Australia)

9 The party system

Rodney Smith

Mass political parties are only 100 years old, but their impact on politics in liberal democracies such as Australia is paramount. As Jaensch (1983: 9) states:

> There can be no argument about the ubiquity, pervasiveness and centrality of party in Australia. The forms, processes and content of politics—executive, parliament, pressure groups, issues and policy-making—are imbued with the influence of party, party rhetoric, party policy and party doctrine.

The other chapters in this book support Jaensch's view. None can avoid discussing parties when explaining the operation of Australia's other political institutions.

What are political parties? They are clearly political organisations, but their defining characteristics are difficult to pin down. What do mass parliamentary parties like the Liberal Party of Australia (LPA) have in common with tiny, secret organisations like the Revolutionary Reunification Party of Korea, or the Communist Party of the Soviet Union, or Sinn Fein in Ireland, or the Democratic Party of the United States? Within Australia, what distinguishes small parties like the Nuclear Disarmament Party (NDP) from organisations like People for Nuclear Disarmament (PND) and the Right to Life Association (RTLA), which are usually seen as pressure groups?

These sorts of questions have caused much debate among political scientists, and answers to them are bound to be controversial. In this chapter, political parties are defined as organisations that aim to influence public policy in favour of an ideology or set of interests primarily by attempting to gain control of public political office.

Several features of this definition deserve brief elaboration. It encompasses large and small organisations, which may be structured in any way. It includes parties with a single aim—for example, the NDP—as well as parties such as the Australian Labor Party (ALP), which has 22 broad objectives and hundreds of more detailed aims (Australian Labor Party, 1986). The aims of parties may be to alter society according to an ideology—for example, liberalism—or to defend a set of interests, such as those of farmers. The distinguishing feature of parties, according to this definition, is their *method*. Any organisation, whether large and complex like the ALP or small and unstructured like the NDP, which uses as its primary method the attempt to control public office is a party. Organisations such as the RTLA or PND, which primarily use methods other than attempted control of public office to influence politics, are properly seen as pressure groups.

A count of all parties that have operated in Australia would run into the hundreds. Jaensch (1984: 132, 133) identifies 82 minor parties in the period 1970 to 1980 alone, most of which have since disappeared. Only three parties—the ALP, the LPA (and its forebears) and the National (formerly Country) Party of Australia (NPA)—have had any major long-term impact on Australian politics and public policy. Two other parties have had smaller but significant impacts for shorter periods—the Democratic Labor Party (DLP) from 1957 to 1974 and the Australian Democrats (AD) since 1977.

Origins, interests and ideologies

What sets of interests or ideologies were these parties established to defend? How have these interests and ideologies shaped the subsequent politics of these parties?

The Australian Labor Party

The ALP is the oldest existing party in Australia, dating back to 1890. The origins of the ALP lie in a mixture of radical, labourist and socialist traditions among workers and middle-class reformers in Australian cities and towns, as well as among rural workers and small farmers. Although some workers were socialists who wished to overthrow the patterns of economic and political power in Australia, most workers held labourist or radical beliefs and simply wanted workers to be represented as another interest in Parliament, alongside those of landowners, traders, industrialists and other capitalists.

The push for workers' interests to be represented at a political level came from three sources. The first was organisations with their roots in Chartist ideas for increasing popular control over politics, such as fair representation, full manhood suffrage with no property qualification on voting for any parliamentary house, and short-term parliaments with paid members. The second and most important was the trade union movement, which from the 1870s saw the need for legislative as well as industrial action to achieve better wages, hours and conditions for workers. Third, revolutionary socialists stressed the need for workers to undertake organised political action if they were to achieve more than slow improvements to industrial conditions.

The early mobilisation of workers' interests through the ALP was quite successful in representative terms. Labor candidates soon won seats on municipal councils. In 1893, sixteen Labor members were elected to the Queensland Parliament, and Labor MPs sat in all state parliaments soon afterwards. Anderson Dawson in Queensland formed the world's first labour government in 1899, and the first ever national labour Government was formed by J.C. Watson in 1904.

This pattern of interest mobilisation had profound influences on the development of the ALP. It led to the formal affiliation of trade unions with the ALP, which gave union leaders extensive power within the party. The collectivist ethos of the working class, combined with chartist and socialist suspicion of the motives of labour leaders, led to the adoption of a pledge binding all members of the party to its policy. Conferences at which unions and rank and file members were represented became the central policy-making bodies within the ALP. Socialists within the party successfully pushed for the early adoption of a socialist objective, but the presence of other ideologies such as radicalism, rural populism and labourism meant that the ALP was never a socialist party. The early parliamentary success of the party gave it a strong pragmatic streak in any case. Its successes before federation meant that its organisation developed along federal rather than centralised lines.

Despite these lasting influences, the present ALP is somewhat different to the party in 1900 or even 1940. The main differences can be traced to a post-World War II middle-classing of the ALP. Public servants, teachers, lawyers and other professionals have entered the ALP in increasing numbers in the last 40 years. They have brought with them a new middle-class radicalism that stresses causes such as the environment, feminism, sexuality, education and the arts, interests that now compete with traditional blue-collar working-class interests on local branch and conference agendas. This middle-classing extends to the parliamentary leadership of the ALP. From being a party of relatively uneducated blue collar workers, the ALP has become a party led by tertiary-educated professionals.

The impact of this middle-classing has been great. It has produced tensions between the trade union and political wings of the labour movement. Middle-class Labor activists sometimes show impatience with the entrenched power of affiliated unions within the ALP. For their part, blue-collar unionists are hostile to the 'trendy' issues pushed by middle-class members within the party. These conflicts have led to debate about the party's very traditions. In recent ALP national conferences, for example, middle-class delegates castigated the Hawke Government for breaking with Labor traditions by allowing uranium exports, even though this 'tradition' only emerged in 1975, 85 years after the party's foundation! Finally, the new middle-class leaders of the parliamentary ALP have sometimes chafed at restrictions imposed on their actions while in government by the power of ALP conferences and caucuses to determine binding party policy. Whitlam, Wran and Hawke, while parliamentary leaders, all took occasional policy decisions that were contrary to or unendorsed by the relevant conference or caucus.

If the ALP is no longer held together by a well-defined social base, it makes sense to ask whether ideology unifies the party. Is the ALP a socialist party?

This is a difficult question, partly because socialism has a variety of meanings that can all claim validity, and partly because a socialism appropriate for the 1890s will inevitably look different to a socialism for the 1980s. Given this, the meaning of the ALP's Socialist Objective, to which it has been formally committed since 1905, deserves attention.

For the early ALP, socialism meant the transfer of productive wealth out of the hands of capitalists. The 1921 National Conference of the ALP, for example, formalised the following objective: 'The socialisation of industry, production, distribution and exchange' (O'Meagher, 1983: 7). Four broad methods would achieve this goal. These were the nationalisation of industries, government of these industries by boards with worker and community representation, industrial coordination by a Supreme Economic Council, and establishing institutions to train workers in management (O'Meagher, 1983: 8). While this concept of socialism is remarkably clear, the same Conference passed the Blackburn Declaration, which effectively made it a future goal rather than an immediate plan of action (Irving, 1983: 42).

Labor's most recently adopted socialist objective of 1981, which proposes '...democratic socialisation...to the extent necessary to eliminate exploitation and other anti-social features...', sets out methods for achieving this quite different to those of 1921. These include equality of opportunity, development of public enterprises, maintenance of a competitive, Australian-owned private sector and the right to own private property (Evans, 1983: 64, 65).

The differences between the 1921 and 1981 objectives are due to a number of factors, including the failure of the Chifley Government's attempts to nationalise medicine and banks in the 1940s, apparent constitutional barriers to nationalisation, the damage caused to the ALP by its opponents linking socialism with communism during the Cold War, the growth of middle-class elements in the party for whom nationalisation was an irrelevance, and a desire to keep people with a broad range of beliefs comfortable within the party. This last factor has been very important, because although the impact of socialists within the ALP should not be underestimated, the party has always included large numbers of radical populists, liberals, social democrats, nationalists and Catholics who would not subscribe to socialism. The ALP maintains its Socialist Objective partly for tradition's sake, partly because the Objective has developed into a flexible commitment to broad principles of social justice, and partly because a significant section of the party remains committed to socialism.

The Liberal Party

The organisation of workers' interests into a party spurred business likewise to protect its interests. Efforts by business to do this produced the three major forerunners of the Liberal Party—the first Liberal Party (1910–1917), the National Party (1917–1931) and the United Australia Party (1931–1944)—and ultimately produced the present party. Prior to 1910, business interests were represented in Parliament by loose groupings of conservative and liberal parliamentarians, but by this time, these groupings and their business backers were in disarray. Union militancy and the early success of the ALP led to reorganisation of business interests, with the formation of national organisations such as the Employers' Federation and the Chamber of Manufacturers, which provided a base for the Liberal Party.

The early liberal parties reflected these business origins in their structures. They had weak branches with no mass base. This meant that the parliamentary party leadership was free from rank and file pressure when formulating policies and in maintaining coalition relations with the Country Party; however, it also made these parties dependent for funding on semi-secret external finance committees run by business groups and individuals. Although not formally affiliated to these parties, business groups exerted strong control on their direction (Starr, 1978: 14–25).

Robert Menzies attempted to broaden the interests represented by the present Liberal Party when it was formed out of the remnants of the UAP and thirteen other anti-Labor organisations in 1944. Menzies pitched the Liberal Party's appeal to 'the forgotten people', the 'middle class' who were neither 'rich and powerful' nor 'the mass of unskilled people' (Menzies, 1943: 1, 2). This middle class was to form a mass-based branch structure and provide rank and file financing for the LPA's operations, which in turn would decrease the direct power of business over the party.

Although the LPA has drawn a wide range of middle and even working-class individuals into its membership, the power of business within the party remains substantial. At parliamentary level, the party is represented by members overwhelmingly drawn from business, farming and the law. Every LPA Federal President has been a prominent businessperson. Much of the party's funding still comes from business, and this affects the LPA's direction and leadership. In 1986, for example, every senior officer of the West Australian division of the LPA was replaced following dissatisfaction and threatened withdrawal of donations by sections of the business community.

The LPA has difficulty in simultaneously articulating the interests of business and those of its middle-class members and supporters. The business community often demands decisive Liberal policy on issues that would alienate other LPA supporters. As with the ALP, the contemporary LPA has to negotiate uneasy compromises between the interests it represents.

It might be argued that the LPA finds this negotiation easier than the ALP because the former is a pragmatic party, unencumbered by the ideological commitment of Labor. Certainly the LPA as a whole has never been concerned with ideology. It has been left to parliamentary leaders like Menzies, Malcolm Fraser and John Howard to set the party's ideological direction. These leaders have in turn relied for inspiration on outside bodies such as the Institute of Public Affairs—whose 1944 statement *Looking Forward* provided the basis for the LPA's philosophical platform until the 1970s—and more recently the intellectual 'think tanks' of the New Right. Although Fraser initiated a Liberal Party philosophy sub-committee in 1976, and other philosophical groups such as the recently established Liberal Forum exist within the LPA, their influence has been small.

The ideology that has emerged from this inattention has been a loose and partly contradictory mixture of liberalism, with its stress on individual freedoms and rights, rational social change through legislation and equality of opportunity, and a conservatism that sees society as harmonious and hierarchical, opposes social change engineered through legislation, and that focusses on individual obligations to the community rather than individual rights. Freedom or obligation? The conflicts in this ideological mix have never been resolved by the LPA. Even recent Liberal soul-searching documents such as the LPA Committee of Review's *Facing the Facts* (1983) offer no ideological clarity or direction. Their real importance is to give a broad ideological home in the party to members from the far-right to the moderate-left.

The National Party

The interests represented by the NPA are best identified by its former name, the Country Party. As with the ALP and the LPA, the Country Party grew out of a sectional pressure group. From the 1890s to the 1910s, farmers and settlers associations and chambers of agriculture formed around Australia to protect farming interests. Some 'country' parliamentarians held seats in this period, but they were not organised into a party. The stimuli to form a country party came from attempts by farmers to prevent large fluctuations in wheat prices and production, opposition to state ALP government controls over agricultural production, lack of interest in rural problems by urban conservatives and, in some states, a push to articulate 'free trade' policies against protectionists. These stimuli led to the formation of the first Country Party in Western Australia in 1914, formation of a federal party in 1920 and divisions in all states by 1922.

Since this time, the Country Party has been very successful in defending rural interests. Although it has electoral and organisational strength only in Queensland, New South Wales and Victoria, its coalition with the LPA has meant the representation of rural interests in federal governments for 50 years since 1920. This coalition also meant it could restrict its electoral efforts to rural seats where it had very good chances of success. In the 1983 federal election, for example, the NPA contested 25 percent and won 14 percent of the House of Representatives seats, mostly in rural areas.

Despite this success, in the last few decades elements within the NPA have attempted to distance the party from its rural base and redefine it as a general conservative party. These moves are reflected in the party's name change to 'National', which occurred in Queensland in 1974 and federally in 1982, following seven years in which the federal party was called 'National Country'. This redefinition has two sources. The first is a fear that with the shrinking rural population, the NPA will disappear if it does not attract non-rural support. This was the motive behind federal leader John McEwen's attempts to attract business support for the party in the 1960s. The second source is confidence among some NPA strategists that the NPA can fill the role of a genuine conservative party for all Australia. This confidence has gained most momentum in Queensland, where the NPA has won a number of urban seats and governed in its own right since 1983 (Costar and Woodward, 1985).

The attempt to replicate this strategy across Australia has not been successful. In the 1984 and 1987 federal elections, the NPA contested 45 percent and 52 percent of House seats respectively, but on both occasions they won 14 percent of seats, failing to expand their parliamentary representation over previous elections. In 1987, attempts by Queensland Premier Bjelke-Petersen to turn the NPA into a national conservative party were resisted by many party members who feared the loss of a distinctly rural party, as much as by

LPA members who wished to retain the urban-rural conservative coalition. Queensland notwithstanding, the NPA remains a party of rural interests.

The NPA has few ideological pretensions. It stresses the moral worth of rural life and sings the praises of farmers as the unappreciated backbone of Australia, but this hardly constitutes systematic ideology. Similarly, although the NPA is avowedly anti-socialist and pro-capitalist, it does not appear to be very clear about what it means by this. There is some truth in the jibe that the NPA aims to capitalise farmers' gains and socialise their losses. Thus, while the NPA supports free markets in principle, it also supports government marketing schemes, low interest rural loans, and subsidies and tariffs to protect uncompetitive rural industries. The rural conservatism of the NPA derives very directly from the interests it seeks to represent.

Minor parties

Beyond the three major parties, hundreds of minor parties have emerged in Australia. These parties fall into three broad categories: doctrinal or ideological parties such as the Communist Party of Australia; single-issue or protest parties such as the Nuclear Disarmament Party; and parties such as the DLP, which emerge when dissenters within a major party split from that party. Most minor parties struggle for survival without much impact on politics, largely because of the far greater power resources of the major parties against whom they compete. Internal factors also contribute to the failure of minor parties. Doctrinal parties fail because their ideology becomes too rigid or irrelevant to sustain supporters' loyalties, single-issue parties struggle because their issues inevitably become less publicly prominent over time, and splitters decline as the anger and disputes that once sustained them fade into memories. Only two minor parties have lasted for any significant time. The first of these was the DLP, which split away from the ALP in the 1950s to help prevent what it saw as a communist-controlled ALP from gaining government, and was primarily supported by upwardly-mobile Catholics (Reynolds 1974). The second is the Australian Democrats.

The ADs began in 1977 as a combination of splitter and protest party. They were a splitter party in the sense that their founder-leader Don Chipp came from the LPA, and a number of early AD members had been Liberals or members of the New Liberal Movement, which had split from the LPA several years earlier. However, the ADs were, and remain, much more importantly a party of protest against the entrenched dominance of the ALP and coalition. Chipp made this clear in founding the party, which he described as a new political force with no vested interests, unlike Labor's union links or those of the coalition to business and farmers. The profile of AD supporters confirms this image: they tend to be young professionals with no previous party identification who vote on issues or as a protest against the major parties. These supporters are regionally diverse and do not constitute a large clearly defined interest with deep loyalties; hence the ADs' inability to win Lower House seats or to poll more than about nine percent in Senate ballots (see chapter 10).

The ADs claim to be a party of liberalism, but they are a party of concerns rather than ideology. These concerns include producing a more harmonious capitalism in Australia by controlling the excesses of business and unions, a strong commitment to environmentalism, increasing Australia's independence in international affairs, and the need to alleviate social inequalities such as poverty and youth unemployment (Australian Democrats, 1987). Until 1986, these ideas reflected divisions within the ADs between former LPA members and more left-wing Democrats. Since then, and especially following the exiting from parliamentary politics of Don Chipp and other prominent founder-members of the party, the ADs appear to have moved toward the left of the political spectrum.

Two themes emerge from this brief survey of party interests and ideology. The first is that the interests represented by all three major parties have become more complex in recent years as class and other social foundations of Australian politics have shifted. For Labor, the crucial change has been the increasing number of workers in 'middle-class' jobs. For the LPA, the problem has been to balance business aspirations with those of its small business, professional, and white-collar supporters and members. For the NPA, it has been the steady decline in Australia's rural population. These changes have all had important consequences.

Second, Australian party politics, even in the ALP, does not revolve around ideology. In comparison with British and European politics, Australian party politics is ideologically pallid. Sectional interests, not ideas, dominate.

Party functions

Parties in liberal democracies have six broad functions. These are: to allow political participation, to recruit political leaders, to form policies, to communicate those policies to the electorate, to contest public office and to initiate policy implementation when in government. How well do Australian parties conform to these expectations?

Participation

Parties are not used as a major form of political participation in Australia. Total party membership is probably about 250 000, comprising 60 000 in the ALP, 90 000 in the LPA, 100 000 in the NPA, 2000 in the AD, and 1000 in other minor parties. As Warhurst (1986: 106) points out, membership of environmentalist pressure groups alone is roughly double this total party membership.

The view is not much sunnier when quality rather than quantity of participation is examined. For many, party membership means simply paying yearly dues. For most who do more than this, participation means staffing fundraising stalls, distributing pamphlets during elections and attending local branch meetings. While branches in all three major parties can pass motions for consideration by party policy-making bodies, the fate of these motions usually remains a mystery to the branch members passing them. Members can attempt to gain election to party policy-making bodies, but the limited places on these are often sewn up by established party powerbrokers. Only in the Democrats is the total membership allowed widespread participation in determining party direction and leadership. Through postal ballots, AD members vote to determine specific party policies, membership of state executives, committees and officers, candidates for the Upper House and the parliamentary leadership. This participation may well be a luxury only a small party can afford, but the wider point remains that few Australian party members enjoy opportunities for other than mundane participation.

Recruitment

If participation is an underdeveloped feature of the Australian party system, formal and informal channels of recruitment for parliamentarians, party leaders and officials are well developed. Apart from Labor Lower House candidates in New South Wales, who are chosen by ballots of the relevant branch members within each electorate, Lower House candidates in all parties are chosen by panels consisting of local branch delegates and central organisational figures. In the LPA and NPA, parliamentary leaders and party presidents keep a close eye on preselection contests, and sometimes recruit attractive candidates from outside the party. In the ALP, factional leaders of the left, centre and right recruit candidates from their factions, particularly in safe Labor electorates, to attempt to alter the factional balance of power within the parliamentary ALP. Factions now form conduits through the ranks of the ALP that reach to the ministry and prime ministership.

Affiliated trade unions provide 60 percent of delegates to state Labor conferences, and hence form the recruiting ground for many party committee members, officials and leaders. Other conference delegates, committee members and so on, come through local branches, as do all position holders in the coalition parties. The recruiting process begins early. All major parties and the Democrats have youth wings where contacts are formed and political skills honed.

Whether these methods of recruitment are adequate is debatable. They tend to exclude certain groups, notably women, blue-collar workers and non-Anglo-Celts, from power in all parties. The altering of ALP rules in 1981 to recruit more women to party positions was strongly resisted, and has had little impact since. No similar rule changes have been attempted in the coalition parties, but women sometimes have held powerful organisational offices in both the LPA and NPA. Factions within the ALP may also prevent the recruitment of valuable parliamentarians or leaders who are not comfortable in any faction. On the coalition side, candidates with business or other skills recruited by Liberal or National leaders from outside their parties have often turned out to be poor parliamentary material.

Policy formation

A liberal democratic party is expected not only to recruit political activists but also to transform the party's ideological beliefs and the demands of its supporting interests into sets of policies. In Australia, the most important parties form these policies in substantially different ways.

In the ALP, policy decisions are made by the National Conference, 'the supreme governing body of the Party' (ALP, 1986: 282). This Conference meets every two years, and is composed of delegates from every state and territory, a delegate from Young Labor, and the party's federal parliamentary leaders as well as those in each state and territory. Trade unions are not directly represented at National Conference, but since they numerically dominate the ALP state conferences, which elect national delegates, trade unionists comprise a large proportion of National Conference delegates.

Although policy decisions of the Conference are 'binding upon every member and every section of the Party' (ALP, 1986: 282), this does not mean that they will automatically be promoted by the party. A smaller body, the National Executive, has the power to interpret policy decisions of the Conference, which leaves considerable scope for flexibility of policy within the often broad resolutions of the Conference. Moreover, the federal Labor caucus—a formal body comprising all federal ALP parliamentarians—is charged with taking 'such action which may be possible to implement the Party's Platform and Conference decisions' (ALP 1986: 283). Again, this leaves room for the parliamentary party to decide that a policy passed at Conference is not feasible and to effectively drop it, although it formally remains part of party policy.

Having noted these limitations on the Conference's policy-making power, it must be stressed that the ALP takes Conference's policy-making role very seriously, often to its electoral detriment. In 1963, newspapers pilloried the ALP, carrying photographs of then Labor parliamentary leader Arthur Calwell and his deputy Gough Whitlam waiting for the '36 faceless men' who comprised the Conference to decide Labor policy on United States bases in Australia. The ALP's parliamentary leadership was seen to be dictated to by a small group of unknown unionists. Since then, Conference has become larger, more representative, open to the media and has included ALP parliamentary leaders *ex officio*. Labor's parliamentary leaders do not determine party policy, but their views have become increasingly important in Conference policy decisions in recent years.

Labor leaders facing a hostile or unpredictable ALP National Conference may well envy Liberal and National party parliamentary leaders, who are formally free to determine their party's policies without interference from the organisational wings of their parties. Thus, while both coalition parties have largish representative bodies called federal councils, these bodies do not make party policy in the way that the ALP National Conference does. Nor can the LPA's Federal Executive direct the parliamentary leadership on policy matters. Although the NPA's Federal Management Committee can direct the parliamentary NPA over policy, it does so very rarely.

This freedom of the parliamentary leadership to determine policy was established from the origins of the LPA's predecessors, and has become part of LPA tradition. It has the important effect of not allowing the party organisations of the coalition partners to lock their parliamentary representatives into damaging policy disputes. The federal councils of these parties are still important, because the policy motions they adopt indicate the climate of opinion within their parties. They may also be used by parliamentary leadership contenders to press their claims, as then Liberal leader Andrew Peacock discovered when John Howard used the 1985 LPA Federal Council to generate support for his leadership challenge.

While the ALP has moved to increase parliamentary input into policy making, in recent years some LPA federal and state presidents have expressed a desire to curtail the policy freedom that Liberal parliamentarians enjoy. These calls have not yet led to formal changes, but they represent important party opinion calling for the LPA to be less reliant on the variable resources of its parliamentary leadership when making policy.

The disadvantages of a lack of formal organisational input into party policy were illustrated prior to the 1987 federal election when federal National leader Ian Sinclair and Queensland National Premier Bjelke-Petersen argued over which of them would determine the NPA's taxation policy, a dispute that diverted opposition energies, divided the coalition and contributed to Labor's subsequent election win. What this dispute also indicated was that any attempt to achieve greater party control over policy-making in the NPA would require a substantial stiffening up of its rather weak federal organisational structure. The same is true of the LPA.

The ALP offers a model of conference-centred policy formation, while the LPA and NPA present leader-centred models. A third model is presented by the Democrats, whose members vote as a whole on policy issues following debate in the party's official journal. The danger here is that policies produced by postal ballot may lack the coherence of those hammered out in the conference room or coordinated by parliamentary leaders.

Party policies reflect much more than these formal structures. They reflect a party's traditions and ideological commitments, the balance of factions within its structures, its attempts to win and maintain federal office, its desire not to harm the electoral prospects of any of its state branches, its loyalty to its primary pressure group, its desire to maintain a committed rank and file membership, its attempts to forge compromises between opposed class interests, or between other interests, both domestic and international. Often these factors will intersect, and the importance of each will vary across different policies. Discovering which are at work in any case requires careful research.

Policy communication

Liberal democratic theory expects citizens to choose rationally between parties on the basis of their policies at elections. Thus, parties need not only to form policies, they need to communicate them to the electorate.

This liberal democratic model is rarely realised in Australia. Parties develop and announce their policies over long periods of time, making it hard for electors to compare them directly. Moreover, outside election policy speeches, which are broadcast in part by the electronic media, parties trying to get their policies across to voters have to rely on whatever publicity journalists see fit to give their announcements (see chapter 19). Thus, a party's timing of policy announcements is crucial. Some policy announcements sink without trace, drowned by other news events of the time. On other occasions, a party may not have fully prepared its policy on an issue that becomes publicly important, losing the opportunity to communicate its own policy and having to watch its opponents gain valuable publicity for their policies. This occurred in 1987, when Liberal leader Howard was unprepared to release his tax policy at a time when taxation was a key issue in political debate.

If the parties do not conform to the liberal democratic model, then neither do voters. No matter how well parties communicate their policies, the electorate does not generally identify parties with particular policies, but rather thinks of parties in terms of broad images (see chapter 20). To attract most voters, communication of party image is more important than policy communication. This is true for minor as well as major parties. In the 1987 election, for example, the Democrats presented 252 policies to the electorate, but these remained almost irrelevant beside the party's image as a watchdog to keep the major parties honest.

Contesting office

In liberal democracies, political parties are expected to present voters with a choice between competing sets of candidates. This certainly is the case in Australia. In the 1987 federal election, for example, the ALP stood candidates in all 148 House of Representatives electorates, the LPA stood candidates in 138 electorates, Democrats stood in 132 electorates, the NPA stood candidates in 82, while 125 candidates were independents or from other minor parties. The ALP, LPA and AD ran candidates for the Senate in every state, and the NPA ran Senate candidates in every state except Tasmania. This high degree of party contest is reflected in the fact that in only twelve electorates were voters restricted to a simple Labor-Coalition choice, while 82 percent of federal Lower House seats were contested by at least the ALP, the coalition and the Democrats.

Australian parties pass the liberal democratic requirement of providing competing sets of candidates for elections, but they less clearly achieve the equally important requirement of providing competing sets of policies. Many observers argue that the policies of the Australian parties have converged markedly since War II.

For some, this convergence is inevitable, due to what they see as the breakdown of the class divisions that once gave the parties different policy orientations (Kemp, 1977). For others, the parties became like Tweedledum and Tweedledee precisely because of class; that is, because the ALP under Whitlam pursued policies that relied heavily on economic planning within capitalism and therefore did not challenge the patterns of class power in Australia. Thus, while ALP and LNP Governments pursued somewhat different socio-economic aims, their policies inevitably became very similar (Catley and McFarlane, 1974). Another widely held convergence theory is that the closeness of Australian electoral competitions forces the major parties to become 'catch-all' parties that cannot afford to alienate any electorally significant section of society. The parties therefore develop an ever-larger and ever-closer set of policies (see Jaensch, 1983: 198–202). A related view sees the parties as converging in response to the demands of increasingly numerous and powerful pressure groups (Marsh, 1983).

While casual evidence for policy convergence has been easy to glean during Bob Hawke's leadership of the ALP, the notion of convergence needs further investigation. First, how much similarity between party policies constitutes evidence of convergence? The Tweedledum-Tweedledee charge in particular is often laid by those on the political left, for whom the ALP would only really be different from the coalition parties if it developed a full-blown revolutionary socialist platform. This view dismisses less dramatic differences as superficial, whereas many see them as genuinely important to the way Australians live. In the 1987 federal election, for example, the broad economic policies, resources and energy policies and immigration policies of the major parties were quite similar, but important differences between the ALP and the coalition parties emerged on taxation, industrial relations, foreign affairs, defence, housing, health, education, women's affairs, aboriginal affairs, broadcasting, welfare, transport, industry and the environment (see *Australian Financial Review* 7 July 1987).

A second problem with convergence theories is that they tend to exaggerate the distance between the major parties' policies in the past and the smooth inevitability of policy convergence. While at some times the major parties' policies have been more divergent than they appear today, at other times they have been equally close.

If the dynamic governing party policies has not been stable convergence, what other explanations exist? One explanation posits the ALP as the party of initiative in Australia, with the coalition parties as parties of resistance. The initiative-resistance thesis suggests that the ALP has been the agenda-setting party in Australian politics, the party that has promoted if not implemented major new policies that changed the shape of Australian society. The coalition parties have resisted these changes (see Mayer, 1966).

Superficial evidence for this thesis is easy to find. Labor partisans can point to the widows' pension, maternity allowances, rehabilitation allowances, funeral benefits, public health systems, QANTAS, TAA, the Commonwealth Shipping Line, the Commonwealth Bank, the Snowy Mountains Scheme, the Australian National University, free tertiary education, opening diplomatic relations with China and the establishment of a Pacific-oriented foreign policy, among other things, as ALP achievements that have changed Australia.

Difficulties with this evidence emerge when it is noted that many of these policies were shared rather than opposed by the coalition parties. Moreover, as the coalition parties have held federal office for much of this century, they have overseen these achievements for longer than Labor. Defenders of the thesis may argue that the vigour of the ALP's policies when not in office forced coalition governments to steal Labor policies, but even if this is accepted, the neat precision of parties of initiative and resistance has become blurred (see Mayer, 1966). The initiative-resistance thesis strikes further trouble in the 1980s, since it could well be argued that the LPA has become the party of initiative in this period with its championing of economic deregulation, privatisation and winding back the welfare state, all policies adopted in muted form by the Hawke Labor Government.

No simple answer is possible to the question of whether the Australian party system provides voters with sufficient scope for policy choice at elections. Similarly, no single, uncomplicated dynamic explains the pattern of policy competition between the major parties. Both of these areas require careful, specific investigation.

Initiating policy implementation

Liberal democracy relies on elections as the principle means of keeping parties in government accountable to the people. Parties can promise whatever they like during elections, but if they do not make every effort to implement those policies when in office, then the party contest could be rightly called a sham.

Very little systematic research exists on the extent to which Australian parties in office achieve their promises. Peter Bowers (1987) drew up a list of 31 promises broken by the ALP in its four years of office from 1983, and Alan Austin (1980) outlined 40 Liberal promises broken by the Fraser Government between 1975 and 1980, but neither of these journalists attempted to state what proportion of the party's total promises these figures represented. Barrett's (1963) study of party promises and performance concludes that the ALP and coalition both fulfilled about 70 percent of their promises between 1928 and 1951, a result that he calls 'remarkably good' (1963: 104).

Some policies are not initiated despite the governing party's efforts, because of obstruction in the Senate, invalidation by the High Court, opposition from state governments, non-cooperation by key pressure groups, or unexpected changes in economic circumstances (see Barrett, 1963: 105–9). Other policies are dropped or reversed because of a lack of political will by a party's parliamentary leadership. When this occurs, there is little the party membership or organisation can do in the short term. In the LPA and NPA, the parliamentary leadership makes policy and so is not directly answerable to anyone for failure to implement policy. ALP governments are bound by their party's platform, but can claim that a broken policy promise could not have been implemented due to changed circumstances. Disgruntled ALP members could attempt to have the relevant ministers expelled from or disciplined by the party, but success would be very unlikely. The ALP Conference might pass motions reaffirming the broken election promise, but conferences occur only every two years and conference delegates may be and have been persuaded not to embarrass the party's parliamentary leadership. Even AD parliamentarians are free to vote against party policy in Parliament, providing they publicly explain that this is what they are doing.

Since minor parties such as the ADs do not form governments, they face additional difficulties getting their policies implemented. If they control the balance of power in the Senate, as the ADs have since 1980, they can combine with the opposition to block policies that they oppose. The ADs have done this on a range of legislation, including the Fraser Government sales tax legislation in 1982 and the Hawke Government's Australia Card legislation in 1987. The ADs have also used the tactic of promising to support government legislation in return for the Government making certain amendments to it. Understandably, the ADs have had almost no success in implementing their own policies (see Strangman, 1983).

Conclusion

The Australian party system only very partially fulfills the requirements of liberal democracy, yet it has remained largely unchanged since the 1920s. It is hard to see dramatic change to the party system in future years. The labels 'Labor', 'Liberal' and 'National' may not mean exactly what what they do now, just as now they do not mean what they meant in the past, but the organisations bearing these labels will remain the central organisations in Australian politics.

References

Austin, A. (1980) 'Promises, Promises...' *Nation Review* April

Australian Democrats (1987) *Platform '87*

Australian Financial Review 7 July 1987

Australian Labor Party (1986) *Platform, Resolutions and Rules* Barton: R.F. McMullan

Barrett, R. (1963) *Promises and Performances in Australian Politics* Vancouver: University of British Columbia

Bowers, P. (1987) 'And What Broken Promises Will Emerge in 1990?' *Sydney Morning Herald*, 4 July

Catley, R. and McFarlane, B. (1974) *From Tweedledum to Tweedledee* Sydney: ANZ Books

Costar, B. and Woodward, D. (eds) (1985) *Country to National* Sydney: George Allen and Unwin

Evans, G. (1983) 'Reshaping the Socialist Objective', in B. O'Meagher (ed.) *The Socialist Objective* Sydney: Hale and Iremonger

Irving, T. (1983) 'Socialism, Working-Class Mobilisation and the Origins of the Labor Party', in B. O'Meagher (ed.) *The Socialist Objective* Sydney: Hale and Iremonger

Jaensch, D. (1983) *The Australian Party System* Sydney: George Allen and Unwin

—— (1984) *An Introduction to Australian Politics* Melbourne: Longman Cheshire

Kemp, D. (1977) 'Political Parties and Australian Culture' *Quadrant* December pp. 3–13

Liberal Party of Australia (1983) *Facing the Facts*

Marsh, I. (1983) 'Politics, Policy Making and Pressure Groups' *Australian Journal of Public Administration* 42, 4, December pp. 433–58

Mayer, H. (1966) 'Parties of Initiative and Resistance', in H. Mayer (ed.) *Australian Politics* Melbourne: Cheshire

Menzies, R. (1943) *The Forgotten People* Sydney: Angus and Robertson

O'Meagher, B. (ed.) (1983) *The Socialist Objective* Sydney: Hale and Iremonger

Reynolds, P. (1974) *The Democratic Labor Party* Milton: Jacaranda

Starr, G. (1978) 'The Liberal Party of Australia', in G. Starr, K. Richmond and G. Maddox *Political Parties in Australia* Richmond: Heinemann
Strangman, D. (1983) 'The Australian Democrats and the Senate', in R. Lucy (ed.) *The Pieces of Politics* Melbourne: Macmillan
Warhurst, J. (1986) 'In Defence of Single Issue Groups' *Australian Quarterly* 58, 1, Autumn pp. 102–09

10 Elections

Martin Painter

Australia is an 'indirect', or 'representative' democracy, in which votes are not normally cast to decide issues directly but to elect representatives who then make decisions in the voters' stead in parliamentary assemblies (see chapter 3). This review of voting systems in Australia, therefore, focusses on the rules governing parliamentary elections.

Elections in Australia are conducted within a framework of widely accepted fundamental political rights that permit free association and free expression. There are very few restrictions on the formation of political groups, the rights of qualified individuals to vote and to stand for election, or their capacity (in principle) to put their point of view to the electorate. Moreover, politics in Australia is, by and large, played within a broadly agreed set of rules of the game, so that, for instance, governments do not call in the army if they lose an election. The rules governing elections, most of which are set out in Acts of Parliament, are administered, for the most part, competently and impartially by people other than politicians, and are subject to interpretation by an independent judiciary.

However, the framing of electoral laws is part of the political process. They are put into place by the governing party of the day. Their content and the way they are administered helps to determine the outcomes of elections, and for this reason tinkering with electoral systems is a favourite pastime of politicians. But there are limits on unrestrained manipulation. If the electorate perceives a system to be grossly biased, it may undermine the legitimacy of government. Moreover, tampering with the 'rules of the game' may rebound on the perpetrators once they lose office. However, while there are such restraints on cynical manipulation, partisan advantage is never far from the surface in any matter of electoral reform.

Different electoral systems have far reaching consequences (Rae, 1967). For this reason decisions about electoral arrangements are not only of partisan interest for the temporary advantages they can confer but are also of constitutional significance. Societies where there are many deep-seated social cleavages, for instance, sometimes adopt an electoral system that guarantees representation of minority groups and parties in the Parliament. These systems then become a more or less permanent part of the constitutional rules that maintain a balance between these interests in the governing process. As such, they embody deep-seated values and beliefs about the rules of the game under which political contests are conducted.

For the political scientist, there are three main aspects to the study of electoral systems: first, an evaluative dimension (for instance, how 'fair' is one system as against another?); secondly, the constitutional dimension; and thirdly, the dimension of partisan advantage and manipulation. All three aspects will be covered in the discussion of Australia's electoral and voting systems that follows.

The franchise (the right to vote)

Australia and New Zealand in the nineteenth century led the world in extending the franchise beyond those with wealth and property. South Australia introduced the right of men to vote (manhood suffrage) in 1856, followed in successive years by Victoria, New South Wales and Queensland respectively. By 1907 all states and the Commonwealth had adult suffrage—that is, votes for women as well as men—with South Australia again being the pioneer in 1894 (Crisp, 1973: 137). South Australia also led the way in 1856 in not permitting plural voting (under which property owners had additional votes). Plural voting was abolished elsewhere around the turn of the century. Various forms of limited franchise remained, however, for some upper houses until very recently (Goot, 1985: 187–8). Limitations on the enfranchisement of aborigines, which were most severe in Western Australia, Northern Territory and Queensland, were not removed until the 1960s (Goot, 1985: 188–9). Until the 1970s, when eighteen-year-olds were given the vote, people were not entitled to vote until they were 21. The only restrictions on the franchise now are for insanity, being guilty of treason and being imprisoned for a serious offence. Voters must be Australian citizens, except for British subjects who were permanent residents in 1983.

Compulsory voting

Compulsory voting is a peculiar, some would say even bizarre, feature of all Australian state and Commonwealth electoral systems. It is also compulsory to enrol or register, although a survey commissioned by the Australian Electoral Office in 1983 found that about 600 000 of those eligible to vote were not enrolled. Compulsory voting was first introduced in Queensland in 1915 and in the Commonwealth in 1924. In the first case, it was introduced partly in the hope of defeating Labor, but Labor won (Goot, 1985: 192). In the Commonwealth, it was also introduced by a conservative Government, but was not seen as a matter of partisan advantage. In the 1922 elections a turnout of 58 percent was achieved, and this was considered disturbingly low by many (although, interestingly enough, this would be considered a high turnout for an American congressional election). Just as persuasive to the legislators were considerations about the costs of campaigning and getting people to the polls (Gow, 1971). Now that it is an accepted part of the Australian political scene, a majority consistently support its retention (according to opinion polls) while the parties are largely content with it because they benefit considerably from not having to go to the expense and trouble of 'getting the vote out'. Arguments for and against compulsory voting are discussed in chapter 3.

Systems of voting and counting the votes

There are three main components of the electoral rules that cover the way voters cast their vote and the way winning candidates are determined: the ballot, the electoral district and the system of counting. In designing electoral systems, each of these components presents a number of choices between alternatives.

The ballot

In the nineteenth century, Australia was a pioneer in the use of the secret ballot (in the United States, it is still often referred to as 'The Australian Ballot'). Voting is a private, personal act conducted in the seclusion of the polling booth. Hence, the voter is free from the possibility of coercion in making a choice.

Essentially, a ballot is a device for presenting the voter with certain choices. There are two kinds of ballot: categorical and ordinal (also called preferential). The first asks the voter to plump for one alternative from a list of candidates on the ballot paper, usually by marking a cross beside the preferred candidate. The second asks the voter to place the candidates in order of preference by writing a number (1, 2, 3, etc.) beside the names on the ballot paper. These different ballots go hand in hand with different ways of counting the votes (see below).

The preferential ballot has been the most commonly used in Australia. There are two varieties: exhaustive and optional. The first asks voters to list their preferences for all candidates, the second does not require the voter to go right down the list expressing preferences. Exhaustive preferential ballots are the most common, but optional preferential voting has been adopted on occasion, for instance by the Labor government for New South Wales elections from 1981. For the Lower House, it is now admissible just to vote '1' or to mark a cross. For the individual voter, the optional preferential ballot has the appeal of greater simplicity and obviates the need to express a preference for some candidates whom one would rather not see on the ballot paper at all.

One of the objectives of some advocates of the exhaustive preferential ballot in the early years of this century was to combat the Labor Party more effectively. Anti-Labor forces were often fragmented into different parties, and were less well disciplined (so that more than one candidate from the same party sometimes stood in a constituency) and a preferential ballot allowed these parties to combine their candidates' votes through the distribution of preferences when the votes were counted (see below).

A further variation in the form of the ballot is the second ballot, which provides for a second election in the shape of a run-off between the top two candidates when none has a majority on the first ballot. This system was used in New South Wales from 1910 to 1918 (Goot, 1985: 221).

The electoral district

The basic choice here is between single-member districts (or constituencies) and multi-member. Both can be combined with either type of ballot. For the Commonwealth House of Representatives, for instance, voters cast a preferential ballot in a single-member constituency, while for the Senate they cast a preferential ballot in a multi-member, state-wide constituency. In Japanese House of Representatives elections, voters cast a single, categorical vote in multi-member districts (Stockwin, 1983) while for the British House of Commons a categorical ballot is combined with single-member constituencies. A natural corollary of multi-member constituencies is that they are larger in size. Proponents of the single member constituency argue that it fosters a one-to-one relationship between elector and representative (although in House of Representative constituencies with an average size of 65 000 electors, the opportunities for direct personal contact must be very limited). However, Australian Senators do not have to be 'constituency minded' in the way local House of Representatives members are expected to be, arguably making them less approachable.

The other important aspect of electoral districts concerns their boundaries. This will be discussed later.

Counting the votes

There are three basic approaches to converting votes cast into seats won: a plurality formula, a majority formula, and a proportionality formula.

- The plurality formula (often called 'first-past-the-post'): the candidate, or candidates, with the most votes is, or are, declared to have won. This system is used in Britain, and was adopted for Australian House of Representatives elections until 1919.
- The majority formula: the winning candidate has to achieve an absolute majority (50 percent +1) of valid votes cast. This is the system now adopted for House of Representative elections and for elections to state lower houses, other than Tasmania.
- The proportionality formula: this system requires multi-member districts. There are several methods of proportional representation (PR), each aiming to allocate seats roughly in proportion to votes cast. In the 'list' system, voters cast a categorical ballot for one of a list of candidates, the lists being drawn up under party labels, with names appearing in an order determined by the party. Each party wins as many seats (with candidates elected in the order they appear on the list) as the proportion of the vote cast for the party entitles them.

Another system is the so-called 'single transferable vote'. Voters cast a preferential ballot, and candidates, in order to win, need only achieve a

Table 10.1 Three electoral systems

	Ballot	District	Method of counting
British House of Commons	categorical	single-member	plurality
Australian House of Representatives	preferential	single-member	majority
Australian Senate	preferential	multi-member	single transferable vote

proportion, or 'quota' of votes. Preferences are distributed in order to avoid 'wasting' their 'surplus' votes. One of its effects is to give groups or parties with a small minority of the vote a good chance of winning seats. The list system has only been used in Australia for the South Australian upper house, while the single transferable vote is used for most other state upper houses and the Senate, as well as for the Tasmanian lower house since 1907.

In order to explain different electoral systems more fully and to observe their effects on electoral outcomes, three actual systems will be outlined and compared: the British House of Commons, the Australian House of Representatives and the Australian Senate (see Table 10.1).

To see how the British system works, look at the example below. Candidate B, who has the most votes (a plurality) is declared the winner:

Candidate A	3500
Candidate B	4000
Candidate C	2000
Candidate D	1000
Total	10500

Note that the winning candidate does not have support from a majority of electors (in fact, it would be theoretically possible to win with 25 percent +1 of the vote). Voters who voted for candidates A, C and D do not have their opinions represented in the Parliament. In effect, the election is a contest between A and B. If candidates C and D represent parties with small but significant support across many seats, their supporters will end up with no direct parliamentary representation of their opinions at all. We can say their votes were 'wasted'.

Remember, the British system is based on single-member constituencies. As a result, the effect is to exaggerate the winning margin of seats in the Parliament compared with the winning margin of votes. If there are ten seats in which the result was similar to above, a small, uniform swing in electoral support at the next election to candidate A's party will result in a transfer of *all* the seats to that party. The Australian House of Representatives electoral system is similar to the British in this respect.

The system thus under-represents the losing parties (especially those that run third or fourth, even with quite significant support)—the 'winner takes all'. But not all seats change hands with a marginal change in support for the major parties across the country. Many seats are considered 'safe', because traditional supporters of one or another of the major parties are concentrated in those seats. The Liberal Party in Australia, for instance, draws heavy support from high-income earners, and they tend to be concentrated in particular suburbs of the capital cities and hence in particular constituencies. Electoral contests are thus determined principally by swings of opinion in a relatively small number of 'marginal' seats. It is somewhat accidental that particular categories of people—for instance, ethnic minorities, or first-home owners in the so-called 'mortgage belt'—are concentrated in such seats rather than others, giving such groups a great deal of potential power. In this way, the electoral system is an important determinant of the kinds of strategies political parties adopt and the kinds of interests they give prominence to in their platforms.

Defenders of the system in Britain, with its traditional pattern of two-party competition, say it ensures strong, stable governments which, however, are vulnerable to small swings of support and are thus likely to be sensitive to public opinion (or rather, to the opinions of those in *marginal* seats). They also argue that it focusses the mind of the electorate on the 'big question' of who should govern, rather than on the representation of their sectional interests, and that it concentrates the minds of party leaders on framing platforms of broad rather than narrow appeal. Critics argue that, far from focussing the minds of the parties on major issues of national significance, it encourages them to bid irresponsibly for support from 'swinging voters' in marginal electorates through making extravagant promises to the particular sectional interests concerned. Moreover, they point out that it entrenches the two-party system and makes it very hard for a new political force to break the mould, as has been the case in Britain in recent years (Jordan and Richardson, 1987: 45–7).

The Australian House of Representatives is elected from 148 single-member constituencies through an exhaustive preferential ballot. The winning candidate in each constituency has to win an absolute majority of votes. In the example given above, no candidate had a majority of primary votes. Candidate D is eliminated, and his ballot papers are inspected to see who each elector has listed as preference number two. These votes are then redistributed to the respective candidates (known as 'distributing the preferences'). Suppose this results in the following:

Candidate A	3600
Candidate B	4100
Candidate C	2800

Still no candidate has an absolute majority (that is 5251 votes). Now candidate C is eliminated. In distributing these preferences, some of the ballot papers will be those from candidate D; now it is the *third* preferences of these voters that are being distributed. Suppose candidate C asked her supporters to give A their second preference, and D asked voters to give their third preference to A as well. If most follow this advice, candidate A will win. Note that A did not receive the most votes, and is in fact elected with the help of votes expressing a third preference (or, to put it another way, A was the second worst option for some voters; and perhaps for others, she was merely a space to fill in so as to make the vote 'formal', or valid).

It is now clear why the fragmented anti-Labor forces early this century advocated the preferential ballot. If B were the Labor candidate, the preferential ballot would enable the others to combine their forces and win the seat. These days, the Liberal and National Parties at Commonwealth House of Representative elections generally stick to an agreement not to contest seats held by a sitting member from the other party, but otherwise they may well each put up a candidate safe in the knowledge that they can exchange preferences and combine their vote against the Labor candidate. If both Liberal and National candidates are popular local figures, their combined vote may be greater than if only one stood. On the other hand, there is always some 'slippage' of preferences to the ALP because not all voters follow the 'how to vote' instructions.

One general effect of this system is to give minority parties a say in the outcome, and a means of influencing the policies of the major parties, even if they do not have much chance of winning seats in their own right. During the 1950s the Labor Party split, resulting in the formation of the Democratic Labor Party, which drew strong support from Catholic Labor voters. The DLP generally directed its voters to express a second preference for the Liberal or Country Parties rather than the ALP, and this was a vital factor in keeping the conservatives in office for many years. However, minority interests only have influence in marginal seats, because if a candidate wins 50 percent +1, preferences are not counted. This gives electors in marginal seats an added source of power. More perversely, the Menzies Government won a very close election in 1961 when the final seat in the balance fell to the Liberals on the preferences of a Communist Party candidate! Recently, the Democrats and minority parties like the Nuclear Disarmament Party have sometimes been of assistance to the ALP in winning seats.

The third system is that used for elections to the Australian Senate. Senators are elected from each state in a state-wide constituency using a proportionality formula, the single transferable vote system of proportional representation (PR). In a full Senate election there are twelve seats per state to be filled. On the ballot paper, candidates are grouped by party, and labelled with the party name. Voters either express their preferences for all candidates (with allowance being made for a limited number of errors to reduce the size of the informal vote) in whatever order they wish, or they can mark a single box next to the party's name, in which case their preferences are considered automatically to follow the party's registered 'how to vote' ticket.

When counting the votes, the first step is to calculate a 'quota' by dividing the total number of votes by the number of senators to be elected plus one (thirteen), and then adding one to the result. The quota is about 7.7 percent of the total valid votes for a full Senate election. Candidates who have votes equal to or in excess of the quota are declared elected. The first candidate listed on the ALP ticket, for instance, is likely to have in excess of 40 percent of the vote; this means that there is a large 'surplus' of votes that are left to be counted, the object of the PR system being not to 'waste' any votes. These surplus votes are sorted into batches according to the second preferences expressed. But not all the votes in each batch are distributed to the number two candidates, only a proportion. A 'transfer value' is calculated by dividing the number of surplus votes by the total number of first preference votes, and then the number of votes in each batch is multiplied by this transfer value. This fraction of each batch is then transferred to the appropriate candidate. Once this is done, some of the candidates who receive these transferred votes now reach the quota, and are declared elected. Surplus votes for these candidates are then dealt with in the same way, with the votes being transferred according to the next preference listed, again after calculating a transfer value. Once all surplus votes have been transferred, and if all seats have not been filled, the candidate with the fewest votes is eliminated and all of his or her preferences are distributed, until enough quotas have been filled and twelve seats determined.

It sounds very complicated, and it is. Indeed, it often takes weeks to work out the result of a full Senate election. But the basic principle behind the complicated mathematics is simple: the aim is to ensure that seats are won in proportion to votes cast for each group of candidates. In our original example above, suppose there are six seats, producing a quota of 1501. A would win two, B two, C one and the final seat would probably be fought out between B and D on the distribution of preferences. In the Australian Senate, this system enables minority parties like the Democrats to win seats, so long as they get to a quota either in primary votes or after the distribution of preferences. This often results in a Senate in which minor party candidates hold a 'balance of power'. Arguably, this strengthens the role of the Upper House as a House of review. On the other hand, it might be argued to place excessive power in the hands of minorities.

In some countries, this system is used to elect the house where a government must have a majority in order to govern, resulting in a situation where minority parties can extract major concessions because they can bring down a government. But it also means that governments formed by coalition directly represent a diversity of opinions rather than just the one partisan point of view. In diverse and fragmented societies, it protects significant minorities and helps build consent and consensus. However, such a system is sometimes prone to chronic parliamentary instability. By contrast, the British and Australian Lower Houses are elected through a system that is far more likely to produce stable, one-party majority governments, with a clear 'mandate' to govern and a solid base of safe parliamentary support.

Some political scientists have suggested that the electoral system is a determinant of the number and type of political parties competing for power: PR encourages the formation of many small parties, while a system such as 'first-past-the-post' in single-member constituencies, because it severely reduces the chance that small parties will win seats, encourages minority interests to coalesce and tends to turn elections into two-party contests. For instance, the 'left' in countries with PR, like Italy and Japan, tends to be fragmented into several parties, each of which attempts to maintain its fragment of left supporters in the electorate. In Britain or Australia, the left has, for the most part, been represented by the one major party. Moreover, due to the need to attract the support of 'swinging voters' in marginal electorates, the ALP and the British Labour Party are under pressure to moderate their more extreme left-wing policies. Where PR exists, the left parties are not only more numerous, but tend to be more doctrinaire.

However, it would be unwise to place too much emphasis on electoral systems as independent determinants of the party system. PR is as much the *result* of the prior existence of many parties representing diverse interests in a particular polity as it is its cause; it is a deliberate choice of constitutional design, often with a view to giving access for these parties to positions of political power. PR in a society that is not deeply divided along several dimensions—ethnic, religious, linguistic, ideological and so on—need not, in itself, cause the formation of a large number of small, but significant, stable political parties, although it provides the favourable conditions for such an outcome. PR in Tasmania, for example, has not resulted in a departure from the pattern of partisan conflict that is found in the rest of Australia. The basis of a country's party system rests on a combination of social, historical, institutional and cultural factors. The voting system is only one factor.

Paradoxes of voting

In the evaluation of alternative systems of voting and election, much debate revolves around how well the result accurately reflects the actual distribution of opinion in a political community. As has been shown, different systems will produce very different results from the same set of figures, and it is possible to line up arguments for and against each. Before one gets too carried away in the search for a 'perfect' system, it has to be recognised that every system of voting yet invented seems to produce paradoxes. There is, it seems, no reliable way of accurately representing collective choices through voting. Arrow's (1951) so-called 'impossibility theorem' showed that there is no way of meeting all five of the following conditions through a system of voting:

- if everyone prefers an option, it should be adopted
- no-one should be able to impose an outcome against the opposition of all the others
- the choices made should not be inconsistent, that is, if A is preferred to B and B to C, then A should be preferred to C
- everyone participating should have the chance to express all possible preferences about the choices on offer
- outcomes should not be affected by irrelevent alternatives

Laver (1983) gives a number of examples of commonly adopted voting procedures that can result in violations of some of these criteria. Consider the example in Table 10.2 (Laver, 1983: 155).

Table 10.2 Paradoxes of voting

Percentage of voters	1st preference	2nd preference	3rd preference
45	A	B	C
30	C	B	A
25	B	C	A

Under a first-past-the-post-system, A wins, yet a majority prefers either B or C. This violates the fifth criterion: faced with the choice between A and C, the presence of B confuses the issue by splitting the vote of those who prefer C to A. Under a preferential system such as operates in the House of Representatives, C would win on B's preferences, yet it is clear that a majority (70 percent) prefers B to C! Again, the fifth criterion is violated. The possibility of this and other paradoxes bedevils all voting systems.

Electoral boundaries

If each vote is to have equal value in a parliamentary election based on electoral districts, then the districts must be of equal size. Clearly, this is not so in the Senate system, for instance, in that Tasmania elects as many senators as New South Wales. The framers of the Constitution saw the Senate as a 'state's house', with equal representation from each of the states to express and protect their individual sovereignty and their distinctive economic and geographic interests (see chapters 5 and 11). In lower houses, the most common form of departure from the one vote one value principle has been what is known as 'rural weighting' (sometimes depicted by its critics as 'one sheep one vote'). Country electorates have frequently been made deliberately smaller in population, often with the justification that the representative would face formidable difficulties in keeping in touch with the electorate in very large and sparsely populated non-urban constituencies. More significant, however, has been the political pressure from rural interests fearful of being dominated by the larger populations of the urban centres and of having their interests ignored. Cooray (1979: 167) suggests a justification for this when he says 'it may be argued that the political future of the country should not rest with the better organised urban majority who enjoy additional amenities and advantages'.

The methods used to build this rural weighting (or malaportionment) into electoral systems have been of two main types: the first allows significant variation in population between electorates and the second is a system of 'zoning'. Before 1974, it was permissible when drawing Commonwealth electoral boundaries to allow for a variation of 20 percent between the population of the largest and smallest (this was reduced to 10 percent in 1974). The area covered by an electorate could also be taken into account. Because electoral redistributions were relatively infrequent, major population changes exaggerated the difference between the smallest rural and the largest urban seats at some elections. In 1972, for instance, the largest seat was 2.9 times the size of the smallest (Blewett, 1973). These provisions were changed by Labor governments (not surprisingly). Now, seats must be as nearly as possible of equal size. Those redrawing the boundaries in the Commonwealth (as is the case in New South Wales) are asked to take account of possible future population trends so that the *next* election will, hopefully, be conducted using roughly equal electorates. The projections are sometimes wrong, however.

The second system, still applied in Queensland and Western Australia, divides the state into zones, and applies different population criteria to each of the zones, so that rural seats have smaller populations. Queensland's system is the most notorious, although Western Australia's is, on most measures, the one that shows the greatest malaportionment. Rural weighting in Queensland has a long history, and originally advantaged the Labor Party, which used to be very strong in outlying rural areas. Bjelke-Petersen's National Party Government inherited the system, and its maintenance (and modification) has been part (but only part) of the reason for its electoral success.

When one takes a close look at the effects of malaportionment in Australia generally, it turns out that its biases on their own explain electoral outcomes in only a very small number of elections (Goot, 1985: 219–20). In Queensland, for instance, Labor's disadvantage has also been a result of the even spread of its votes across most constituencies (Hughes, 1980: 102–4). Remember that under a single-member constituency system, running even a close second in a large number of seats does not win any of them, and failure to convert votes into seats for this reason is a feature of all such systems. There is a tendency (e.g., in Jaensch, 1985) to blame all of the distortions apparent in Queensland's electoral system on the one clearly identifiable source of bias—the zoning system—to the exclusion of others that would apply in the absence of malaportionment (but are not subject to the same degree of disapprobation). The National Party in 1980 won 39 percent of the vote and 50 percent of the seats (but only stood candidates in 72 of the 82 constituencies). At the 1983 elections in Britain, the Conservatives won 42.4 percent of the votes cast and 61 percent of the seats (Jordan and Richardson, 1987: 45), without the aid of any form of zoning, but due to the 'winner takes all' effect discussed earlier. Moreover, is the 'over-representation' of views of those in marginal seats any more defensible than over-representation due to malaportionment?

The genius of the Queensland Government's manipulation of the electoral system is that it seems to have been designed in such a way that *all* the biases work in its favour, and against the interest of both Labor and Liberal. The benefit to the Nationals of the zoning system, for instance, is that it ensures that in the rural areas, in which it will be over-represented in any case, because of its consistent margin of support over the other parties from constituency to constituency, it is even more over-represented because of malaportionment. It is highly probable that the only way Labor could have won office in its own right in the last twenty or thirty years, given its performance in terms of votes won, would have been if the electoral system had been deliberately manipulated in *its* favour.

Manipulation of and tinkering with electoral boundaries for partisan advantage does not require 'political interference' in the actual process of electoral redistribution, which has long been conducted by public servants or independent commissioners. Partisan advantage has been achieved by framing the guidelines within which these people work. The trend over many years in the states and the Commonwealth has been to enhance the independence and impartiality of those given the work of electoral administration, to the point where their procedures have taken on a quasi-judicial character.

The system established by the 1960s for Commonwealth electorates provided for a committee of public servants headed by the Chief Electoral Officer, to draw new boundaries when required. This was done by publishing provisional boundaries, calling for submissions, amending the boundaries, if necessary, in the light of these, and then sending them to Parliament for approval (at which point Parliament had the power to reject them). In the 1960s, changes were introduced to allow submissions to be made before provisional boundaries were released, as well objections after their publication. A new Electoral Commission was set up in 1983 to distance electoral administration even further from politics. Public hearings are now held at the objections stage of a redistribution process. The whole procedure was thus given an even more judicial appearance (particularly as a judge of the Federal Court was added to the body finally determining the boundaries). Parliament can no longer disallow the final determination, but MPs and the political parties make most of the submissions and lodge most of the objections, and get a chance to influence outcomes in this way.

Election finances

Political parties have traditionally had the job of raising their own funds. The Labor Party has relied a lot (but not exclusively) on levies on union members and union donations, but the very high cost of campaigns in the age of the mass media has led them to seek greater support from elsewhere, including private corporations. The conservative parties have been better placed to call on business corporations and wealthy individuals for a regular supply of funds, and as a result they seem to have had less trouble in raising large amounts of money (although the veil of secrecy behind which this area of political activity has been conducted in the past makes it difficult to be certain). Not surprisingly, perhaps, the Labor Party has been the strongest advocate of public funding for election purposes, which was introduced in New South Wales in 1981 and for the Commonwealth in 1983.

In both cases the measures were brought in by Labor Governments against conservative opposition. Prior to this, most states and the Commonwealth had laws limiting election expenses, but they were widely and openly breached and loosely enforced. The New South Wales provisions establish a fund equalling 22 cents per enrolled voter. The fund is in two parts: a central fund, which is distributed to the parties according to their statewide share of the vote for the Legislative Council, and a constituency fund divided among lower house candidates. Two-thirds of the money goes into the central fund, the rest into the constituency fund. In addition there are provisions requiring public disclosure of election expenses and financial contributions to candidates and parties. The Commonwealth system is similar, but there is no separate constituency fund and the amounts involved per enrolled elector are larger (Chaples, forthcoming).

The conservative parties opposed public funding and disclosure on the grounds that it was an improper call on the public purse and that individuals and parties had a right to preserve confidentiality. Contributors, if their donations are made public, might fear victimisation from the other side if they 'back the wrong horse'. On the other side of the argument, public funding may reduce the possibility of influence being 'bought' improperly. Disclosure at least goes some way to reassuring the public that secret deals are not being made. It has also demonstrated what has been suspected for some time, that many large private donors have a 'bob each way', and contribute funds both to the conservative and Labor parties.

The disclosure provisions are not easily enforced. Ways have been devised of 'laundering' contributions through 'front organisations' so that details can remain secret. Labor, Liberal and National Parties have each exploited loopholes to accommodate the wish for secrecy of large contributors (Chaples, forthcoming). At the other end of the scale, the provisions provide a recipe for red tape to little purpose. Barry Gration, candidate for the Imperial British Conservative Party for the Victorian seat of Chisholm submitted a return for the 1987 Commonwealth election disclosing that he had spent $81 on his campaign and that the sole contribution to his campaign fund had been two donuts, with a declared monetary value of 45 cents.

Despite administrative difficulties, public funding and disclosure provisions are probably here to stay. They can be seen as providing one further application of notions of fair play and equity in electoral systems. Some still argue, however, that the competition for votes and the organisation and financial basis of political parties are matters best left to the 'free play' of the political marketplace rather than being subsidised from the public purse. Like compulsory voting, public funding may make parties and candidates less active in selling their wares and less responsive to public demands.

Conclusion

Electoral systems are part of a polity's 'rules of the game' that shape political behaviour and political outcomes. All electoral systems have biases and produce inescapable paradoxes of some sort or another. Partisan advantage aside, criteria of judgement that most of us would accept as having some justification are often contradictory, and it is a matter of arriving at compromises. There are no simple answers and no hard and fast formulae.

References

Arrow, Kenneth (1951) *Social Choice and Individual Values* New York: Wiley

Blewett, N. (1973) 'Redistribution Procedures', in Henry Mayer & Helen Nelson *Australian Politics A Third Reader* Melbourne: Cheshire

Chaples, E.A. (forthcoming) 'Public Funding of Elections in Australia', in H. Alexander (ed.) *Comparative Political Finançe* Cambridge: Cambridge University Press

Cooray, L.J.M. (1979) *Conventions, The Australian Constitution and The Future* Sydney: Legal Books

Crisp, L.F. (1973) *Australian National Government* 3rd edn, Melbourne: Cheshire

Goot, M. (1985) 'Electoral Systems', in Don Aitken (ed.) *Surveys of Australian Political Science* Sydney: George Allen and Unwin

Gow, N. (1971) 'The Introduction of Compulsory Voting', *Politics* 6, 2, pp. 201–10

Hughes, C.A. (1980) *The Government of Queensland* St Lucia: University of Queensland Press

Jaensch, D. (1985) 'The "Bjelke-mander"', in Allan Patience (ed.) *The Bjelke-Petersen Premiership 1968–1983 Issues in Public Policy* Melbourne: Longman Cheshire

Jordon, A. and Richardson, J. (1987) *British Politics and the Policy Process* London: Allen and Unwin

Laver, M. (1983) *Invitation to Politics* Oxford: Martin Robertson

Rae, D.W. (1967) *The Political Consequences of Electoral Laws* New Haven: Yale University Press

Stockwin, J.A.A. (1983) 'Japan' in V. Bogdanor and D. Butler (eds) *Democracy and Elections: Electoral Systems and their Political Consequences* Cambridge: Cambridge University Press

11 Australian federalism

Karen Wilcox

Australia is a federation. Its political system is divided by the constitution into two tiers, with the Commonwealth Government forming the first tier and the state governments forming the second. Therefore, each Australian citizen obeys the laws of two governments, is represented by members of two parliaments and is likely to come into contact with the bureaucracies of both levels.

The relationship between these two levels has been of much interest to Australian political scientists. Indeed, writings on federalism in Australia have given rise to a lively and vigorous debate, with descriptions, definitions and evaluations of Australian federalism still unsettled. As a result, newcomers to the field would be excused for feeling baffled and confused about the nature of the federal relationship and the implications of federalism for the political system as a whole.

What is federalism? Features of a federation

Federalism refers to a system of government whereby power and responsibility are formally (that is, constitutionally) divided between two tiers. This formal division distinguishes federalism from unitary or 'one-tiered' political systems, where ultimate power and authority is vested in a single government. In practice, administrative responsibility in unitary systems may be devolved to smaller units of government such as regional or county councils, but the power of these smaller units is assigned to them by the national government, and hence can be removed or reconstituted by that government at will. The autonomy and existence of the sub-units of a decentralised unitary administration is not guaranteed, as they are units of that administration, rather than legally constituted tiers of government. For example, in Britain (a unitary system) the national government is legally empowered to dissolve the regional councils. In 1985, the Thatcher Government created considerable controversy by choosing to exercise this power, and dismantling the Greater London Council.

The political features that constitute and define a federation are themselves the subject of some controversy within the discourse of political science. In general though, most scholars of federalism would suggest that the following features distinguish a federal political system:

- a formal division of government into two tiers;
- the maintenance, by each tier, of political and legal autonomy in certain fields of government activity;
- separate bureaucratic systems to administer the areas of government within each tier's jurisdiction;
- in western liberal democracies separate legislatures and executives for each tier of government; and
- recognition by each of the tiers of the jurisdictional autonomy of the other (some would argue that an equality of status must also be recognised for the system to be considered federal).

In Australia, the structure of government is complicated further by the devolution of many state responsibilities to local councils. Although not part of the constitutional arrangements of federalism, local councils form a 'de facto' third tier of government.

Scholars of federalism are wont to classify federal systems into types, depending on the nature of intergovernmental relations within that system (in particular, the extent of conflict or compromise that is apparent, the relative strength of each of the partners in the federal relationship, and the changes to the relationship that may occur over a period of time). Indeed, Frenkel has found that there are 460 'types' of federal systems used within the literature on federalism (Frenkel, 1986: 78). In discussions of Australian federalism, Sawer's three categories of coordinate federalism, cooperative federalism and organic federalism, are widely used (Sawer, 1976: 98). Coordinate federalism refers to a system whereby the partners in the federal relationship are formally equal (although Sawer notes that in practice the Commonwealth or central government will always be stronger than the regional or state governments, if only because the central government represents a larger number of people) (Sawer, 1976: 98). The second type of federal system, cooperative federalism, is distinguished by mechanisms which are available for joint centre/region agreement over programmes and policies (Sawer, 1976: 101). Organic federalism refers to a federal relationship where the central government plays a strong and directive role (Sawer, 1976: 104). However, there is a need to exercise caution when using descriptive labels to categorise styles or phases of federalism. As Frenkel suggests, they 'do not really inform us about the matter at hand—creativity, co-operation, rigidity, competition, etc. may be found everywhere—but indicate an author's basic opinion of [the] subject' (Frenkel, 1986: 78).

A number of federations exist in the world today, including West Germany, Canada and the United States. However, the unitary or 'one-tiered' political system, the alternative to a federation, is by far the most common form of government.

Federations have been formed for a number of reasons, but are most usually the result of a movement for unification within a region amongst existing political bodies wishing to retain some of their powers. Movements to federate often have been accompanied by a corresponding movement, within the colonies of an imperial power, for some degree of political independence from the 'parent' nation (e.g., the United States, Canada, Australia, India). The adoption of a federal form of government by these newly created nations enabled the translation of a nationalist spirit into political reality amongst previously disunited polities, which had been unwilling to sacrifice entirely their political authority to a national body politic. Federations may also be formed in recognition of the cultural, ethnic, linguistic or geographical diversity within a nation. In this sense, they are a compromise—an attempt to maintain diversity in unity.

The relationships among constituent states or provinces, and between these and the national government are often precarious, reflecting the conflicting needs of unification and separation. This has certainly been true of Australia, as will be discussed later in this chapter. Because of this, federations include a written constitution outlining at least some of the rules through which the autonomy of each of the tiers is to be maintained. Hence federal relationships within nations such as Australia have developed within a legal, as well as political, framework.

The development of Australian federalism

Discussion of federalism in Australia must to some extent be focussed historically. English occupation of the Australian continent began with the establishment of colonies that were independent of each other in most respects. This resulted in the development of separate bureaucratic systems and eventually, separate legislatures within each of the colonies. The movement for unity and nationhood must be considered within this context. Colonial politicians, bureaucrats (and others whose personal power depended on the continuing existence of the colonies as political systems) were unwilling to relinquish their positions within established political institutions as a sacrifice to the developing nation. Given these political realities, it was to some extent inevitable that the 'national movement' would embody federalism.

The Australian constitution was an attempt to accommodate the requirements of the colonial governments that their political strength be maintained (see chapter 5). The authors of Australia's constitution, following the United States' rather than Canada's example, drafted a document designed to give the new states guaranteed strength, if not the upper hand, in the federal system. Hence Commonwealth powers and responsibilities (including responsibility for trade and commerce, postal, telegraphic and telephonic matters, currency, marriage, divorce, external affairs and railways) were listed, in an attempt to limit them. The assumption of the authors of the constitution was that textual definition of the responsibilities for the Commonwealth would provide a means for limiting Commonwealth power. The responsibilities of the states were assumed to be comprised of the residue of unnamed government activity, including education, health, roads, housing and the maintenance of police forces. The powers of the states were undefined within the constitution and therefore, with a few exceptions (Sections 90, 114 and 115), intended to be unlimited.

The bulk of the Commonwealth powers were outlined chapter 1, part 4 and chapter 4 of the Australian consitution. As most of these powers are not exclusive to the Commonwealth, the states, as well, are legally empowered to legislate in these fields. Nevertheless, the extent to which these powers (such as the trade, commerce, taxation, and race relations powers) can be considered concurrent in practice has been limited by the operation of section 109, which states that Commonwealth law prevails over state law where both have legislated (provided the Commonwealth legislation falls validly within one of the enumerated Commonwealth powers). Indeed, section 109, in conjunction with liberal interpretation of the Commonwealth powers, has rendered ineffective the supposed guarantee of state strength that the authors of the constitution envisaged it would provide. Thus, while the wording of the constitution has remained fundamentally consistent over the past 90 years (see chapter 5), the federal relationship has not.

Factors contributing to Australian federalism

A number of factors have contributed to the development of a distinctively Australian version of federalism. The relationships between the Commonwealth and states have been affected by most of the political agencies in Australia.

Perhaps the most significant force to have shaped the federal relationship has been that of the process of judicial review—the combined force of Commonwealth or state challenges to the legislative actions of each other and judgement of those challenges by the High Court. Through a series of constitutional cases (most importantly the Engineers, Garnishee, Burgess, Uniform Tax, Offshore Sovereignty, Koowarta and the Gordon River Dam cases), Commonwealth activity in an increasing range of areas became constitutionally legitimate (see chapter 5).

The political parties have provided much of the impetus for changes to federalism. In a sense, they are the main actors within the federal relationship. Legislative activity in both tiers of government develops from political party programmes. For example, as a result of the ALP's urban renewal and welfare orientations in the early 1970s, legislation was passed by the Whitlam Government that expanded the Commonwealth's role in areas such as education (disadvantaged schools, higher education), health (Medibank, community health programmes, hospital development) and community relations, thereby affecting the direction of state activities in these fields. In this sense, the character of the federal relationship is dynamic and likely to alter in accordance with changes in party priorities and the electoral arena.

Conflict within the federal relationship is often the product of party conflict. If opposing political parties are in power at both state and Commonwealth Government level then disagreements over policies and priorities will often arise. This inter-party conflict, which is evident even within the coalition, may be expressed in the language of federalism. For example, the Garnishee Case (NSW Labor vs Commonwealth UAP), Koowarta (Queensland National

Party vs Commonwealth Liberal) and the Gordon River Dam Case (Tasmania Liberal vs Commonwealth Labor) arose out of inter-party policy discordance, which was translated into disputes about the nature of Australian federalism. In the most recent of these cases, the Gordon River Dam Case, the policy conflict generated by differing party priorities was clear. The Tasmanian Liberal government passed the 'Gordon River Hydro-Electric Power Development Act' in 1982 to begin construction on a dam that was designed to add to Tasmania's generator capacity, and hence lower electricity costs in Tasmania. The national conference of the Labor Party had adopted an environmentally sensitive platform, which was expressed in the Party's 1983 election promise to halt dam construction and protect the rainforest and aboriginal sites facing imminent flooding. Upon being elected, the Hawke Government passed the World Heritage Properties Conservation Act 1983, and the opposing party priorities manifested in the conflicting Tasmanian and Commonwealth legislation became embroiled in the agenda of federalism.

These factors together have enabled growth and change within the federal relationship. Most works on Australian federalism suggest that the changes to Australian federalism can be viewed as expansion of the powers of the Commonwealth, vis-a-vis the states. The Commonwealth Government is now responsible for a wider range of legislative and financial activity than was necessary or politically possible at federation. A glance at the 'Commonwealth Government' section of the Canberra phone book provides an indication of the current scope of Commonwealth activity. There are now Commonwealth administrative bodies responsible for a diverse range of activities such as affirmative action, business and consumer affairs, education, training and crime. Nevertheless, changes to the federal relationship that have enabled a general growth in Commonwealth activity have not arisen without difficulty.

Current financial arrangements

Any discussion of contemporary federalism must involve analysis of the financial aspects of the federal relationship. It is in this field that many of the problems within intergovernmental relations are apparent. Over the period since federation, state governments have become increasingly dependent on the Commonwealth for the revenue required to finance the day to day government activities for which they are largely responsible. There is a clear disparity between the responsibilities of the state governments and the avenues for revenue raising available to them. These avenues have been limited by the impact of judicial review, in particular, the uniform tax decisions, which effectively prevented state governments from raising revenue from income tax, leaving the Commonwealth to control this important revenue source.

State governments themselves can raise money through various charges and fees, including fines for traffic offences, vehicle registration and driver's licence fees, gambling and alcohol taxes, petrol tax, payroll tax and road and bridge tolls. These sources provide them with approximately one-third of their total revenue (Mcmillan et al., 1983: 117).

The states rely on the Commonwealth for the remainder of their revenue, and this is granted in the following ways:

- General 'tax reimbursement' grants: these have been provided to the state governments since the first Uniform Tax Case to compensate for the revenue shortfall created when the states were forced to abandon income tax.
- Equalisation grants to individual claimant states: these have been provided to those state governments that have made a special application on the basis of need or financial difficulty. They are designed to equalise financial conditions amongst the states.
- Specific purpose or section 96 grants: the Commonwealth may provide grants to the states 'on such terms and conditions as the Parliament thinks fit' (section 96, constitution). These include funds for housing, roads, health and education and may be tied to specific programmes (such as AIDS education) or organisations (such as universities).

The 'mix' of these grants varies in accordance with the objectives of the Commonwealth Government, as does the overall level of funding. The past three Canberra Governments employed differing approaches to grant arrangements. The Whitlam Labor Government developed a new approach to federal financial arrangements as a means of implementing their social policy objectives. These objectives focussed on a more equitable provision of government services throughout Australia, in particular in health, education, housing, transport and social services. As the state governments had been responsible for most of the administration and policy making in these fields, the Commonwealth Government was required to restructure funding arrangements to ensure the success of their various programmes. Specific purpose grants, directed at equalising the provision of these services throughout Australia, were greatly increased during the Whitlam years. They rose from 2.1 percent of the Gross Domestic Product in the 1972/73 financial year, to 5.8 percent of GDP in 1975/76 (Mathews, 1982: 162), with health grants, for example, rising from 21 million dollars to one billion dollars, and grants for urban and regional development rising from 1 million to 263 million dollars (Mathews, 1977: 14). Specific purpose grants were also used to enhance the role of local councils, via the states. Community level funding via the Australian Assistance Plan, established under section 81 of the constitution, was introduced to enable the implementation of social welfare programmes at a regional (sub-state) level, funded directly by the Commonwealth. As well as increasing specific purpose payments, and expanding the functions of regional and local administration, the Whitlam Government greatly increased the total funds available to the states. In 1973/74 this amounted to a 20.6 percent increase over the previous year's funding. In 1974/75, the increase was by 50.6 percent (Australia, 1976: 4).

Under the succeeding Fraser Coalition Government, increases in the overall level of funding were less significant, dropping to 4.6 percent in 1978/79. During these years, Specific Purpose grants steadily declined as a proportion of total grants to the states (Australia, 1982). In place of this, general grants were distributed under new guidelines—the so-called 'tax sharing' arrangements, whereby a proportion of Commonwealth tax collected in each state was returned to each state, to be used in ways determined by the state. In addition, states were permitted to impose additional surcharges on the income tax collected within their borders, so that citizens potentially would have paid income tax to both Commonwealth and state governments. Nonetheless, 'piggy-back' taxation of this kind was not adopted by the states. Conventional wisdom suggested that such a move would be electorally damaging to any state government attempting to boost their finances in this way.

Fiscal arrangements under the Hawke administration have diverged from those of its Labor predecessor. Indeed, the Government's orientations in this area most closely resemble those of the Fraser Coalition Government. Although the 'tax-sharing' arrangements have been abandoned, general grants have continued to dominate financial assistance to the states, whilst Specific Purpose grants have steadily declined as a proportion of overall funding (Australia, 1987: 131, 132). There has been a reduction in the level of financial assistance both as expressed as a percentage of GDP and in net terms. (Australia, 1987: 4, 16). (In the 1986/87 budget, net funding to the states was 1.8 percent *less* than in the previous year) (Australia, 1987: 4). The Hawke Government appears to be committed to a policy of reducing the Commonwealth budget deficit by either maintaining or reducing assistance to the states. This is likely to cause further tension in the federal relationship, particularly where non-Labor states are concerned (given that inter-party conflict exacerbates difficulties in state/Commonwealth relations).

The Commonwealth raises its own revenue through such sources as income tax, company tax, customs and excise duties and sales tax. Again, the governing party's policies and its interpretation of the mood of the electorate and the economy affects the finer details of Commonwealth revenue raising.

Several institutions have been created to administer and organise the financial arrangements of federalism. The most prominent of these is the annual Premiers' Conference. This meeting of Commonwealth and state leaders of government includes on its agenda the discussion of state financial needs and the transfer of funds to the states. Nevertheless, much of the lobbying for funds occurs in advance of the Premiers' Conference, so that it has become something of a media spectacle.

Another financial institution of federalism is the Loans Council, which began as an informal institution, but by 1928 was constitutionally entrenched by an amendment to section 105. The purpose of the Loans Council is to coordinate borrowings by Commonwealth and state governments and government corporations and to prevent the competition that would otherwise ensue if all governments aimed to raise funds from the same sources. The Loans Council is comprised of a representative from each of the states (usually the Premier or Treasurer) and the Commonwealth Prime Minister and Treasurer.

The states have one vote each and the Commonwealth two votes, plus the casting vote.

The federal financial relationship has also given rise to the Grants Commission, which was formed in 1933 to determine and administer Commonwealth equalisation grants for the less populous and prosperous states. However, in the last decade, these grants have become unnecessary, and with the decline in the use of equalisation grants, the functions of the Grants Commission have altered somewhat. Equalisation grants were initially established to ensure that the less populous states would not suffer fiscal disadvantage in relation to New South Wales and Victoria, but in this sense they have outlived their purpose. The Fraser Government's tax-sharing arrangements for the distribution of general revenue funds and the Hawke Government's general revenue distribution arrangements were both designed to ensure fiscal equalisation across the states, eliminating the need for additional equalisation grants. Indeed, it became clear that on the basis of the criteria used for the assessment of general revenue distribution (in summary, population, expenditure per capita, revenue raising capacity, differential costs of providing standard services), the *most* populous states were financially weak relative to the smaller states—the opposite situation to that which necessitated the establishment of the Grants Commission (Mathews, 1982: 159, 160).

The Grants Commission has become involved in several reviews of intergovernmental financial arrangements in recent years. These have included an inquiry into tax-sharing arrangements, presented in 1981, which Mathews has suggested 'was probably the most extensive and exhaustive fiscal equalisation study which has ever been attempted in a federal country' (Mathews, 1982: 158). A further inquiry of per capita relativities (that is, the per capita funding required to finance similar services within each state) was conducted by the Commission in 1985, and provided the basis for general revenue distribution under the Hawke Government, in place of the tax-sharing formula (Australia, 1987: 38).

Effective control of each of these three institutions of federalism seems to rest with the Commonwealth. Although the state governments are represented in each of the bodies, the states do not make unified requests, so are weakened by their individual and varying priorities and applications. In addition, because of the Commonwealth's superior fundraising capabilities, it is responsible for appropriating much of the revenue available for state purposes. This places Canberra in an advantageous bargaining position vis-a-vis the states, particularly in setting the overall levels of funding and borrowing.

Problems in the federal relationship

Numerous arguments have been posited concerning the problems of Australian federalism. Although there is no apparent consensus about the nature of these problems, the varying approaches to the problems of federalism can be grouped broadly into two political positions: arguments supportive of federalism, and arguments that consider federalism problematic by nature.

Arguments supportive of federalism, but critical of current arrangements

Most of the problems identified by those who maintain this position concern the division of responsibilities between state and Federal Government. Generally, critics suggest that there has been sufficient change in the federal balance to warrant concern. This concern can be divided into several general lines of argument.

The first argument is that which is articulated by states' rights proponents. It rests on the assumption that changes within the federal relationship are *per se* problematic. They can be seen to challenge the autonomy of the states (the Commonwealth being involved in government activities that were the alluded to responsibilities of the states at federation). The 'right' alluded to is based on the assumption that certain responsibilities have been reserved for the states. This position involves an implicit veneration of the authors of the constitution and of their concept of federalism. The right of the states to maintain responsibility in education, health and human rights (to name a few areas that have caused concern to states' righters) only make sense if definitions of federalism other than the 'strong states/weak Commonwealth' (envisaged by the authors of the constitution) are less valid. The states' rights argument is based on an understanding of the federal relationship, which is fixed in a particular historical period, namely that of federation.

The second argument is concerned with the financial difficulties that have arisen out of changes to the federal relationship. State governments have the responsibility for the administration of the costly, non-productive, yet essential, government activities such as hospitals, schools and railways. Yet they no longer have the means for funding these activities and must rely on the Commonwealth. This financial dependency is viewed as undermining state autonomy and the principles of federalism and in this sense is similar to the states' rights position, in that the states are considered to be disadvantaged partners in the federal relationship (although the language of 'rights' is seldom employed in this case). Those who argue this position conclude that the equality of status afforded to both central and regional governments in a federal system has not been evident in Australia since the Uniform Tax decisions.

The third argument similarly recognises the finance/responsibility disparity characteristic of contemporary Australian federalism as problematic. However, this argument considers the Commonwealth to be burdened by the cost of running the states. The argument might be viewed as a 'Commonwealth rights' position, insofar as it is an attempt to demonstrate that while the Commonwealth has become involved in the funding of an increasing range of government services at state level, this has not been to its advantage (Sharman, 1986: 108–20). The state governments have the legislative and administrative control of these services, and perhaps more importantly, have been able to take the credit for their provision in areas affecting the everyday lives of citizens; for example, education, law, health, transport. Sharman suggests that Commonwealth funding of the states has in fact restricted its own policy making, by greatly reducing the funding available for Commonwealth purposes (Sharman, 1985: 112–14). The Commonwealth must budget for state financing, yet often has little real say over spending priorities. Conditional grants have proven to be 'a clumsy way of achieving policy goals in areas of state jurisdiction' (Sharman, 1986: 113). Overall, the current federal relationship is an unsatisfactory one according to those who support the general position outlined above. The state governments (and to a lesser extent, the Commonwealth) are increasingly unable to meet the demands and needs of the electorate as contradictions between fiscal and administrative responsibility for the functions of government have developed. Scholars of federalism who maintain this position suggest that the Commonwealth domination of the financial arrangements of Australian federalism has almost destroyed the federal character of government in Australia.

Arguments that consider federalism problematic by nature

Another approach to the problems of federalism suggests that difficulties within the contemporary federal relationship are inherent to all federations. This approach is based on the assumption that government activity within one region (Australia) and with respect to the same citizens (Australians) cannot be divided amongst two supposedly autonomous tiers.

These arguments consider that, in practice, an enormous range of legislative responsibilities must be shared by both Commonwealth and state governments. There are further responsibilities that are at the moment purely within state jurisdictions, however, these are often regulated by divergent codes, regulations and standards in each state. These state/state and state/Commonwealth inconsistencies have led to inefficiency, duplication of activity, and inequity among states, causing considerable frustration to industries, unions, consumers and individual citizens who must work within these confusing jurisdictional frameworks. For example, industries involved in the manufacture and distribution of dangerous goods must deal with varying state interpretations of the Commonwealth Transport of Dangerous Goods Code. This code is enforced by different legislation in each state and is administered by different bureaucracies from state to state (for example, the Department of Industrial Relations in New South Wales, the Department of Mines and Energy in Western Australia), each of which has created a disparate array of rules and regulations. Industries located within, and dealing across, several states are forced to make sense of this regulatory maze. Similarly, pollution controls differ from state to state, so that industrialists and environmentalists alike must battle with varying requirements as they cross state borders.

It is also argued that federalism leads to serious inconsistencies and anomalies across states. The field of law provides numerous examples (McMillan et al., 1983: chapter 4). Anti-discrimination legislation is not consistent from state to state, so a disabled individual residing in Tweed Heads would receive legislative protection over employment applications on one side of the border (New South Wales) but not the other (Queensland). Although a federal system may provide some scope for legislative innovation and experimentation (by a single state) in 'new' fields (such as anti-discrimination), those who consider federalism undesirable protest against the legal inequality that is an inevitable result.

Within the Australian federal system, there is the potential for much repetition of work as a result of federalism, in particular at the level of research and policy formulation (although the extent of this is difficult to establish, given the added variable of complex interdepartmental relations within each level (see chapter 10)). Cooperation between tiers of government working in the same field may not always be effective and is often contingent on the ad hoc 'networking' instigated by individual government officers.

The entanglement of responsibility for government activity that is apparent in a federal system has led to a further criticism regarding the absence of accountability in federal systems. The federal financial arrangements have been the cause of much 'buck passing', which has developed because of the 'sharing' of responsibilities between both partners. This situation causes difficulties for Australian citizens, who often will be left with an impression that neither of their governments are accountable for problems that arise in their day to day contact with government agencies. Individuals affected by the problems of bed and staff shortages within the hospital system are likely to become confused, for on the one hand, they are told it is a state government responsibility and the states ought to 'organise their priorities', yet on the other hand are given by the states to believe that state revenues are insufficient to deal with these problems singlehandedly because of insufficient Commonwealth funding of the states.

It is likely that the problems of accountability and 'buck-passing' that plague the current federal relationship will increase as the spectre of the 'small government' movement and the accompanying spending and legislative cutbacks for which this movement has lobbied, place a greater strain on federalism. For example, Commonwealth funding of universities has been limited in the wake of the emerging dominance of this movement in public discourse. This has caused disruption to progress on the western Sydney university proposal in New South Wales, resulting in 'buck-passing' of the financial responsibility for the proposal between state and Commonwealth education departments.

The myths of federalism

In political science, the term 'myth' does not denote a challenge to the veracity of a statement. Rather, the habitual use of figures of speech and of assumptions about political events create a political myth.

Several popular and scholarly myths have emerged within federalism discourse. Some of these have been outlined by Crisp (1971: 94–104) and by Maddox (1973: 92–100). The substance of these myths needs to be investigated, as they have contributed to the legitimacy and endurance of the federal form of government in Australia.

The beliefs and assumptions that have legitimised federalism usually deal with the nature and functions of the states. For example, implicit in most discussion of federalism is the notion that 'the states' exist as a single political entity with a common purpose, and can be considered vis-a-vis the Commonwealth in that manner. However, 'the states' are in fact six separate bodies, each with its own set of priorities and policies. Moreover, the priorities of each state change over time, depending on the priorities of the political party in office. Crisp suggests that the six states have never operated as a 'monolith', or even a 'self-disciplined coalition' (Crisp, 1971: 96). Although it is convenient to discuss federalism as a single relationship, federalism is actually a complex network of relationships, between each state and the Commonwealth, and amongst each of the states.

Also relevant to the base upon which the continuing credibility of the states rests is the notion of state 'sovereignty'. This depends upon an assumption that states are sovereign bodies politic, hence maintain legitimate and absolute authority in certain preserved areas of government activity. The argument is similar to that of states' rights, mentioned earlier, insofar as it is supported by the now discredited belief that certain government functions are 'reserved' for state governments, (the 'reserved powers' doctrine), and within this range of activities, the states are sovereign. In Koowarta, Justice Mason noted that:

> . . . the rejection of the doctrine (of reserved powers) was a fundamental and decisive event in the evolution of this Courts' interpretation of the Constitution. . . The consequence is that it is quite illegitimate to approach any question of the interpretation of Commonwealth power on the footing that an expansive construction should be rejected because it will effectively deprive the States of power which has hitherto been exercised or could be exercised by them. (Mason, 1982: 650)

In fact, it is difficult to conceive of the states as being jointly sovereign with the Commonwealth over shared territory, given the rejection of the reserved powers doctrine. The notion that sovereignty can be divided and applied to various areas of government activity does not withstand practical application. Actual pieces of legislation and political issues cannot be categorised neatly into distinctively Commonwealth or state powers, as they usually embrace several subjects. Was the construction of the Gordon River dam an issue regarding Tasmania's energy needs, or was it a conservation, aboriginal rights or property rights issue? Of course, it was all of these, hence can be viewed as straddling both Commonwealth and state jurisdictions. Section 109 ensures Commonwealth legislative supremacy, so the actual sovereignty of the states is an untenable concept.

Although the myth of state sovereignty can be questioned on these grounds, it persists within federalism discourse (and indeed, is essential to federal theory). Tasmania's Premier Gray's remonstrances against Commonwealth regulation of the Gordon Dam project and the woodchipping industry were based on the notion of sovereign states, which assumes that Commonwealth activity in these fields is a challenge to this. It seems that much of the state sovereignty rhetoric used in political discourse serves effectively to screen the entrenched interests of state governments and their agencies.

The endurance of federalism has also been supported by a persistent assumption that federalism provides a structure of government that represents fundamental divisions within Australian society. This is based on a belief that the states reflect the regional and cultural diversity of the nation as a whole. Holmes and Sharman have argued that the federal structure of government in Australia reflects the cultural differences apparent between the states (Holmes and Sharman, 1977: chapter 2). This argument has been supported by Kemp, who has found that different voting patterns are discernable within each state, (Kemp, 1978: 239–57), and by popular stereotypes of state inhabitants that are commonly found in the media—Queenslanders as conservative, Western Australians as entreprenuerial, and so forth. Nevertheless, divergent state political cultures may be artificial. Australia is culturally and regionally heterogeneous, but these social divisions are not essentially represented by current state boundaries. Differences between the states do not equate with the fundamental cleavages in Australian society. The ethnic, age and urban/rural mix coincidentally grouped within each state may well have determined the differing value systems have been shown by researchers to characterise individual state cultures. Aitkin has found that urban/rural variations in political attitudes are more important than those found amongst the states, and that interstate variations are explained by 'the complex interactions of social, economic and political variables' (Aitkin, 1982: 185). Farmers of the Murray region have a good deal in common with each other in spite of the region's division between three states. It would appear that the residents of Melbourne likewise would have more in common with their counterparts in Adelaide than with their fellow statesfolk in the Mallee scrub. Although many aspects of Australian society are organised federally (for example, state-based media, political parties, sporting organisations), it is impossible to establish whether these divisions cause, or are caused by a federally divided culture.

Conclusion

In the final analysis, the endurance of federalism is a result of its interpenetration within so many areas of Australian political and social life. The federal system has not been challenged seriously, because it is entrenched within numerous institutions with a ninety year lineage. Thus Australia is likely to remain a federation for some time.

References

Aitkin, D. (1982) *Stability and Change in Australian Politics* ANU Press: Canberra
Australia (1976) *1975–1976 Budget Paper no. 7* Canberra: AGPS
—— (1982) *1981–1982 Budget Paper no. 7* Canberra: AGPS
—— (1987) *1986–1987 Budget Paper no. 4* Canberra: AGPS
Crisp, L.F. (1971) *Australian National Government* Melbourne: Longman
Frenkel, M. (1986) *Federal Theory* Canberra: Centre for Research on Federal Financial Relations

Holmes, J. and Sharman, C. (1977) *The Australian Federal System* Sydney: George Allen and Unwin
Kemp, D. (1978) *Society and Electoral Behaviour in Australia* St Lucia: University of Queensland Press
McMillan, J., Storey, H. and Evans, G. (1983) *Australia's Constitution: Time for Change?* Sydney: George Allen and Unwin
Maddox, G, (1973) 'Federalism: Or Government Frustrated?', in *Australian Quarterly* September, pp. 92–100
Mason, J. (1982) 'Koowarta v Bjelke-Petersen and Ors; State of Queensland v Commonwealth of Australia' *AJLR* 56
Mathews, R. (1977) 'Innovations and Developments in Australian Federalism' *Publius*
—— (1982) 'Intergovernmental Financial Arrangements and Taxation', in R. Mathews (ed.) *Public Policy in Two Federal Countries: Australia and Canada* Canberra: Centre for Research on Federal Financial Relations
Sawer, G. (1976) *Modern Federalism* Melbourne: Pitman
Sharman, C. (1985) 'The Commonwealth, the States and Federalism', in D. Woodward et al. (eds) *Government, Politics and Power in Australia* Melbourne: Longman Cheshire

12 State politics

Helen Nelson

Why states? Riker poses the question less bluntly:

> The divisions in Australian culture seem to be economic and religious with hardly any geographical base. Hence there also seems to be an Australian patriotism unobstructed by loyalties to the states. . . One wonders, indeed, why they bother with federalism in Australia. (1964: 113)

Accidents of history, the boundaries of the Australian states mark none of the social or economic cleavages that commonly lend political rationality to federal systems. Why then do Australians tolerate a system of government that gives them eight parliaments (that is, including the Northern Territory), eight public services and all the concomitant costs in duplication, overlap and over-government? In brief, what is it that sustains the Australian federation?

In the balance of power between the Commonwealth and state governments, time has favoured the central Government. The major centralising force has been the Commonwealth's financial dominance. As early as 1909, the Commonwealth showed its financial muscle when, following the conclusion of the ten-year Braddon clause (section 87 of the constitution), it ceased refunding to the states three-quarters of customs and excise revenue. The Commonwealth consolidated its position when it took over the monopoly in income taxation in 1942. Today, the Commonwealth's financial supremacy is seen most clearly in its control over the allocation of federal-state funding and its use of specific purpose payments, taxation incentives, subsidies and other financial instruments to enter public policy areas not formally assigned to it in the constitution. Financial control has provided the counterforce to ease the constitutional constraints on Commonwealth policy making.

Less tangible, and less well documented, factors in the broadening of the foci of federal politics have included the breakdown of the 'tyranny of distance', the need for a 'national' voice in times of national and international crises, the new nationalism of the 1970s and 1980s, and the linkages and increasing overlap between policy areas. More recently, the liberal judicial interpretation given to the external affairs power (see chapter 11) has enhanced further the Commonwealth's policy-making potential. There are now few areas of public policy in which the Federal Government does not have some impact, even if its reach is often confined to its financial influence.

Federal–state relations are not, however, a zero-sum game. When the

Commonwealth spreads itself into areas previously regarded as solely state domains, the states do not retire from the arena. Rather, there is a redistribution of power to accommodate the new player. The new player might have the dollar backing and the international reputation, but the old players retain some strengths. In Australian federal–state politics, the boundaries, the rules of the game and the crowd are still on the side of the states.

This chapter examines the sources of state strength. It surveys the centrifugal forces that balance the centralising drifts in modern Australian federal politics. It focusses on the boundaries, the rules of the game and the crowd. The account of the strategies, the high kicks, the drop-passes and the injuries will have to wait for another time.

The boundaries

The primary function of constitution makers is to decide upon the distribution of power, that is, to set the boundaries for the use of power. For the Australian constitution makers, the prospect of all power concentrated in the hands of a central, unitary government was never an option. From the beginning, the efficacy of the already-established state governments had to be preserved. Federalism provided the framework for a mutually beneficial union, but federal powers were carefully selected. The Commonwealth was allocated postal and telegraph powers, but not the powers to regulate the economy; it gained control over weights and measures, but not over industrial conditions and standards; it gained lighthouses, but control over territorial waters had to await a High Court decision in 1975 (which was subsequently ameliorated by a process of political bargaining. See Galligan, 1986: 228–30). In brief, the constitutional division of powers was weighted in favour of the states, which were given the residual powers, that is, those not specifically mentioned in the constitution. Commonwealth powers were specified and limited mainly to those that were necessary to ensure a national defence effort and coordinated administrative action in the interests of the smooth running of the economic activities of the states.

There has been no major revision of the original division of powers, although in 1988 a Constitutional Commission has the matter under consideration. Time has reconfirmed the mean bargain. All federations have some agreed-upon method of constitutional change, and the Australian constitution makers ensured that their nineteenth century priorities would rule well beyond the grave. Section 128 of the constitution requires that amendment proposals be ratified not only by a majority of electors, but by a majority in the majority of states. Only eight of the 38 constitutional referendums have passed the test. The changes have been only minor in terms of their impact on the original division of powers. Further, an analysis of the changing patterns of referendum voting in the individual states suggests that there is a state 'interest' at work so that support and opposition to referendum proposals waxes and wanes according to changing positions in the balance of power between the states in the federation (Sharman and Stuart, 1981).

The original division of powers remains the states' greatest source of strength. From this constitutional base, the states have the 'inside running' not only in those areas of primary electoral importance, such as education, housing, transport and health, but also their residual powers give them immediate access to all new issue areas. They can thwart Commonwealth action by, for instance, anticipating it or blocking it. Given the political will, they can, and do, enact legislation and implement policies that stamp a state 'style' on their territories (see Holmes and Sharman, 1977).

The significance of the boundaries can, however, be overemphasised. The division of powers does not denote a monopoly of policy making in specific areas. As stated above, the Commonwealth's financial dominance gives it access to most areas. What it cannot manage directly, it can control through the use of financial incentives and sanctions. The states also have room for manoeuvre, even in areas of Commonwealth exclusivity. For instance, in external affairs, the states still have their own overseas representation (see Ravenhill, 1988); in defence matters, a state government can still plan development of a space launching pad and state governments still compete for defence contracts; and in communications, different state censorship and taxation laws have an impact on media operations within the individual states. Further blurring of functional distinctions arises from the linkages and overlaps between policy areas (Wiltshire, 1986). Environment and conservation laws, whether enacted by federal or state governments, cannot be implemented in isolation from laws regarding irrigation practices, rural usage and development schemes. Similarly, federal marriage and divorce laws inevitably overlap with state laws regarding adoption, inheritance, bankruptcy and de facto relationships.

The result is reflected in the legislative agendas of the federal and state governments. Both types of government are active across the range of policy areas. The constitutional division becomes evident more in the *content* of their respective lawmaking than in their functional classifications. Both make policy, but whereas the Commonwealth is biased towards measures that relate to financial resources and means, the states tend to be more concerned with rules and regulations, and organisational structures (Nelson, 1988). Primary industry, for instance, is an area governed by *federal* laws relating to export schemes and controls, levies, subsidies and concessions, and *state* laws relating to marketing boards and controls, land settlement and development, pest control, daylight saving, irrigation schemes and conservation. In another example, public housing policies comprise a combination of the provisions of the Commonwealth–State Housing Agreement, setting out the broad financial ambits, and widely different state measures concerning the criteria for housing assistance, the balance between housing for sale to prospective buyers and rental accommodation, provisions for relief housing assistance and other specific requirements (Parkin, 1988).

The mix of federal and state laws that now characterises most policy areas in the federation presents a benefit–cost ratio that depends upon the eye of the beholder, specifically, it depends upon where one draws the line between national priorities and state priorities. In the above examples, in primary industry, the federal role has evolved out of federal export powers, while state priorities continue to dictate domestic marketing structures, and land usage and development issues. In public housing, the Commonwealth–State Housing Agreement has not been the vehicle for social reform envisaged by the reconstructionists of the Chifley Government era. Policy has evolved so that whereas the Federal Government has retained its financial role, state priorities guide the forms of service delivery.

Two current issues illustrate the difficulties that arise when federal and state priorities clash: environment conservation and aboriginal land rights. Both issues entail conflicting territorial claims. Environmental issues are state issues. The Commonwealth has no direct powers, but is already active in the area in various ways through its powers in external affairs, export controls and taxation. Aboriginal affairs has been an area of federal–state concurrent power since 1967, when a referendum granted the Commonwealth jurisdiction in what had been previously a solely state domain. In environment conservation, the case for a 'national' solution has the advantage of an established national network of supporting interests. It is unlikely that the extraordinary example of the Tasmanian Gordon-below-Franklin Dam, where Tasmania was granted monetary compensation for foregoing state development plans, can be the precedent for future federal involvement in the environment area. Rather, federal involvement will probably depend upon the ability of the national network of interests to sustain its electoral impact long enough for national priorities to be worked out and established, either in conjunction with or superimposed upon state priorities. The process began with the Labor Party's wooing of the national environmental vote through its promises to act on the Franklin Dam issue at the 1983 elections. The Hawke Government repeated the approach prior to the 1987 election, when it promised to seek World Heritage listing for the Daintree rainforest area in Queensland, again in return for electoral support from the environmentalist lobby.

The land rights issue presents a different scenario. The Federal Government has withdrawn from its National Aboriginal Land Rights Legislation proposal presented in 1985. In this case, the supporting interests lack the national electoral support similar to that developed by the environmentalist lobby. The issue has reverted to state level, where it inevitably becomes entangled in questions about property rights. With the issue so defined in state terms, it might be anticipated that when it re-emerges as an issue at federal level, state priorities will be a major consideration in the policy formulation process. Land rights might well be defined in property terms—rather than, say, as a human rights issue—and, perhaps, with the onus put on the Commonwealth Government to purchase the relevant land from state sources.

The tussle between federal and state priorities is part of the fascination of the study of federal systems. In the Australian federation, the federal and state roles in public policy making appear generally to have evolved out of their financial and constitutional powers respectively. Most significantly, in the context of this chapter, the states' role has been to put a brake on the rate of social change. Federal governments can prompt, persuade, plead and even enforce reformist policies, but, as in the case of Medibank and Medicare, such changes enforced at federal level require a concerted financial, organisational and political commitment. When the states have primary carriage for an issue area—as they do for the vast range of policies—reform proposals will sooner or later require state legislation, either in a form complementary with the Commonwealth and other states or else on the initiative of the states individually. States vary in their rates of policy innovation and in their emphases. Policy innovation at state level is time-specific and issue-specific (Nelson, 1985). The states therefore have the effect of staggering the rate of social change. The reform debate becomes dispersed at state level and fragmented. It is particularly in the areas of policy innovation and policy change that the original division of powers and its impact in maintaining the states' presence becomes most evident.

The rules of the game

Federal and state lawmaking takes place within the framework of the constitutional division of powers. In the section above, emphasis is given to the degree to which both levels of government have legislative input into the range of public policy areas. Should either level of government step over the constitutional line, however, the High Court is there to blow the whistle.

There is no similar umpire to regulate the rough and tumble of intergovernmental administrative and financial relations. The array of arrangements for federal–state cooperation derive generally from informal agreements between governments. The constitution makes only very limited provision for intergovernmental machinery (see Saunders, 1986: 170) and few such bodies and agreements are subject to parliamentary examination.

The major forms of intergovernmental cooperation are summarised in Chapman (1988) and Saunders (1986: 170–5). The former includes an outline of the more than 40 ministerial councils, comprising the relevant ministers from federal and state levels, set up to exchange information and coordinate activities in the various subject areas. Chapman's account of the River Murray Commission, established in 1914 by the Commonwealth, New South Wales, Victorian and South Australian governments, provides a good example of the capacity for state priorities (in this case, irrigation and settlement schemes in New South Wales and Victoria) to override national concerns (conservation of the River Murray resources). Saunders' assessment of existing intergovernmental arrangements points to the problems they create for public accountability and the degree to which their poor organisational structures, including, in many instances, the lack of a permanent secretariat, place limitations on opportunities for effective policy-making. Even the 'peak' intergovernmental body, the Premiers' Conference, is subject to ad hocery in its procedures.

Informality and ad hocery in intergovernmental relations work in favour of the states. As Saunders notes, intergovernmental arrangements often have the impact of constitutional change by effecting national policy without going through the process of constitutional transfer (1986: 172). By assigning intergovernmental relations to the political arena, unburdened by formal institutional machinery, national priorities are more easily displaced by the politically pertinent state questions: 'What is in it for us? What will it cost us?'. One gains the impression that if the respective answers are 'Nothing' and 'Plenty', then 'cooperation' is unlikely to go far—but that proposition has yet to be tested. The point is that there are few incentives for state governments to participate in, or seek to improve the status of, intergovernmental structures.

The states are more vulnerable in the area of federal–state financial relations. State rhetoric allows that a financially dominant Commonwealth Government deals poorly with the cap-in-hand state governments. Yet, when the Fraser Government's New Federalism provided states with the opportunity to levy their own income tax, no state government pursued the offer. The present arrangements hold one clear advantage for state governments: they relieve states from the burden of, and financial responsibility of, collecting their own taxation revenue. Sharman (1980: 12–14) argues that, despite the Commonwealth Government's financial superiority, its manoeuvrability is nevertheless reduced by the extent of its commitments to its own public service and to the state governments, and further, that state governments manipulate the present system for their own political gain. By claiming credit for Commonwealth-funded projects, by blaming the Commonwealth when projects fail or funding declines, and with similar tactics, 'the states have continued to ensure that a disproportionate share of the political costs of raising funds falls on the national government while the political benefits accrue to the states' (1980: 14).

Tactics, strategies, political ploys are part of the 'sport' of federal–state relations. It is not stretching the analogy too far to include here the play of the team captains, the Premiers. In the small pool of state politics, successful Premiers can achieve an ascendancy that allows them to stamp their own style on the politics of their respective states. Nationally, they can come to personify their states' politics. Successful Premiers reinforce the image through their energetic promotion of the interests of their states. In the process, the Federal Government can become a useful punching bag. If the Premiers' Conference fails as an occasion for the advancement of intergovernmental cooperation, it is partly because it is also an occasion when Premiers can grandstand and fly their state flags. In doing so, they not only promote their states' interests—they also remind us of the saliency of the state presence.

The crowd

A sense of territorial identity is an essential component of regional viability in federal systems. Riker's observation, quoted at the opening of this chapter, that there appears to be an Australian patriotism 'unobstructed' by state loyalties, is not incompatible with the notion of coexisting state identities. The important point is that the political rationale for a division of powers includes the notion of cultural 'separateness'.

Defining what comprises the condition of 'separateness' is a more difficult task, but we might expect it to include a 'federal sentiment', or attitudinal support for the federal structure, and, in more tangible form, political institutions and social sub-structures that exist independently of the national structures.

'Federal sentiment' is an elusive quality. Miller (1959: 138–40, 152) included it in his list of possible explanations for the resistance to constitutional change, as shown in referendum results. The analysis of referendum voting statistics in the Sharman and Stuart study (1981), cited earlier, suggests that referendum voters might indeed be prompted by a desire to preserve state integrity. Certainly, state Premiers play up the idea of 'stateness'. It also finds expression in the artefacts of the civilisation, for instance, car number plates that proclaim 'The State of Excitement', 'The Sunshine State', 'The Garden State', 'The Premier State', and so on.

The most comprehensive endeavour to date to 'nail' the characteristics that distinguish the citizens of the different states is contained in Holmes and Sharman's survey (1977: 34–59) of opinion polls showing the state differences in attitudes towards various issues. Although no clear state 'profiles' emerge, there are significant differences in the results from the various states. Berry's often-quoted study, published in 1969, reported that his sample of tertiary students were able to identify state stereotypes: Tasmanians were identified as quiet, conservative, provincial, friendly and hospitable; South Australians as conservative, cultured, artistic, religious and respectable; Western Australians as active, outdoor, adventurous, friendly and pioneering; Queenslanders as casual, outdoor, friendly, easygoing and carefree; the New South Welsh as commercial, competitive, cosmopolitan, materialistic and suburban; and Victorians as conservative, aloof, formal and narrow minded. The Berry study is two decades old, but we can still recognise the state types. If we can identify 'them', then we must also have an idea of a separate 'us'.

State political structures are more readily identifiable than state attitudes. The state political systems were in place before federation, and have developed surprisingly untouched by the federal superstructure. At their heart are the state parliaments. Modelled on the Westminster system and dominated by the demands of the two-party structure, most sit for an average of less than two months a year and their agendas and proceedings are controlled by their respective executives. When in office, no state party has been too embarrassed to press home its advantage by manipulation of the legislative agenda and revision of standing orders to suit their own immediate purpose.

In more recent years, the reformist breeze has touched the state legislatures. There has been no lessening of executive control and most reforms have been in the direction of reinforcing the two-party domination. The main foci of parliamentary reform have been the upper houses and the committee systems. With the exception of Queensland's legislative council, which was abolished in 1922, the state upper houses survived into the 1960s protected by restrictive electoral systems and made strong by rights of veto. Since then, all states have acted successfully to introduce adult franchise, although, as Rydon has observed, 'The extension of the franchise unaccompanied by any move towards equality of votes has not made Councils genuinely democratic. It has tended to make them more party political' (1983: 31). The councils in all states except New South Wales have retained the right to refuse supply. The Victorian Cain Government's Constitution (Council Powers) Bill 1983 proposed the removal of the power, but was amended in the Council so that a refusal of supply would entail both houses going to an election.

There has also been a revival of interest in state parliamentary committee systems. The success of the Victorian Public Bodies Review Committee has inspired an overhaul of that parliament's committee system and has provided a model for the other states (Holmes, Halligan and Hay, 1986: 36–8). In New South Wales, the Public Accounts Committee has been revived, with widened powers, and in 1982, the first Standing Committee (on Road Safety) was established. In 1980, South Australia established two Estimates Committees to examine the state budget. Select committees have also been active. In recent years, state parliamentary select committees have investigated topics such as: bushfires, alcohol and drugs, the fruit and vegetable industry, and sport and recreation (Western Australia); random breath testing, parliamentary reform and prostitution (South Australia); and parliamentary privilege, workers' compensation and prostitution (New South Wales). When Premier Holgate prorogued the Tasmanian parliament in December 1981, he also terminated the work of eleven select committees. Only Queensland appears to have resisted the committee revival.

Throughout, even in the more moribund periods of the more moribund parliaments, the legislative output has been maintained. The state parliaments average an output of more than 100 new Acts annually. Most of these make minor policy or administrative adjustments to existing arrangements. Only a small proportion are concerned with new or other major policy matters. In recent years, these have included legislation in such critical new areas as in-vitro fertilisation, transplant surgery, AIDS, environmental protection, control of hazardous chemicals, firearms control and equal employment opportunity (Nelson, 1988). The output reflects the important, independent place that state lawmaking retains in the federal system.

Federal–state matters are a very minor concern in the life of the state parliaments. They are dominated by purely state matters. More relevant in terms of the 'state separateness' theme, the state parliaments provide career structures that are entirely independent of parliamentary career structures at federal level. In practice, there are even disincentives for those who might contemplate moving from one level to the other: 'To do so is likely to entail a loss of seniority and add more years to the apprenticeship stage at the legislative level' (Sharman, Hughes and Tuffin, 1986: 232). The system reinforces the federal–state division. Also, it must bring to federal–state negotiations that same vested interest in favour of the upholding of state rights that dominated the early federal conventions.

The careers of state public servants are similarly fully contained at state level. Again, it is difficult not to see a vested interest in retaining state career opportunities as a factor contributing to a states' rights stance when intergovernmental matters arise. But also again, although there are extensive contacts between the federal and state public services (for example, see Warhurst, 1983), these contacts are of secondary concern to state public servants. Their careers, and their business, are focussed primarily at state level.

State governments have been notable in their longevity (Davis, 1960: 631). A major factor in their ability to retain office once elected has been their readiness to manipulate the state electoral systems with gerrymandering, changes in voting systems and regular tinkering with the rules and regulations (see chapter 10). As in the case of control of the state legislatures, we can see here the hand of the state political parties.

The state party systems have their origins in the pre-federation era (see, Loveday, Martin and Parker, 1977). The present-day structures of the Labor and conservative parties reflect their state-based origins. All three major political parties—Labor, Liberal and National Party—share a similar organisational format, based on the federal principle. In each case, however, the respective state branches differ widely in their political styles, forms and procedures, factional politics and extent of success in gaining office at state level. For instance, during the years 1910–1987, Labor was in office in Tasmania and New South Wales for about two-thirds of the period (66.0 percent and 60.9 percent of the 78 years respectively), about half the total number of years in Queensland and Western Australia (50.0 percent and 49.6 percent respectively), and considerably less than half the period in South Australia and Victoria (35.0 percent and 18.6 percent). These differences denote differences in the ability to appeal to different electorates. The achievement of, or failure to gain, electoral success is a major influence on the internal structure of the parties, in particular, on the relationship between the parliamentary party and the party machine (see, for example, Davis, 1960: 603–12). Differences in electoral record at both state and federal levels is mentioned by Warhurst as a source of the differences between the various state Labor parties. He mentions also membership size, relationship to the trade union movement and the influence of individual personalities (Warhurst, 1983a: 257–72).

Despite the marked differences between and within the major parties, it is the similarity in organisational format that is most pertinent to this chapter. All the major political parties are state based. Their memberships and their branch structures are state based. Their major fundraising has been at state level. Until the 1970s their election campaigns, even for federal elections, were funded and organised mainly at state level. In the last decade, the parties have upgraded their federal organisations. Their memberships remain, however, state based, supported by long-established state party machines. The party organisations replicate the federal structure. Representation on the parties' federal bodies follows the Senate principle of an equal number of representatives from each state, regardless of population size, regardless of the number of state seats in the House of Representatives, regardless of the federal vote in the respective states and regardless of the number of party members in each state.

The pattern reinforces the federal–state structure of the federation. In addition, it creates within the political parties themselves a vested interest in retention of the federal system. In Riker's view, parties structured on the federal principle were the single most influential factor in the maintenance of the American federal system (1964: 101). Certainly, in recent Australian political experience, the most overtly centralist Prime Ministers, Gorton (Liberal) and Whitlam (Labor), suffered heavily for their centralist sentiments by criticism from their own state party machines (Reid, 1971: 177–82; Lloyd and Reid, 1974: 231–2).

The federal party structures are repeated in the organisational structures of the array of voluntary organisations, professional associations, sporting bodies and suchlike that make up the social sub-structure. Most non-government organisations are primarily state based, with their organisational and financial resources concentrated at state level. Although the expansion of Commonwealth government activity has been accompanied by an increase in the federal organisational and lobbying efforts of the major groups (see chapter 16), most retain structures that repeat the Senate principle of equal state representation at federal level, regardless of state inequalities in size of membership and other resources.

It is these social underpinnings and the vested interests that they denote, that contribute most to the sense of state identity, and that are perhaps the states' greatest survival resource.

Reference has been made already to the current (1987) considerations of the Constitutional Commission established in 1985. Its terms of reference include review of the present constitutional division of powers. As a final tribute to the staying power of the states, it is worth noting that the terms of reference do not include any questioning of the viability of federalism or the efficacy of a system of state governments.

References

Berry, J. (1969) 'The Stereotypes of Australian States' *Australian Journal of Psychology*, 21, 3, December, pp. 227–33

Chapman, Ralph (1988) 'Intergovernmental Relations', in B. Galligan (ed.) *Comparative State Policies* Melbourne: Longman Cheshire

Davis, S.R. (ed.) (1960) *The Government of the Australian States* Melbourne: Longmans

Galligan, B. (1986) *The Politics of the High Court* St Lucia: University of Queensland Press

Holmes, J., Halligan, J. and Hay, P. (1986) 'Victoria', in B. Galligan (ed.) *Australian State Politics* Melbourne: Longman Cheshire

Holmes, J. and Sharman, C. (1977) *The Australian Federal System* Sydney: George Allen and Unwin

Lloyd, C.J. and Reid, G.S. (1974) *Out of the Wilderness* Melbourne: Cassell

Loveday, P. Martin, A.W. and Parker, R.S. (eds) (1977) *The Emergence of the Australian Party System* Sydney: Hale and Iremonger

Miller, J.D.B. (1959) *Australian Government and Politics* 2nd edn, London: Duckworth

Nelson, H. (1985) 'Policy Innovation in the Australian States' *Politics*, 20, 2, November, pp. 77–88

—— (1988) 'Legislative Outputs', in B. Galligan (ed.) *Comparative State Policies* Melbourne: Longman Cheshire

Parkin, Andrew (1988) 'Housing Policies', in B. Galligan (ed.) *Comparative State Policies* Melbourne: Longman Cheshire

Ravenhill, J.R. (1988) 'Australia', in H.J. Michelman and P. Soldatos (eds) *Federalism and International Relations: The Role of Subnational Units* Oxford: Oxford University Press

Reid, A. (1971) *The Gorton Experiment* Sydney: Shakespeare Head

Riker, William H. (1964) *Federalism: Origin, Operation, Significance* Boston: Little Brown

Rydon, J. (1983) 'Upper Houses—the Australian Experience', in Reid, G.S. (ed.) *The Role of Upper Houses Today* Proceedings of the Fourth Annual Workshop of the Australasian Study of Parliament Group, pp. 22–42

Saunders, C. (1986) 'The Federal System', in B. Galligan (ed.) *Australian State Politics* Melbourne: Longman Cheshire

Sharman, C. (1980) 'Fraser, the states and federalism' *Australian Quarterly*, 52, 1, Autumn, pp. 9–19

Sharman, C. Hughes, O. and Tuffin, K. (1986) 'State Premiers', in B. Galligan (ed.) *Australian State Politics* Melbourne: Longman Cheshire

Sharman, C. and Stuart, J. (1981) 'Patterns of State Voting in National Referendums' *Politics*, 16, 2, November, pp. 261–70

Warhurst, J. (1983) *Central Agencies, Intergovernmental Managers, and Australian Federal–State Relations* Occasional Paper 29, Canberra: Centre for Research on Federal Financial Relations, Australian National University

—— (1983a) 'One party or eight? the State & Territory Labor Parties', in A. Parkin and J. Warhurst (eds) *Machine Politics in the Australian Labor Party* Sydney: Allen & Unwin

Wiltshire, K. (1986) *Planning and Federalism* St Lucia: University of Queensland Press

13 Local government

Martin Painter

Local government is Australia's third tier of government. Local councils are elected, general purpose authorities, each with jurisdiction over a local area. In each state, legislation passed by state parliament gives councils their powers, defines their boundaries and regulates their activities. There are over 800 local governments in Australia and approximately 8300 elected councillors (in some councils they are called aldermen). Table 13.1 shows the numbers of councils in each state and the Northern Territory. In most states, urban councils are called municipalities or cities and those in the country are shires or districts. The smallest have populations of less than 500, while the boundaries of the largest, the City of Brisbane, encompass a population of over 700 000. In terms of area, the smallest, Peppermint Grove (Western Australia), is only 1 square kilometre, while the largest, East Pilbara (Western Australia), covers 377 637 square kilometres. Table 13.2 groups local councils by population. Most councils have populations of under 10 000. Most of Australia's population, however, lives in the larger, metropolitan or fringe metropolitan local government areas.

When compared with state and Commonwealth governments, local government plays a small, but not unimportant, part. For each $100 spent by Australian governments, the Commonwealth spends approximately $52, the states $42 and local government $6; for each $100 in tax collected, the Commonwealth levies approximately $79, the states $17 and local government $4 (National Inquiry into Local Government Finance, 1985).

The status and powers of local government

Local government authorities are creatures of state governments, established and operating under the provisions of local government Acts, which are very long and specify in great detail what councils may do and how they may do it. Many other Acts also impinge on and constrain their activities.

The subordinate legal status of local councils does not mean that they can be treated merely as administrative extensions of state governments. Being elected, councils are directly accountable to a local populace; as general purpose bodies they have the power to make choices about the quantity and quality of various services. In addition, they are able to levy certain taxes and charges. Councils can also have their own 'by-laws' enacted to give them legal

Table 13.1 Number of local governments

State	Cities	Municipalities*	Shires**	Total
NSW	30	32	113	175
VIC.	66	11	133	210
QLD	19	3	112	134
SA	27	10	87	124
WA	15	12	113	139
TAS.	4	43		47
NT	1	5	1	7
TOTAL	162	115	559	836

Note: * Includes towns and boroughs
** Includes districts
Source: Australian Council of Local Government Associations *List of Local Governments in Australia* June 1986

Table 13.2 Local governments grouped by population

Population	NSW	VIC.	QLD	WA	SA	TAS.	NT	TOTAL	%
0– 500	—	—	5	10	3	3	—	21	2.5
500– 749	1	1	3	5	6	2	—	18	2.1
750– 999	—	—	4	10	3	—	—	17	2.0
1000– 2499	12	27	22	49	34	14	2	160	19.1
2500– 4999	35	54	34	14	30	7	2	176	21.0
5000– 9999	32	41	29	20	17	10	—	149	17.8
10 000– 14 999	15	18	9	10	6	4	1	63	7.5
15 000– 24 999	22	16	10	7	8	3	1	67	8.0
25 000– 49 999	26	27	10	8	9	3	—	83	9.9
50 000– 99 999	16	23	8	4	7	1	1	60	7.2
100 000–249 999	16	3	2	2	—	—	—	23	2.7
250 000+	—	—	1	—	—	—	—	1	0.1

Source: Australian Council of Local Government Associations *List of Local Governments in Australia* June 1986

powers to govern local matters, such as the keeping of dogs by local residents and the control of local building and development.

Local councils, then, are in a somewhat anomolous position. On the one hand, they have the appearance of a fully-fledged level of government; on the other, they operate within the constraints of enacted powers and the constant oversight of state governments. A feature of most local government Acts is the power vested in the Governor to dismiss a council and replace it with an appointed administrator. Although dismissals are rare, the power has been used most frequently in New South Wales, sometimes where corruption has been revealed (Power et al., 1981: 114–6).

The origins of Australian local government in the 1840s reflect this tension between local autonomy and central control. At that time, many of local government's proponents saw it as part of the movement for greater popular representation in the government of the colonies (Power et al., 1981: 9). Some argued that local self government provided an ideal 'training ground' for

Table 13.3 Purpose classification of local government outlays 1975/76–1984/85 (%)*

	75/76	78/79	81/82	84/85
Road transport	45	41	36	36
General public services	21	24	23	17
Recreation, culture	17	17	18	20
Sanitation and protection of environment	6	6	8	12
Education, health & welfare	5	6	6	7
Housing and community development	2	3	4	3
Other	3	3	5	5

Note: * Includes final consumption expenditure and expenditure on new fixed assets
Source: National Inquiry into Local Government Finance; Australian Bureau of Statistics, cat. 5504

democratic citizenship and that councils could also act as bulwarks against the dangers of central government domination. However, a major reason behind the establishment of local bodies was to relieve some of the administrative burden on central authorities and to raise funds through local taxation. In fact, some early proposals for establishing municipal councils were fostered more enthusiastically by the central authorities than by local populations, who resisted the imposition of another taxing body. However, recent studies of the development of local government have revised earlier views that local government was largely imposed on a reluctant populace (Power et al., 1981: 20–2). There were many early failures and setbacks, but they were due as much to inappropriate legal and financial frameworks in the Acts as to lack of local enthusiasm. From the beginning, however, the operations of local bodies were frequently accompanied by controversy, scandal and inefficiency. This, in turn, encouraged the central authorities' view that close supervision and constraints were needed, despite the elected status of local bodies.

By the early years of the twentieth century, Victoria, Tasmania, Western Australia and Queensland had established systems of local government covering the whole of their states. In New South Wales and South Australia, large, sparsely populated areas were left under the administration of state government agencies. In the Northern Territory, local government in Darwin goes back to 1874, but it was not until 1971 that a second council, in Alice Springs, was established.

Functions and finance

Most people probably associate local government with roads, kerbs and gutters and garbage collection; they are not too far off the mark. Particularly in rural areas, local road construction and maintenance take up a very large proportion of council expenditures. But expenditure on personal welfare services (like 'meals on wheels' and home nursing) and facilities for recreational and other community purposes have shown slow but steady growth (see Table 13.3).

Local government performs a variety of regulatory functions in the public health, building and town planning fields. To some extent, these activities involve the administration of uniform, statewide legislation, but local by-laws also exist. Councils, where they have the power, can exercise considerable influence on the kind of building and other development that takes place through drawing up local land-use planning schemes. However, here as in so much else, state government planning authorities limit the discretion of councils so that overall land-use and planning policies are not undermined.

Local government Acts grant councils the power to provide a wide variety of services, but many of these are only rarely taken up. Just to name a few, councils in various states have the power to operate gymnasiums, morgues, creches, public conveniences and aerodromes; run dental services, kindergartens and camping sites; employ nurses, parking-meter attendants and dog catchers; regulate scaffolding, fairgrounds, vehicles plying for hire and noxious weeds; and undertake trading activities in afforestation, ferries, trolley buses and sheep dips.

There is an enormous variation between councils in the range of services and facilities provided. The bulk of councils are too small to do much more than the minimum. Better-off or larger councils often provide a wide range, including libraries, community centres, sporting and recreation facilities and so on. Variety is due not only to capacity but also to choice and need. A rural shire is likely to have a very different set of priorities from a metropolitan municipality, for instance.

All councils complain that the funds and powers available to them are insufficient to allow them to do all they would like. More to the point, councils on the whole have tended to adopt a rather unambitious view of their responsibilities. While attitudes have changed considerably in recent years, this tradition of limited service is worth exploring.

In the first place, local councils have developed under the shadow of the states. Many 'municipal' functions familiar to people in Britain or the United States are provided by the states in Australia: education, health, police, most public transport and so on. Where councils have failed to take initiatives, state authorities have often stepped in, as has been the case with water supply and sewerage in the metropolitan areas. Some state departments have been reluctant to see local councils having discretionary powers over matters that they see as their responsibility. Health departments, for instance, have tended to impose strict and pettifogging controls 'even to the extent of determining the colour of lavatory doors in municipal baby health centres' (Bowman, 1983: 172). At the same time, they have extended local health services through regional offices of their own.

Limited views about council responsibilities also have origins in local government itself. There is a strong tradition that the essential purpose of councils is to provide 'services to property', such as streets, footpaths and garbage collection. This stems to a large extent from the character of the single most important source of local revenue—the rate on property. In 1985/86 around 42 percent of local government revenue in Victoria and New South Wales came from rates. Each parcel of land is given a valuation and its owner is then taxed by the council on the basis of so many cents per dollar of value. Councillors have tended to be particularly sensitive to the 'hip pocket nerve' of ratepayers. One of the features of land rates is that they are a once a year lump sum demand, and hence highly visible and painful, making ratepayers particularly sensitive to the purported 'extravagances' of local councils.

Despite this traditional focus on 'essential services', local councils are increasingly important for the delivery of commmunity services of various kinds. Over the years, rates have declined as a proportion of income, particularly as grants from state and Commonwealth governments have grown, weakening the 'services for property' argument. For instance, under the Libraries Act 1939, the New South Wales government pays a matching subsidy for library operating costs. Commonwealth grants for local government only reached significant proportions in the early 1970s, when the Whitlam Labor Government took a number of initiatives (National Inquiry into Local Government Finance, 1985). Between 1972 and 1985 income from state and Commonwealth grants increased from 18 to 25 percent of total funds. In 1973/74 Commonwealth grants for local government totalled about $90 million; by 1983/84 this had risen to nearly $900 million (taking account of inflation, the increase was just over threefold). Many of the Whitlam grants were for specific purposes, but since 1976 general-purpose grants have become much more significant. In that year the Fraser Government decided to grant local government (through the states) an amount equivalent to 1.52 percent of income tax collections; this percentage increased to 1.75 in 1979/80 and to 2.0 in 1980/81. One of the provisions attached to these funds was that each council would receive an amount according to population. The bulk, however, would be distributed by state Local Government Grants Commissions, which have adopted various 'equalising' formulae aimed at giving more money to those councils with the greatest need. Most councils have used these grants more to balance their budgets than to undertake new initiatives (National Inquiry into Local Government Finance, 1985: 65–100).

An 'equalisation principle' was first introduced in local government grants by the Whitlam Government. It acknowledges one of the fundamental problems of local finance—the great disparity in the 'fiscal capacity' of councils. Poorer councils, where land values are lower, have to strike a higher rate to raise their income, while the residents possess a lower capacity to pay. Acute problems are faced, for instance, by some fast-developing outer suburbs where demands for services are high and the capacity to pay low. An additional problem for all councils in New South Wales is that since 1977 the state government has imposed 'rate-pegging', which limits the annual increase in any property owner's rate (for 1988 the increase is limited to 6.5 percent).

Local politics

The conventional wisdom in local government circles has tended to be that too much politics (especially party politics) is a bad thing. Much of this is a case of hiding one's head in the sand, for councils allocate important scarce resources for highly valued community purposes, and hence must become the focus for political conflict. In part, it is also self-serving, for the attack on politics is frequently associated with an attack on Labor Party participation in local government. A large proportion of councillors call themselves 'independents' and condemn the influence of party, which is seen to be inimical to the representation of 'true' community interests. However, some of these self-styled 'independents' are, in fact, partisan activists themselves on the conservative side of politics. Nevertheless, the fact that many 'independents' get elected to local councils indicates some important facts about local politics that distinguish them from politics elsewhere.

An important difference is that councillors are not 'professional politicians' but part-time, unpaid volunteers (only on the Brisbane city council are they paid a salary; elsewhere they may claim relatively small amounts in expenses). Local social and economic elites—farmers, local businesspeople and those in administrative and executive occupations—provide the recruiting ground for most councillors (Wild, 1974; Chapman and Wood, 1984: 49). At state and national levels the political parties are the primary channels of political recruitment. In local politics, the channels are more diverse. Studies of local political recruitment show that previous participation in voluntary associations like community service or sporting clubs is a very common stepping-stone to service on the council (Painter, 1973; Chapman and Wood, 1984: 49–51).

An important prerequisite for getting elected is being well known in the community. A feature of local elections is the importance of being able to muster a personal following, particularly as electorates are numbered in their hundreds or thousands rather than tens of thousands. A strong 'friends and neighbours' element has been observed in patterns of support for some candidates (Painter, 1974). In some cases, major local issues give rise to what might be termed 'local parties', for instance ratepayers' organisations protesting at rate rises, or resident action groups protesting at urban development. Groups like progress associations or chambers of commerce will sometimes sponsor individual candidates. Each local area has its own character and is, in some sense, a distinct political community in its own right.

In sum, local politics are different. Three central facts about local government decision making are important for understanding this. First, the duties and functions of councils are very much 'down to earth' matters. Whether councils are deciding on the programming of street works, the location of public facilities, the granting or refusal of a building or development application or the kind of rubbish bin to be used for garbage collection, the matters are, from the local population's point of view, very immediate and specific. From the viewpoint of state or Commonwealth politicians, such decisions would mostly seem matters of administrative detail, but they are the essence of local politics.

Here, the second fact about local government decision making comes into play. The council as a whole is formally responsible for every decision taken by the council, and particularly in the smaller councils, personal oversight by councillors is quite feasible (see page 173). Thirdly, councillors are accessible and have close links with their local communities. Faced with representations from members of the public individually affected by decisions, councillors often exercise their decision making powers to the full and may become closely involved in detail (for instance, not only how much to spend on kerbs and gutters but which streets to kerb and gutter and when). Much of local council decision making is case by case, detailed consideration of 'minor' matters; it is highly parochial and 'particularistic' (Painter, 1975). Councillors are sometimes found 'bending' the rules (for instance, those governing building development), responding to parochial political demands and 'doing favours' as a result of their personal involvement. This occasionally shades into outright corruption, particularly where councils exercise discretion over major development projects, as several cases of council dismissals have revealed. While it is easy to exaggerate the extent of local government corruption, council affairs do provide a happy hunting ground for a small minority of self-seeking individuals.

Although council politics are different simply by virtue of being local, the major political parties have not entirely ignored local government. Particularly in the metropolitan central cities and larger suburban and town councils, parties have stood candidates and sought to gain control. One of the reasons behind Labor Party participation has been to combat the power of local social and economic elites. Until quite recently, the Liberal Party eschewed formal participation in local politics, probably because its natural supporters were already in control. Partly in response to Labor Party involvement, there has been a trend towards more overt participation by the conservative parties.

The parties have often faced the embarrassment of a poor showing against groups of local 'independents' because local issues and personal followings cut across patterns of partisan allegiance. This is symptomatic of a wider dilemma. Party ideologies and policies are not always directly relevant in local matters and most party activists with political ambitions set their sights on higher things. In fact, those who stand under the party banner are often motivated as much by local as by party concerns. This raises difficulties for party organisations in council politics, as local allegiances and parochial issues will sometimes be a more pressing influence on party councillors than 'party policy'. In recent years, for instance, a number of Labor Party councillors on the City of Sydney council have openly rebelled against the party, largely for these reasons. In the inner cities, 'grass roots' movements of resident action groups protesting at city development and poor services have arisen outside the party political framework, providing a new 'progressive' vehicle for urban reform and adding fuel to internal factional disputes in the Labor Party.

Thus, local issues do spill over into other political arenas. Social movements arising from local protests against urban development in the 1970s became significant forces in state politics (Painter, 1977). Sometimes, councils represent these political interests in broader conflicts. As local government has acquired important functions in the town planning sphere and expanded its involvement in social expenditures, its political profile has been raised. There have been particularly fierce battles over planning issues between state governments and councils governing the central districts of Melbourne and Sydney, leading to the dismissal of these city councils (Melbourne in 1981 and Sydney in 1987). In both cases, councillors representing residents of inner suburbs resisted schemes for intensive redevelopment in the central business districts, and business interests lobbied successfully for state government intervention.

Local democracy

Advocates of local government have always highlighted its special virtues as a democratic institution because, to use a common cliché, it is 'close to the people' and permits local choice and diversity. However, Australian local government does not measure up well by some of these criteria. While most councils are small and hence, in a literal sense, 'close to the people', they have limited powers and capacity for local choice, and are constrained by state government oversight. As to accessibility and responsiveness, the record is uneven.

In a representative democracy politicians are expected to be responsive partly because of their fear of not being re-elected. This model of electoral accountability requires, among other things, an electorate that is active and interested, and elections that are competitive. Neither is always true of local government. Where voting at local elections is voluntary (Victoria South Australia, Western Australia and Tasmania), average turnouts vary between 5 and 45 percent (Chapman and Wood, 1984: 57). Even compulsory voting in New South Wales rarely encourages more than 70 percent to vote. In addition, except in metropolitan councils, where elections are often fiercely contested, uncontested elections are common due to a dearth of candidates. In 1976/78 only 35 percent of vacancies were contested in Victoria; in the same period in New South Wales 39 percent of New South Wales councillors were returned unopposed, as were 70 percent in Tasmania at the 1980 elections, when there was a 29 percent turnout in contested seats (Chapman and Wood, 1984: 54). Small, rural councils in particular normally attract little active participation; on the other hand, some metropolitan council elections are fiercely contested and local issues can transform a relatively docile political community into a volatile, active one.

While the electoral sanction cannot always be relied upon to ensure responsiveness in local representatives, theories of representation suggest other ways that responsiveness may be assured. It has often been suggested that the best hope for democracy lies not in an active citizenry but in a political elite that espouses a 'democratic culture': representatives will fulfil their democratic obligations because they believe they should or because they are conforming to a norm. Here, the crux of the matter is whether we can have faith in the character of councillors as representatives who accept the necessary restraints and obligations. In fact, councils contain both the selfless community servant and the venal self-server, and all shades in between. Councillors can sometimes be responsive to and generously supportive of community groups and residents and at other times arrogant and exclusive or involved in somewhat shady deals with their powerful friends. The picture varies enormously across local government and over time. In sum, it is very hard to sustain the generalisations often made about the 'special virtues' of local government as a democratic institution.

Council management

Local government Acts prescribe quite closely the way local governments are organised and staffed, with only a few variations from state to state. Councils are usually quite small bodies, most falling in the range of between six and thirteen elected members. The mayor, who chairs council meetings and sometimes acts as a de facto chief executive, is, on most councils, elected each year by the council from among its members. There is no distinct, formally constituted political executive like a cabinet or ministry. Instead, it is common for councils to divide into committees, each responsible for a particular field of administration—like engineering works or planning and building controls. Committees consider matters in detail and make recommendations to the whole council, which meets every few weeks. The permanent staff is responsible to the council and is normally divided into a number of departments under chief officers who have specialised qualifications, for instance in engineering or town planning. The chief administrative officer is the council clerk.

Within the council, chief officers, the mayor and councillors who chair committees are normally the key decision makers. The clerk in particular, being at the centre of communications and in constant touch with both staff and councillors, is in a position of great potential influence.

One of the principle management problems is that councillors are not prepared to delegate powers over detailed decisions to officials. The result is often delays, inconsistent application of policies and clogged decision-making processes, while skilled staff feel frustrated at the 'meddling' of amateurs in their spheres of technical competence.

A number of official inquiries into local council management have claimed that councils lack management direction and have no effective procedures for formulating objectives, determining policy priorites or reviewing performance (Bains, 1978; Victoria, 1979). Recommendations include a clearer delineation between the respective roles of elected councillors, who should set objectives and exercise corporate oversight, and officials, who should be left to manage, preferably through a central management team to overcome departmental fragmentation (Bains, 1978). Change has been slow, partly because councillors often have little acquaintance with modern management methods. Many of them take the view that 'strategy', 'forward planning' and the like are far less important than the kind of detailed case work that directly assists their constituents.

Local government boundaries

As with all other matters relating to local government, the boundaries of councils are subject to state legislation. It has long been argued that many councils are too small or that particular boundaries are illogical. However, proposals to amalgamate councils often provoke fierce opposition, and schemes of wholesale boundary reform have rarely borne fruit. Some changes have been brought about. For instance, in New South Wales, a permanent Local Government Boundaries Commission has achieved amalgamations, resulting in a reduction in the number of councils between 1972 and 1986 from 223 to 175.

Most proposals to reduce the number of councils rest on arguments about administrative efficiency and economies of scale (ACIR, 1984). Thus, it is claimed that the large number of small councils, each with its basic complement of officials, duplicates administrative expenses (Easton and Thomson, 1987). For some services, there may be 'economies of scale' to be achieved in a larger area, for instance through the ability to purchase more cost-effective modern equipment or to employ more specialised staff than smaller councils can afford. However, the evidence on this is not conclusive, and there is no universal 'optimal' size of a local council (National Inquiry into Local Government Finance, 1985: 372–3).

Efficiency is not the only criterion. A common claim is that smaller councils are 'more democratic'—a dubious proposition, as already discussed. The claim often comes from local elites with vested interests in local control. The current trend is towards piecemeal amalgamations, particularly under the stimulus of Local Government Grants Commissions, which have argued that grants to local government should not be used to prop up small, inefficient councils.

At various times, suggestions have been made that regional bodies would be a good idea. Gough Whitlam (1971: 11) foresaw them replacing state governments. The Whitlam Government encouraged councils to get together in regional organisations in order to coordinate some planning and expenditure, but only a few of these organisations developed a life of their own. It is highly unlikely that a fourth tier of government is viable, and it is probably unnecessary. However, state governments and departments have made frequent use of regional advisory bodies for such things as regional planning.

In theory, considerable benefits would flow from cooperation between adjoining councils for specific purposes where local areas are too small for effective administration but where amalgamation is considered undesirable and a separate regional body would be an unnecessary duplication. Councils often need advice, encouragement or stronger measures to get them to join together in this way, and disputes and demarcation squabbles are common. The New South Wales Local Government Act permits the formation of single-purpose county councils to facilitate joint action. Electricity sales and distribution have been organised in this way. For some other major regional services, such as water and sewerage or waste disposal in metropolitan areas, special purpose regional bodies have been set up over and above local government.

Ultimately, the issue of local government boundaries is a political one. Successful campaigns of resistance often result in proposals being placed in the 'too hard basket' by state governments. The political considerations at play include party advantage. In New South Wales, successive Liberal/Country Party and Labor governments have quite cynically redrawn the boundaries of the City of Sydney council to ensure a majority for their respective parties.

Conclusion

The importance of local government is far greater than the figures on its limited role in the overall system of government would suggest. Councils are sometimes aloof and insensitive to community interests and even, on occasion, corrupt. But an active, concerned citizenry would probably have more chance of remedying such ills in local government than in the more distant, large-scale and bureaucratic systems of public administration that exist at other levels of government.

References

Australian Council for Inter-government Relations (ACIR) (1984) *Local Government Boundary Reorganisation* Hobart: ACIR

Bains, M.A. (1978) *Report to the Minister for Local Government into Local Authority Management in New South Wales* Sydney: Government Printer

Bowman, M. (1983) 'Local government in Australia', in M. Bowman and W. Hampton (eds) *Local Democracies* Melbourne: Longman Cheshire

Chapman, R.J.K. and Wood, M. (1984) *Australian Local Government: The Federal Dimension* Sydney: George Allen and Unwin

Easton, S.A. and Thomson, N.J. (1987) 'Scale economies in the administration of local government' *Australian Journal of Public Administration* 46, 3, pp. 293–300

National Inquiry into Local Government Finance (1985) *Report* Canberra: AGPS

Painter, M. (1973) *A Comparative Analysis of the Decision Making Process in Six Local Government Councils in Sydney* Ph.D. Thesis, Australian National University

—— (1974) 'Parochialism and localism in local council elections in suburban Sydney' *Public Administration* (Sydney) 33, 4, pp. 346–59

—— (1975) 'Parochialism, particularism and maladministration in local government', in R.N. Spann, G.R. Curnow (eds) *Public Policy and Administration in Australia: A Reader* Sydney: John Wiley

—— (1977) 'New forces in state politics' *Current Affairs Bulletin* 53, 8, pp. 16–28

Power, J., Wettenhal, R. and Halligan, J. (eds) (1981) *Local Government Systems of Australia* Canberra: Advisory Council for Inter-government Relations, Information Paper No. 7

Whitlam, E.G. (1971) 'A New Federalism' *Australian Quarterly* 43(3), pp. 6–17

Wild, R.A. (1974) *Bradstow* Sydney: Angus and Robertson

Part Three

SOCIO-POLITICAL FORCES

14 The structures of inequality

Michael Hogan

'We hold these truths to be self evident', proclaims the United States' Declaration of Independence, 'that all men are created equal, that they are endowed by their Creator with certain unalienable Rights...' These are stirring sentiments in one of the foundation documents of modern liberalism and they certainly represent the aspirations of millions of people throughout the world. Unfortunately, however, the fundamental equality of people is not nearly as self-evident as Thomas Jefferson and his colleagues were claiming on 4 July 1776. Much more obvious is the fact that, however they were created, people in virtually every society are very unequal according to almost any measure imaginable. Putting aside questions of the inequality of people according to their age, health, strength, beauty or intelligence, the more directly political problems are associated with inequalities of income, wealth, legal status, social prestige and political influence. These are often referred to by the general term: 'social inequality'.

If the equality of people is not obvious in fact, then neither is it obvious what should be the correct attitude to take towards social inequality. Is it good or bad? Should societies promote inequality or struggle to reduce it? These are normative questions about which people can be expected to disagree—and in fact do disagree, often violently. The discussion in this chapter cannot solve those disagreements, but it can help to clarify some of the points about the nature of inequality upon which such value judgements are often based.

The first thing that needs to be said is that any discussion of power and politics assumes that social inequalities exist. The first three chapters of this book would make no sense at all if political resources were distributed equally between people and if there could be no changes in such a distribution. Without at least the possibility of social inequality there would be no role for politics; and once there is any kind of political process some unequal distribution of political resources is inevitable.

The fundamental questions being asked in this chapter are about the nature of social inequality. Is it something, like beauty or intelligence, which seems to be fairly randomly distributed? If this is the case then most of the heat goes out of the debate about equality; individuals with few resources may complain of their lot, but they cannot blame anything in the political system for their situation. Or is social inequality, as many theorists claim, something which is distributed in such a way as to allot more resources systematically to some groups of people rather than to others? Do all citizens have equal access to the arenas in which important social and political decisions are made, or do some groups of people always tend to have better access? If this latter is the case, then the normative question follows: what should be the attitude of people to the structures of society that enshrine such inequality and give greater power to some over others?

These arguments do not take place just in the realm of ideas—which one can debate backwards and forwards in a fairly dispassionate manner. The term 'social theory' often seems to have that purely intellectual connotation. Yet, all the theories discussed below also have an ideological dimension. They contain, implicitly or explictly, sets of values about how society should be arranged. Many of their proponents are quite open in admitting that there is a political programme attached to their preferred theory. As Karl Marx proclaimed in the last of his Theses on Feuerbach, written in 1845: 'The philosophers have only interpreted the world, in various ways; the point, however, is to change it' (Tucker, 1972: 109).

Theories of elitism

Throughout history the overwhelmingly dominant attitude to social inequality has been to accept it as normal and even to embrace it as something desirable. In this respect the words of the American Declaration of Independence that head this chapter expressed a point of view which, for its own time and for most previous eras, was quite revolutionary. As shall be seen, however, the liberal doctrine it enshrines itself accepts the inevitability of many forms of social inequality and is by no means the most radical challenge to inequality in the contemporary world. At the heart of elitism is a denial that all men are equal—at least in their political capabilities. As Geraint Parry wrote (1969: 30): 'The core of the elitist doctrine is that there may exist in any society a minority of the population which takes the major decisions in society'.

Before the age of the American and French Revolutions it was accepted by all but a few people on the fringes of European society that some people should have more power, prestige and wealth than others. Kings should rule; aristocrats should be influential and wealthy; the common people should leave politics to their betters and not put on airs above their station. Writers from the Greek philosopher Plato in the fourth century BC through to the grandfather of English liberalism, John Locke in the seventeenth century AD, provided philosophical justification for various forms of inequality. There have been egalitarian and democratic ideas expressed throughout history, but it was only after the age of revolutions opened up the possibility of forms of democracy in which the common people could share in state power that such ideas gained effective political force.

The first reaction to democratic egalitarianism was fundamentally conservative, and this remains today one of the founts of elitist thought. The political leaders who opposed the various reform bills, which extended the franchise in nineteenth century Britain, appealed to a set of ideas that can be traced back at least as far as Plato: the common people are politically incompetent; government is a business that requires education, breeding, and people with sufficient wealth to be able to devote themselves selflessly to public service; the inevitable consequence of unbridled democracy will be chaos and the breakdown of civil order in which the common people themselves will be worse off. There have been many variations of such conservative attitudes. Many quite liberal politicians of nineteenth-century Britain and Australia, for example, accepted some of these ideas at the same time as they accepted some democratic principles. The terms of the Australian constitution were hammered out in committees of such men in the 1890s. Hence the inclusion in the constitution of residual executive powers to the Crown—which reflected the political realities of a pre-democratic era. The common people, in this way of thinking, are not to be trusted with ultimate power.

Conservative values are by no means the most important source of elitist ideas. During the nineteenth century a new reaction to the existence of social inequality emerged, partly as a natural development of the now dominant economic system in Europe and America—capitalism. It was also influenced by a new scientific approach to the study of society, which borrowed some of the ideas of the biologist Charles Darwin. One of the assumptions of capitalism is that the system works by the cooperation of capital (amalgamated into the control of a relatively small section of the community) and labour (represented in the mass of people who comprise the wage-earning workforce). There is another assumption that within the section of society that possesses capital people will compete against each other to achieve profit. Some will succeed; others will fail. The ideas of what became known as 'social Darwinism' fitted in very well with this ideology. Part of Darwin's theory of the evolution of species was an explanation of progress by the natural selection of individuals and species who were better adapted to the environment. The British sociologist, Herbert Spencer, was only one of many writers of the late nineteenth century who translated this into a theory of the survival of the fittest and the law of the jungle in an economic and social environment. Entrepreneurs who adapt themselves well to the economic conditions become successful, rich and powerful; those who do not are weeded out. Workers with appropriate skills will make a good living; those who cannot or will not adapt themselves will go to the wall. Moreover, that is the way things should be. For the community or the state to come to the assistance of the weaker participants is to prevent the effective working of the marketplace, to impede economic progress, and ultimately to work against the interests even of the weaker members of society. In contemporary Australia this way of thinking is espoused by economic rationalists of the so-called New Right. Far from being conservative, it is quite radical in its insistence that the motor of progress for society as a whole is the incentive that can make a small proportion of the society very rich or very powerful. Those who miss out are encouraged to compete harder.

At the same time as this harsh economic doctrine of the survival of the fittest was becoming popular, another way of understanding society, which was just as elitist in the political arena, was gaining strength. Among academics who were inventing the modern discipline of sociology it was customary to explain many of the characteristics of society by using a simple analogy of a living organism. These 'organicist' social theorists, given respectability by Auguste Comte and Herbert Spencer, and represented most explicitly by nineteenth century French sociologist Emile Durkheim, compared society with a human body. Like a body it has different parts and organs. Like a body some parts are more important than others. The basic political function of decision making—of ruling—is exercised by the head of the body. Parts of the body with other functions should get on with the job of being hands or eyes and should leave the business of politics to those members who make up the head. With proper direction from the head, all the other parts and organs will work in harmony and the society will be healthy. Without this there will be disorder and collapse. This social theory was in direct conflict with assumptions of liberal democracy such as widespread franchise and the principle of majority rule. It was to find its political application in the fascist and authoritarian regimes of Italy's Mussolini and Spain's Franco in the first half of the twentieth century. Newer versions of organicist or corporatist ways of thinking, seen in Australia in such experiments of industrial cooperation as the National Summit and the Accord sponsored by Prime Minister Bob Hawke after his first electoral victory in 1983, are not so explicitly elitist.

The golden age of elite theory in the modern world lasted from the end of the nineteenth century through to World War II. It owed its strength to political conditions in Europe at the time rather than to conservative, Darwinian, organicist or any other set of social doctrines. The circumstance was the fact that most of the European nations that had experimented with democratic forms of government were experiencing considerable political turmoil. Many observers contrasted this with the highly successful, and quite authoritarian, Prussian regime of Bismarck at the height of his power. A number of authors argued that the turmoil of democratic politics was only to be expected since, in the very nature of the exercise of power, only elites can or should rule. In this period, Italian theorist Gaetano Mosca, one of the ideological sources for fascism, argued in *The Ruling Class* (1939; originally published in 1896) that mass rule is both impossible and undesirable. Rule should be by political elites, not by the 'people'. A more complex argument with a similar conclusion was presented by Mosca's compatriot Vilfredo Pareto, who added an explanation of the 'circulation of elites' (1935). The fact that some elites lose power was no obstacle to a general argument that elites will always rule. A study by German sociologist Robert Michels of the internal workings of political parties seemed to confirm his 'iron law of oligarchy' when, even in a supposedly democratic socialist political party, actual control was exercised by the few rather than the many. His *Political Parties*, first published in 1911, does not rejoice in elitism but pessimistically examines '. . . if, and in what degree, democracy is an ideal which we can never hope to realize in practice' (1962: 368).

So all-pervasive was the elitist argument in the first half of the twentieth century that some democratic theorists believed that its principles had to be incorporated, rather than opposed. Probably the most representative of this brand of 'democratic elitism' was Joseph Schumpeter, whose *Capitalism, Socialism and Democracy* argued that 'the democratic method is that institutional arrangement for arriving at political decisions in which individuals acquire the power to decide by means of a competitive struggle for the people's vote' (1943: 269). Democracy in this vision means voting—nothing more. Elections decide which elites will rule and the people have no other role in the democratic process till the next election.

Schumpeter's argument marked the high water mark of the acceptance of elitism as an unchallengeable doctrine. World War II made people wary of the political consequences of elitism when translated into the authoritarian regimes of Hitler, Mussolini or Stalin. One direction of attack came out of an appreciation of the role of pressure groups influencing government decisions at times other than when elections were due. This became part of the wider liberal doctrine of pluralism, which is discussed separately below. A completely different approach was to accept the existence of, or tendency towards, elite power, yet to repudiate the normative aspects of elitism. Commenting on the American democratic system, C. Wright Mills described the leaders of the major political and ideological institutions, together with those of the military–industrial complex, as *The Power Elite* (1956), whose power, he argued, should be restrained and balanced by better democratic forms. An Australian version of this thesis can be found in E.W. Campbell's book, *The 60 Rich Families Who Own Australia* (1963). Although works like these tend to come out of a Marxist tradition, they emphasise the personal power of a group of individuals rather than the more structural class analysis of classic Marxism. Common to most elitist theories is an assumption that the individual members of the elite act in some concerted fashion. In its extreme form this becomes a theory of actual conspiracy among those members to exclude others and to counteract any mass influences. This sometimes causes confusion for students who think that if there is no conspiracy then there can be no elite. An elitist argument does not need to be justified by some assertion about smoke-filled rooms.

Elite theories cannot simply be brushed away. In contemporary Australia they are still important—if not as completely dominant as in the first half of the twentieth century. They take two main forms. It is clear that theories of class (whether radical or conservative) are elitist. These are discussed separately below. Otherwise the principal contemporary source of elite theory and research is in the behavioural tradition of social sciences such as sociology, political science and economics. It is commonplace for researchers to try to identify key personnel in different institutions or decision-making processes. The assumption, even when not stated, is that it is the few, not the many, who are of interest in understanding society. The most extensive Australian study that explores the theoretical and political implications of this form of elitism is a major work by John Higley, Desley Deacon and Don Smart, entitled *Elites in Australia* (1979). In contemporary debate the strongest alternative to this style of elite theory is the dominant ideology of pluralism. However, even before pluralism became so popular, a defence of more democratic forms of rule had been given powerful support in the classic doctrines of nineteenth-century liberalism.

Political implications of liberalism

A key to an understanding of liberalism is the emphasis that it places on the role of the individual in society. The ideology had its origins in the social ideas of the European enlightenment, which fed into the great political revolutions at the end of the eighteenth century in America and France. In this sense its earliest ideas—individual freedom and equality of all people before the law—were a direct challenge to established elitist principles and provided part of the driving force of the American and French Revolutions. However, liberalism became a full-blown social theory only when its principles were seen as complementary to the new economic system that was being ushered in at the same time; liberalism became the ideology of nineteenth-century capitalism. Individual freedom achieved a context; it was for the purpose of fostering individual initiative and competition, thus providing the economic engine of capitalism and the social and political dynamism of liberal democracy. Liberalism is not a theory or ideology that can be simply defined and nailed down. It has no bible. Rather, it has had various writers (for example, Locke, Bentham, James Mill and J.S. Mill) who have contributed something to its development at different stages. As capitalism has gone through a number of distinct phases since the early nineteenth century, and as the forms of modern democracy have developed over the same period, so liberalism has adjusted and taken on various forms.

In Australia the political campaigns in the first half of the nineteenth century to achieve some measure of self-government for the colonies from Britain were led by men like W.C. Wentworth who were happy to describe themselves as 'liberals'. The term at that time tended to be used to distinguish them from other colonial 'conservatives' who resisted the pressures towards democracy and colonial autonomy. By the second half of the nineteenth century virtually all elected politicians in the Australian colonies regarded themselves as liberals. Quite clearly, however, the term covered a very wide range of opinion on matters of economic and social policy, and the range could be appreciated in the different personality and policy factions of colonial politics during that era. By the beginning of the twentieth century the term 'liberal' was being used increasingly to distinguish the established elites of the colonial parliaments from the challenge of 'radicals' such as the new representatives of the trade union and socialist movements who were creating the modern Australian Labor Party. The antecedents of the contemporary Liberal Party, which in its present form was founded by R.G. Menzies in 1944, date from this period. By the second half of the twentieth century an ideology of liberal democracy—which is supported in some form by virtually all Australian members of Parliament of whatever party—expresses the main alternative to communist or socialist forms of democracy. Liberalism is part of the ideology of the 'first world' (capitalist, economically developed, with some form of party competition) as opposed to the 'second world' (socialist, economically developed, with one unchallengeable party). The 'first' and the 'second world' compete to export their economic and political forms to the 'third world'.

Although liberalism is primarily a set of assertions about the role of the individual in society, these carry important implications for related notions of the proper role of the state. One of the basic liberal principles has always been that the distribution of resources in society should be determined by the laws of the marketplace, rather than by government intervention. Socially and politically the principle came to be expressed in terms of a minimal, non-interfering, role for the state in all areas of human life. People should be able to lead their own lives without having to worry about the state telling them, for example, what church they could attend, what books they could read, what friends they could associate with, or what kind of sexual life they could lead. It is a principle of the political autonomy of each area of human endeavour. Some common liberal dogmas are: the separation of church and state, that politics should not be brought into sport, that there must be a free press, and that the law should not trespass into the bedrooms of citizens. People should also, of course, be able to become rich or poor, successful or not, and powerful or powerless, without interference by governments.

Although liberalism in its eighteenth century origins was an ideology of individual equality, its evolution has highlighted the fact that this is a very restricted notion of equality. Equality of opportunity, yes; actual equality, no. In Australia during the 1960s many observers began to point to the obvious inequalities of wealth, income, education, health care, housing, access to community services and general lifestyle. One product of this concern was the Australian Government's Commission of Inquiry into Poverty, whose First Main Report asserted that: 'Poverty is not just a personal attribute; it arises out of the organisation of society' (1975: 1). It is clear that what is meant is that the pursuance of liberal principles of competition, free enterprise, and non-interference by the state will inevitably lead to noticeable levels of social disadvantage for some members of society. One way of expressing this is to say that there is a price to pay to maintain the esteemed value of freedom for all; the price is—poverty for some.

One liberal response to the perceived dilemma of having to choose between freedom and equality in a liberal society is to emphasise equality of opportunity. The Whitlam Labor Government from 1972 till 1975 tried to reform liberal Australia by introducing policies aimed at restoring genuine equality of opportunity by restructuring areas such as health care, education, public housing and social welfare. But more radical critics of Australian liberalism have challenged even the reality of the original fundamental value. Is there really freedom for all if some citizens can afford to pay for almost unlimited choices, while others can scarcely afford to stay alive? Consequently, proponents of a more radical class analysis of Australian society (see below) suggest that the only way out is to dismantle some of the liberal structure—to demand greater state intervention, even at the cost of some individual freedom—in order to eliminate structural disadvantage and inequality. At the same time, not surprisingly, there has been a reaction from more traditional supporters of liberalism. The argument of economic rationalists in the so-called New Right of Australian politics is that the worst inequalities are the product of government restriction on free enterprise. Let governments stop penalising initiative by heavy taxation, which is wasted on the non-productive disadvantaged section of society. The result, they argue, will be a richer Australia for all. With a larger cake even the smallest slices will be bigger than the present crumbs distributed by the welfare state. Quite clearly this fundamental dilemma of liberalism provides much of the agenda for contemporary Australian political debate.

Theories of class

Not all theories of class are radical. The conservative reaction to democratic movements mentioned above assumed that a class structure was desirable in society. People belong to separate classes, with different levels of access to power—and this is the way things should be. People in any society will be and should be different in their social origins, their wealth and income, their education, their styles of dress, their accents and even in their dreams and aspirations. In all European countries this was plainly the situation during the nineteenth century. The fundamental idea in all theories of class is that society is best understood by looking at the way people are grouped rather than by focussing on the role of individuals. The word 'class' gained currency from the European experience at the beginning of the Industrial Revolution. Previously the basic divisions in European society tended to be referred to as distinct 'orders' or 'estates'. Outside Europe there were similar assumptions about the necessity of some fundamental system of social inequality. Sometimes different names are used. The caste system in India, for example, was based upon a set of beliefs about the hierarchical nature of social relationships. People share characteristics with other people in their own social group; they are quite different from people in other classes or castes; this pattern is reinforced by the social values propagated by the dominant religious institutions and by traditional political authority.

This way of thinking was not new in the period of the industrial and political revolutions in Europe. What was new was that there had been quite radical changes in the traditional pattern of religious and political authority since the sixteenth century and now a class vision of a properly ordered Christendom had to contend with a number of other ways of understanding society. One radical and secular alternative was liberalism, which denied the whole set of ideas and asserted that it is the individual, not social class, which is at the heart of the dynamism of modern society. At another extreme were the theories of radicals who asserted that the class nature of modern society was still fundamental, but that it needed in some way to be destroyed or overturned. The most influential figure in this tradition was Karl Marx, whose writings date from the 1840s to the 1880s. Insofar as he accepted that there were fundamental inequalities in society he fits into one part of the elitist tradition. But his attitude to inequality was that it should be fought against, not meekly accepted as the only way that society could be organised. The importance of Marx and his colleague Friedrich Engels was that they took the current conservative ideas about the class nature of society, refined them, turned them on their head, and used the resulting class analysis as an explanation of the way that capitalist society worked and as a means of predicting the way that it was likely to develop. It became much more than simply a description of the way in which some groups of people are richer, more powerful, better educated or better dressed than others. The theory had at its centre an assertion that capitalist society is driven by conflict; not the random competition between free-enterprise entrepreneurs, as liberal ideologists claimed, but a structured division of society in which one set of forces (a ruling, bourgeois, class) finds itself opposed to another (a wage-earning working class or proletariat). Their interests are irreconcileably in conflict because of the system's non-negotiable need for continuing profit. Yet capitalist society needs both classes. It can only survive by the exploitation of the working class by the ruling class. The source of profit is the value imparted by the worker, and the employer must return less than that value to the worker if any profit is to be made. Moreover, the logic of continued exploitation, added to the increasing difficulty of maintaining an adequate rate of profit, will result in the collapse of capitalism, the revolutionary replacement of the ruling class by the proletariat, and eventually the inauguration of a classless 'communist' society. This Marxist version of class was a considerable refinement of the conservative description. For Marx, the fact that people wore different clothes, went to different schools, spoke with different class accents or even had vast differences of political power was simply describing secondary characteristics. The fundamental difference between classes could be seen in their relationship with the basic structure of capitalism. Class is primarily about the economic structure, and all other aspects (social, educational, religious, political) pertain to the realm of 'superstructure', which is secondary, dependent or derivative of the economic structure. The great economic division is between that section of society that owns capital in some form, and the other section that does not—and has to sell its labour below its true value in order that capital may generate profit. Class is important not simply because it describes how people have different kinds of economic power, but because the relationship between classes in society provides the dynamism of capitalist society and, according to Marx, will eventually bring about its collapse. This is an oversimplified portrayal of the foundations of Marxist class analysis, but it does give some idea of the powerful set of ideas that were to be so influential in world history till the present day.

As with liberalism, Marxism has undergone many modifications and revisions since the mid-nineteenth century. It also has had to come to terms with the fact that capitalism has been very resourceful in adapting to changing circumstances, and especially with the much more dominant role that the state has exercised over every aspect of twentieth-century society. There are now socialist governments in many nations that claim some version of Marxism as their ruling ideology. Marx himself would be dismayed with many of the developments in so-called Marxist or communist states. Nevertheless, even within the world of liberal democracy, various versions of Marxism provide a challenging set of critical social ideas.

In Australia it has been radical critics from a Marxist tradition such as R.W. Connell who have been most assiduous in pointing out the structures of inequality in most aspects of Australian social, political and economic life. The conservative and radical traditions of class analysis have been strongest in Europe where, even today, many of the social characteristics of class-divided societies are apparent in differing accents, clothes, occupations and lifestyles. In less traditional societies, such as those of North America or Australia, class differences seem to be less obvious to the casual observer. Yet trends in behaviour can be detected when people are grouped according to various social characteristics. It is possible to make generalisations about the likely political behaviour, for example, of recently-arrived migrants, pentecostal Christians, or factory workers. Many authors use some classification of an individual's occupation in this way and use the word 'class' to describe the result. Don Aitkin, for example, in *Stability and Change in Australian Politics* (1982: 118) uses both a six-grade division of occupation (ranging from professional to unskilled manual) and a simpler two-grade classification (non-manual and manual) in order to describe aspects of the influence of class on political values and behaviour. More fundamentally, however, he depends upon the class grouping that people are prepared to use about themselves when they answer question 62(a) in his survey: 'First of all, to what class would you say you belong?' (Upper 1 percent; middle 56 percent; lower 4 percent; working 26 percent; other 2 percent; doesn't belong to any 4 percent; no such thing as social classes 3 percent; don't know 4 percent) (1982: 389). This is normally spoken of as subjective or self-perceived class. In a similar way, David Kemp, in his *Society and Electoral Behaviour in Australia*, uses both crude and sophisticated measures of class, ranging from the manual/non-manual or blue-collar/white-collar division to a complex correlation of occupation with other indicators of class such as residence, economic level, subjective class, union membership and education level (1978: 45).

It is important to recognise that the word 'class' is being used in a number of different senses. Class means something different for a Marxist scholar and for a conventional behavioural social scientist like Aitkin or Kemp. For most class theorists in the European tradition, radical and conservative, the concept is part of the central explanation of how society works. It is a dynamic concept. In the behavioural tradition the word applies to only one of many possible characteristics that must be examined to provide a portrait of the state of society at any point in time. It is a much more static concept, which does not in itself claim to explain anything. Most researchers will try to use the concept to make assertions about causal relationships within a society, but the hypotheses upon which such assertions are founded need to be introduced from outside—perhaps from guesses based on earlier studies, or even as responses to ideological assertions of radical scholars. Class is a tool for testing an extremely wide variety of possible explanations, rather than being an explanation itself as it is in the earlier sense. Many modern studies in the behavioural tradition attempt to avoid the ambiguity built in to the word by choosing a different word, such as 'occupational class', 'subjective class' or, very commonly, 'socio-economic status'. This last term, sometimes contracted to its initials SES, refers to more sophisticated analyses, customarily compiled with the help of computers, which involve relationships between a number of different yet related characteristics such as occupation, education, ethnic origin, place or style of residence, and subjective class. This attempt of scholars to distance themselves from such ambiguities can be seen in the massive Australian Values Study Survey (1983), where questions were asked about the occupation, income, residence, education and values of respondents—so that it would be quite simple for researchers to compile any number of categories of SES. Yet the authors of the study leave them as separate variables; there is no attempt to specify any variables as measures of 'class' or 'SES'.

The behavioural approach to the study of class or SES shares some characteristics with the liberal tradition of scholarship in which it flourishes. There is an assumption that the fundamental unit of analysis is the individual. The typical research tool is the computer-processed questionnaire survey in which different categories are simply amalgamations of individuals. The amalgamations are expressed in percentage terms, with the expectation that the percentages will change in surveys taken at a different time or for a different place, as individuals cross from one category to another. There is also an assumption that the research is objective and 'value-free'. In this, the behavioural approach is directly opposed by most radical versions of class analysis, which explictly recognise the ideological content of social research and deny that any such studies can be free of the value biases of their authors. Probably the most powerful development of liberal thinking, which also assumes that people are grouped into categories, but which provides a more dynamic and explanatory alternative to radical class theory than do behavioural versions of socio-economic status, is modern political pluralism.

The pluralist alternative

It was not surprising that, after World War II, with its discredited totalitarian governments, a reaction against elitist theories of rule gained momentum. One source of this reaction was among American liberal scholars who examined the actual distribution of power in cities and local communities and seemed to find that power was not narrowly concentrated into the hands of a few key decision makers, but was shared among a wide spectrum of influential people. Scholars such as Robert Dahl (1967) and Robert Presthus (1970) argued that power is diffuse, not concentrated. Other scholars, in Europe and America, examined the growth of pressure groups in order to argue that governments, although they may have a central position in any system of power, do not have control. Instead, so it was argued, they merely respond to the powerful forces acting on them.

In some ways the theory of pluralism, now dominant in conventional analyses of politics in societies like Australia, is best understood as a twentieth-century refinement of liberalism that has placed the emphasis in social and economic competition on large and small groups rather than on isolated individuals. The theory took on its inevitable ideological dimension when pluralism was presented as the ideal model of democracy: the 'people' have real power because they influence government decisions at every stage of the life of a government; it is not just at election times that the people rule. As a refinement of liberalism it can be regarded as the political and social ideology that accompanies the versions of capitalism in the second half of the twentieth century. Pluralism has become the dominant ideology of the anti-communist west.

Pluralism shares with liberalism a normative assertion about the minimal role of the state. Yes, the state appears to be more important than any that the laissez-faire theorists had known, but the appearence is deceptive. For pluralists, the state acts as a referee between important associations, who interact in a the complex web of self-interested pressure groups. The closer the state approaches the level of these competing groups, so the theory goes, the better it can exercise this role. So, governments are best when they are broken up into small units, decentralised, and closer to the people. Again, pluralism shares with liberalism a belief that that the dynamism in modern capitalist society comes from free-enterprise competition. But the main competitive actors are companies, corporations and pressure groups rather than individuals. (This emphasis on the integration of individuals into society through a multitude of voluntary associations was borrowed from the classic French sociologist Emile Durkheim rather than from the liberal tradition.)

Pluralism also shares with liberalism the confidence that competition within society is benign. Many pluralist theorists assumed that competing groups would tend to balance one another in a political variation on a Newtonian principle: that to every action there is a nearly equal and approximately opposite reaction. Along with this notion of countervailing power comes a democratic assertion that is much stronger than some earlier liberal theory, which concentrated on justifications of electoral and franchise reform. For pluralists the right to vote in elections is only one small part of a very wide spectrum of political participation. Moreover, the concentration on pressure groups seemed to provide a further guarantee of freedom, which is contrasted with the alleged lack of freedom in the communist world: legal rights are protected by the people themselves through their competitive political activity.

As with all important theories about society, there is no one satisfactory definition of pluralism. Often, for example, the word is used in modern writing to express a less explicitly political ideology. It is used to describe a characteristic of societies such as the United States or Australia where there can be found people with widely different ethnic origins or religious beliefs. In this sense a pluralist society is contrasted with a culturally homogeneous society. In Australia in recent years the word 'multiculturalism' has become more popular to express the social theory that approves cultural diversity, even if only for the cultural richness with which it is claimed to be associated. More fundamentally, the key political implication of this version of pluralism is that there is, or there should be, tolerance of cultural differences and acceptance of diversity. Some relationship of this with the political ideology of pluralism is clear enough, but its emphasis is on the need for social harmony between culturally distinct sections of society rather than on the political value of competition and conflict.

More than any other important contemporary ideology pluralism denies that there is significant structured inequality in its host nations. As in classic liberalism there will be actual inequalities between people according to wealth or power; otherwise, competition would be meaningless. Yet, so it is claimed, a genuinely pluralist society provides structural mechanisms whose primary functions are to break down concentrations of power and to distribute political influence as widely as possible throughout the community. The more pluralist a society is, the more equal will be the distribution of power. It should come as no surprise to find that it is precisely here that the critics of pluralism have concentrated their attack. If the principle is valid then it should be possible to test it empirically: does a pluralist society like America or Australia have a relatively egalitarian division of power? Moreover, neither should it be surprising that the most vigorous criticisms of pluralism come from a radical and Marxist tradition that has always asserted an exactly opposite principle: the more capitalist a society is, the more unequal will be its distribution of power.

Attacks on pluralism

Modern critics of pluralism have refused to accept either the descriptive or the normative aspects of pluralism. It is undeniable that there are, in societies like Australia, many pressure groups that seek to influence government policy on almost every aspect of life. In this respect pluralist theorists have added to the accepted body of knowledge about the working of politics. But almost every step past that is strongly contested. Does the existence of all these pressure groups mean that power is widely distributed in society? Is participation, in fact, as widespread as the pluralists would contend? Are all such groups notionally equal in resources, or do some always tend to win and others always tend to lose? Is there still an elite that dictates the fundamental nature of government decisions? Are the roles of governments and the state as neutral as pluralists argue?

One obvious attack on pluralism is simply a refinement of earlier elitist theories such as Michels' 'iron law of oligarchy'. There may be a multiplicity of pressure groups, but in any of them the executive decision makers are a very small proportion of the total membership. According to this view, at the top of any significant pressure group, such as a trade union, employers' organisation or environmental association, there will be an elite that really runs things. The president of the Australian Council of Trade Unions has more power in the ACTU than most members of the executive for whom that forum is only one of their concerns, and any member of the executive has much more power over trade union affairs than the majority of trade union rank and file members, who do not even bother to vote in union elections. All that pluralism would mean, if this attack is successful, is that an observer has to look a little harder in order to find the members of the elite in any society. Pluralism becomes merely a smokescreen concealing the basically elite nature of modern society.

A more radical attack would suggest that the very multiplicity of pressure groups is itself an illusion. Some pressure groups have more power, or a more direct access to influence, than others. The function of the pressure group system is seen as deceiving the majority of the population that participation is widespread, while allowing the reality that, for example, the representatives of big business will usually get what they want and environmental protesters will be fobbed off with an occasional symbolic victory. According to this criticism, expressed clearly by Playford (1968), the pluralist assumption of countervailing power or the analogy of 'equal and opposite' power is fundamentally wrong. Moreover, by successfully propagating an ideology of such balance of power, pluralism legitimises the actual unequal distribution and persuades members of the community to continue playing a game that they can never hope to win.

A further focus of criticism is that shared with earlier versions of liberalism—the role given to the state in pluralist ideology. It is, in fact, quite difficult to sustain an argument that governments have only a minimal and adjudicating role in modern capitalist societies. The reality in most developed nations is that the state is getting more and more involved in 'big government', rather than withdrawing into some impartial referee role between competing interest groups. In Australia, for example, the European settlement began as a government initiative in the colonial era, and private enterprise followed. In the modern Australian economy the state is called upon to defend the interests of almost all exporting primary producers, with a resulting flood of legislation and regulation about tariff protection, quality control, credit facilities, and an infrastructure for international marketing. Moreover, the state competes with private enterprise in areas such as banking, airlines, housing, health care and education. All successful capitalist economies are mixed economies, with the state and private enterprise cooperating and competing in the marketplace. Nevertheless, there is a very strong pluralist and liberal normative counter-attack to this trend, with 'New Right' and monetarist theorists arguing that capitalism will work even better when governments withdraw from the market place and go back to their adjudicating role. Part of the contemporary Australian argument about 'privatisation' is made according to these principles—that governments should sell off profit-making state enterprises in order that the private sector may become stronger and healthier. It is only part of the argument; privatisation is also attractive for some government leaders because the sale of such assets brings increased revenue in the short term to government itself. In this latter view, and in the opinion of many opponents of privatisation policies, especially within the labour movement, the state is not merely a referee; it is one of the dominant players in the game. The state is in the game either to protect its own interests (the opinion of many bureaucrats and government ministers) or to protect the weak in society from the depredations of an unfettered private sector (the argument of many on the left of the labour movement).

The fundamental nature of most attacks on pluralist ideology lies in the rejection of pluralist claims that advanced capitalism has swept away earlier structured forms of inequality in society and replaced them with an open, multi-competitive society in which almost all members have a chance of access to wealth, power and prestige. In post-war Australia the years of prosperity and improving standards of living seemed to indicate that, at least in Australia, there might be something in the pluralist doctrine. By the end of the 1960s, however, society started to be made aware of the intractable nature of social inequalities. The Henderson Report on poverty in Australia, for example, made a strong argument that the prosperity had by no means been equally shared and that large sections of society were systematically disadvantaged by the pluralist rules of play. In recent years pluralists have hit back with a new argument that the structures of inequality survive precisely because pluralism has not been allowed to flourish in its pure form. Let the state get out of the business of employing, producing, investing, borrowing, regulating and taxing—or so it is argued—and a truly pluralist system will emerge.

Who to believe?

With contrasting theories about the nature of social inequality, how is one to decide which one or which combination to choose? Where does the truth lie? In the first place a student should be aware that all these theories have a strong ideological content. Like proselytising religions, ideologies are about convincing people. In a similar sense, the word 'belief' is an appropriate word. Whatever the truth or falsity of the many contradictory claims of different ideologies, many people will give their allegiance almost by a leap of faith. The reasons for belief lie partly in the realm of emotions, traditional inclinations, family or social cohesion, or camouflaged self-interest. If this is the only basis for belief then rational arguments are irrelevant to the person concerned. One believes because one wants to. One is a pluralist, a Marxist, a liberal, an elitist...by conviction.

Yet, to continue the analogy with religious belief, there may well be a rational, arguable, basis for belief. Is one ideology demonstrably true and the others as demonstrably false? This is a quite complicated matter to sort out. The first thing that needs to be said is that most of these theories are important because they attempt to explain some of the important characteristics of society. An explanation is not true or false; it can be an adequate or less than adequate explanation, depending on how successful it is in explaining a very complicated set of features in society. It can never be a completely adequate explanation because, in the nature of human knowledge, it is impossible to be sure that someone will not discover something about society tomorrow which will make necessary a complete revision of today's assumptions. Explanations are the product of people's brains; they do not inhere in physical things or in communities of people. There is, however, at least one customary test of the adequacy of any explanation. If it can successfully predict what is likely to happen in the future, then it will be more acceptable than a theory that continually fails in its predictions. Unfortunately, however, this is a very slippery tool to use. Any theory that has survived for a length of time will have had successes and failures of prediction based on its principles. What happens then is that later proponents of the theory modify it or revise it to take account of why some predictions were off target. Both liberalism and Marxism, for example, have gone through numerous revisions in this way. The failure to predict, in fact, is precisely the incentive for the development of stronger social theories.

The arguments used to support explanations often resort to details that claim to be factual. Here, at least, it is possible, sometimes, to test the worth of arguments. The book *Elites in Australia* claims to identify elite positions in business, trade unions, the public service, politics and other areas about which there is a strong measure of consensus in the community (Higley, Deacon and Smart, 1979: 25–74). It should be possible to repeat the study, using the same methods (accepting, for the sake of this exercise, that the original research methods were appropriate) and decide whether or not these are the key positions about which there is community agreement. There are elements of all theories that are like this. There are explicit and implicit assumptions, as well as statements about historical fact that can be challenged. In a similar way, the various arguments used to support any social theory can be scrutinised to see if there is anything which is internally contradictory. Few social theories can escape some charge of logical inconsistency.

In the ultimate analysis, however, all social theories are ideological. The discussion in this chapter, for example, is clearly in a pluralist mould—insofar as it assumes that no one theory can monopolise the truth and that there is a free market of ideas in which students may shop at will. Many Marxists would respond by asserting that the market of ideas is not free; that ideas and values are moulded by society, and that ideas and values supporting the reigning disposition of power will always have an advantage. They may well be right.

References

Aitkin, D. (1982) *Stability and Change in Australian Politics 2nd edn*, Canberra: ANU Press

Australia. Commission of Inquiry into Poverty (1975) *Poverty in Australia* Canberra: AGPS

Australian Values Study Survey (1983) *User's Guide for the Machine-Readable Data File* Canberra: Social Science Data Archives

Campbell, E.W. (1963) *The 60 Rich Families Who Own Australia* Sydney: Current Book Distributers

Connell, R.W. (1977) *Ruling Class, Ruling Culture* Cambridge: Cambridge University Press

Dahl, R. (1967) *Pluralist Democracy in the United States* Chicago: Rand McNally

Higley, J., Deacon, D. and Smart, D. (1979) *Elites in Australia* London: Routledge and Kegan Paul
Kemp, D.A. (1978) *Society and Electoral Behaviour in Australia* St Lucia Qld.: University of Queensland Press
Michels, R. (1962) *Political Parties* Glencoe, Ill.: Free Press Paperback
Mosca, G. (1939) *The Ruling Class* New York: McGraw-Hill
Pareto, V. (1935) *The Mind and Society* New York: Harcourt-Brace
Parry, G. (1969) *Political Elites* London: George Allen and Unwin
Playford, J. (1968) 'The Myth of Pluralism', in *Arena* No. 15, pp. 34–47
Presthus, R. (1970) 'The Pluralist Framework', in Kariel, H.S. (ed.) *Frontiers of Democratic Theory* New York: Random House, pp. 274–304
Schumpeter, J. (1942) *Capitalism, Socialism and Democracy* New York: Harper and Row
Tucker, R.C. (ed.) (1972) *The Marx-Engels Reader* New York: Norton
Wright Mills, C. (1956) *The Power Elite* New York: Oxford University Press

15 Gender and patriarchy

Sue Outhwaite

Conventional wisdom has it that women and men now compete in Australian society on fairly equal terms. Extensions of the idea of citizenship, the expansion and modification of legal rights for women and extension of social justice through equality of opportunity have all led to a fairer and more equitable position for the average woman. Feminist political action and general social change has led to the breakdown of sex role stereotypes and has helped to ensure that many areas of disadvantage have been alleviated by ensuring that governments fulfill their responsibilities to half the population—women.

Recent years have seen considerable change in many areas of social life where women were once entirely unrepresented or where inequities existed in the treatment of women and the treatment of men. However, the links between gender and the operation and distribution of social power is a central dynamic in Australian society. This power relationship, which feminists have labelled patriarchy, continues to operate in an organised and structured way to benefit men and disadvantage women. Patriarchal power is evident in both the institutional structures of a society and in the formation of cultural beliefs and values. This chapter examines the major dimensions of women's subordination in Australia and documents the forms of political action that have been undertaken to combat them.

The dimensions of inequality

The major social, political and economic institutions of Australian society show continued inequalities on gender lines. These inequalities, which are generally a matter of public record, do not present a full account of women's subordination, but do present some background on the place of women in liberal democratic societies like Australia. Despite the fact that women have the same legal, civil and political rights as men, major discrepancies between the position of the sexes exist.

Work

Most Australian women engage in paid work for some part of their adult lives. One of the most striking features of the post-war labour market in Australia has been the growing participation of women, especially married women, in paid employment. This has been aided by a variety of legislative changes like the enactment of the Equal Pay Principle (1972), maternity leave provisions and—more recently—Sex Discrimination legislation (1984) and Affirmative Action legislation (1986).

Despite these changes, women and men do not compete in the labour market on anything like equal terms. The Australian labour market, like labour markets in other OECD countries, is characterised by a high degree of sex segmentation, which results in particular consequences for women's employment. In Australia, 54 percent of women workers are concentrated into just two broad occupational categories, clerk and salesperson/personnel worker (ABS, 1986). Within these broad categories 81 percent of all tellers, cashiers and ticket sellers are women, but only 19 percent of sales representatives are women. Women are under-represented in the professions and in managerial positions. While 12 percent of women work as professionals, 48 percent of these are school teachers. Of 6 percent of women engaged as managers, 43 percent work as farmers or farm managers (Ronalds, 1987: 4).

In general, the jobs done by women are characterised by lower pay, poorer conditions, less mobility, limited access to training programmes and less effective trade union support than traditionally male areas of the labour market.

These general conditions of disadvantage have been compounded by the onset of economic recession in the mid 1970s and the current role of technological change, which has made many areas of women's work vulnerable. Although male and female unemployment rates vary, in August 1986 the unemployment rate for women was proportionately higher than the unemployment rate for men. Women looking for work comprised 8.4 percent of the labour force as compared to 7.7 percent for men. (ABS, 1986). The situation is worse for both young women and young men but young women suffer slightly more disadvantage than young men. Official statistics on unemployment severely underestimate the rate of female unemployment. If estimates are made to include the 'hidden unemployment' (discouraged job seekers) and estimates of underemployment (those in part-time employment who would like full-time employment), the unemployment rate among Australian women is at least 42 percent (Power et al., 1984: 69).

As well as unemployment, recession conditions and technological change have also seen a loss of full-time work opportunities, especially for young women, and an increase in part-time and casual work. 19 percent of all employed persons are in the part-time workforce. Women comprise 79 percent of all part-time workers, with 27 percent employed as clerks and 29 percent in sales and personnel work. Although many women prefer part-time work because of childcare and family responsibilities, it does not carry the same advantages as full-time work. Women in part-time work have even less money, poorer conditions and less chance of advancement than their counterparts in the full-time workforce. Feminists have suggested that part-time work as a principle is not to be dismissed but that the introduction of better conditions for these women is necessary. Demands for change have met with little success.

Although the pattern and results of sex segmentation in Australia are well understood, satisfactory explanations for its persistence have not been reached. Feminists (and some labour economists), stress that women's role in paid work cannot be understood apart from the primary responsibilities women hold in the home and in child raising. These responsibilities undermine women's ability to undertake jobs with demanding hours and affect women's attitude to education and training. To combat structured inequalities in the workplace, inequalities in the home must also be addressed.

Poverty

Poverty in Australia is overwhelmingly a female problem. Because large numbers of women work intermittently, are susceptible to unemployment, and earn low wages in relation to men, the ability of many women to earn a 'living wage' is limited. The Poverty Report (1975) observed that a female shop assistant was eleven times more likely to have an income below the poverty line as a male shop assistant, and female factory and service workers were four times as likely to be very poor as men working in these occupations.

The recent dramatic increase in the number of sole-parent families—combined with continued sex segregation in the labour market and a recession economy—has increased the number of impoverished women and children (Power et al., 1984: 79). Sole-parent families constitute 14 percent of all families with dependent children, 84 percent of these families are headed by women. A sole-parent family with two children that depends on social security for its income must survive on 44 percent of average weekly earnings, 20 percent below the poverty line (ACOSS, 1983 (3): 114). Such families cannot maintain an adequate standard of living.

Sole parents with jobs have income levels about 30 percent higher than other sole parents, but because of childcare costs and high rates of taxation, the average family income is still low (Power et al., 1984: 82).

Aged women are also disadvantaged. Social security payments are the principle source of income for many aged pensioners. Because women have fewer opportunities than men to benefit from superannuation, women are less able than men to take advantage of institutional arrangements that could make their life in retirement more comfortable. Rosenman and Leeds (1984) point out that 15 percent of women working in retailing are members of a superannuation scheme, as compared to 34 percent of men. Women's lack of access to superannuation payments is partly a reflection of the concentration of women in part-time work.

Some feminists argue that structured inequalities in society that lead to poverty for women reinforce the dependent status of women. Because many women's access to economic resources is limited, women are forced into dependence either on a male breadwinner with greater earning capacity or onto dependence on the state in the form of welfare payments. Both types of dependency reinforce the social belief that women lack autonomy and power, and must rely on the paternalism of either a man or the state for their continued well being.

Political participation

The relationship between sex and political participation has received little attention from Australian political scientists (Sawer and Simms, 1984: 155). However, as with conventional studies of political participation, two major issues emerge.

The first concerns women's participation in political elites, particularly the parliamentary arena. The aim of studying women here is based on the idea that more equitable representation in Parliament between women and men will result is issues central to women being considered more favourably. A Parliament with a high percentage of women might consider childcare or sexual assault less marginal issues.

Despite women's formal rights to compete equally with men for political office, women remain under-represented in both state and Federal Parliaments. In the 1974 Federal Parliament, there was one woman member in the House of Representatives and four women in the Senate. By 1985, there had been a steady increase to eight women in the House of Representatives and fourteen women in the Senate. This represents an improvement, but nothing like equal representation between the sexes.

Low participation rates do not merely reflect a lack of interest by women in participation in formal politics, but reflect a number of structural barriers that impede women's access to the parliamentary arena. In both party preselection and election campaigns, women are deemed to be out of place, because they are women. A woman must perform to a higher standard than a male candidate and women are regarded as not being 'tough' enough for the electoral battle. Within the Liberal Party, women are further disadvantaged because the cultural norms of the party present a strong bias against the participation of married women, and especially those with young children. Where women candidates are endorsed, it is rarely for safe seats. These go to male party stalwarts with strong career aspirations. Typically, women are endorsed for unwinnable marginal seats (Sawer and Simms, 1984: 120–23). Political parties are, however, more willing to endorse women candidates for the Senate, where twelve members stand on a state basis.

Political scientists have also examined women's participation in 'grass roots' politics, defined as voting behaviour and party identification. In the 1960s and the 1970s it was concluded that women, on average, were more conservative than men. Women's conservatism was reflected in the greater likelihood of women to support non-labour parties. More recently, public opinion polls have shown a declining gender gap in conservatism, with some groups of young women being more radical than young men (Office of the Status of Women, 1986: 51). Political scientists explain the difference in terms of social changes in women's role and self perceptions.

Overall, studies of women's political participation reinforce the idea that women are less interested in politics than men. In fact, Australian women have a long history of political activity, but the male bias of researchers and narrow definitions of political behaviour has resulted in the invisibility of women in the political arena. Although few women have achieved legislative office, they have been very active in extra-parliamentary politics, through political parties, pressure groups and political movements. Such activities often involve issues pertaining directly to the lives of women, like the welfare of children, domestic violence or issues of sexuality (Sawer and Simms, 1984: 22–4).

Media

The media is a powerful determinant of attitudes in society (see chapter 19). For this reason, media images play an important role in shaping the social values concerning women and men. The stereotypic roles associated with what it is to be a man or a woman portrayed in advertising, film, television and print media affect people's thinking about the place of women and men in society. Wherever media images present outdated or unrealistic images of women, or fail to reflect the current status of women, or project women as sex objects rather than people, or portray women as foolish and incompetent, power relations between the sexes are reinforced (Office of the Status of Women, 1983). In presenting these images, the media adds to a social belief in the superiority of men and the inferiority of women.

In relation to advertising, it is not only the image presented that affect the social place of women, but also the fact that the majority of advertisements are directed at women. This is because women control 80 percent or more of consumption decisions (Game and Pringle, 1984: 69).

Advertising works in both conscious and unconscious ways, manipulating and promoting particular definitions of femininity. The notion that a woman should be slim, attractive to men, a good homemaker and a 'supermum' are all promoted through advertising. Unstated messages in many advertisements aim to exploit a woman's need to please the important people in her life. It is suggested that a product will win approval of either boyfriend or husband or will show a woman's family what a 'good' wife and mother she is. Buying the product reinforces her own and other people's definition of what it is to be a woman. This is not to suggest that women are entirely manipulated. They do not buy indiscrimately, but make conscious decisions between products, taking pride in sound household economic management (Game and Pringle, 1984: 70)

Media treatment of women as sex objects has been of particular concern to women (Office of the Status of Women, 1986: 39). Such images occur in some advertising, in girlie magazines and in pornography. The main objection to such images is based firstly on the way women are belittled by suggesting that they have bodies but not minds, and secondly because they reinforce the idea that women derive pleasure from male aggression and violence. This has been a major concern to some parts of the feminist movement in the 1980s.

Government responses

Government responses to discrimination against women and inequality between the sexes has been aimed at reducing the most obvious inequities in line with the ideal that a liberal democracy should promote equality of opportunity to all citizens. Since the initiatives introduced by the Whitlam Labor Government, in conjuction with the growth of feminist activity in Australia, women's issues have been firmly, if sometimes contentiously and marginally, on the political agenda.

Both state and Federal Governments have introduced a variety of legislative changes aimed to improve the position of women, and an array of bureaucratic machinery also exists to advise on women's policy issues. Support for issues specific to women has bipartisan agreement, although Labor governments have tended to be more sympathetic than Liberal Governments. At the federal level, recent minor initiatives to improve the position of women range from changes to guidelines to eliminate sexist language from Commonwealth legislation, to a voice for women at the 1985 National Tax Summit, to changes in parental leave for Commonwealth public servants. State governments have initiated similar changes in line with state responsibilities and have also provided funding for a variety of women's services like rape crisis centres, women's refuges and women's health centres. Specific arrangements vary from state to state.

The Federal Government's major response to gender inequality is the Sex Discrimination Act (1984). The legislation sets up standards of behaviour applicable throughout Australia to eliminate discrimination on the basis of sex, martial status or pregnancy in areas like employment, education, accommodation and the provision of goods and services. It provides a complaint-based mechanism for the handling of grievances that stresses negotiation between parties, provides access to a quasi-judicial tribunal to hear the complaint publicly and provides further access to the courts if necessary.

The legislation functions on the basis of individual complaints and therefore remedies individual rather than structural discrimination, however, the farmers of the legislation claim that it also services a symbolic or declaratory function. Anti-discrimination legislation indicates to Australians that certain forms of behaviour are no longer socially acceptable and therefore reinforces particular rights and freedoms in society at large (Ronalds, 1987: 10).

Governments have also recognised the need to address structural inequalities, particularly in relation to the workforce. In 1986, following a pilot programme, the Federal Government introduced the Affirmative Action (Equal Employment Opportunity for Women) Act. This legislation aims to breakdown labour market segmentation and give women and other disadvantaged groups access to senior and management positions. The Affirmative Action Act aims to fill the gaps that complaint-based anti-discrimination legislation and the Equal Pay Principle have been unable to reach.

The aim of affirmative action is to achieve equality of opportunity in employment. According to the legislators this occurs where access to jobs is not biased by a person's race or sex or because of physical disability. To attain this goal, the legislation has established mechanisms for the review and reassessment of employment policies to eliminate discriminatory practices that have disadvantaged women. For example, employers can no longer advertise specifically for a man or a woman to fill a job vacnacy, but must advertise for a person; promotion is to be based on merit rather than seniority; an employer cannot inquire into a woman's childcare and family responsibilities, only her ability to do the job is at issue. The onus is on the employer to change organisational institutional arrangements and to encourage women applicants into areas where they are currently under-represented. The employer is held publicly accountable for the elimination of any discriminatory practices through a system of reporting to a government agency. Most states have enacted similar legislation.

The rise in importance of women as a social group has also encouraged changes in the bureaucracy. Since the appointment of Elizabeth Reid as Women's Adviser to Prime Minister Gough Whitlam in 1973, both Federal and state governments have established a network of women's advisory units attached to various bureaucratic departments. These units, staffed by women who have become known as femocrats, (feminist bureaucrats), provide policy advice to aid women's access to economic and social resources and to ensure the full participation of women in society.

Women's advisory units exist in the Premier's departments in Victoria, South Australia and Western Australia, and existed in the New South Wales Premier's Department until 1988 (when the new Greiner Government moved the unit out of the Premier's Department). Neither Tasmania nor Queensland have such units. Various state departments—typically employment and industrial relations, education, health and TAFE—have also established units. At the federal level, the Departments of Prime Minister and Cabinet, Employment and Industrial Relations, Education and Immigration also have provisions.

Women's units, which operate on very small budgets, tend to be more visible than other sections of the bureaucracy. They take public positions on issues, participate in public forums and publish material in the name of the unit, not the minister. By definition, their interests are wide ranging, they therefore threaten the entrenched positions of other departments (Summers, 1986: 61). Despite difficulties, these units function to provide substantial policy advice on the place of women.

With the election of the Hawke Government in 1983, women's issues have taken on a new political importance. The ALP is very aware of the importance of 'the women's vote' to its electoral success. A major initiative of the Hawke Government has been the introduction of the Women's Budget Programme. First produced in 1984, this document demands that all government departments monitor women's access to the programmes and policies they administer. The publication provides an overview of the effects of government policy on women and also puts pressure on departments to consider how their policies impact on women. The Women's Budget Programme is an attempt to place women's policy issues within the mainstream of government policy making.

Feminist responses

Feminist responses to the problem of patriarchy have taken a wide variety of forms. Feminism, like most social movements, is not a monolithic entity, and a diverse range of theories and practical responses to patriarchal power relations now exist. The Australian women's movement is a loose coalition of forces that aims to combat gender power relations, but represents no unified front on basic issues explanations or strategies.

Radical feminism

As a movement for social change radical feminism represents the visionary or utopian strand of the current women's movement (Ferree and Hess, 1985: 160). Originally having the most impact on Australian feminist thought, a defining feature of the radical feminist position is the idea that sex is the fundamental power division is society. Based around the analysis of American writers like Firestone (1970) and Millet (1970), and later Daly (1978) and Rich (1979), radical feminists see patriarchy as a universal power in the hands of all men that enables them to dominate and control women. This is the underlying power relation that undercuts and permeates all other forms of social power. It is more important than class or race as a social cleavage. Within this view of male power, radical feminists have emphasised men's use of force and violence as a method of subordinating women, sometimes claiming that masculinity and violence are integrally linked.

Patriarchal power, which exists in the hands of all men, is manifest in both the institutional structures of society and in individual attitude or belief formation. To radical feminists, *all* institutions, from the state, police force and military to medicine, schools and the family, are definitionally patriarchal.

Radical feminists reject the pluralist view of government and the modification of public policy as a method to end women's subordination. State institutions and accompanying bureaucratic hierarchies are seen as synonymous with male power and control. Radical feminists stress that women must free *themselves* from patriarchal rule. In order to do this women must not attempt to achieve in the male world, but must reject both the institutions and values of a male-dominated society. By rejecting current social definitions of femininity and by creating alternative structures and communities, radical feminists aim to challenge the basis of social patterns that devalue and subordinate women. According to radical feminists power can be reclaimed through the celebration of women's differences to men and support of other women in this transformation.

In order to achieve their ends radical feminists have adopted an organisational form that stresses process as well as ends. They organise in autonomous, non-hierarchical collectives, which form on an ad hoc basis to develop political strategies around single issues. A collective will form to organise the publication of a women's newsletter or magazine, to organise and run a crisis centre for rape victims or a demonstration against public acceptance of pornography. Activity is centred around small, local group planning without formal rules or leadership. In theory, members of the group all have the opportunity to participate and hence develop self-awareness, political insight and basic political skills. In practice, genuinely egalitarian structures are difficult to implement. Collectives tend to form their own de facto hierarchies and ideological attacks on group members occur. Feminists are well aware that in their attempts to combat power alternative power structures emerge.

A loose network of collectives with no centralised organising body is a defining feature of the current women's movement. It has enabled the fostering of a diverse range of strategies and ensures that the basic initiative for change eminates from the grass roots. In contrast to organised pressure-group activity, feminist politics can appear amorphous, disorganised and haphazard (Sawer and Simms, 1984: 174). However, feminists argue that this non-hierarchical mode of organisation is a central tool in combatting male power and authority.

Issues relating to sexuality and the body have been particularly important to radical feminist politics. This has involved theorising the links between sexuality and male power through analyses of pornography (see Dworkin, 1981; Griffin, 1981), rape (see Brownmiller, 1975) and the institution of heterosexuality (see Rich, 1980), but has also involved a practical politics aimed at increasing autonomy and control in women's lives. Here for example, the women's health movement in Australia has been dominated by radical feminism.

Based on the strategies of self-help and a challenge to the masculine domination of the institution of medicine, radical feminists have been responsible for the establishment of specific women's health centres such as the Liverpool Women's Health Centre in New South Wales. Despite the radical feminist stance that all institutions, including the state, are definitionally sites of male power, the practical need for funding to establish health centres and also refuges has meant that feminists working in these areas have turned to the bureaucracy to provide the money for a wide variety of services. This particular coalition between the state and grass-roots feminist action has now gained a certain legitimacy but has also been fraught with tensions on both sides. In general, these services have been beset with funding difficulties, but public support and pressure-group action has ensured that governments do not completely ignore their demands. In recent years, with tighter monetary policy and consequent efforts by governments to restrict spending, there has been little growth in new initiatives, but already established centres have generally managed to survive. Even with government funding, such centres have retained their autonomy and continue to operate on principles informed by a broad feminist politics. This use of state resources is generally seen as legitimate by the broad women's movement.

Because violence is seen as central to male domination, radical feminists have also been particularly concerned to combat this aspect of women's subordination. Anti-violence groups have campaigned against pornography and have established both rape crisis centres and women's refuges for victims of domestic violence. The first women's refuge to be established in Australia involved direct action from feminist groups with the seizure of government property on the Glebe Estate in Sydney in March, 1974. Here a group of women squatted to make political statements about the homelessness of women and the related issue of domestic violence. The squat resulted in the establishment of the Elsie Women's Refuge (Dowse, 1984: 148).

For radical feminists, the politics of anti-violence also involves environmental and anti-war activities. In Australia this has involved protests against United States military bases at Pine Gap and Cockburn Sound and the 'Wimmin for Survival Peace Camp' outside Parliament House, Canberra, October 1986.

From a theoretical perspective, the major difficulty with the radical feminist approach rises from the inadequate conception of power employed within the model. This model, which can be called the oppressor/oppressed or victim/aggressor, model presents two monolithic entities: 'men', who have power, autonomy and control, and 'women' who are denied power and are subject to male constraint so that men may define themselves superior. Patriarchy becomes a deliberate exercise of power that men consciously impose on women, often through physical force. Within this framework, which sees male power as universal, radical feminists are unable to account adequately for structural and cultural changes in women's lives or for the complex social divisions that exist between disparate groups of women and men. The need to differentiate between groups in terms of history, culture, class or race is not ignored but is given minimal importance. For example, cultural and social differences between aboriginal women and white Australian women are seen to be overcome by their common oppression *as women*. The specific relationship of other groups to the operation of social power is overcome by an all encompassing male power, which pervades, fashions and distorts the social fabric.

Socialist feminism

Like radical feminists, socialist feminists also envisage broad social change. But unlike their radical sisters socialist feminists believe that the fight to end women's subordination cannot be achieved in isolation but must be linked to other struggles against inequality. Whereas radical feminists concentrate on the power of patriarchy, socialist feminists also consider the importance of race and class in a system of subordination.

Socialist feminists argue that Australian society is organised on both capitalist *and* patriarchal lines. Patriarchy or male domination takes on a specific institutional form under capitalism that leads to women being both economically exploited and dominated by men.

To explain women's subordination under capitalism socialist feminists use the concept of the sexual division of labour. This refers to the allocation of work on the basis of sex in both home and workplace, and to the division between home and workplace, which is a central feature of capitalism (Game and Pringle, 1983: 14). For socialist feminists then, women's subordination is closely linked to women's role within the family, particularly as unpaid domestic workers and in women's primary responsibility for childrearing. This basic division of labour within the home limits the opportunity of women to participate fully in paid work and leaves them subordinate to men in both home and workplace.

As its name implies, socialist feminism has drawn and extended on Marxism as a theory of domination and social change. Socialist feminists have analysed the role of domestic labour, the relationship between women, capitalism and the family, and have attempted to chart the relationship between sex and class (see Burton, 1985).

In recent years, women's relationship to paid work has become a central concern of both socialist feminist theory and socialist feminist practice. Analyses range from the impact of unemployment and recession on women workers (see Power, 1980) to charting the relationship between sex and skill (see Phillips and Taylor 1980) and the effects of technological change on the gender composition of the workforce (see Game and Pringle, 1983), to the relationship between gender, education and the labour market (see O'Donnell, 1984). Within this literature, explanations for women's continued subordination in the workforce are not decisive, but socialist feminists argue that the distinction between men's work and women's work is a central feature in maintaining patriarchal power.

Because socialist feminists believe that theories of subordination and political practice are integrally linked, they have also developed a range of practical strategies to improve women's disadvantaged labour market status. This has included support for affirmative action legislation and particularly the encouragement of women into non-traditional trades, reviews of protective legislation excluding women from various areas of the labour market, input into wage-fixing guidelines and, most importantly, active participation in trade unions. Trade union activity through bodies like the Melbourne Working Women's Centre under the auspices of the ACTU has helped create increased union involvement in working women's issues. This has been particularly successful in the skilled occupations like nursing, teaching and social work (Curthoys, 1984: 172).

Closely related to the issue of paid work is that of female poverty. Here socialist feminists see immediate solutions in the provision of low-cost childcare, affordable housing, rises in social security payments and higher wages and better access to jobs for women.

Although socialist feminists have campaigned for changes in public policy as a means of alleviating the disadvantaged status of women, they hold a deep mistrust of the state and emphasise its limitations in ending women's subordination. They argue that the incorporation of women into Parliament and the bureaucracy, for example, will benefit middle-class women at the expense of their less fortunate working-class sisters. Because the relationship between class and sex is central to the socialist feminist framework, gains that benefit one class of women over another reinforce rather than end exploitative relationships. To socialist feminists the growth of the femocracy or the increased participation of women in Parliament has done little to improve the position of the average Australian woman. Rather is has provided a few middle-class women with career aspirations with a place in the dominant capitalist and patriarchal order.

To end the exploitation of patriarcal capitalism socialist feminists believe that women must align themselves with other movements for social justice. Strategically then socialist feminists align with the broad left, where they believe that feminist aims and goals can be attained through placing women's issues at the centre of a progressive political platform for social change (Eisenstein, 1984: 143).

In this strategy for change socialist feminists stress not only alignment but also autonomy. There is a need for women to organise separately as women but also a need to feed back into other movements with related goals. Importantly, socialist feminists have worked within the anti-nuclear movement, environmental groups, gay liberation, left trade unions and also within the Labor Party. Although the male-dominated left has not always been sensitive to gender issues, socialist feminists argue that a politics of social change informed by gender offers the best chance of a humane and equitable future.

Two major problems currently exist within the socialist feminist enterprise. The first concerns the viability of a theoretical alliance with Marxism. Because Marxism is a theory of power based on the ownership of the means of production, it definitionally casts class power as central. Other expressions of power are then by-products of the central class dynamic. Within this framework gender-based power is not ignored, but there is a tendency for it to be marginalised. The question for feminists then becomes whether it is possible for a genuinely feminist position to exist within the Marxist framework or whether feminism needs a different definition of power. Here power would be seen to emanate from social relations in general rather than from a Marxist economic base (Game and Pringle, 1986: 281).

The second major problem currently facing socialist feminism concerns the narrowness of focus of the socialist feminist enterprise. Although socialist feminism originally offered the most sophisticated accounts of women's oppression through the analysis of specific historical periods and the changing institutional forms of patriarchal rule, the framework has emphasised economic and social issues at the expense of the politics of personal experience, culture and the role of sexuality. Radical feminists in particular have emphasised that a full understanding of women's oppression cannot be reached without analysing the centrality of these issues to a system of patriarchal power.

Liberal feminism

In contrast to their more radical sisters, liberal feminists present a limited platform for social change. Whereas radical and socialist feminists demand fundamental changes in society and politics, liberal feminists believe that women's disadvantaged status can be remedied by reforms to the existing system.

Liberal feminists see the disadvantage of women not in terms of patriarchal rule, but resulting from the traditional liberal's exclusion of women. Women are disadvantaged because the liberal democratic system has not considered women's civil, legal and political rights in the same way that men's have been considered.

To ensure equality between the sexes, liberal feminists stress equal rights before the law, changes to the division of labour within households, the elimination of stereotypes in education and increased personal choice in childbearing and childrearing. In general Australian society seems willing to absorb the kind of change liberal feminists suggest.

As its name implies, liberal feminism fully accepts the liberal democratic ideal that underlies Australia's existing socio-political system and believes that social justice for women can be achieved through the normal political channels this system provides. Liberal feminists accept the pluralist model of power and therefore attempt change through the lobbying and influencing of government. Although they see women's disadvantage as deep seated and widespread, liberal feminists believe that social equality between women and men can be achieved through the existing party political system.

This model, which takes the notion of individual liberties and civil rights as its base, argues that a liberal democracy cannot logically extend civil rights to men without also considering parallel rights for women. As Sawer and Simms (1984) point out a major strength of the approach is that it presents a case that supporters of the liberal democratic ideal cannot logically refute.

In Australia, liberal feminism has been represented by a specific organisation—the Women's Electoral Lobby (WEL). A group of Australian women founded WEL in 1972, modelling it on a United States counterpart. Since its inception, WEL has campaigned vigorously to maintain legal, social, political and economic rights for women as an important electoral issue. As a tactic this has been moderately successful. In 1972, for example, WEL implemented a skilful tactic of rating prospective MPs on women's issues (Sawer and Simms, 1984: 191). However, WEL has not always campaigned in isolation. In the Melbourne 1980 election campaign, WEL worked together with other groups from the women's movement and the ALP in the 'Right to Choose' campaign. This campaign aimed to reduce the effectiveness of the Right to Life Association, who were targetting candidates seen as being pro-abortion (Sawer and Simms, 1984: 186).

Whereas radical and socialist feminists organise collectively, WEL, as an established pressure group, has adopted a formal constitution, elects committees, has official spokeswomen and a national coordinator. Although this parallels other pressure-group organisations, WEL has tried to avoid the hierarchical principles of many male pressure groups and WEL women have also been aware of the importance of feminist beliefs to the feminist cause. They have therefore attempted to diseminate feminist ideas with their pressure-group activity (Sawer and Simms, 1984: 189).

In general liberal feminists have organised around a wide variety of related issues. As the state is seen as the appropriate vehicle for social change, liberal feminist strategies concentrate on the modification of public policy to ensure the protection and promotion of women's rights. Liberal feminists have set the agenda for reform of existing rape laws, feminist reform of the tax system and have made women's disadvantage in relation to superannuation payments a political issue.

Liberal feminists consider Anti-Discrimination legislation and Affirmative Action policies as major advances for women. The growth of Women's Units and Women's Policy Advisers is also a logical extension of the liberal feminist platform for change.

However, other feminists have not always greeted these changes warmly. Affirmative Action has been criticised for reinforcing a masculine work ethic and for benefitting only a few middle-class women whilst leaving the underlying problem of labour market segmentation virtually untouched (see Game, 1984).

The rise of the femocracy has also caused debate. Whereas liberal feminists see the femocracy as feminist infiltration of a key arena of power and influence in society which aids the redistribution of important social resources along more equitable lines, radical and socialist feminists are less optimistic (see above).

In general, the liberal feminist perspective, with its emphasis on state intervention, has been criticised for efforts to modify rather than transform the masculine institutions of public life. It is argued that the incorporation of women into the male political system reinforces rather than challenges a masculine value system where masculine modes of organisation and male activities continue to dominate social organisation. The state can only incorporate women as 'pseudo-men', a new form of patriarchal domination. In this view, formal equality is unable to guarantee either social justice for women or an end to patriarchal power relations.

References

ABS (1986) *Average Weekly Earnings, States and Australia* Canberra: AGPS, November

ACOSS (1983) 'Submission to the National Economic Summit Conference, NESC, *Documents and Proceedings* (3)—*Documents Submitted: Participants and Observers*, Canberra: AGPS

Brownmiller, S. (1975) *Against our Will: Men, Women and Rape* New York: Simon and Schuster

Burton, C. (1985) *Subordination: Feminism and Social Theory* Sydney: George Allen and Unwin

Curthoys, A. (1984) 'The women's movement and social justice', in D. Broom (ed.) *Unfinished Business: Social Justice for Women in Australia* Sydney: George Allen and Unwin

Daly, M. (1978) *Gyn/Ecology: The Metaethics of Radical Feminism* Boston: Beacon Press

Dowse, S. (1984) 'The bureaucrat as unsurer', in D. Broom (ed.) *Unfinished Business: Social Justice for Women in Australia* Sydney: George Allen and Unwin

Dworkin, A. (1981) *Pornography: Men Possessing Women* New York: Perigree

Eisenstein, H. (1984) *Contemporary Feminist Thought* Sydney: George Allen and Unwin

Ferree, M.M. and Hess, B.B. (1985) *Controversy and Coalition: The New Feminist Movement* Boston: Twayne Publishers

Firestone, S. (1970) *The Dialectic of Sex: The Case for Feminist Revolution* New York: Bantam Books

Game, A. (1984) 'Affirmative Action: Liberal rationality or challenge to patriarchy?' *Legal Service Bulletin*, No. 6, Vol. 19

Game, A. and Pringle, R. (1983) *Gender at Work* Sydney: George Allen and Unwin
—— (1984) 'Production and consumption: Public versus private', in D. Broom *Unfinished Business: Social Justice for Women in Australia* Sydney: George Allen and Unwin
—— (1986) 'Beyond Gender at Work: Secretaries', in N. Grieve and A. Burns (eds) *Australian Women: New Feminist Perspectives* Melbourne: Oxford University Press
Griffin, S. (1981) *Pornography and Silence* London: The Women's Press
Millet, K. (1970) *Sexual Politics* New York: Avon Books
O'Donnell, C. (1984) *The Basis of the Bargain* Sydney: George Allen and Unwin
Office of the Status of Women, Department of Prime Minister and Cabinet (1983) *Fair Exposure* Canberra: AGPS
—— (1986) *Convention on the Elimination of Discrimination against Women* Report to Australia Canberra: AGPS
Phillips, A. and Taylor, B. (1980) 'Sex and Skill: Notes towards a Feminist Economics' *Feminist Review* No. 6
Power, M. (1980) 'Women and Economic Crisis: the Great Depression and the Present Crisis', in E. Windschuttle (ed.) *Women, Class and History* Melbourne: Fontana
Power, M., Wallace, C., Outhwaite, S., Rosewarne, S. (1984) *Women, Work and Labour Market Programs* Sydney: Commissioned by the Committee of Inquiry into Labour Market Programs
Rich, A. (1979) *On Lies, Secrets and Silences: Selected Prose,* 1966–1978 New York: W.W. Norton
—— (1980) 'Compulsory Heterosexuality and Lesbian Existence' *Signs* Vol. 5 No. 4
Ronalds, C. (1987) *Affirmative Action and Sex Discrimination: A Handbook of Legal Rights for Women* Australia: Pluto Press
Rosenman, L. and Leeds, M. (1984) *Women and the Retirement Age Income Scheme* SWRC Report No. 42 University of New South Wales: Social Welfare Research Centre
Sawer, M. and Simms, M. (1984) *A Woman's Place* Sydney: George Allen and Unwin
Summers, A. (1986) 'Mandarins or Missionaries: Women and the Federal Bureaucracy', in N. Grieve and A. Burns (eds) *Australian Women: New Feminist Perspectives* Melbourne: Oxford University Press

16 Interest Groups

Trevor Matthews

Look at any Australian newspaper and you will find items like this:

'National Farmers' Federation organises march on Canberra'

'Business Council of Australia calls for welfare cuts'

'ACTU adopts anti-uranium policy'

'Gun lobby musters vote in country electorates'

'New Right group presses Liberals for tax reform'

'Conservationists launch High Court appeal'

These headlines illustrate political action by interest groups; that is, private associations that attempt to influence public policy without (unlike political parties) wanting to become the government.

The variety of interest groups is enormous. The field covers groups as diverse as the Australian Council of Trade Unions and the Australian Council of Churches; the Returned Services League and the Right to Life Association; the Business Council of Australia and the Refugee Council of Australia; the Australian Chiropractors' Association and the Australian Mushroom Growers' Association; the Friends of the Earth and the Friends of the ABC.

These groups clearly differ in size, wealth, aims, effectiveness and 'politicisation'. Faced with such a catch-all category as 'interest group', political scientists have suggested that the field should be subject to systematic subdivision. They have proposed a number of ways to classify interest groups. Their aim has not only been to sort and arrange but also to suggest hypotheses to explain the behaviour and influence of interest groups. Their assumption has been that different *types* of interest groups will also differ in their political strategies and their effectiveness.

Most of the classifications have been simple dichotomies: an interest group is placed into one of two boxes depending on whether or not it possesses a given characteristic. Among the characteristics that political scientists use to distinguish types of interest groups are:

- aims: to distinguish *sectional* groups, which seek to further the interests of a section of society (e.g., Australian Council of Trade Unions), from *promotional* groups, which seek to advance a cause (e.g., Friends of the Earth). It is a line between groups *of* and groups *for*.

- support: to distinguish *closed* groups, whose membership is restricted to those who belong to a certain section of society (e.g., Australian Medical Association), from *open* groups, whose membership is open to anyone who espouses the belief or cause that the group champions (e.g., Movement Against Uranium Mining).
- status: to distinguish *insider* groups, whom government officials judge to be representative and responsible, from *outsider* groups, which are not accorded a regularised, consultative status either because their demands are seen as too uncompromising or because they are judged not to have much to contribute that is of any use to policy makers.
- beneficiaries: to distinguish groups that concentrate on lobbying for *collective* benefits (which will favour all who share a particular interest, whether or not they are dues-paying members of the group) from groups that concentrate on providing *selective* benefits (which are only available to members of the group).
- economic function: to distinguish *corporate* (or producer) groups, which represent the interests of producers of goods and providers of services, from *attitude* (or consumer) groups, which advocate particular attitudes, beliefs, values, preferences, tastes, or interests shared by its individual members.

There are, of course, boundary problems with these attempts to classify interest groups. This will be especially so when the two categories are not mutually exclusive. It is easy, for example, to point to sectional groups that promote a cause (e.g., the RSL's advocacy of the 'White Australia' policy in the 1950s) and to promotional groups that are fronts for sectional interests (e.g., smokers' rights groups that are financed by the tobacco industry). Despite such evidence of hard-to-classify cases, the evidence from Western Europe, Britain and North America suggests that the different classificatory schemes tend, in fact, to divide groups in broadly similar ways. Sectional groups tend to have closed memberships and insider status while promotional groups tend to be open and to be treated by governments as outsiders. Likewise sectional groups tend to provide selective incentives and to be financed by their members while promotional groups tend to focus on collective benefits and to rely on patrons for funds. Similarly, corporate groups tend to be insiders while attitude groups tend to be outsiders (see Jordan and Richardson, 1987: chapter 1).

Why join an interest group?

The authors of the early interest group studies in the 1950s did not see this question as particularly troublesome. Rather, they gave a simple, self-evident answer: people form interest groups to protect or further their common interests and people join these groups because they agree with their goals (Truman, 1951). These studies assume a pluralist structure of society: society consists of a multitude of overlapping interests; *any* of these interests will, when required, organise as an interest group to protect the shared interests of its members; competition and struggle between this plurality of interest groups is what politics is all about.

Mancur Olson (1965) challenged these common sense assumptions. Olson argued that it is simply not rational for self-interested individuals to join a *large* interest group in order to promote a common goal. This is because an individual will realise (i) that the potential contribution of any single member will not significantly affect the group's chances of success; and (ii) that even if the group's goal is attained, non-members will also enjoy the benefit along with members. In short, they calculate that it is more rational to 'free-ride' than to join. For instance, if a dairy farmers' organisation persuades the government to increase the price of milk, all dairy farmers will benefit whether or not they are members of the organisation.

Why then does anyone go to the trouble of joining an interest group? According to Olson, it is rational for an individual to do so only if certain conditions hold. These conditions are:

- if the group is small—an individual may reasonably calculate that his or her failure to join could adversely affect the group's chances of success;
- if the group can coerce members to join—e.g., by denying workers the right to work in an industry unless they join a union; or
- if the group can offer certain incentives that are available only to dues-paying members—here it is rational to join the group if these 'selective incentives' outweigh the costs of joining. The NRMA in New South Wales provides a forceful example of such incentives at work. Unlike most consumers' groups, which normally manage to recruit only a tiny fraction of their constituency, the NRMA has a membership of 1.8 million. Most of its members join for one reason: to take advantage of the free break-down services that membership entitles them to.

Some organisational features of Australian interest groups

Olson's 'logic of collective action' helps explain a distinctive organisational characteristic of interest groups in Australia; namely, the relatively high rate of trade union membership. According to Olson, if a high proportion of a country's workforce belongs to trade unions this will either be because the unions are able to offer attractive selective incentives or because membership is mandatory. The latter has been important in Australia (see chapter 18). Although Australian trade unions are technically voluntary organisations, rulings of Commonwealth and state arbitration tribunals have granted preference in employment to members of the trade union that is party to a relevant award. This has been a powerful disincentive to 'free-riders'.

Australian unions are linked together both at the state and federal level in various 'peak' or 'umbrella' associations. At the state level are the trades and labour councils. At the national level is the Australian Council of Trade Unions. Almost all important unions are now affiliated with the ACTU, which can claim to speak for over 90 percent of Australia's trade unionists. Thus with around 56 percent of the workforce unionised, and with 90 percent of them in unions affiliated with the ACTU, labour in Australia is, in international terms, highly mobilised.

What of the other corporate (i.e., producer) groups? Like the ACTU most national peak organisations representing business, farmers and the professions have federal structures. Two important exceptions are the Business Council of Australia and the Australian Mining Industry Council. The adoption of federal structures is just one example of the way in which the structure of government influences pressure-group activities and organisation. But federal associations are not without their problems. The main one is cohesion, for state branches of a federally organised association are often powerful in their own right. This potential for weak cohesion is especially realised when social and economic conditions differ from state to state. In such cases there are likely to be strong conflicts of interests among the state branches. If the federal body has a rule preventing it from acting unless the state branches are unanimous, it is clear that the scope for action by the association as a whole can be severely limited. On the other hand, if the federal association is able to bind its members—when, for example, policies and courses of action are decided by a majority vote—it is able to present a united front, but only at the risk of dissension and threats of secession.

Other corporate sectors have single national peak organisations to speak for their sectoral interests. Farmers are represented by the National Farmers' Federation (NFF). Formed in 1979, the NFF is made up of ten national commodity groups as well as ten state-based general farmers' organisations. It claims to cover about 80 percent of Australia's 174 000 farms.

Among the professions, the largest and most important group has been the Australian Medical Association (AMA), though it has fallen on hard times in recent years. Its membership has declined dramatically from 90 percent of Australia's doctors in 1970 to only 50 percent in 1987 (in New South Wales it is below 40 percent). The AMA has been subject to tensions caused by increasing specialisation in the medical profession and by conflicts between the national organisation and the state branches. The AMA's public reputation has been damaged in recent years by internal dissention.

Business interests in Australia have been characterised by their diversity and their disunion (see chapter 17 and Matthews, 1983). The large number and variety of trade associations illustrates this diversity. The long history of organisational rivalry between peak business associations and the lack of any national peak organisation with the authority to speak as the single voice of business illustrates the disunion.

That situation seemed to change in 1977 with the formation of the Confederation of Australian Industry (CAI). The CAI, however, was never fully representative of Australian employers or business. From the beginning there were important omissions from its ranks, such as the Australian Mining Industry Council. More recently it has been further weakened by the loss of important affiliates such as the Metal Trades Industry Association and by tension between big and small business interests. This is seen in the emergence of two new business groups: the Business Council of Australia (BCA), representing Australia's 70 largest companies, and the Australian Federation of Employers, representing the hardline anti-union views of groups of small employers.

Determinants of strategy and tactics

What determines how an interest group goes about attempting to influence public policy? What channels is it likely to use? Which policy makers will it set its sights upon?

Three broad strategies of influence are available to interest groups: persuasion, coercion, and inducement. Despite the connotations of 'pressure' in the term 'pressure group', most groups choose to persuade rather than to threaten, to convince rather than to coerce. They present submissions, give testimony, supply evidence and make requests.

Nonetheless, threats are often embedded in arguments. A warning about the consequences of a policy may also be a warning that the group will make life difficult for the government. Once this happens, coercion takes over from persuasion. For example, the group may threaten to challenge a decision in the High Court; to campaign against the government at the next election; to close down a factory; to move investment overseas; to sabotage the implementation of a programme; or to go public with information that will embarrass the government.

Sometimes groups will seek to sway decision makers by promising rewards. This is the strategy of inducement. Some inducements are administrative: the promise to assist in the smooth administration of a scheme. Others clearly smack of bribery and corruption.

Given these broad strategies, the particular tactics or techniques that a group will use and the target it will attempt to influence depend on four factors. Two of these relate to stable features of the political system:

- the structure of the decision-making processes which groups seek to influence; and
- the characteristic style of a country's decision making and the general attitudes towards legitimate political behaviour.

Two are situational:

- the issues at stake and the stage they have reached in the policy process; and
- the resources that the group has at its disposal.

Of these the most important are the first two: the structure and operating style of the decision making system. Interest groups gravitate to where effective decision-making lies. If the Executive dominates the legislature and if the permanent bureaucracy is a key factor in policy making, interest groups will try to influence ministers and their departments. If, on the other hand, the legislature shares power with the Executive (as occurs in the United States), groups will direct their lobbying as much to Congress as towards the Presidency. Likewise, in federal countries (such as Australia), where significant powers are shared with state governments, groups have a broader range of targets to aim at than do groups in unitary countries. One of these targets in Australia is the High Court, which has the power to rule on the constitutionality of actions of Federal and state governments.

Interest groups will also tend to conform to generally accepted political values that give legitimacy to certain types of activity (such as preparing well-researched submissions and giving evidence to official committees). Similarly they will steer away from those activities deemed to be illegitimate (such as violent protests) or illegal (such as bribery, fraud, and blackmail). Political values also shape the predominant style of policy making in a country (Richardson, 1982). The bias towards bureaucratic decision making involving consultation with knowledgeable, 'responsible', 'useful' insider groups is based in part on a cultural norm that governing should be built on consent. In their efforts to generate support for their work, bureaucrats take steps to foster contact with their 'clientele'. One result, in Canberra as well as elsewhere, has been the rise in significance of what political scientists refer to as 'policy communities', 'issue networks' and 'subgovernments' (see chapter 4). For an interest group to be an integral part of a policy community—to be accorded 'insider status'—is a sign that it conforms to the bureaucratic standards of 'responsible' behaviour. Some interest groups are as much concerned with securing (and keeping) this status as they are with pursuing substantive policy goals.

While a country's structure of government and predominant style of policy making will set the broad constraints on interest groups strategies, the actual tactics a group will adopt will also be shaped by two situational factors: the character of the issue and the resources at the group's disposal.

Certain features of an issue will deflect an interest group away from bureaucratic channels. The first of these is if the issue is not yet on the political agenda. Getting an issue onto the political agenda—i.e., placing it on the list of problems that politicians and officials are paying serious attention to—is the first stage in the policy-making process. Second, the issue may belong to the realm of 'high' rather than 'routine' politics. Routine politics deals with the normal, day to day decision making and administration in a policy area. It is concerned with technical matters and with detail. Solutions often lie in incremental adjustments to existing policy. High politics, in contrast, deals with issues of principle and consequence, with major questions concerning the nation's economy and its place in world politics, and with issues that fundamentally divide the political parties. Even if it is conceded that a matter of detail for one person can be a matter of high principle for another, the two types of issues tend to be settled in different political arenas. The former in bureaucratically-dominated policy communities; the latter in top-level interdepartmental committees, in Cabinet, in the Prime Minister's office, or in Parliament. An interest group will find itself being drawn into these arenas if it is embroiled in an issue of high politics.

The third feature occurs when the issue has already been decided and the interest group has suffered defeat. If the group wishes to challenge the decision it will find it has to use quite different tactics to those that are appropriate when discussing an issue with officials in a government department. The group may ask an MP to raise the issue in Parliament; it may protest against the decision in public; it may fight the issue during an election campaign (as the gun lobby did during the 1988 New South Wales elections); or it may challenge the decision in the courts.

Similarly, the resources at the group's disposal may determine the tactics it uses and the target it focusses upon. In general, the fewer resources available to a group, the narrower the menu of strategies and tactics it can choose from. For example, if a group lacks 'insider' status and a reputation among policy makers for reliability and credibility, it may not be able to use the strategy of bureaucratic persuasion; if it lacks a geographically concentrated and politically aroused membership, it will not be able to mobilise its members electorally; and if it lacks funds it will not be able to undertake an ambitious advertising campaign or to engage in expensive litigation.

Arenas for interest-group politics

The Executive

At the present time in Australia most interest groups that seek to influence public policy direct their activities toward the Executive branch of government. This is because most of the decisions that concern interest groups are made by ministers (the political executive) or public servants (the bureaucratic executive). The best way to influence ministers is to influence the advice they receive. For that reason the public service has become a key target for most interest groups. The bureaucracy's significance for interest groups is reinforced by its policy-making and policy-implementing roles (see chapter 8). Many 'routine', 'technical' and 'less important' decisions of vital concern to interest groups are actually made by public servants.

But the relationship between interest groups and the Executive is not all one-sided. Ministers and bureaucrats also need the groups. Groups can tell the government how a proposed policy is likely to affect or be regarded by certain sections of the population. They not only furnish opinions: some can supply facts, figures and research results that a department might lack. In addition, an interest group's cooperation may be essential for the smooth implementation of a programme and its approval may be crucial in selling a policy to the public. They are useful sounding boards.

To solicit this information, governments employ a variety of advisory devices. There are, for instance, formal, continuing committees on which groups are represented. An example is the National Labour Consultative Council representing the ACTU and the Confederation of Australian Industry. There are also ad hoc committees set up to report on particular topics. They include Royal Commissions, task forces and inter-departmental committees. These committees frequently invite interest groups to present submissions, although such invitations tend to elicit responses only from the organised and the articulate.

There is marked bias in favour of producer groups on Commonwealth advisory committees (Matthews, 1976: 339–42). Not only is representation on advisory committees biased in favour of clientele producer groups. So too is access to departments. Moreover, the two are mutually reinforcing. Groups that have access are frequently appointed to advisory committees; and groups that are appointed to such committees gain official contacts and a certain 'standing', which further facilitates their access.

Trade unions have not enjoyed this kind of patron–client access. Except for the RSL, Aboriginal and conservation groups, all of which have patron departments, no non-producer associations have been able to establish quite the sort of close, institutionalised client relations with departments that trade associations and farmers' groups possess. This is largely because they lack the socio-economic leverage of producer groups. It is also because they lack other resources: particularly large, stable memberships and money.

Quasi-judicial tribunals

If the structure of decision making in Australia has a distinctive character, it lies in the prominent place occupied by adjudicative tribunals and boards. The Arbitration Commission and the Industries Assistance Commission are two such bodies. Given the significance of the decisions of the Arbitration Commission (not only on wage levels but also on such questions as working hours, paid leave, and superannuation), it is a major target for the ACTU and the CAI (see chapters 17 and 18).

Parliament

One result of Parliament's eclipse by the Executive as a maker of public policy (see chapter 6) has been the decline in the importance and frequency of parliamentary activities in the strategy of most interest groups.

Parliament is now used mainly as a second resort when efforts to influence ministers or the bureaucracy have failed. Intensive lobbying against a bill generally indicates that the hostile pressure groups have been unsuccessful in their representations to the relevant minister. In Canberra such lobbying tends to focus on the Senate, where the government's control has on occasion been weaker. The Whitlam Government, for example, lacked a majority in the Senate.

Most parliamentary activity by pressure groups in Canberra, however, relates not to legislation but to two of Parliament's other functions: criticising the Executive and gathering information. Some groups use the services of friendly MPs to question a minister about administrative and policy issues during question time. Others give evidence and present submissions to inquiries that are held by parliamentary committees. The Senate gave a boost to the information-gathering function of parliament in the late 1960s with its greater use of select committees and its decision to set up a number of standing committees.

Litigation

Going to court is a tactic sometimes used by interest groups. The court system is available as a channel for interest-group activity mainly because the constitution gives the High Court the power of judicial review; that is, the power to rule on the constitutionality of legislation and decisions of the Federal and state governments. This gives interest groups whose claims have been rebuffed by Parliament, Cabinet or the bureaucracy a further decision-making arena to turn to.

Not surprisingly, High Court litigation has been used by groups who wish to challenge a governmental decision. Employers' groups successfully used this tactic in the early decades of the century by sponsoring challenges to the constitutional validity of awards and rulings of the Commonwealth Arbitration Court as well as to industrial legislation passed by the Commonwealth Parliament.

Two considerable barriers exist to limit interest-group use of litigation. One is cost. Litigation can be extremely expensive, especially as the losers must generally pay the costs of the winning side as well as their own. The second is standing. This refers to the rules that determine whether a person or body initiating legal proceedings is an appropriate party to do so. These rules in Australia have required that the instigator must establish some personal stake or material interest in the subject matter of the case. If this cannot be done, the proceeding fails. The relevance of these rules is to make it difficult for groups (especially public interest groups) to initiate proceedings. The High Court, for instance, recently ruled that the Australian Conservation Foundation lacked standing to take action under environmental protection legislation to restrain Alcoa from erecting a smelter at Portland in Victoria.

Voters

Except for trade unions affiliated to the ALP, it is now rare for sectional groups to campaign openly for one political party at elections. When they do, it is almost always to oppose the party in office and it indicates a high level of dissatisfaction with the government. A recent example was the NFF's opposition to ALP candidates in 22 marginal rural electorates at the 1987 federal election.

In general, promotional rather than sectional groups employ electoral tactics. Causes promoted in this way have included opposition to state aid for private schools and to Australia's participation in the Vietnam War (in the 1960s); to uranium mining (in the 1970s); and to dams, legalised abortion and gun control (in the 1980s). Single-issue groups have used the technique of asking their supporters to vote only for the candidates who have 'acceptable' views on the issue. The Victorian Right to Life Association has recently given a new twist to the technique: using what it calls 'punishment politics' it has campaigned intensively *against* candidates with pro-abortion views (Warhurst: 1983).

Public Campaigns

When a pressure group's direct approaches to the government or Parliament are unsuccessful, it often resorts to a public campaign in the hope that public opinion will achieve what it, through direct channels, was unable to secure. There are two types of public campaign. The first is a short run campaign to influence a decision about to be taken or to a decision recently taken. The second is a longer run campaign to create a favourable public image or slogan for a group, or to create a public demand for a certain type of policy.

The first of these types is most graphically illustrated by the campaign waged in 1947 against the Chifley Labor Government's proposed legislation for nationalising the private banks. This was probably the most intense and concentrated campaign ever experienced in Australia.

The second type of campaign has been waged in the 1980s by the National Farmers' Federation. With a budget of $3.8 million, the NFF launched a massive series of media advertisements stressing that agriculture affects the lives of all Australians. Its jingle 'You Can't Take the Country out of Our Country' was heard in 40 000 radio and TV advertisements. The campaign was launched to counter what opinion polls showed to be an outdated and unsympathetic public image of farming (NFF, 1987).

Small promotional groups often attempt to create the semblance of intense support for their cause by writing letters to newspapers and participating in talkback radio programmes. One index of the use of letter-writing campaigns is the size of the Prime Minister's morning mail. Not only is the number staggering (133 000, or over 500 letters each working day, in 1985–86) but a good proportion is orchestrated. In 1978, 40 percent of the letters were 'campaign' letters dealing with such issues as uranium mining, pensions, family allowances, and whaling (Department PM & C, 1986: 27; 1979: 25).

Political Parties

The only interest groups that are formally affiliated to a political party in Australia are the trade unions. Although the ACTU is not affiliated to the ALP, about 60 percent of unionists belong to unions that are ALP-affiliated (see chapter 18 and Rawson, 1986: 49). In New South Wales and Western Australia farmers' groups were formally affiliated to the Country Party until the 1940s. By then, however, these groups had come to view their affiliation as a hindrance to their pressure-group activities with other parties. Likewise the Country Party itself realised that its organisational dependence on primary producers' associations was preventing it from becoming more broadly based. Accordingly the two sides agreed upon a friendly separation. Since then no farmers' groups have been formally affiliated to the successor of the Country Party—the National Party.

The Liberal Party and its predecessors, unlike the ALP and the National Party, have never had outside organisations as formal affiliates. There were, however, a number of clandestine cabals of big businessmen, which collected and distributed political funds for the Liberal Party's predecessors. This practice ended in 1945 (see chapter 9).

From time to time interest groups that are not affiliated to a political party will attempt to influence public policy indirectly by working through the party channel. An example was the Australian Council of Churches successful campaign to get the ALP's Federal Conference to adopt a policy resolution recognising aboriginal land (and mineral) rights.

How influential are interest groups?

The concepts 'power' and 'influence' are among the most debated in political science (see chapter 2). Because of these disputes, any question about interest-group influence hides a minefield of methodological difficulties. Each path towards a possible answer has its own risks. All that can be done here is to signpost some of these dangerous paths.

Inferring influence from outcomes

This is the sort of argument that says that the government's adoption of a policy demonstrates the influence wielded by the interest groups which had been campaigning for that policy. But does it? Not necessarily, for the interest-group input may not have been the decisive factor that 'caused' the government to act. More important may have been a party's own policy commitment; the arguments put forward by departmental advisers; the climate of opinion; the views of foreign governments; and so on. Indeed, the government may well have used the group to give the appearance that it acted in accord with organised opinion. Arguments that infer influence from outcomes neglect to consider the full context of a decision; forget that pressure groups are often 'pressured groups' (Hayward, 1984); and commit the logical fallacy of *post hoc ergo propter hoc* (i.e., of reasoning that if Y follows X, Y is therefore caused by X).

Inferring influence from a group's internal resources

This is the sort of argument that says trade unions are powerful: just look at the ACTU's massive membership and its annual income; its personal links with Prime Minister Hawke; its cohesion; and its highly professional staff and leadership. But arguments like these run into difficulties. First, God is not always on the side of the big battalions. To concentrate only on a group's aggregate resources would not enable us to explain cases where an asset-rich Goliath is defeated by a puny David. Second, it is not self-evident how different sorts of resources are to be measured and then totalled or how one group's 'total' is to be compared to another group's 'total'. How, for example, is membership to be compared with expertise, and expertise with cohesion? Third, the value to a group of certain resources depends on the strategy that group wishes to pursue in the political contest. It is a case of horses for courses. A reputation for always producing accurate scientific data may be more important than sheer membership size when giving evidence to a technical commission of inquiry. But membership size may be of crucial importance if the group is contemplating a letter-writing campaign. An intimate relationship with one political party may be counter-productive if that party's opponents are in office. Fourth, a focus on the group's internal assets (membership, wealth, staff expertise, cohesion, members' commitment) overlooks two assets that are external: access to government and socio-economic leverage.

Inferring influence from access

This is the sort of argument that suggests that 'insider' groups are more effective than 'outsider' ones. It is the argument that accounts for the political influence of big business by pointing to its representation on governmental advisory committees (see Playford, 1969: 7). But access does not equal influence. Mere representation on advisory committees neither demonstrates nor guarantees that the interests represented share in the exercise of state power. There are a number of reasons for this. First, all the committees are multipartite. Business representatives, for example have to compete not only with bureaucrats but with the representatives of other interests. Secondly, their proceedings can be used by departmental officials to engineer support for departmentally-formed policies. In the 1960s the Manufacturing Industry Advisory Council 'became as much a departmental arm as a voice of industry within the government' (Glezer, 1982: 247). Thirdly, having access to one's 'own' department or membership on a high-level standing advisory committee does not ensure that the group will be listened to (or consulted), even on issues of fundamental importance to its members.

Inferring influence by observing who prevails in decision making

According to Dahl (1983: chapters 3 and 4), A has power over B if A can get B to something B would not otherwise do. If an interest group (A) can, despite governmental resistance, get the government (B) to shift its position, the group can be said to have exercised influence. This behavioural interpretation has come under much criticism. One criticism concerns the difficulty of gaining conclusive evidence: 'Although we can discover that A wanted B to take a certain action, and we can observe that A has certain resources of potential power and used the available means to bring them to bear on B, and we can observe that B took the action that A intended, we still cannot be sure that B would not have taken the action without A's efforts' (Derthick, 1965: 7). This criticism is obviously less valid in cases where a government is forced to back down. Here it is more certain that the government would not have suffered the humiliation of conceding defeat were it not for A's efforts.

Another criticism concerns influence that cannot be observed by considering only the formal decision-making process. An interest group may, for example, be able to prevent a threatening issue from even getting onto the political agenda. Another group may have influence although it does not participate in the decision-making process. This occurs when a government takes that group's interests into account by anticipating what would happen if those interests were ignored (see chapter 2). To deal with such situations, some political analysts have rejected behavioural interpretations of power in favour of ones that give priority to a group's socio-economic leverage.

Inferring influence from structural position in the economy

This is the sort of argument that says that the political power of producer groups lies in the strategic positions they occupy in the economy. This structural position gives them the ability to disrupt economic life and causes governments to be mindful of the threat of such action. Such arguments have been applied to trade unions (Finer, 1973) and to business (Lindblom, 1977: 170–233). Unions exercise socio-economic leverage by threatening to strike; business by threatening an 'investment strike'. More generally, business exercises structural influence because its employment and investment decisions affect the health of the economy, which in turn affects the government's electoral chances. Governments consequently anxiously court 'business confidence'.

Useful as these contributions are in pointing to a structural bias in the politics of interest groups, they fail to account for variations in business (or trade union) power over time and between countries. Their analysis is too blunt for this. These problems have led a number of Marxist analysts to examine the mechanisms whereby the class interests of capital are accorded disproportionate weight by governments. In doing so they have brought organisational questions and interest groups back into their analyses, particularly in their discussions of corporatism (Panitch, 1979; Offe, 1985: chapters 7, 8).

Corporatism and interest group/government relations

Some commentators assert that interest group/government relations in Australia are now corporatist. Katharine West (1984) writes of a corporatist 'revolution' having occurred under the Hawke Government. Other commentators, while avoiding the impression that the Hawke Government has wrought a wholesale shift from pluralist to corporatist politics, use the idea of corporatism to explain aspects of recent policy making, such as the prices and incomes Accord between the ACTU and the ALP (Stewart, 1984; Gerritsen, 1986).

Two basic uses underlie most political science discussions of corporatism. One treats corporatism as a way in which producer interests are structured: here the stress is on each functional area (e.g., business, agriculture) possessing a peak organisation that has the authority to commit its members and is granted a representational monopoly by the state. The other treats corporatism as a way in which interest groups are incorporated into the policy-making process: here the stress is on collaboration between antagonistic producer interests and their joint participation with government officials in the making and administering of public policy (the typical form involving tripartite co-operation between the state, business and labour).

Corporatist analysis (see chapter 4) has been valuable in focussing attention on the links between economics and politics; on the interpretation of governments and interest groups; on interest group collusion and collaboration; on the unequal participation and influence of producer groups in the making and implementation of public policy; and on the ways groups (especially trade unions) are co-opted by governments to exercise control over their members. To this extent a corporatist approach has been a valuable corrective to much pluralist imagery of a multiplicity of competing groups, each 'representing' its members, and exerting one-way pressure on governments.

How valid is it to portray interest group/government relations in Australia as 'corporatist'? Three aspects need to be examined: 'consensus politics', preconditions for corporatism, and the shift from pluralism.

The Hawke Government's 'consensus politics'

'Corporatists' point to the Accord, the Economic Summit, and the Economic Planning Advisory Council (EPAC) as evidence of corporatist structures and arrangements in Australia. Superficially these arrangements seem to illustrate Panitch's notion of corporatist practices—ones that 'integrate trade unions with the state/executive bureaucracy and associations of business in forming, legitimating and administering public policy' (Panitch, 1981: 29). But closer examination shows these arrangements hardly support a corporatist interpretation (Singleton, 1985; McEachern, 1986):

- business is not a party to the Accord
- thus the Accord is not an instance of mutual collaboration among interest groups
- business was not represented by a single group at the Summit or on EPAC
- EPAC does not make and administer economic policy; it advises on policy and legitimises policy made elsewhere
- EPAC is not strictly tripartite: consumers and the welfare sector are represented; business representation is fragmented; and government representation is divided between federal, state and local governments
- EPAC is prevented by the Accord from considering incomes policy (said to be a 'core domain' of corporatism)
- business is unwilling for political reasons to be a partner to tripartite arrangements between the ACTU and a *Labor* government
- the Accord is essentially an agreement between organised labour and a *political party* (not 'the state'); and it has been legitimised 'through the party and parliamentary system' (not through private tripartite interaction) (Singleton, 1985: 22–4)

The preconditions for corporatism

Corporatism as a form of policy formation presupposes a strong, cohesive government able to negotiate with producer groups. As a form of interest mediation it presupposes single, cohesive peak organisations able to negotiate on behalf of their constituents. In Australia, however, governmental and group structures are in many ways incompatible with corporatism:

- federalism fractures and divides 'the state'. Many powers are shared between the Commonwealth Government and the states
- the constitution limits the Commonwealth Government's powers over incomes policies. This is because the principal agency for a national wages policy is not the government but the Arbitration Commission, whose quasi-judicial status gives it an independence from governmental direction
- many other statutory bodies are also independent of government (i.e., Cabinet or ministerial) direction
- the Arbitration Commission's use of adversarial procedures and public hearings is inconsistent with the collaborative, closed-door, tripartite procedures characteristic of corporatism
- the High Court and the Senate have the constitutional power to check and balance the government of the day
- business is organisationally disunited. No single group has achieved the authority to speak for business

A shift from a pluralist pattern

It is factually wrong to argue that, until the Hawke Government, Australia had a 'pluralist kind of pressure group politics' where groups 'were clearly separate from the government they were trying to pressure' (West 1984: 3). Such an assertion ignores the close (and often closed) clientele relations that have existed between some government departments and 'their' interest groups; the Department of Veterans' Affairs and the RSL; and, during the Menzies' years, the Department of Health and the Australian Medical Association. Far from being 'clearly separate', these groups were said to be in 'co-operative partnership' with their sponsor departments. It also ignores the distinctive place in Australian politics of special bodies designed to cater to the needs of interest groups. Examples include the numerous bodies established to market Australian primary products. In all cases, the relevant farmers' groups are represented on, and in some cases they control, the board.

To treat interest group/government relations as being *either* pluralist *or* corporatist is misleading in three ways. First, many frequently observed group/government relations cannot be easily labelled as pluralist or corporatist because they share characteristics of both. Examples include policy committees, bargaining between producer groups and governments, and clientele relations between departments and the groups they serve. Pluralism and corporatism are not mutually exclusive. More useful is the image of group/government relations as a continuum with competitive pressure-group 'contestation' at one end and collaborative corporatism at the other, with various forms of 'corporate pluralism' lying between (Crouch, 1983).

Second, pluralist and corporatist relations can coexist in the same political system. Corporate arrangements might apply, for example, to trade unions and business on questions of incomes policy, while pluralist politics will characterise other issues such as abortion, gun control and conservation.

Finally, to think of interest group/government relations as either pluralist or corporatist runs the risk of exaggerating the role of interest groups in the policy process. In some policy areas interest groups may play *no* significant role at all. Defence, foreign policy and fiscal policy are such areas in Australia.

References

Crouch, C. (1983) 'Pluralism and the New Corporatism: A Rejoinder' *Political Studies* 31, pp. 452–460

Dahl, R.A. (1983) *Modern Political Analysis* Englewood Cliffs: Prentice Hall, fourth edn

Department of the Prime Minister and Cabinet (1979) *Annual Report 1978–79* Canberra: AGPS

—— (1986) *Annual Report 1985–86* Canberra: AGPS

Derthick, M. (1965) *The National Guard in Politics* Cambridge: Harvard University Press

Finer, S.E. (1973) 'The Political Power of Organised Labour' *Government and Opposition* 8, 4, pp. 391–406

Gerritsen, R. (1986) 'The Necessity of "Corporatism": the Case of the Hawke Government' *Politics* 21, 1, pp. 45–54

Glezer, L. (1982) *Tariff Politics* Melbourne: Melbourne University Press

Hayward, J.E.S. (1984) 'Pressure Groups and Pressured Groups in Franco-British Perspective' in D. Kavanagh and G. Peele (eds) *Comparative Government and Politics* London: Heinemann

Jordan, A.G. and Richardson, J.J. (1987) *Government and Pressure Groups in Britain* Oxford: Clarendon Press

Lindblom, C. (1977) *Politics and Markets* New York: Basic Books

McEachern, D. (1986) 'Corporatism and Business Responses to the Hawke Government' *Politics* 21, 1, pp. 19–27

Matthews, T.V. (1976) 'Interest Group Access to the Australian Government Bureaucracy', in Royal Commission on Australian Government Administration *Appendices to the Report: Volume 2* Canberra: AGPS

—— (1983) 'Business Associations and the State, 1850–1979', in B.W. Head (ed.) *State and Economy in Australia* Melbourne: Oxford University Press

NFF (1987) *Australian Agriculture* Camberwell: National Farmers' Federation

Offe, C. (1985) *Disorganised Capitalism* Oxford: Polity Press

Olson, M. (1965) *The Logic of Collective Action* Cambridge: Harvard University Press

Panitch, L. (1979) 'The Development of Corporatism in Liberal Democracies', in P.C. Schmitter and G. Lehmbruch (eds) *Trends Towards Corporatist Intermediation* Beverly Hills: Sage

—— (1981) 'Trade Unions and the Capitalist State' *New Left Review* 125, pp. 21–45

Playford, J. (1969) *Neo-Capitalism in Australia* Melbourne: Arena

Rawson, D.W. (1986) *Unions and Unionists in Australia* Sydney: George Allen and Unwin, revised edn

Richardson, J. (ed.) (1982) *Policy Styles in Western Europe* London: George Allen and Unwin

Singleton, G. (1985) 'The Economic Planning Advisory Council: The Reality of Consensus' *Politics* 20, 1, pp. 12–25

Stewart, R. (1984) 'The Politics of the Accord: Does Corporatism Explain It?' *Politics* 20, 1, pp. 26–36
Truman, D.B. (1951) *The Governmental Process* New York: Alfred A. Knopf
Warhurst, J. (1983) 'Single Issue Politics: The Impact of Conservation and Anti-Abortion Groups in Politics' *Current Affairs Bulletin* 60, 2, pp. 19–31
West, K. (1984) *The Revolution in Australian Politics* Ringwood: Penguin

17 Business and politics

John Ravenhill

In his influential book, *Politics and Markets*, Charles Lindblom (1977) asserted that business enjoys a 'privileged' position in the liberal democratic political systems of all capitalist states. His argument rested not on the perceived existence of a ruling class or power elite, nor on some conspiratorial notion of the relationship between members of the business and political elites. Rather, he saw the 'privileged' position of business as a function of three factors.

The first and by far the most important factor is the location that business occupies in the structure of capitalist economies. In capitalist systems many of the most important economic decisions are not directly under government control: it is the private sector that decides whether to undertake the further investment that is essential for the generation of employment and income, and of the new technology on which a country's future prosperity depends. Governments cannot legislate new investment by the private sector but have to induce it by creating a favourable investment climate and by maintaining business confidence. Governments (especially in Australia, given its heavy reliance on foreign investment) must retain the support not only of local business but also that of the international business community. In an era in which the international financial system has become increasingly integrated, and speculative flows of capital can quickly undermine government policy, no administration can afford to ignore the sentiment of the foreign exchange markets—as seen, for instance, in the Hawke Labor Government's preoccupation with the size of the budget deficit (Steketee, 1984).

Governments will always be mindful of the potential threat to close plants or withhold investment that business can wield. And because businessmen and women take decisions that are crucial to the welfare of the whole society they appear to government officials not 'simply as the representatives of a special interest, as representatives of interest groups do. They appear as functionaries performing functions that government officials regard as indispensable' (Lindblom, 1977: 175). As a consequence, business is given a privileged role in the policy-making process: it enjoys 'insider' status that is not accorded to other organised interests.

The second factor that Lindblom identified as contributing to the privileged position of business is its success in pressure group and electoral politics. Here business groups again are often advantaged compared to other interests:

they frequently have specific expertise that is of value to governments, and the organisational base and financial resources to lobby effectively for their cause. Olson's (1971) theory of collective goods (see chapter 10) predicts that interest groups will be easier to organise and better financed where there are only a few rather than many members (a lobby of large manufacturing companies should be easier to arrange than a consumers' group, for instance). Some companies may be of sufficient size and importance to the economy that they do not need to join with others in order for their voice to be heard; this contrasts with the situation of individual workers who must organise and act together through a trade union if they are to be effective (Offe, 1985). A recent example of the power of the business lobby and its ability to cause a change in government policy was the withdrawal by the Hawke Government of its Industrial Relations Bill in May 1987 following business threats to launch a half-million dollar advertising campaign against it.

The final factor that contributes to business's privileged position, Lindblom argues, is the control that it is able to exercise over public opinion. Business simply has the ability to keep what Lindblom (1977; 205) terms 'grand' issues of politico-economic organisation, such as the maintenance of the private enterprise system, off the political agenda (compare Connell, 1977). This control of parts of the political agenda is what Bachrach and Baratz (1963) refer to as the 'second face' of power. A principal means of sustaining a capitalist ethos is of course through the privately-owned media (chapter 19).

Lindblom's structural approach makes an important contribution to studies of the political power of business and goes beyond the previously dominant pluralist approach that focussed primarily on the role of business interest groups. Yet although Lindblom makes a powerful case that business generally enjoys a unique position in liberal democratic political systems, he does not address the question of how the power of business differs from one liberal democracy to the next or across time periods, nor identify the factors that might explain such variations. These questions are examined below. Before they are explored, however, an important qualification needs to be added. Up until this point we have written of business as if it is a single entity. This is convenient shorthand but can be extremely misleading, particularly in a diverse economy like that of Australia.

The diversity of business

Agriculture, industry, mining, and services all make important contributions to Australia's Gross Domestic Product; each sector has distinct economic interests. On major economic issues such as the level of tariffs, the appropriate exchange rate for the Australian dollar, and the desirability of foreign investment, considerable disagreement has occurred between the 'peak' organisations that represent companies and industry associations in the four economic sectors. Most agricultural organisations and mining companies have been opposed to high levels of protection; high tariffs, however, have traditionally been supported by most of the manufacturing groups. At times, two of the most important manufacturers' organisations, the Associated Chambers of Manufacturers and the Australian Industries Development Association, opposed an open-door policy towards foreign investment as did many rural organisations. Increased foreign investment was welcomed, however, by the mining industry, and by the financial sector (which stood to profit through acting as intermediaries). The support by the financial sector for the admission of overseas capital did not extend, however, to the admission of foreign banks to Australia (Glezer, 1982, and Tsokhas, 1984).

Not only are there significant differences between the economic interests of the four sectors, but there are often divisions *within* them. Dairy farmers, for example, who produce largely for the domestic market have interests that diverge from wheat farmers who produce primarily for export. Foreign-owned companies in any sector may have different views—particularly on the issue of foreign investment—to their domestically-owned counterparts. And there are frequently variations in perspective between large and small companies in the same sector. One of the best examples of this in recent years has been the dissension between the Associated Chambers of Commerce of Australia (representing, among others, many small companies) and the Business Council of Australia (which groups Australia's largest corporations) on the approach that should be adopted towards trade unions.

The political power of business in comparative perspective

What factors determine how the power of business varies from one country to the next? Are there unique features of the Australian economic and political systems that affect the political influence of business? We will examine four factors: business unity and organisation; the structure of the political system; the strength and cohesion of other interests; and the structure of interest intermediation. Another relevant factor—the structure of the economy—has already been noted.

Business unity and organisation

The sectoral divisions within business that were noted above are reproduced in the organisations that lobby on its behalf; this fragmentation is further complicated by Australia's federal system as most business associations are organised on a federal basis. Unlike Britain, for instance, business associations in Australia 'are characterised by a striking lack of amalgamation' (Matthews, 1976: 334). The inability of business to speak with one voice inevitably affects its capacity to influence government policy. On several occasions Liberal and Labor Commonwealth governments alike have added their voices to those of significant members of the business community in deploring the failure of business to present a united front in negotiations.

The better that business groups are organised and financed then, other things being equal, the more effective lobbies one would expect them to be. But the financial and membership strength of an interest group does not necessarily tell us how effective it will be in influencing policy (see chapter

16). A relatively poorly-organised but united group that enjoys 'insider' status may have more influence in policy making than a better-financed outsider. Moran (1984), for example, attributes the success of British banks in influencing financial policy to the 'insider' status that they enjoyed through their ties with the Bank of England, and contrasts it with the relative ineffectiveness of the much better-financed (but internally divided) American Bankers Association.

Parliamentary and congressional systems

The contrast between Britain and the United States points to a second factor that may influence the political power of business. In parliamentary systems, like Australia and Britain, the legislature is relatively unimportant as a source of policy. In contrast, in the United States and similar systems in which the constitution guarantees a balance of power between the executive and the legislative branches of government, the legislature (Congress in the United States) retains an important policy-making role and is consequently a principal focus for interest-group activity.

Which type of system is more advantageous to business? There is no simple answer to this question. In a parliamentary system, where much of the detailed policy making and implementation is in the hands of government departments, 'insider' status is particularly important to having one's voice heard in the policy process. This, of course, is an area where business often enjoys an advantage over other groups. In contrast, although business lobbies, because of the financial and organisational advantages they enjoy, may not have to compete on equal terms in congressional systems, this form of government is more open to other groups. The parliamentary system, beside generally necessitating lower lobbying expenditures for business than a congressional system, also advantages business in that much of the lobbying takes place behind closed doors; it is less likely to have a negative impact on business legitimacy than a perception of an expensively-acquired congressional vote. Business in the United States has utilised means such as political action committees (through which funds are channelled to favoured candidates) to circumvent this problem. In countries where the legislature plays an important policy-making role, local business may also benefit from the ability of legislators to promote their interests through distributive politics (pork-barrelling).

The strength and status of other interests

In arguing that business enjoys a privileged position in liberal democratic systems, Lindblom pays little attention to the possibility that other interest groups might enjoy similar status. In particular, he largely ignores organised labour—the group that often (but not always) has an adversarial relationship with business. In the United States, Lindblom's principal focus, organised labour is relatively weak and his lack of attention to its institutionalised role in policy making is perhaps of minor consequence. But not so in Australia, where more than 50 percent of the workforce is unionised (twice the figure of the United States). Finer (1973) (writing with the British experience in mind) made the case that the union movement enjoys a privileged position in the political system as it possesses 'socio-economic leverage', the product of its ability to call strikes that can potentially undermine a government's economic strategy. Organised labour's privileged role would appear to be reinforced in political systems like Australia's where there is a powerful Labor Party to which trade unions are affiliated.

To do a thorough job in evaluating the relative influence of business and labour within the Australian political system would take far more space than is available here. Generalisation is dangerous in that different policy communities and decision-making processes operate in various issue areas; the relative influence of the two groups is likely to differ not only according to the policy issue but also from one time period to the next. The ability of some sectors of business to threaten to withhold investment appears to be matched by the capacity of strategically-located unions to disrupt the economy through their withdrawal of labour. In contrast to the fragmentation that has plagued the business lobby, the ACTU has been relatively cohesive in recent years—and in the figures of Bob Hawke and Simon Crean has had particularly effective advocates. The principal advantage that some business groups appear to hold lies in the 'insider' status they enjoy with key government departments—which trade unions do not possess to the same extent.

The mode of interest intermediation

The 'mode of interest intermediation' is the term given to the institutional arrangements for linking organised interests in society with the decision-making structures of the state. Political scientists have differentiated several 'ideal types' of modes of interest intermediation according to the number of interest groups within the political system, whether membership in these groups is compulsory, and whether these groups have been created and/or licensed by the state (Schmitter, 1979). 'Ideal types' are methodological devices (associated with the German sociologist Max Weber) in which the key features of phenomena are abstracted and deliberately exaggerated in order to provide a benchmark against which *real* societies can be measured. Although the characteristics of one ideal type may be predominant in a given country, all *real* societies are 'mixed' in that they contain elements from each ideal type. Political scientists usually contrast two ideal types of interest intermediation. At one end of the spectrum is *corporatism*, approximated by countries such as Austria, where 'peak' associations of interest groups organise a large proportion of producers and workers, and cooperation (particularly in the field of prices and incomes policies) between the peak associations and the government is institutionalised through commissions. At the other end of the spectrum is *pluralism*, of which the United States is the closest approximation in real life, where there are multiple competing interest groups that embrace only a small percentage of employers and employees, and where there are few institutionalised procedures for bringing the groups together in the policy-making process.

Which mode of interest intermediation is most advantageous to business? Again there is no simple answer to this question. Pluralist systems enable business groups to capitalise on their organisational and financial strength; in pluralist systems 'insider' status will be particularly important in influencing policy implementation. Organised labour may be outgunned in the lobbying arena, lack the insider status accorded business, and thus, depending on the strength of its membership and organisation, may be denied an institutionalised role in the policy process. But the benefits to business may be offset by the adversarial relationship that frequently exists between it and organised labour in pluralist systems. In corporatist systems, on the other hand, labour enjoys an institutionalised role in policy making equivalent to that of business. This undoubtedly affords it legitimacy. But corporatist systems offer the advantage to business that organised labour may be co-opted by giving it interests in the system: relations between business and labour therefore may be more harmonious than in pluralist systems (as is suggested by data on the frequency of strikes in the two types of system).

Like all *real* societies, Australia contains elements of both pluralism and corporatism. It is inaccurate to argue that Australia under the Hawke Government has swung markedly towards the corporatist end of the spectrum (chapter 16). The Australian political system lacks the tripartite institutions that characterise corporatist societies. Australia does, however, have some special institutions that play a major role in policy making in areas central to business concerns. These institutions, which Miller (1959: 128) termed 'organs of syndical satisfaction', were designed both to meet the needs of certain organised interests and to create 'a buffer' between sectional interests on the one hand and parliaments and governments on the other (Crisp, 1975: 176). Governments in the first quarter of a century after federation wished to insulate themselves from struggles between organised economic interests, yet, in Emy's (1974) terms, create an environment of equal opportunity in which all major groups would be given a 'fair go'. To achieve this, three types of bodies were created, each intended to cater to the particular needs of one economic group: arbitration tribunals in response to labour's demands for a fair wage; the Tariff Board to accommodate industry's desire for tariff protection; and marketing boards to attend to the special needs of rural producers.

How do these bodies affect the role of business in the Australian political system? First it is important to distinguish between the three types of institution in terms of their constitutional status and powers, as these determine the autonomy of the bodies from the government of the day—to lump them together as 'quasi-legislative' (Emy, 1974) or 'quasi-judicial' institutions is unhelpful. Another important difference between them is in the composition of their membership, as this affects the extent to which the bodies will act primarily to further the interests of one economic sector.

The most important of these institutions is the arbitration system—which *is* composed of quasi-judicial bodies. The uniqueness of the system of industrial tribunals lies in the independent role the tribunals play as arbiter between business and labour. Unlike some corporatist systems, they do not depend on business and labour to negotiate their own compromise outcomes. Nor, unlike some other systems, does the government of the day act as the mediator between the two adversaries (in the arbitration system it is the *state* rather than the *government* that plays a mediating role). Which economic sector is the primary beneficiary? Although an argument can be made that business benefits from the arbitration system in that it provides a mechanism for attempting to restrain industrial conflict—in Miller's (1959: 132) analogy, the tribunals provide a ring to fight in and a referee who ensures that neither party knocks the other out—labour would appear to gain the major benefit. This is particularly true for the weaker sections of the labour movement because the practice of permitting wage awards in one industry to flow-on to others enables weaker unions to share the benefits that have been obtained by their colleagues who are better placed to bargain. The very existence of the arbitration system also strengthens organised labour by providing an incentive to workers to join trade unions—the high rate of unionism among white collar workers in Australia can be explained by the advantages that are obtained from union representation before the arbitration tribunals.

The other two categories of 'organs of syndical satisfaction' lack the quasi-judicial powers of the arbitration tribunals. The Tariff Board (and its successor, the Industries Assistance Commission) and the marketing boards are all statutory authorities but they differ significantly in the extent of their policy-making autonomy. Marketing boards are a common feature of liberal democratic systems, their aim being to regulate production and sales of agricultural commodities in order to stabilise and enhance the incomes of producers. In Australia they enjoy a a great deal of discretionary authority in regulating the production and marketing of agricultural produce. Of their benefit to the rural sector, especially smaller producers, there is little question. Unlike the arbitration system, many marketing boards—particularly at the state level—contain representatives only of producer groups and the government. Consumers are represented on some boards but usually only in a token manner. Marketing boards thus provide rural producers with a privileged position in policy making in a number of areas that are central to their concerns.

Manufacturers lack a similar institution to cater to their interests. Until the mid-1960s, the Tariff Board was perceived to play this role. High levels of tariff protection was the compensation given to local manufacturers to enable them to pay the 'living wage' determined by the arbitration system. The Board's responsibility was to *advise* the government on the tariff protection that should be given to Australian industry—unlike the marketing boards, the Tariff Board did not itself have policy-making powers. The Board grew in importance after 1960 when the system of import licensing was abolished. References to the Board were controlled by the Department of Trade, whose minister throughout the 1960s was Sir John McEwen, leader of the Country Party. As the social base of the Country Party declined, McEwen had sought to forge links with manufacturers. The trade-off for manufacturers' political and financial support was 'made-to-measure' protection, a policy best summed up in the phrase of Sir Frank Meere, 'You make it and I'll protect it' (quoted in Glezer, 1982: 71).

In the mid-1960s, however, the Tariff Board began to advocate a policy line that was increasingly independent from that of the Department of Trade and of the manufacturing lobbies. The Board subsequently became a principal advocate within the bureaucracy of economic rationalism. With the removal of the Tariff Board from the control of the Department of Trade to that of the Department of Prime Minister and Cabinet under the Whitlam Government, the independence of the Board (subsequently the Industries Assistance Commission [IAC]) was enhanced. In the following decade the IAC had a number of ministerial homes. Its autonomy, however, had been sufficiently well established so as not to be seriously threatened by protectionist interests (see Glezer, 1982; Warhurst, 1982; and Rattigan, 1986). After the 1987 election, the IAC was removed from the control of the Department of Industry and Commerce and placed under the Treasury, a move that was intended to increase its freedom to comment critically on the overall structure of industry assistance policies.

Although the IAC has only an advisory role (and some of its most important recommendations were ignored during the Fraser period), its publicising of the costs of tariff protection and its advocacy of lower tariffs have been a continuing thorn in the flesh of manufacturing industry. From being an organ of syndical satisfaction, the Tariff Board and its IAC successor turned into an organ of syndical frustration—the IAC being dubbed the 'Industries Assassination Commission'. Most manufacturers would undoubtedly have preferred not to have had a largely autonomous body scrutinising tariffs. Again, a pluralist system would appear to have been more advantageous for business: manufacturers would have been able to exploit the close ties and client status that they had built up over the years with the Department of Trade—which had been largely sympathetic to protectionism. But some companies (especially those producing for export markets) that depended extensively on inputs from heavily-protected domestic industries supported the IAC's push for lower tariffs, as did most of the agribusiness sector.

In sum, Australia's unusual 'organs of syndical satisfaction'—the arbitration system and the Tariff Board/Industries Assistance Commission—on balance appear to have had an adverse effect on the 'privileged' role of business in the political system. The marketing boards, however, like their overseas counterparts, have played an important role in institutionalising the insider status enjoyed by agricultural producers.

Does business power vary across time?

In asserting that business enjoys a 'privileged position' in liberal democratic political systems, Lindblom (1977) did not address the question of whether the power of business—both in terms of control over agendas and control over policy outcomes—varies from one period to the next. Nor has this issue been examined in any detail by political scientists interested in the role of business in Australia (Abbey, 1987). Among the factors that would be expected to affect the influence of business from one time period to the next are the climate of elite and public opinion, the state of the economy, and the political complexion of the party that is in office.

The climate of opinion

Business might be expected to be better able to control the political agenda and gain favourable policy outcomes when elite and public opinion is sympathetic to its preferred options on issues of particular concern—deregulation, for example. A multitude of factors would have to be examined to determine why the climate of public opinion changes. These include the state of the domestic and international economy, international influences such as public perceptions of the results of policies implemented overseas, and the lobbying done by business and other organisations. Vogel (1983) suggested that business in the United States lost control of the political agenda in the late 1960s and early 1970s as other groups, such as environmentalists, organised and were successful in placing issues of concern to them on the political agenda. By the late 1970s, however, business had regained the initiative as a consequence of better organised and financed lobbying, and changes in the domestic and international economic climates. Australia appears to be following a similar pattern—although lagging a few years behind the United States.

The state of the economy

If the threat to withhold or withdraw investment (a 'capital strike') is one of the principal sources of leverage available to business, when is it most effective? A plausible *a priori* argument would be that a threat of this nature will have least effect when the economy is booming, that is, when there is full employment and high levels of economic growth. In a period of economic crisis the credibility of business may be diminished and the government enjoy a popular mandate to interfere with business activity. At other stages of the economic cycle, however, potential new investment may be of much greater economic and political importance to the government of the day. The credibility of a threat to withdraw/withhold investment also has to be taken into account. This would be determined in part by the nature of the company making the threat. For example, a transnational corporation usually would have more options available to it than a company operating primarily within the Australian market. Similarly, a manufacturing concern would usually have more alternative locations for its investment than would a mining company.

The political party in power

Business in Australia has traditionally been seen as having a natural affinity with the Liberal Party. In Jaensch's (1985) words, it has been a matter of like talking to like. In contrast, the origins of the ALP, coupled with the continuing affiliation of trade unions to the party, suggest that business will enjoy less of a privileged role under a Labor government. Certainly the Chifley and Whitlam Labor Governments both lost the confidence of business amidst complaints that they had pursued policies that were hostile to business, and had excluded business from policy decisions.

But is this well established image relevant to contemporary Australia, where the idea of politics as a class struggle has largely faded? The professional managers of today's large corporations may have more in common with the technocrats that figure prominently in today's ALP leadership (and the Hawke Cabinet) than they do with the traditional Liberal political elite. And despite the empathy of the Liberal Party for the concerns of business, it would be entirely misleading to perceive the Liberals as puppets dancing to the tune of a business master (see chapter 9). The Liberals in fact were not always sympathetic to the demands from the manufacturing sector for high tariffs (Glezer, 1982: 198) (which opened the way for the National Party under McEwen to cultivate the manufacturing constituency). And business has not been uncritically supportive of the Liberal Party. Both the Gorton and McMahon Governments were publicly reproached by sections of the business community for their handling of the foreign investment issue and the apparent lack of coherence in their general economic policies (Connell, 1977: chapter 5). In consequence, the business community provided financial support for Labor at the 1972 election, mistakenly anticipating that the ALP would be more sympathetic towards requests for higher tariffs.

Although the Whitlam Labor administration subsequently alienated most elements of the business community, the economic recession of the early 1980s generated substantial business support for the ALP in the 1983 election. In the subsequent period big business has been fulsome at times in its praise of the Hawke Government and critical of the policy alternatives offered by the coalition. A series of advertisements from Australia's largest corporation, BHP, in support of a consensus approach to economic policy making was widely perceived to be thinly-disguised praise for the Accord. These advertisements led Ian Sinclair, the National Party leader, to issue a press release criticising 'the sycophantic attitude of some big businesses towards the Hawke Government' (Steketee, 1984). In the 1987 election campaign some of Australia's best-known entrepreneurs publicly endorsed the re-election of the Hawke Government; criticism by business groups, such as the Confederation of Australian Industry, of Liberal plans to cut subsidies to manufacturing industry contributed to the destruction of the credibility of the much-vaunted Liberal tax plan. Although electoral spending laws in Australia are so riddled with loopholes that an accurate estimate of business contributions to parties' electoral funding is impossible to obtain, the information that is available suggests that many companies have a two-way bet by providing finance to both major parties.

Some observers perceived the Accord signed between the Labor Party and the ACTU in February 1983 as undercutting the influence of business in the political system (West, 1984). Certainly this was the fear of business—expressed in an analogy by Sir Peter Abeles at the National Economic Summit that it had been invited 'to play singles tennis against a championship doubles combination' (quoted in McEachern, 1986: 24). These fears proved to be greatly exaggerated. The summits turned the bipartite Accord into a tripartite arrangement (Randall and Williams, 1986) and led to a watering down of the Government's commitment to control prices as well as incomes. Indeed, critics of the Accord on the left of the political spectrum have asserted that it has been transformed into a mechanism to hold down wages while allowing the share of profits in national income to increase (Stilwell, 1986).

These comments suggest that no *a priori* assumptions should be made that the political complexion of an Australian government will determine the warmth of the relationship that business enjoys with it, or indeed, the access of business leaders to key decision makers. Certainly, business enjoyed much better relations with government during the Menzies period that it did during the Whitlam years. But representatives of the business community have noted that Bob Hawke is far more willing to consult with and listen to the views of the business community than was his Liberal Party predecessor, Malcolm Fraser (Westfield, 1983). Another sign of the close relations between business and the Hawke Government has been the increasing complaints from within the ALP at the frequency with which Prime Minister Hawke and Treasurer Keating are seen in the company of prominent business leaders.

How autonomous is the state from business?

Up to this point this chapter has focussed on the role of business in policy making. Although the privileged positions of other interests in the political system have been briefly examined, no attention has yet been given to the role of the state. Yet it would be profoundly mistaken to perceive the state as a neutral arbiter between conflicting pressure groups. The various organs that constitute the state have their own interests to pursue, which do not necessarily coincide with those of business.

The question of the extent to which the state can act independently (enjoy autonomy) from major private economic interests has long been of concern to political scientists, particularly those adopting a Marxist perspective. For the latter the puzzle has been why capitalism, given its internal contradictions, has managed to survive. To answer this question they have increasingly focussed on the role of the state. Inevitably, they argue, the state must act in the long-term interests of the dominant capitalist class even though the necessary policies may come at the expense of the short-term interests of individual companies. The problem with this argument is that it is non-falsifiable: any action by the state, however hostile it may appear to the short-term interests of business, can be asserted to be serving the long-term objectives of capitalist survival (for a good introduction to Marxist theories of the state, see Head, 1983).

A more useful starting point is to acknowledge that state bureaucracies are powerful actors in their own right and have their own interests to pursue. The state has to be concerned not only with managing competing domestic interests but also must take the necessary actions to survive in an often hostile external environment. In doing so, the state has considerable power resources at its disposal—personnel, finance, and, particularly, information—which place it in an advantageous position compared to most interest groups. The fact that the state is subjected to numerous, conflicting pressures from various groups also gives it autonomy from the demands of business (Nordlinger 1981: 66–7). And, as has already been noted, business is itself divided on many of the major policy issues.

For all of these reasons, the policies pursued by the state at any one time may not be those that some sections of the business community would prefer. Indeed, it is not unreasonable to suggest that some policies pursued by state bureaucracies will be harmful to business interests—whether these are conceived in terms of the short or the long run (Jessop, 1983). The extent of state autonomy from societal interests is, however, not static, but will vary according to the respective resources possessed by the state and societal interests at any particular time, and the opportunity that circumstances offer for their exercise (for further discussion see Block [1977] and Evans, Rueschemeyer and Skocpol [1985]). Two of the best known instances where the Australian state has taken important economic decisions without even *consulting* business organisations are the abolition of import licensing in 1960, and the 25 percent tariff cut that the Whitlam Government implemented in 1973 (Glezer, 1982: 284).

States, themselves, however, are not unified actors. Differences between various bureaucracies afford opportunities to interest groups to seek allies within the state in pursuit of their particular cause. On most policy issues there are likely to be at least two coalitions—one pro and one against—composed of some elements of the state, some business sectors, and other interest groups.

State policies affect the activities of business in numerous ways. The whole range of macro- and micro-economic policies has an impact on business, as do attempts by the state at economic planning and promoting structural adjustment. Similarly, the decision by the state to reserve certain economic activities to itself, and the charges that these enterprises (railways, utilities, etc.) levy directly affect the opportunities and profitability of the private sector. State declarations of wilderness areas and national parks may inhibit some parts of the private sector, e.g., logging interests, while assisting others such as tourism. In the last part of this chapter the focus will be on two broad areas of interaction between the state and business: state promotion of and state regulation of business activities.

Government promotion of business

Australia has had a long tradition of government intervention in the economy in support of the private sector. From the middle of the nineteenth century through the 1930s successive governments undertook much of the expenditure, e.g., financing railways, that was necessary to open up the country (Butlin, Barnard, and Pincus, 1982). Although government investment in infrastructure declined in relative importance after World War II, public power continued to be employed to support private interests. Menzies (1964: 5)—not known for his interventionist views—asserted that laissez-faire was obsolete: 'Industrial activities are, in the modern world, no longer purely private matters, to be resolved by private decision alone in the light of unfettered competition'.

One of the most important roles played by the state has been to serve as a guarantor of economic rents to the private sector (economic rents are enjoyed when companies earn profits that are derived from artificially-induced scarcities that typically are generated by government actions to limit competition—see Krueger [1974]). Through its imposition of tariff barriers, licensing, and its toleration of restrictive practices, governments have enabled companies to enjoy higher profits than would have been the case if free competition had prevailed. Legislation has sustained oligopolies rather than a free market in many sectors of the Australian economy. Examples range from the two-airline policy to the licensing of TV and radio stations to the regulation of bread prices.

Governments provide a wide array of other services aimed directly at supporting the private sector. Many of these are information services such as the provision of statistical data and details of export opportunities. Others aim at facilitating structural adjustment, at enhancing export opportunities, and at providing industry with a workforce with the necessary skills (Loveday, 1982; and Warhurst, 1986).

Government regulation of business

Australia has had an undistinguished history in the field of government regulation of business. The concern of the Menzies Governments during the 'second long boom' of the 1950s and 1960s to promote industrialisation, economic growth and population increase produced a climate in which government regulation of business was perceived to be desirable only if it had the potential to promote business activities. Regulation has been complicated by the country's federal system in which the states enjoy some important powers over corporations and mining. Some states have appeared to be more enamoured of the myth of free enterprise than business itself.

Government regulation has frequently been undertaken to protect existing businesses rather than to force competition (Hogan, 1983). Regulatory activities in many cases have also appeared to serve the purpose of disarming critics by giving the appearance of taking action rather than actually promoting change. In some cases, agencies appear to have been 'captured' by the businesses that they were supposed to regulate. This has been facilitated by what has been termed the 'revolving door': the movement of civil servants from a regulatory agency into the business sector with which they were previously dealing, and the practice of staffing regulatory agencies with recruits from the relevant business sector.

Grabosky and Braithwaite (1986), on the basis of a survey of 96 Commonwealth, state and local government agencies, suggest that business regulation in Australia has generally been benign. Rather than using the powers available to them, regulatory agencies have operated in an ad hoc manner and have relied primarily on platitudinous appeals to industry to act responsibly. Token enforcement is frequent; agencies are preoccupied with keeping the lid on potential scandals. Three of the most significant areas of regulatory activities are briefly reviewed below.

Trade practices

Numerous commentators pointed to the ineffectiveness of attempts to control restrictive trade practices in Australia before the 1970s. Walker (quoted in Wheelwright, 1970) wrote of the 'unrestrained monopoly' that characterised Australian business. Emy (1974) pointed out that Australia was almost the only developed economy not to attempt to restrain restrictive practices. When proposals for trade practices regulation were made in 1962 by the Menzies Government, business was successful in diluting the legislation to such an extent that one commentator termed it a 'fantasy' (Lamond, 1970; see also Walker, 1976). Although a far more effective Trade Practices Act was passed by the Whitlam Government in 1974, there have been persistent criticisms that the Trade Practices Commission has failed to adequately enforce the Act (Venturini, 1980; Hopkins, 1983). Grabosky and Braithwaite (1986: 93) argue that the Commission has been quite successful in controlling the actual conduct of companies in areas such as price-fixing but has had a negligible effect in acting to prevent mergers that create/reinforce monopolies in particular industries.

Corporate affairs

Company law is an area where regulation has been particularly handicapped by Australia's federal system. There was no uniform company law before 1962; until 1978 companies and securities regulation was the responsibility of states. A conference between the Commonwealth and state governments in December of that year, however, produced a 'Formal Agreement' that provided for a National Co-operative Scheme under the control of the National Companies and Securities Commission (NCSC). The NCSC's principal responsibility is to administer codes of conduct for companies, the securities industry, and for takeovers. In the spirit of the cooperative scheme, however, the actual enforcement of the three codes rests primarily with the states—which on occasion have shown considerable reluctance to take the action that the NCSC desired. Neither the NCSC nor the state corporate affairs offices appear adequately staffed to cope with the workloads they face in an environment that is rapidly changing as a consequence of the deregulation of the financial industry. With only 75 staff, the NCSC's resources have been so severely stretched that it has had to abandon some important investigations.

In 1987, the Commonwealth Government proposed the abandonment of the cooperative scheme and its replacement by an Australian Securities Commission. The securities industry would be largely responsible for its own regulation. Critics have charged that the proposed scheme will inhibit government supervision—and that it was introduced because the NCSC's investigations of takeovers had become increasingly irksome to some sectors of business.

Prices surveillance

Establishment of a pricing authority was one of the commitments made by the ALP as part of its Accord with the ACTU. The proposal met with considerable opposition from the business community. One of the few dissenting notes in the National Economic Summit Communique was the statement that: 'The employers accept that the Government has a mandate to establish a price surveillance mechanism. Many employers believe this is unnecessary...' (in Stilwell, 1986: Appendix B, p. 179). The Prices Surveillance Authority [PSA], established in March 1984, is mandated to monitor and examine prices rather than attempt to control them directly. The Treasurer determines which goods, services, and companies will be monitored. The PSA is also authorised to conduct public inquiries, again at the discretion of the Treasurer. In his speech during the second reading of the bill establishing the Authority, the Treasurer asserted that the Government's view was that the best form of price restraint comes from the effective operation of competitive market forces. Those companies that operated in competitive market environments would therefore not be subject to surveillance by the Authority (Prices Surveillance Authority, 1984: 5).

Unlike the Prices Justification Tribunal established by the Whitlam Government (Nieuwenhuysen and Daly, 1977), the PSA relies entirely on moral suasion; the Authority has no power to enforce its recommendations. A Democrat-sponsored amendment to the legislation for the PSA, which would have given it the same powers as the Prices Justification Tribunal had enjoyed, was rejected by the Government. For many observers, the PSA is a classic example of 'symbolism' in regulation: with a staff of only 32, and few products referred to it for monitoring, the PSA has been judged the 'most toothless' regulatory agency in the country (Grabosky and Braithwaite, 1986: 95).

Conclusion

Two misconceptions often exist about the relationship of business to government. The first is that government always acts in the interests of business. The second is that the relationship between business and government is primarily adversarial. It is impossible for governments always to act in the interests of business because on many issues there is no such thing as *a* business interest: different sectors of business have their own concerns which are not uncommonly in conflict. On the other hand, the relationship between business and government is not primarily adversarial, because governments and the business community have a common interest in economic prosperity.

References

Abbey, B. (1987) 'Power, Politics and Business' *Politics* 22, 2 (November) pp. 46–54

Bachrach, P. and Baratz, M.S. (1962) 'The Two Faces of Power' *American Political Science Review* 56 (December) pp. 947–52

Butlin, N.G., Barnard, A. and Pincus, J.J. (1982) *Government and Capitalism* Sydney: George Allen and Unwin

Connell, R.W. (1977) *Ruling Class, Ruling Culture* Cambridge: Cambridge University Press

Crisp, L.F. (1975) *Australian National Government* Melbourne: Longman
Emy, H.V. (1974) *The Politics of Australian Democracy* Melbourne: Macmillan
Finer, S.E. (1973) 'The Political Power of Organised Labour' *Government and Opposition* 8, 4, pp. 391–406
Glezer, L. (1982) *Tariff Politics* Melbourne: Melbourne University Press
Grabosky, P. and Braithwaite, J. (1986) *Of Manners Gentle* Melbourne: Oxford University Press
Head, B.W. (1983) 'State and Economy: Theories and Problems', in Head (ed.) *State and Economy in Australia* Melbourne: Oxford University Press
Hogan, W.P. (1983) 'Government and Business Links' *Australian Journal of Public Administration* XLII, 1, pp. 53–72
Hopkins, A. (1983) 'Marxist Theory and Australian Monopoly Law', in E.L. Wheelwright and K. Buckley (eds) *Essays in the Political Economy of Australian Capitalism Vol. 5* Sydney: ANZ Books
Jaensch, D. (1985) 'The Liberal Party', in D. Woodward, A. Parkin and J. Summers (eds) *Government Politics and Power in Australia* Melbourne: Longman pp. 137–52
Jessop, B. (1983) 'The Capitalist State and the Rule of Capital: Problems in the Analysis of Business Associations', in D. Marsh (ed.) *Capital and Politics in Western Europe* London: Cass pp. 139–62
Krueger, A.O. (1974) 'The Political Economy of the Rent-Seeking Society' *American Economic Review* LXIV
Lamond, T. (1970) 'Discussion' in G.G. Masterman (ed.) *Big Business in Australia* Sydney: Angus and Robertson, pp. 162–3
Lindblom, C.E. (1977) *Politics and Markets* New York: Basic Books
Loveday, P. (1982) *Promoting Industry* St Lucia: University of Queensland Press
Matthews, T.V. (1976) 'Interest Group Access to the Australian Government Bureaucracy', in *Royal Commission on Australian Government* Canberra: AGPS, Vol. 2 pp. 332–65
McEachern, D. (1986) 'Corporatism and Business Responses to the Hawke Government' *Politics* 21, 1 pp. 19–27
Menzies, R. (1964) *The Interdependence of Political and Industrial Leadership in the Modern State* London: British Institute of Management
Miller, J.D.B. (1959) *Australian Government and Politics* London: Gerald Duckworth
Moran, M. (1984) 'Politics, Banks and Markets: An Anglo-American Comparison' *Political Studies* 32 pp. 173–89
Nieuwenhuysen, J.P. and Daly, A.E. (1977) *The Australian Prices Justification Tribunal* Melbourne: Melbourne University Press
Nordlinger, E.A. (1981) *On the Autonomy of the Democratic State* Cambridge, Mass.: Harvard University Press
Offe, C. (1985) 'The Attribution of Public Status to Interest Groups', in Offe *Disorganised Capitalism* Cambridge, Mass.: MIT Press
Olson, M. (1971) *The Logic of Collective Action* Cambridge, Mass.: Harvard University Press
Prices Surveillance Authority (1984) *First Annual Report of the Prices Surveillance Authority* Canberra: AGPS
Randall, K. and Williams, P. (1986) 'Labor's New Business Deal' *Business Review Weekly* 3 October pp. 17–21
Rattigan, A. (1986) *Industry Assistance* Melbourne: Melbourne University Press
Schmitter, P.C. (1979) 'Still the Century of Corporatism', in Schmitter and G. Lehmbruch (eds) *Trends Towards Corporatist Intermediation* Beverly Hills: Sage
Steketee, M. (1984) 'Big Business and Labor: How times have changed' *Sydney Morning Herald* 3 August
Stilwell, F. (1986) *The Accord and Beyond* Sydney: Pluto

Tsokhas, K. (1984) *A Class Apart? Businessmen and Australian Politics 1970–1980* Melbourne: Oxford University Press

Venturini, V.G. (1980) *Malpractice: The Administration of the Murphy Trade Practices Act* Sydney: Non Mollare

Vogel, D. (1983) 'The Power of Business in America: A Re-appraisal' *British Journal of Political Science* 13 pp. 19–43

Walker, G. deQ. (1976) 'The Trade Practices Act at Work', in J.P. Nieuwenhuysen (ed.) *Australian Trade Practices Readings* [2nd edn] London: Croom Helm

Warhurst, J. (1982) *Jobs or Dogma? The Industries Assistance Commission and Australian Politics* St Lucia: University of Queensland Press

—— (1986) 'Industry assistance issues: state and federal governments', in B.W. Head (ed.) *The Politics of Development in Australia* Sydney: George Allen and Unwin

West, K. (1984) *The Revolution in Australian Politics* Ringwood: Penguin

Westfield, N. (1983) 'Why Business Backs Hawke' *Business Review Weekly* 2 November pp. 12–17

Wheelwright, E.L. (1970) 'Discussion' in G.G. Masterman (ed.) *Big Business in Australia* Sydney: Angus and Robertson, pp. 55–64

18 Trade unions

Marian Simms

Trade unions have a major impact upon Australian politics. They have visibility and influence through different means and in different arenas. The most important of these are the links with the Australian Labor Party (ALP), the arbitration system, direct industrial action and lobbying governments.

Four areas of union influence

In the first instance there is the unions' ALP connection. The ALP was set up by Australian unions in order to gain a political voice after the severe and often unsuccessful industrial conflict of the 1880s and 1890s. About 60 percent of Australian unionists belong to unions affiliated with the ALP.

Secondly, there is the arbitration system. Wages tribunals had been set up before federation. In 1901 the Australian constitution gave the Federal Government the following power: 'Conciliation and arbitration for the prevention and settlement of industrial disputes extending beyond the limits of any one state' (section 51 [XXXV]). Then the Conciliation and Arbitration Act of 1904 set up the federal conciliation and arbitration machinery. According to H.B. Higgins, one of the early presidents of the Commonwealth Court of Conciliation and Arbitration, 'The system of arbitration adopted by the Act is based on unionism. Indeed, without unions it is hard to conceive how arbitration could be worked' (quoted in Rawson, 1978: 24).

Thirdly, unions may engage in strikes and other forms of direct industrial action. Strike action gives the unions involved high visibility—and indeed notoriety—but not necessarily influence. In fact, the use of the strike weapon may constitute a sign of lack of influence. It is also not always realised that most forms of industrial action in Australia 'are unlawful at common law and very often under statute law as well' (Creighton et al., 1983: 792). The existence of those so-called 'penal clauses' has in turn led to major conflict between unions, employers and governments.

Fourthly, trade unions lobby state and federal governments. Working with a Labor government has often been an advantage but can have its own complications. The Administrative and Clerical Officers' Association's (ACOA) Peter Paramore said that dealing with the Hawke Government was a 'double-edged sword' (Simms, 1987). Lobbying may be done by individual unions, but more often it is done through the major peak organisations.

The structure and composition of Australian unionism

Capital cities and some provincial centres have union Trades and Labor Councils (TLCs), sometimes known as Trades Hall Councils (THCs). The Australian Council of Trade Unions (ACTU), formed in 1927, is the federal peak organisation of all its affiliates who join via the metropolitan TLC (or equivalent). It is important to realise that not all unions are affiliated to TLCs. For many years the large and powerful rural-based Australian Workers' Union (AWU) stayed outside. Martin (1971) noted the reluctance—until recent decades—of most non-manual unions to identify themselves too closely with the blue collar-dominated ACTU. Their objections have melted away since, and one by one the white-collar public sector unions have affiliated with the metropolitan TLCs. Until the late 1970s, most such unions were affiliated to specific peak organisations. The two major groupings, the Australian Council of Salaried and Professional Associations and the Council of Australian Government Employee Organisations, dissolved into the ACTU in 1979 and 1981, respectively.

Most white-collar public sector unions have held back from the next political step, namely affiliation with the ALP. Some have given other assistance to the ALP. At a state level, the Public Service Association (PSA) of New South Wales, for example, has a long history of surveying the views of parties and candidates at election times and of publishing the results. This often meant that it had given de facto electoral support to the ALP. During the 1961 federal elections, the normally non-partisan ACOA had 'campaigned against the Minister for Labour and National Service, with the financial support of other associations' (Martin 1962: p. 64). In 1982, the Victorian Branch of the Teachers Federation gave substantial financial support to the Victorian Labor Party led by John Cain in tacit exchange for favours from the Cain Government.

Affiliation with the ALP is a significant step that most blue-collar and a few white-collar unions have taken. It is a landmark, as is a union's first strike.

Australia is one of the most highly unionised countries in the world. About 55 percent of wage and salary earners are union members. This percentage has changed only moderately from 1969 to 1983, 'but "trade unionism" in 1983 was made up of very different people from trade unionists of 1969' (Rawson and Wrightson, 1985: 1).

> Between 1976 and 1983, very many unions of manual workers declined in size. . . The changing occupational character of unionism is related to another consistent change which has continued into the most recent period—the increased proportion of unionists are women. . . According to the ABS (Australian Bureau of Statistics), in December 1983 the proportion of unionists who were women was 33 percent. This compares with 24 percent in 1969 and 30 percent in 1979. (Rawson and Wrightson, 1985: 13)

The changing occupational character of Australian trade unionism is also indicated by those large unions that had the highest rate of growth in the period 1976–83. Of the largest ten, the Federated Miscellaneous Workers' Union and the Transport Workers' Union were the only non-white-collar unions, while teachers and public-sector clerical workers unions were predominant (Rawson and Wrightson, 1985: 11).

One of the fastest growing areas of employment for women has been the public sector, both federal and state. In May 1985, for example, for the first time, the number of female members of the PSA of New South Wales exceeded the number of males. In a similiar fashion, in 1984 women constituted 37 percent of all federal public servants (those employed under the Federal Public Service Act) working in New South Wales, and they constituted a similar proportion (36 percent) of all financial members of the New South Wales Branch of the ACOA. Nationally, women comprised one-third of ACOA's membership. In the ACT, however, it was down to 20 percent, reflecting the number of head offices in Canberra and hence the higher percentage of senior middle management positions that are generally held by men. Overall, these figures suggest a solid union involvement by women public servants. Nonetheless, female membership has not translated into female participation. The New South Wales ACOA figures show that women comprised less than 25 percent of all ACOA delegates in that state. These figures are similar to those in other unions with substantial female memberships.

Most Australian unions use a delegate system based on the shop steward model, which has been used for a long time by the traditional blue-collar unions. The shop steward was the foundation of internal union democracy, representing the members' grievances both to management and to the union hierarchy.

The majority of Australian trade unions are craft-type unions; that is, their members share similar occupations or skills. In the case of the ACOA, members are administrators and/or clerks. It is conventional to distinguish between 'three main types of unions—craft unions, industrial unions and general unions' (Plowman et al., 1980: chapter 8):

- *Craft unions* are those which organise workers on the basis of a particular craft or trade, whatever they may be employed in . . . Australia's earliest trade unions were craft unions which formed amongst printers, stonemasons, carpenters, plasterers and the like.
- *Industrial unions* are those which organise all workers in a given industry, irrespective of the job they perform. There is no true industrial union in Australia. Unions such as the Australian Bank Employees' Union, the Australasian Meat Industry Employees' Union and the Australian Tramways and Motor Omnibus Union come the closest, as they represent most of the employees in their respective industries.
- *General unions* are those that organise workers regardless of skill, occupation or industry. There are few unions of this type in Australia, although the Australian Workers' Union, and the Federated Miscellaneous Workers' Union can be described as general unions.

The ACTU and other sections of the trade union movement have long wished to have fewer unions, and those organised on an industry basis. Moves in this direction face two major obstacles. First, it has been argued that the arbitration system, which requires the registration of unions, has encouraged the proliferation of unions (Plowman et al., 1981: chapter 8). Second, political and ideological differences among powerful unions in the same industry also make amalgamation difficult. The Builders Labourers' Federation and the Building Workers' Industrial Union, for example, are linked with different and antagonistic communist parties, and have a history of industrial and political clashes.

Smaller unions are easier targets for amalgamation. The Hancock Inquiry, which was set up by the Hawke Government and reported in 1985, recommended *inter alia* that the minimum size of federally-registered unions be lifted from 100 to 1000. If implemented this would have reduced the number of unions from just over 300 to about 180.

It is important to realise that Australian trade unions do not constitute a monolith. They are probably more coherent and cohesive than are their employer counterparts (see chapter 17), but they have important industrial and political differences. They do share one feature. They are primarily reactors in the industrial and political spheres, rather than initiators of change to these spheres (Martin, 1980). To survive, unions regularly need to respond to a number of forces, including economic conditions, the views and legislation of government, the determination of the various industrial tribunals and, last but not least, the actions of management.

Employer organisations have generally maintained lower profiles than have employee groups. In recent years, however, there have been exceptions. The National Farmers' Federation (NFF) has held major demonstrations, and in 1985 spearheaded successful legal action against the Australasian Meat Industry Employees Union in the highly significant Mudginberri Dispute:

> The dispute became a symbol for one possible direction that could be taken by Australian industrial relations: a direction characterised by greater legal regulation (of union activities), direct bargaining between employers and employees without the participation of trade unions or employers associations and reduced trade union power. (Kitay and Powe, 1987: 365)

The Mudginberri case and several other industrial struggles within a two-year period stood out for two main reasons. In the first instance, the Hawke Government's industrial relations package—known as the Accord—had brought relative industrial harmony since 1983. Secondly, the Mudginberri dispute, the Dollar Sweets case and the SEQEB dispute (between the Bjelke-Petersen Government and Queensland electricity workers), among other industrial disputes, seemed to signal an onset of greater employer strength and the capitulation of union power (Kitay and Powe, 1987). In all cases, the unions involved were reactors to employer and/or government actions, and not initiators. The paradox is, however, that most Australians want to curb the power of unions.

The Hawke Government's Hancock Inquiry commissioned a major survey of Australian public opinion on unions and discovered the following:

> Only 28 percent of Australians favour the strike as an acceptable union activity, and only 14 percent accept the use of work bans. Most favoured some kind of disciplinary power over unions—47 percent favoured fines, 43 percent favoured stopping a union representing its members, 34 percent favoured abolishing the union, 21 percent favoured removing part of the benefits of an award, and 17 percent favoured jailing union leaders (some favoured more than one of these). (*Australian Financial Review* 21 May 1985)

The survey essentially showed that the majority of Australians polled favoured the maintenance of the existing system of arbitration. Penalties were advocated, however, for participants who refused to abide by the umpire's rulings. Strikes were often negatively viewed as reflecting the refusal of unionists to stay within the system.

The union–ALP connection

More generally, personal hostility towards trade unions has been closely correlated, at least from the 1970s through to the 1980s, with the likelihood of voting Liberal or National (Bean and Kelley, 1988). This feature has led some (for example, Kemp, 1977) to argue that the ALP's links with the union movement are anachronistic and constitute a major electoral liability. In Kemp's view, the volatile voters of the new suburbia are likely to be put off voting Labor because of their perception of trade unions as a too powerful influence on the ALP.

Within the ALP, too, there has been concern that the trade union movement has had a disproportionate influence on the party. In 1977, for example, the ALP's historic National Committee of Inquiry recognised that the party was too 'male' and too 'trade union dominated' and that this was bad for its image, particularly among women voters. Consequently the ALP set up an internal Affirmative Action policy designed to increase women's participation in many internal decision-making structures. The National Conference, held every two years, was broadened and expanded. It should be emphasised, however, that as at 1988 most ALP state constitutions provide for affiliated unions to send 60 percent of the delegates to state conferences, which normally elect each state's delegates to the Party's National Conference (see chapter 9). The bulk of these affiliated unions are unions which, if not male-dominated in their membership, are male-dominated in their leadership. Even unions like the Shop, Distributive and Allied Employees' Association (SDA) and the Federated Liquor and Allied Industries Employees' Union of Australia, whose membership is predominantly female, have predominantly male executives and send predominantly male delegates to the ALP conferences. The more feminised white-collar public sector-unions, as is noted above, have been slower to affiliate with the ALP. They have pursued their various agendas through the relevant TLCs and via the ACTU.

Whether a trade union affiliates with the ALP—which is normally done on a state by state basis—is, of course, a highly political question. It may, on the one hand, reflect the political will of the dominant group in the union. When the New South Wales Branch of the Australasian Public Service Association (APSA) affiliated with the New South Wales ALP, it was the result of a left-wing group taking over the union's state branch. For many years the APSA had been dominated by more conservative elements. On the other hand, the decision to affiliate or disaffiliate may also reflect the attitude of the ALP to that particular union, and the prevailing balance of power within the party. During the early years of the Hawke Government, for example, several 'right wing' unions were allowed to reaffiliate with the Victorian branch of the ALP, despite left-wing opposition to this within the party. Those unions, most notably the SDA, had left the ALP during the 'split' of the mid-1950s and had been closely associated with the Catholic-oriented Democratic Labor Party (DLP), which emerged to the right of the mainstream ALP as a result of the split. These divisions were strongest in Victoria, but also occurred in Queensland. In other states, most notably New South Wales, conservative elements stayed within the Labor Party and right wing unions also retained their affiliation. The reaffiliations in Victoria were allowed partly because they strengthened the position of the non-left-wing factions in the Victorian branch of the ALP.

The balance of political and ideological power within the trade union movement is normally reflected in the composition of the executive of the ACTU. In July 1988, the fear was expressed by John McBean, the Senior Vice-President of the ACTU, the President of the New South Wales ALP and the Secretary of the New South Wales Labor Council, that the organised left was becoming too powerful within the union movement. McBean called for 'a national meeting of key party and union leaders to galvanise his side of the Labor (sic) movement against the rising tide of left-wing influence' (*The Australian* 28 July 1988). Left-wing dominance, it was feared, would lead to the defeat of the Hawke Government.

Several left unions, in an opposing move, actually disaffiliated from the ALP in 1988 because of the Hawke Government's alleged failure to deliver policies favourable to the particular unions. According to a leader of the left-wing Miners' Federation: 'There is no doubt that the Labor Party has been moving further to the Right and discriminated against workers in favour of the corporate sector...we are not likely to overcome this in the period between now and the next election' (*The Australian* 11 August 1988).

The arbitration system

The arbitration system provides an arena within which conflict between labour and capital are mediated. In order for matters to come before the federal arbitration system there has to have been a 'dispute' 'extending beyond the limits of any one state'. The High Court's intepretation of this condition has been very broad and so-called 'paper disputes' between unions, or between unions and management, are taken to federal arbitration. The High Court had traditionally taken a narrow view of the definition of what constituted an 'industrial' dispute. This changed in 1983 when it declared that social welfare workers, covered by the Australian Social Welfare Union, were engaged in an 'industry' and hence were eligible for federal registration.

Industrial relations in Australia cover both what happens in the formal arbitration system and so-called collective bargaining, which, unlike arbitration, does not involve arbitrating bodies as third parties. Under collective bargaining, unions and management face each other directly and negotiate contracts covering conditions of employment and wages. Governments have tried to influence wage levels by making submissions to arbitration and conciliation bodies, but often they have been unsuccessful. The arbitration system is relatively autonomous from government efforts to influence it. Furthermore, with collective bargaining, governments have even less influence over outcomes.

If governments cannot control, or even have a determining influence on, wage levels, wages policy can help to undermine federal governments. In 1929, for example, the conservative Bruce–Page Federal Government fell and the Prime Minister Stanley Melbourne Bruce lost his seat, partly because of his plans to dismantle arbitration. Inflation, often alleged to have been caused by a union 'wages push', was a factor in the downfall of the McMahon Government in 1972 and then the Whitlam Government in 1975. Bad relations with unions can mar a government's image as a successful manager of the economy. The Fraser Government (1975–83) gambled with this fate by adopting a confrontationist stance with the trade union movement in general and with the public service unions in particular. Dabscheck and Niland (1981: 105–6) explained this as part of a conservative tradition:

> Non-Labor governments typically refer to the emotive issue of 'who is running the country', and the importance of constitutional government. By adopting such a stance a government may seek to distract attention from other more burning issues. In the extreme, such a government could precipitate a strike, a task more easily achieved with a government's own employees than those in the private sector. . . as again a government may introduce, or thereafter threaten to introduce, legislation which will curb the irresponsible behaviour of militant unions.

The Fraser Government was widely criticised for interfering with the arbitration system, for ignoring the umpires' decisions and for overturning decisions through legislation (Simms, 1987: chapter 3). The Federal Government, however, does have the right to make submissions to the Conciliation and Arbitration Commission and has greater powers in respect of its own employees, those in the the Commonwealth public service.

The Arbitration Commission has adopted certain broad perspectives on wages. In 1907, under Higgins, the Commission's predecessor handed down the landmark Harvester Judgement. The judgement enshrined the concept of the 'family wage', which has been seen as a major factor in the long and continued existence of low wages for females. Furthermore, it emphasised the needs of workers (and their families) rather than the capacity of industry to pay. Subsequently these two concepts, 'needs' and 'capacity to pay', were to battle it out in the confines of the arbitration system.

Collective bargaining has sometimes replaced arbitration as the major source of wage levels depending on the state of the economy and the strength of unions in particular industries. Most recently this has occurred in the early 1970s and then again in the early 1980s. For a time in the intervening period indexation was tried. This occurs when wages are automatically increased in line with the Consumer Price Index (CPI). When this failed and was overtaken by collective bargaining and the resultant 'wages explosion', the Fraser government introduced the wages pause.

The Accord

The development of the Accord between the ACTU and the ALP reflected the desire of the ACTU from the late 1970s onward to develop stability in industrial relations. It effectively involved the ACTU eschewing direct action on the part of its member unions. The Accord is thus an example of the way unions may be aware of the limitations of direct industrial action and develop alternative strategies. Once the ALP was elected to government in March 1983, it became 'locked into' the provisions of the Accord. The history of the Accord thus becomes a prime example of the successful lobbying of the government by the union movement.

The Hayden-led ALP, while in Opposition, had been developing an alternative approach to industrial relations policy generally and to containing wages specifically. In 1983 this was promulgated by the Labor Opposition (with Bob Hawke as the new leader) and the ACTU as the 'Statement of Accord'. It was promoted as a way out of the trap of simultaneous high inflation and high unemployment. The Accord (1983: 3) attacked the 'wages freeze' as an 'inequitable wages policy' requiring 'sacrifice' from wage earners but not from 'non-wage income earners'. The Accord effectively guaranteed a lower rate of wage increases (lower than the CPI) in return for other policy considerations, especially those associated with the 'social wage', namely 'expenditure by governments that affect the living standards of the people by direct income transfers or provision of services' (The Accord, 1983: 6). The process by which these policies were to be made was also discussed in the Accord. 'Co-operation' was the keyword rather than 'confrontation'.

The Accord has been interpreted variously. At one level it has delivered relative industrial peace and harmony (see Stilwell, 1986). Key disputes such as Mudginberri have stood out conspciuously in this context. At another level the Accord has been seen as part of a corporatist or partial corporatist strategy by the Hawke Government (see chapter 16 and Stewart, 1984). According to this view, during periods of economic instability or crisis corporatism may emerge, usually focussing on the question of incomes policy. Politics within corporatist institutions are 'simulated' rather than real, with the usual open business–union conflicts hidden from the public. The interest groups, normally 'big business' and 'big unions', that engineer this process are seen to be organised on a hierarchical basis and are concerned to exclude other interests from the process (see chapter 16).

Conclusion

Although trade unions are important actors in Australian politics, their power is most often exhibited in their reactions to other political actor's initiatives, rather than in initiatives of their own. Despite public perceptions and distrust of the power of unions, trade union power is generally reactive in each of the four arenas discussed above—in the ALP, the arbitration system, industrial action and lobbying governments.

References

The Accord (1983) The ALP and the ACTU

Bean, C. and Kelley, J. (1988) 'Partisan Stability and Short-Term Change in the 1987 Federal Election' *Politics* 23, 2, November

Creighton, W.B. et al., (1983) *Labour Law* Sydney: Law Book Co.

Dabscheck, B. and Niland, J. (1981) *Industrial Relations in Australia* Sydney: George Allen and Unwin

Kemp, D. (1977) 'Political Parties and Australian Culture' *Quadrant* 21, 12, December, pp. 3–13

Kitay, G.B. and Powe, R. (1987) 'Exploitation at $1,000 per Week? The Mudginberri Dispute' *The Journal of Industrial Relations* 29, 3, pp. 365–400

Martin, R.M. (1962) 'Australian Trade Unionism, 1961' *The Journal of Industrial Relations*, 4, 1, pp. 1–9

—— (1971) 'Australian Professional and White Collar Unions', in J.E. Isaac and G.W. Ford (eds) *Australian Labor Relations* Melbourne: Sun Books

—— (1980) *Trade Unions in Australia* Ringwood: Penguin

Plowman, D. et al. (1981) *Australian Industrial Relations* revised edn, Sydney: McGraw Hill

Rawson, D.W. (1978) *Unions and Unionists in Australia* Sydney: George Allen and Unwin

Rawson, D.W. and Wrightson, S. (1985) *Australian Unions 1984* Sydney: Croom Helm

Simms, M. (1987) *Militant Public Servants* Sydney: Macmillan

Stewart, R. (1984) 'The Politics of the Accord: Does Corporatism Explain It' *Politics* 20, 1, May, pp. 26–36

Stilwell, F. (1986) *The Accord and Beyond* London: Pluto Press

19 The news media

Rodney Smith

The power of the media is a subject that excites more political debate than most others in Australia. Often this debate is confused, ranging indiscriminately across questions such as whether news media owners like Rupert Murdoch have too much power, whether the words of journalists determine which party wins elections and whether government controls over the media are too strong or too weak. This confusion arises largely because the simple phrase 'the power of the media' hides a complex range of power relationships involving media owners and managers, advertisers and sponsors, governments, media workers and audiences. It is only by examining these relationships that media power can be adequately understood. Although all media involve politics, this chapter focusses on the media power relationships that are most obviously political—those of the news media.

Media ownership

Some critics think that understanding the power of the media can be reduced to the question of who owns the media. Australia's media are owned by a few wealthy businessmen; these businessmen therefore exercise the media's power (McQueen, 1977).

Australian news media ownership certainly is highly oligopolised. Australian print media ownership is the most concentrated among OECD countries. In January 1988, Murdoch's News Limited owned ten of Australia's nineteen metropolitan daily papers, while John Fairfax Ltd owned five, Robert Holmes à Court's Bell Publishing owned two and Kerry Packer's Australian Consolidated Press (ACP) one. All four companies also owned groups of suburban and/or provincial newspapers. ACP owned 45 percent of Australian magazines, while News owned 40 percent. At the time, the three commercial metropolitan television networks, on whom the regional commercial stations relied for almost of their programming, were dominated by four owners. Bond Media owned four of the five metropolitan Nine channels and Sky satellite television, Northern Star Holdings/Westfield Capital Corporation owned four of the five Ten channels, while Christopher Skase's Qintex and Bell between them controlled the five Seven stations. Radio station ownership was somewhat more diverse, although Bond, Holmes à Court and Northern Star were among owners with five or more stations.

Australian news media ownership was not always as concentrated as it is today. In 1903, Australia's 21 metropolitan daily newspapers were owned by seventeen companies. By 1950, the fifteen metropolitans were owned by ten companies, a ratio that rose to fourteen owned by six in 1963. By 1972, every metropolitan paper was published by either Herald and Weekly Times (HWT), Fairfax or Murdoch (McQueen, 1977: 36). Until 1986, these three companies, along with ACP, formed a stable oligopoly that owned the lion's share of newspapers, magazines and metropolitan television stations.

Between 1986 and 1988, four factors disrupted this stable oligopoly, without fundamentally altering the concentrated nature of Australian news media ownership.

First, HWT, which controlled half of Australia's daily newspapers, came under stockmarket pressure from Holmes à Court and ACP in 1985, and was finally taken over and divided among a number of new and old media organisations between November 1986 and February 1987. The major result of this takeover was that Rupert Murdoch extended his ownership to 74 percent of the metropolitan daily newspaper market.

Second, between 1986 and 1988 the Hawke Government introduced changes to the regulations controlling television licences (see below) to allow companies to own stations covering up to 60 percent of the national audience, but preventing them from owning stations where they also owned newspapers. These changes resulted in fifteen stations changing owners between January and September 1987, and the development for the first time of national television networks dominated by single companies.

Third, the launching of Australia's domestic satellites (AUSSAT) between 1985 and 1987, combined with the Hawke Government's policy of equalising rural and urban television services, meant that rural television audiences, which had previously been limited at most to one local channel and the ABC, came within reach of the major commercial networks. As a result of these developments, a number of rural stations changed hands and almost all of them affiliated with one of the metropolitan networks.

The fourth factor was the attempt in 1987–88 by Warwick Fairfax to buy back complete ownership of the Fairfax company. To finance this, Fairfax was forced to close down two of its metropolitan newspapers and to sell other newspapers as well as its magazine holdings and the Macquarie radio retwork, leaving it a shell of its former self.

Australia's media oligopoly has developed partly due to political factors such as the granting of television licences to certain companies (see below), but it has primarily occurred because of economic factors. To take newspapers as an example, concentration has occurred partly because of their high production costs, and partly because newspapers gain over half their income from advertising. Existing newspapers that fail to maintain a large readership steadily lose corporate and private advertisers to their competitors until they are no longer profitable. In four months to March 1988, Perth's *Western Mail*, Brisbane's *Telegraph*, the Sydney *Sun* and *The Times on Sunday* were all closed due to financial problems. New newspapers are rarely launched because to return a profit they must first build a substantial readership for advertisers. *The Australian*, for example, ran for twenty years before showing a profit for News Ltd. Large companies like News Ltd may be able to absorb the substantial costs of starting a new paper, but small companies cannot. *Business Daily*, launched by a group of journalists in 1987, folded after only 38 issues because of financial difficulties. Similar dynamics of production costs and advertising share operate to produce oligopolies in the television and radio industries, with the added factor in these industries of government licencing (see below).

An Australian news media oligopoly certainly exists, but what impact does it have on the political news consumed by Australian citizens? How much power do news media owners really have? Four broad effects can be identified.

The first and most obvious effect is a strong limitation on the ability of citizens to choose between alternative accounts of Australian politics. This is particularly true of newspapers. Australians who start the day with tea, toast and the metropolitan newspaper in Hobart, Adelaide, Perth, Canberra and Darwin have no choice as to which newspaper they will buy. These cities all have only one morning newspaper.

Moreover, a news media owner decides the particular audience at which a newspaper or news programme is to be aimed, in order to maximise advertising revenue. This in turn affects the emphasis that newspaper or news programme gives to political as opposed to sporting or social news, as well as the approach to politics taken by its reporters. Newspapers or news programmes aimed at serious, well-educated audiences give lengthier treatment to political news and provide more substantial analysis of politics compared with those aimed at popular, less-educated audiences.

This audience targetting means that in cities with alternative morning newspapers, the two papers do not truly compete. Brisbane's *Courier Mail*, the *Sydney Morning Herald* and Melbourne's *Age* are aimed at one market, Brisbane's *Daily Sun*, Sydney's *Daily Telegraph* and Melbourne's *Sun-News Pictorial* are aimed at another. Citizens wanting a serious metropolitan newspaper, or a popular metropolitan newspaper, are left with no consumer choice.

Second, news media owners and their managers sometimes act directly to ensure that particular news stories, editorial comment or even the whole coverage of news events reflect a particular viewpoint or protect a particular set of interests. In newspaper companies, for example, owners and managers have occupied the positions of 'managing editor', 'executive editor' or 'chief editorial executive' to exercise control over their papers' news coverage. Sir Warwick Fairfax, for example, while chairman of Fairfax, was also managing editor of the *Sydney Morning Herald*, and regularly used to impose his views on the *Herald's* reporting. Rupert Murdoch used the *Australian* to help Labor's federal election chances in 1972, before turning the paper against the ALP in 1975.

Some critics argue that this type of direct intervention becomes more likely when media owners are involved in other forms of business. Most of the newer Australian media owners, as well as Murdoch and Packer, also pursue other business activities. Holmes à Court, for example, has large investments in industries including transport, mining and banking. As Chadwick (1987: 6) notes: 'Potential conflicts of interest abound. Imagine: a *Financial Review* journalist learns of an impending Holmes à Court takeover bid, but disclosure would ruin the plan or, at best, cost Holmes à Court millions by pushing up the target's share price. Will the story be published? When?' Such situations are not hypothetical. In 1986, Holmes à Court's *Western Mail* apparently suppressed stories that reflected unfavourably on fellow West Australian Alan Bond's taxation and share dealings.

Nonetheless, intervention of this sort is less common than is popularly believed, primarily because media owners with large business interests simply can not be in every news room they own on every day to ensure that the news is written the way they want it to be. For the most part, the power they have is exercised indirectly, through the hiring and firing of news staff.

The third effect of the concentration of media organisations into a few hands is to make this indirect power over news staff easier for owners to exert. A newspaper editor is unlikely to risk being sacked for acting against the interests of her or his paper's owner if that owner can ensure that the editor cannot find work in two-thirds of the metropolitan papers in the country. Editors who want to keep their jobs thus become attuned to their owners' often implicit views:

> You can see the way the wind blows from the remarks of Peter Wylie, then editor of Murdoch's *Daily Mirror*, on *Four Corners* some years ago. 'I don't particularly follow Murdoch's policies. . . I know where we stand politically—the last federal election here we supported the Fraser government, its return. But I understand what Rupert Murdoch's feelings are in his business interests; I would know where we stand. Question: Would you go against them? Wylie: No, I wouldn't. (Bowman, 1987: 5)

The final effect of media oligopoly is to reduce the variety of sources and points of view gaining media access. Articles written for one newspaper are then used by other papers in the same company. Rather than maintain full news staffs, media organisations tend to take the cheaper option of using the same syndicated material from Australian and overseas news services. The recent development of national television networks makes it possible to produce one news programme for broadcasting nationwide. This is cheaper than producing one programme per state capital, but it means the loss of distinct state and local perspectives on news events. Australian news becomes Sydney-centric.

Government involvement in news media

Broadcasting

The most obvious government involvement in the news media occurs via the Australian Broadcasting Corporation (ABC). The Corporation (Commission before 1983), a government-funded statutory authority, is Australia's only nationwide broadcaster, and, through Radio Australia, Australia's voice to surrounding countries. Among its programmes, the ABC broadcasts each session of Federal Parliament on radio, and provides the widest range of news and current affairs programmes of any Australian electronic news media organisation. Since the 1960s, ABC news services have been widely heralded for their critical and sometimes radical treatment of politics.

The critical spirit of ABC programmes that date from the 1960s, such as 'Four Corners', 'AM' and 'PM', combined with the regular complaints by politicians about the treatment they receive on the ABC, may suggest an image of the ABC as timelessly independent, beholden to no one but itself. This image is false. Until the 1960s, ABC news reflected an orthodoxly conservative world view. Since 1975, many of the more radical, adventurous ABC programming ideas developed in the 1960s and early 1970s have disappeared or come under threat. These changing directions of ABC news reflect the fact that the ABC comprises a set of power relations—primarily between its staff, its management and the government—similar to those that operate in the commercial news media.

The government can exercise very direct power over the ABC. Under the Australian Broadcasting Corporation Act, the relevant government minister has power to direct the ABC to broadcast, or refrain from broadcasting, material if this is deemed to be 'in the national interest'. Intervention of this sort is rare but not unheard of (Ashbolt, 1987: 82–85). The indirect exercise of power by governments over the ABC has been much more widespread.

One major form of indirect government power over the ABC is its ability to choose the Chairman (sic) and commissioners who comprise the ABC Board. As Ashbolt (1987: 102) notes, ABC chairmen and commissioners historically have been establishment figures with 'a tight class loyalty' to the values of Australian capitalism. Current Chairman Robert Somervaille, for example, is a senior partner at law and a former director of News Ltd.

Prime Ministers and cabinets have not shied away from appointing chairmen who share their general views. Malcolm Fraser, for example, wanted to curb innovative ABC programmes in 1976, and chose conservative former public service head Sir Harry Bland to attack this task as ABC Chairman (Harding, 1979: chapter 5). In 1986, the Hawke Government appointed former Neville Wran adviser David Hill as Chairman.

The composition of ABC boards appointed by Labor governments is usually somewhat broader than it is under coalition governments. The Board appointed by Labor in 1983, for example, included several prominent social reformers, three women and an aborigine. The commissioners came from a range of occupations (although none were blue-collar workers).

The combination of loyalties toward the establishment and toward particular parties has meant that the ABC Board and the management beneath it have been extremely cautious about news and current affairs programmes that threaten establishment values or party fortunes. On occasions, this has meant removal of reporters (as when George Negus was removed from TDT following an allegedly aggressive interview with Malcolm Fraser), the vetting of scripts by management (as occured prior to the 1972 election) and the suppression of whole programmes (as ABC Chairman Ken Myer attempted with a 'Four Corners' report on Papua New Guinea in 1984). Sometimes these actions have followed direct pressure from the government or political parties. On many occasions, they have been pre-emptive actions taken by ABC controllers who have learned to anticipate government and establishment wishes in the same way that editors in commercial news media organisations anticipate their owners' wishes: '. . . much of the conformism, repression and self-censorship within the ABC comes about less by direct, straightforward government interference than by the constant striving of the governing body, managerial staff and producers to anticipate, interpret and fulfil government expectations' (Ashbolt, 1987: 85). This explains much government power over the ABC, but even ABC boards and managements that resist outside expectations cannot escape the most important control that governments exercise over the ABC—control over funding.

One of the first actions of the Fraser Government was to cut funding for what it saw as a hostile ABC, an action that was repeated almost every year thereafter by the Coalition Government. The Hawke Government has increased ABC funding only slightly since it came to office. In 1981, the Dix Committee of Inquiry into the ABC suggested that the ABC should not rely on public funding, but should accept corporate sponsorship to pay for some programming. Although this idea was not incorporated into the 1983 Australian Broadcasting Corporation Bill, it has re-emerged intermittently since. From being seen as an instrument of national culture worth preserving for its own sake, the ABC is now regarded by many on both sides of Parliament as an institution that must prove its worth by competing against commercial electronic news media.

The effects of these financial challenges on ABC news and current affairs programmes has been threefold. First, it has meant reductions in news staff and the retention of increasingly outdated equipment, leaving the ABC well behind commercial news media in its capacity to process news quickly and efficiently.

Second, the ABC's management has been unwilling to risk further funding cuts sparked by government dissatisfaction with programming that is too 'radical' or serves very small audiences. Thus, it has concentrated its diminishing resources on producing mainstream news programmes. Programming giving access to groups usually not heard on the airwaves has suffered accordingly. In its attempts to provide less controversial news in the 1980s, the ABC has lost much of its direction without escaping controversy, as the axing of 'Nationwide', the short-lived 'National' programme, the restructuring of ABC radio and several public disputes between management and prominent journalists attest. Third, better conditions, equipment and salaries have lured many of Australia's best electronic journalists from the ABC to commercial news media.

The net result of these developments is that while the ABC still manages to provide a broader news and current affairs service than commercial media, much of the qualitative difference between the ABC and commercial news has closed in recent years.

Since 1977, Australian governments have also funded the Special Broadcasting Service (SBS) to provide multicultural broadcasting. Initially limited to radio, SBS has broadcast television programmes in Sydney and Melbourne from 1979 and to all major cities from 1986. With its small news staff, SBS concentrates on international news events, combining foreign commercial video footage with its own commentary. Perhaps because of its tiny audiences and less varied formats, SBS news and current affairs have attracted less criticism than those of the ABC.

Legislation

Governments also exert power over all Australian news media through legislation. Some of this legislation has quite specific effects on the shape of Australian politics, such as the legislation, repealed in 1983, that prevented the electronic news media from broadcasting any material relating to an election from midnight on the Wednesday before polling day to the close of polling. Other legislation, such as that governing media ownership, has less direct effects.

Until 1987, no government legislation existed restricting the ownership of newspapers. Television station owners were restricted to two metropolitan stations, while radio station owners were limited to no more than one metropolitan station in each state, four stations across any state and eight across Australia. These regulations limited oligopolies within the electronic media, but they did not bar large newspaper owners like Fairfax from television and radio ownership.

Cross-media ownership was limited in 1987 by the Broadcasting (Ownership and Control) Act, which prohibited owners of more than 15 percent of shares in a newspaper or ownership of a radio station with a commercial monopoly in an area from holding more than a 5 percent share in a television station covering the same audience as that newspaper or radio station. The same legislation expanded permissable television ownership from the two-station limit to stations reaching a maximum of 60 percent of the Australian population. These legislative changes originated in pressure from corporations wanting to expand their television holdings into metropolitan networks, and were resisted by public-interest groups concerned to prevent the concentration of television ownership.

Effective legislation requires policing. The body most concerned with policing electronic media ownership is the Australian Broadcasting Tribunal (ABT). The Tribunal, which replaced the Australian Broadcasting Control Board in 1976, is a quasi-judicial body which, among other tasks, holds inquiries into the granting and renewal of television and radio licences. The ABT may refuse to grant or renew a licence, or it may shorten the period for which a licence is granted. In practice, the former action is unheard of and the latter very rare. Moreover, the Tribunal's powers were reduced in 1981 when it was prevented from investigating licence transfers between companies *before* they occurred. As a result, at the end of 1987 the ABT was just beginning to examine the rapid succession of television licence transfers which took place in late 1986, leading its chairperson, Dierdre O'Connor, to describe it as a 'toothless tiger' (*Australian Financial Review* 9 November 1987).

ABT hearings are sometimes further hampered by lack of cooperation from licence holders under scrutiny and by the Tribunal's need to wait on Federal and High Court rulings on legal points arising from hearings. These problems were both illustrated in the ABT's investigation into whether American citizen Murdoch had broken the law prohibiting more than 15 percent foreign ownership of television stations. This investigation began in April 1986, but was not concluded by early 1988, many months after Murdoch's News Ltd sold the stations under question.

Despite these problems, the ABT helps to keep electronic news media owners within the broad bounds of the law. Its hearings also reveal information that would not otherwise be widely known, such as the alleged collusion between media-owners Bond and Holmes à Court to attempt to remove West Australian Premier Brian Burke from office and the alleged $400 000 secret defamation payment made by Bond to Joh Bjelke-Petersen for a programme shown on QTQ9. Finally, the Tribunal's public inquiries into matters such as Australian content and children's programming provide a forum for media consumers to make their voices heard.

News as bureaucratic work

Media oligopoly and government intervention set the broad constraints on news, but they only tell part of the story. Owners, managers and politicians do not write the news. The view of politics that the media present is fundamentally the work of journalists, editors, photographers, camera and sound operators, producers and other media workers. To understand the role of the media in Australian politics therefore requires an understanding of this work.

A fundamental question in any such understanding is 'What is news?' The apparently flippant response to this question—'Whatever is in the newspapers'—is not far from the truth. Newspapers and news programmes never cover all the events, or even all of the 'important' events, in a day. They present some events and omit others, include some points of view about the events presented and exclude others. Thus they can never be said to be 'objective' records of the day's events. In this sense, all news is biased. As Barr (1977: 77) writes: 'Of course the press is biased. How, indeed could it not be? How could anyone publish a value-free newspaper? The gathering, editing and publishing of news involves decisions by people who inevitably bring their own background, values and prejudices to bear on deciding what to select, emphasise and colour as news'.

The choice and presentation of certain events and views as news and others as not is not primarily a matter of deliberate bias and inaccurate reporting by journalists, although examples of these are easy to find. Nor does it stem primarily from the sociological background of news staff—who tend to be middle class, male and anglo-celtic (Henningham, 1981)—although this certainly has an impact on their choice of news. Rather, the two strongest influences on news selection are socialisation, which takes place on the journalistic job, and the bureaucratic nature of news organisations and news gathering.

Socialisation in news organisations is very strong, since it comes with a system of direct rewards and punishments. News staff beginning as cadets or junior reporters soon find out which stories get printed and which get rejected by sub-editors. To keep their jobs they have to respond correctly to these messages from sub-editors about what is news and what is not. Some news organisations have house journals that help to reinforce the organisation's approach to news. At higher levels, staff discuss approaches to events and issues. In these formal and informal ways, news staff learn what can be termed 'news sense' or a 'news formula'. They apply this news formula to the multifarious events of any day to decide which of them are news and which are not. According to Windschuttle (1984: 278–99), the news formula that provides the core of most news stories in the Australian media comprises the following elements: celebrities (political leaders, the royal family, sporting heroes and entertainers); death and disaster (murders, shark attacks, bushfires, car smashes); and deviance (criminals, protesters, the unemployed, homosexuals). Examination of any news media for a few days suggests the truth of Windschuttle's claim.

The bureaucratic nature of news is determined by the time constraints under which news staff work. They have 20 pages or 30 minutes of news to produce every day, and to cope with the pressure of this daily deadline, they produce it in manageable, predictable ways. A morning newspaper will, for example, always have three pages of international news, three of national news, an editorial page, a features page, a 'lifestyle' or 'human interest' page, three pages of business news, three sports pages, and so on. The specific content on these pages will vary from day to day, but unless a very important news story such as an election or stock market crash temporarily dominates the paper, these emphases on different types of news remain fixed (Tuchman, 1978: chapter 2).

Most news is not even 'new' in the sense of being unexpected. The dates of parliamentary sittings, budget speeches, elections, party conferences, as well as football finals, Christmas road tolls and other events are all known well in advance, allowing journalists to anticipate and manage the news (Tuchman, 1978: chapter 3). In other cases, news staff do not even have to look for news. Political parties, pressure groups, companies and so on all want publicity for their actions and regularly contact media organisations in the hope of gaining it. As well as receiving this public relations material, most news organisations subscribe to wire services like Australian Associated Press, which provide them with hundreds of news stories every day.

Major news organisations divide their staff to cover particular specialist 'rounds'; for example, federal politics, state politics, education, police, courts, ethnic affairs and business. These reporters develop a deeper knowledge of their round, as well as close contacts with sources in a particular area of news, on whom they rely for most of their stories. This relationship between reporters and sources is perhaps most obvious in the operation of the parliamentary press galleries (see Edgar, 1979: chapter 4).

In sum, news making is bureaucratic work. News organisations cope with the apparent chaos and infinite number of events in each day by developing routines and specialisation. This bureaucratisation has important effects on news. It favours the views of other organisations that operate bureaucratically; that is, groups with enough resources to maintain full-time spokespeople and to provide journalists with regular publicity handouts. Groups that are diverse and unorganised, or do not possess these resources, receive little or no coverage. In demonstrations, for example, it is the comments of police spokespeople and not those of the demonstrators that are reported. In biotechnological experimentation, the comments of research teams and the church receive coverage, but the views of women do not.

Repeated use of particular news sources in turn patterns the way in which news is defined over time. News about demonstrations becomes news of disruptions to traffic, violence and arrests, because these are matters important to police. The causes for which the demonstrators are protesting gain almost no coverage. Similarly, news about in vitro fertilisation becomes news about scientific breakthroughs and religious morality, rather than news about changed possibilities for women. News becomes defined in terms of the dominant organisations in society, in terms of the status quo (Tuchman, 1978: 209–16).

The power of news sources

The above account of journalists' work suggests that the 'power of the media' encompasses the power of news sources over each other and over news staff. Journalists want news; news sources compete with each other to provide that news. The results of this competition are determined by the resources of the various sources and their skill in using those resources. Some of these resources, like money, are general in nature (see chapter 2). Others, which are discussed below, relate specifically to the operation of the news media.

The first and most important resources are press secretaries and media-liaison units. Government ministers have always had officials to deal with the press, but the expansion of news media demands on politicians in the last twenty years has meant an increase in the size and importance of government media-liason units. In line with this development, Opposition leaders, political parties, public service departments and even some businesses and pressure groups have introduced or increased their publicity staff in recent years, recognising the need to deal with the media in a professional way if they are to get their messages across. Because press secretaries and publicity officers must understand the needs of the news media, they are often former journalists. This can lead to cosy circles developing between journalists and press secretaries who were formerly colleagues, circles into which it is hard for other potential news sources to break.

The major tool of news sources is the well written press release, which requires little adaption by journalists before it can be run as a news story. News organisations with small staffs rely on press releases to fill much of their news space, since without them they simply could not cover all the major stories in a day. Even large news organisations rely on press releases to make work easier. Providing Queensland's news media with plentiful press releases and pre-filmed interviews was one of the main ways in which Joh Bjelke-Petersen ensured favourable coverage for his state government (Wallace, 1980: 211–13). As Tiffen (1985) writes: '. . . a well-fed press will have less time and inclination to search for other stories'.

Different news media require different approaches by sources. The number of words in an average television or radio news bulletin would not even fill the front page of a newspaper. News sources using these media therefore have to keep their announcements brief and simple. The politicians most successful at using the electronic news media have been those such as Neville Wran, who learned to speak in twenty-second 'grabs' that could be slotted easily into short news broadcasts.

Television news demands interesting visual footage, something that most politics lacks. This demand can sometimes be met by staging actions for television such as the signing of documents or the gathering of politicians at a meeting. Politicians rarely miss opportunities to appear at events that are themselves visually interesting, a practice epitomised by Bob Hawke's ubiquitous attendances at sporting events. Nonetheless, institutional politics remains fundamentally unsuited to television, a fact that helps to explain the prominence television news gives to alternative, more colourful forms of politics such as demonstrations, pickets and marches.

A political actor's timing of events and statements is crucial to his or her success or failure as news. News organisations have 'slow' days like Sunday and slow periods such as the Christmas 'silly season', during which it is much easier for political actors to make news than it is on a weekday full of potentially newsworthy events. The opponents of the Australia Card generated much publicity for their cause in 1987 largely by releasing accusations about the Card on successive Sundays, when few other events clamoured for attention. Timing within each day is also important. A political actor holding a press conference late in the afternoon not only provides fresh news and footage for the widely-watched evening television news, but does so without giving his or her opponents time to present well-formulated responses.

Since many news organisations only have one reporter or news team assigned to state or federal politics, parties knowing that their opposition is about to make a policy announcement can time announcements of their own for the same time in order to minimise their opponent's coverage. Wran did this in 1981, drawing journalists away from the New South Wales Opposition leader's press conference on the film industry policy by staging a press conference to announce hospital fees at the same time (Tiffen, 1985: 152).

Governments wishing to defuse potentially controversial actions will introduce them when the news media's attention is focussed on other events. On the other hand, good news can be released in stages to maximise its impact.

Australian governments have developed an art form out of opening projects several times—at their inception, half way thorough completion, and when they are finished—to create an impression of achievement. Similarly, political actors with allegations damaging to their opponents can release these gradually rather than all at once. This creates 'new allegations' and 'further developments' for journalists to report each day and maximises the impact of the allegations.

Sources can develop good personal relationships with news staff and news media managements. Politicians can 'play favourites' with journalists, selectively leaking information in advance to journalists who have given them favourable coverage in the past and 'freezing out' critical journalists. They can court journalists by providing them with food, alcohol and access to events. Journalists invited to accompany government ministers on overseas trips will inevitably file regular stories about these trips, if only to justify their own participation on them. The generally favourable news media coverage of the Hawke Government can be partly explained by Hawke's assiduous efforts to maintain good personal relationships with most news media staff. In 1986, for example, when the news media began to take a critical view of his Government, Hawke initiated a series of dinners at the Lodge with senior news reporters.

Coalition governments have usually had fairly friendly relationships with news media owners and managers, perhaps best typified by the Menzies Government's granting of Australia's first television licence to newspaper magnate Frank Packer. Historically, the ALP has been suspicious of media owners, a suspicion vindicated for many Labor activists by the media's role in the Whitlam Government's 1975 fall. Despite, or perhaps because of, this role, recent ALP governments have moved close to media owners. Hawke proudly describes media owners such as Bond and Packer as great Australians, a complete reversal of his views fifteen years ago. In 1986, the Hawke Government smoothed the way for the tax-free sale of television stations owned by Packer and Murdoch. At state level, the Wran New South Wales government made several decisions favouring media owners, such as including Packer and Murdoch as partners with the government in Lotto, extending Packer's monopoly on two ski resorts until the year 2025, and providing millions of dollars to help decentralise Australian Newsprint Mills, then owned by HWT and Fairfax (see Tiffen, 1985: 163–65). ALP and coalition governments at state and federal levels now both have close relations with media owners. The voice most critical of Australia's media oligopolies in recent years has not been Labor's, but that of Liberal backbencher Ian Macphee. Whether Labor's new chumminess has influenced the media is difficult to determine unequivocably, but media coverage of recent ALP governments appears to have been more favourable than in the past.

The above points suggest why some political actors are able to generate more favourable news than others. They possess more of the relevant resources and utilise them more skillfully (see chapter 2). Governments dominate the news because they control a large number of key resources—time, press secretaries, information and largesse. Other actors such as Opposition parties, business, unions and some pressure groups have the resources to get their views across the media regularly, while groups with fewer resources are rarely and fleetingly heard.

Newsmedia audiences

The extent to which audiences are influenced by news media messages is central to understanding the news media's political impact. This is particularly true in liberal democracies such as Australia, where a high proportion of those audiences comprise voters who periodically judge the performance of governments at elections. If audiences completely ignore or reject news media messages when forming electoral judgements and other political attitudes, then it does not matter whether the news media are owned by one company or many, how the government regulates the media, or which sources gain access to the news. If, at the other extreme, audiences uncritically suck in every news media message, then control of the news media would mean control of the political system. Four broad schools of thinkers have developed competing models of the power relationship between news media and audiences.

The free market or pluralist school claims that the media have very little impact on their audiences. Indeed, the audience has the power of the marketplace over news media organisations. If consumers do not like the news they get from one organisation, they will find another one they prefer. Any media organisation that does not give the public what it wants will go out of business (see Windschuttle, 1984: 261–63).

The second school, most often associated with vulgar Marxist class analysis, argues that the news media simply legitimate the status quo for their audiences. Workers, and other subordinate groups in society take their political views directly from the news media, which themselves serve the interests of capitalists and other dominant social forces. Consequently, subordinate groups adopt the views of these dominant forces themselves, and become diverted from taking political action in their own interests. The news media are a contemporary opiate of the masses (see Windschuttle, 1984: 263–65).

The third school, the hegemonic school, is a refinement of the vulgar Marxist school. According to this school, news media cannot simply impose the alien views of dominant social groups on the working class and other subordinate groups, since these groups have attitudes and values of their own. Rather, the news media respond to subordinate attitudes and values in such a way as to accommodate them within the framework of the dominant social groups. The news is not manipulated from above as the vulgar Marxists argue, or directed from below as the free market school claims, but is the result of an uneasy and shifting compromise between dominant and subordinate groups (see Windschuttle, 1984: 273–76).

The final school, associated with critical pluralist studies of politics, contends that the media '. . . may not be successful much of the time in telling people what to think, but it is stunningly successful in telling its readers what to think about' (Cohen, 1963: 120). The power of the media over audiences lies in agenda setting; that is, rather than news media changing attitudes over the short term, they are able, consciously or unconsciously, to suggest to audiences what events and issues are important.

Despite the importance of the news media-audience relationship and the development of these four schools, very few researchers have investigated exactly what impact news media have on the political attitudes, values and behaviour of Australian citizens. There are two broad reasons for this. One is that media effects on audiences are difficult to define. Should researchers be interested in investigating possible short-term effects, such as whether the news media coverage of an election campaign causes some voters to change their votes? Or are the more important questions whether the media help to maintain long-term support for the very institutions of elections and parties and prevent people from conceiving of and working towards alternative political arrangements? The second reason is methodological: it is extremely difficult to devise ways of isolating the impact of media from the impact of other socio-political factors on citizens' behaviour. Studying electoral behaviour, for example, it is very difficult to determine whether voter X changed her vote because of the news media, or discussions with her friends, or meeting the local candidate, or dissatisfaction with the policies of the party she previously supported.

In the absence of good, direct evidence of news media effects on audiences, news media critics from the four schools often argue from indirect evidence. Supporters of the free market school argue that high media consumption shows audience satisfaction with Australian news media. News media usage in Australia is certainly extensive. A 1979 survey revealed that almost 100 percent of households possessed a radio and a television, and large proportions used these media for their news coverage (Western and Hughes, 1983: 16, 52–8). Although newspaper consumption has fallen in recent decades, 70 percent of Australians still bought a newspaper every day in 1979 (Western and Hughes, 1983: 16). In 1987, the metropolitan daily newspapers had a combined circulation of 4 137 000.

The vulgar Marxist response is that this media consumption is almost all consumption of media owned by large corporations. Against this consumption, the audiences for alternative media like *Tribune* (circulation 10 000), feminist magazines, gay newspapers, community access radio stations such as 4ZZZ, 2RSR and 3CR, and even Australia's ethnic presses (combined circulation 800 000) are small beer. Most Australians get their political views from the mainstream, capitalist media.

If almost all Australians use mainstream commercial and ABC news media, it is by no means clear that the effect of this is the uncritical acceptance suggested by vulgar Marxist theorists. The 1984 Australian Values Study showed that while Australians had moderate to high levels of confidence in institutions such as the banking system (86 percent), police (81 percent), the education system (64 percent), the legal system (62 percent), the church (56 percent) and the Federal Government (56 percent), confidence in the press was a very low 28 percent. Moreover, overseas studies suggest that news audiences react to and interpret the news in the light of experiences and values that they draw from their immediate environment. Thus, for example, workers who have themselves been on strike are sceptical of negative presentations of other strikers and unions (Windschuttle, 1984: 343–45). Similarly, audiences differentiate between the sources to whose views they are exposed by the media, embracing some and rejecting others (Page et al., 1987). While the news media may initially push their audience's perceptions of events in one direction, those audiences later begin to re-evaluate their views and the media's impact becomes much weaker (Page et al., 1987). Finally, research such as that by Chamberlain (1983) indicates a much greater divergence of political attitudes and values between members of different classes in Australia than would be expected if the media had successfully seduced workers with capitalist ideology.

The hegemonic and agenda-setting schools are also somewhat stuck for evidence on their central claims. Hegemonic school researchers have identified some working-class values taken up by the news media (see Windschuttle, 1984: chapters 6, 10); however, they have not presented evidence that working-class audiences actually *accept* the transformation of these values that takes place in the media. While agenda-setting research has shown that the media do create agendas, no research has been done to see whether audiences actually adopt these news media agendas, whether audiences construct their own agendas that the media then take up, or whether the media's agenda and the public's agenda remain quite independent.

All of this is not to suggest that the news media do not help to shape the political attitudes and behaviour of individuals and groups in Australian society, but it does suggest that the power relationship between the news media and their audiences is the least understood of all of the power relationships embodied in the news media. Until this relationship is better understood, the precise position and power of Australia's news media, and the implications of this power for Australian liberal democracy, cannot be traced adequately.

References

Ashbolt, A. (1987) 'The ABC in Political Society: the relation the government', in E. Wheelwright and K. Buckley (eds) *Communications and Media in Australia* Sydney: Allen and Unwin

Barr, T. (1977) *Reflections of Reality* Adelaide: Rigby

Bowman, D. (1987) 'Fourth Estate' *Australian Society* 6, 12 December, p. 5

Chadwick, P. (1987) 'A Charter for Independence' *Australian Society* 6, 12 December, pp. 5–7

Chamberlain, C. (1983) *Class Consciousness in Australia* Sydney: George Allen and Unwin

Cohen, B. (1963) *The Press and Foreign Policy* Princeton: Princeton University Press

Edgar, P. (1979) *The Politics of the Press* Melbourne: Sun

Harding, R. (1979) *Outside Interference* Melbourne: Sun

Henningham, J. (1981) 'The Television Journalist: A Profile' *Media Information Australia* 22, November, pp. 3–7

McQueen, H. (1977) *Australia's Media Monopolies* Camberwell: Widescope

Page, B., Shapiro, R. and Dempsey, G. (1987) 'What Moves Public Opinion' *American Political Science Review* 81, 1 March, pp. 23–44

Tiffen, R. (1985) 'The Dynamics of Dominance: Wran and the Media, 1981', in E. Chaples, H. Nelson and K. Turner (eds) *The Wran Model* Melbourne: Oxford University Press

Tuchman, G. (1978) *Making News* New York: Free Press

Wallace, J. (1980) 'Reporting the Joh Show: The Queensland Media', in M. Cribb and P. Boyce (eds) *Politics in Queensland: 1977 and Beyond* St Lucia: University of Queensland Press

Western, J. and Hughes, C. (1983) *The Mass Media in Australia* St Lucia: University of Queensland Press

Windschuttle, K. (1984) *The Media* Ringwood: Penguin

20 The Australian voters

Ernie Chaples

Participation in politics, at least at first glance, would appear to be relatively high in Australia. In the federal election of 11 July 1987, the Australian Electoral office estimates that about 95 percent of the almost 10 million eligible voters actually had their names on the electoral rolls, and of those about 94.5 percent voted in the election.

But while figures concerning enrolment and voting always appear impressive for Australia (among the liberal democracies only Belgium has higher voter turnout figures in recent elections), other forms of political involvement by most Australians are much more limited.

Don Aitkin, in his book *Stability and Change in Australian Politics* (1982: chapter 18), divides Australians into three basic types of citizens: the politically active, the spectators, and the apathetic. In his 1967 national survey, only 27 percent qualified as being politically active, while 35 percent were apathetic. By 1979, however, the number of actives had risen to 43 percent, while the apathetics had fallen to 20 percent (the spectators remained steady at 38 percent in 1967 and 37 percent in 1979). Aitkin (1982: 273) speculates that the reasons for this new awareness are that 'anxiety and criticism have replaced complacence and euphoria', in the twelve years separating his two surveys.

Yet Aitkin's criteria for participation are very limited indeed. To be politically active for Aitkin requires only that a voter talk politics with others or follow politics in the media. If a somewhat greater effort is required by voters to classify them as 'actives', only 2 percent are regularly active in political parties and only 4 percent are even financial members of parties.

In a study of Brisbane voters, Wilson and Western (1973) found that 80 percent of the voters had never worked in a political campaign, 72 percent had never written to a member of Parliament, and 67 percent had never signed a petition. The number of people who had often participated was very low indeed; 7 percent had worked regularly in campaigns, 4 percent regularly write to MPs, 10 percent regularly attend political meetings.

So it seems justified to say that while most Australians are willing to accept compulsory enrolment and voting (Aitkin, 1982), and that voting is about as far as participation goes for the large majority of people. Active forms of politics, particularly as they involve running for office and belonging to political groups, is left to a small group of politically-active 'junkies'.

Who are the joiners?

The data on political activists in Australia is similar to most other western countries where political activity is valued in the political culture. The people most involved in politics are most likely to come from upper-income groups, are most likely to have benefitted from high levels of formal education and are generally drawn from occupation groups that directly benefit from and therefore attach more importance to political activity. In contrast, those with the lowest levels of personal wealth, the least education and those who either work in unskilled jobs or are unemployed are the citizens least likely to be politically active.

The results of this bias in favour of high status citizens correlating strongly with high political activity is described in Verba and Nie's study of participation in the United States (1972). The picture they paint is one in which a self-perpetuating cycle exists with those of high social status (i.e. those with money and education) having their strong tendencies to participate in politics reinforced by the social system. The result is that the privileged largely control the political system and tend to have a monopoly on the decision-making mechanisms of government, regardless of which political party controls government or which leader heads the government.

In contrast, those least privileged in society come from groups that are least likely to participate in politics, and these people end up having the least access to political leaders and the least influence on established, formal politics.

This is a pattern that is deeply reinforced by the Australian political culture but which contradicts liberal democratic notions of having citizens treated equally within the political process.

The voters and how they decide

The literature on voting in Australia is generally agreed on one basic proposition. In the words of Aitkin (1982: 353), 'The key to understanding stability and change in Australian politics is the continuing attachment of Australians to one or other of the political parties'.

Aitkin found that 85 percent of his respondents in 1979 possessed a psychological loyalty to one of the major parties, with most identifying themselves as being either Labor or Liberal. This is only slightly less than the 87 percent who demonstrated a clear party identification in Aitkin's 1967 survey. In addition, the strength of this party identification in 1979 was just about identical to the strength of attachment he discovered in 1967 (Aitkin, 1982, chapter 19).

The importance of party identification is also clearly indicated by the proportion of Aitkin's respondents who remembered voting in the last federal election for the House of Representatives in agreement with their normal party identification. A total of 93 percent remembered voting consistent with their party ID while only 5 percent remembered voting differently. In

Table 20.1 Strength of party identification, 1967 and 1979

	1967	1979
Party ID and strength	*(n = 2021)* %	*(n = 1982)* %
very strong	29	29
fairly strong	38	40
not very strong	20	16
'closer to' a party	5	7
no party identification	8	8

Source: Aitkin (1982: 287)

addition, there is virtually no difference in the tendency for either Labor partisans or for Liberal/National Party identifiers to vote according to their psychological identification with their party (Aitkin, 1982, pp. 288–89).

Who decides elections?

Given the apparent strength of party identification in Australia in recent decades, which voters decide which party will form a government? Basically, it comes down to two groups of voters: the 15 percent of the electorate that is not psychologically aligned with either major party and the estimated 5 percent of major party identifiers that for one reason or another abandons its normal allegiance and votes in opposition to its normally preferred party at any election.

In House of Representatives elections, the two major party groups start off with very similar numbers of supporters. Both Labor and the non-Labor parties consistently command about 40 percent of the national vote, even when there is a landslide by one side or the other in parliamentary seats won at the election.

But a word of caution needs to be entered here. Results in voting for state parliament or for the Australian Senate do not necessarily parallel voting for the House of Representatives. Since 1975, the number of voters who give a first preference to someone other than the Labor or Liberal/National Party candidates in Senate polling has about doubled.

The Senate is elected according to proportional representation, and in recent decades neither the Labor Party nor the Liberal and National Parties in coalition have generally been able to elect a majority of members of the Senate. The Australian Democrats have exercised a balance-of-power position in the Senate since 1980, much as the Democratic Labor Party did in the late 1960s and early 1970s. In addition, several independents have been elected to the Senate, including Tasmanian Brian Harradine, who was first elected in 1975 and has been re-elected every time he has stood for re-election since then. Peace candidate Senator Jo Vallentine was first elected in Western Australia in 1984 and was re-elected again in 1987. Senator Robert Wood was elected under proportional representation as a candidate for the Nuclear

Table 20.2 First preference votes by party for the House and Senate, 1975–87

Nationwide percentages: Federal elections 1975–84					
Election	Chamber	ALP	Lib./Nat.	Aust. Dems	Other
1975	House	42.8	53.1		4.0
	Senate	40.9	51.7		7.4
1977	House	39.6	48.1	9.4	2.8
	Senate	36.8	45.6	11.1	6.6
1980	House	45.1	46.3	6.6	2.0
	Senate	42.3	43.5	9.3	5.0
1983	House	49.5	43.6	5.0	1.9
	Senate	45.5	39.8	9.6	5.1
1984	House	47.5	45.0	5.4	2.0
	Senate	42.2	39.5	7.6	10.6
1987	House	45.8	45.9	6.0	2.3
	Senate	42.8	42.0	8.5	6.7

Source: Legislative Research Service, *Basic Paper No. 3: Federal Election Results, 1949–1984*; for 1987, Australian Electoral Commission preliminary results.

Disarmament Party, despite getting only 1.5 percent of the primary votes in the 1987 New South Wales Senate ballot.

Aitkin (1982: 47) also reports that while 66 percent of the respondents in his 1967 survey had always voted for the same party in both federal and state elections, 34 percent had not done so. This tendency for large numbers of people to vote for different parties in federal and state politics or for different parties at the same election in the House and Senate adds substantially to the uncertainty in the outcomes of Australian elections.

Uncertainty in voting behaviour

This pool of voters who are not particularly loyal to either the Labor Party or their Liberal/National opponents has been the major objective of most political campaigning in recent decades.

These voters are often referred to as 'swinging voters' or softly-committed voters. Here the term describes voters who deviate from their normal party identification and, of course, voters with no party identification. Rod Cameron, the Labor Party's national pollster since the 1972 elections, calls the swinging voter 'The VIP of Australian politics. . . A major part of the (parties') creative effort, budget allowance and media planning is directed at this prestigious swinger' (Cameron, 1973: 275).

The research that I have done on softly-committed voters in recent elections suggests that there are four basic types of voters who are not entirely predictable in national elections. They are the true swingers, those with weak party identifications who decide between the two major party groupings; the local candidate inconsistents, who vote in House elections because of their preference for a local candidate above other considerations; the party waverers; and the Senate protestors. Both the true swingers and Senate protestors include important sub-groups of voters, as follows:

- Swinging voters in Lower House elections
  - Major-party swingers—no party identification
  - Third-party voters
  - Alienated voters
  - Airheads and drongos
- Local candidate inconsistents
- Party waverers
- Senate protestors
  - Left-Labor Senate protestors
  - 'Keep the bastards honest' protestors
  - Religious fundamentalist protestors
  - Liberal progressive protestors

The true swinging voter can actually be found in four major varieties. The first sub-type is loyal to neither Labor or the Liberals but chooses exclusively from among these two parties. They are the ultimate rationalists in our electorate. These major party swinging voters know that either the ALP or Liberal Party (with the Nationals) will form the next government, they look at each party to decide which suits them best at a given election and they then cast their vote accordingly.

A second brand of swinging voter is really anti-major party. This type of voter nearly always prefers giving a first preference to the Australian Democrats or to another independent or minor party candidate. In New South Wales elections, their choice of candidates may well stop after casting this first preference since numbering other choices is not required.

But in federal politics, a valid formal vote requires the third-party voter to decide between Labor and Liberal (or National) if their ballot is to be counted as formal. So in federal politics at least, their House vote is cast on similar grounds to the true major-party swinger. The third-party swinger almost always gives a first preference for minor parties in Senate and other Upper House elections.

An increasing number of swinging voters in Australia are alienated voters. These voters decide on candidates largely for negative reasons, usually voting to punish a party or a candidate. More often than not, an alienated swinger will end up voting against the government of the day in House of Representatives elections although in some cases they may cast a conscious informal vote rather than support either the government or the equally distrusted opposition.

The airheads and drongos are the apoliticals of our society. They don't know much about politics, and they care even less. If it were not for compulsory enrolment and voting, this group would hardly matter as they would hardly ever show up at the polls. But in the Australian system, these voters may cast a donkey vote (vote all the numbers in order either up or down the ballot), vote informal, vote the name they like best, vote the how-to-vote ticket on the top of those given to them at the voting booth, or who knows what? Often, the drongos and airheads don't even know how they voted once the exercise is completed. It makes the task of studying their 'preferences' very difficult indeed.

The local candidate inconsistents often have a party identification, but more importantly, they are personality-oriented voters. This group votes primarily for the local candidate—very often the sitting MP—whom they know and support. Often this voter is returning a favour done by that MP in the past.A good 'personal vote' of 3 to 5 percent can often help a locally-popular MP withstand a general swing against his or her party in the area. In 1987, for example, the sitting Labor MP for Phillip (the Bondi–Randwick area of Sydney), Jeanette McHugh, ran 10 percent ahead of her party's Senate ticket and easily retained her seat, despite swings against the ALP in all neighbouring seats. Interviews by the Sydney University Voter Research Project after both the 1984 and 1987 elections showed that McHugh was able to retain support among softly-committed voters that might have been lost to a different Labor candidate, especially among left-wing voters with strong views on peace-related issues, on environmental issues and amongst women with a feminist orientation.

Another group of waverers at any election become disenchanted with their 'normal' party and entertain the possibility of a switch in their support. Generally the power of their Labor or Liberal loyalties keeps them with their preferred party, usually in both the House and Senate elections. Sometimes, however, even lifetime loyalists will desert their party on a single issue that is particularly salient to them personally. For example, after the 1984 election the Sydney University Voter Research Project interviewed several lifetime Labor pensioners who had abandoned the ALP due to the Labor Government's assets test on pensions, which was a major factor in the Liberal campaign advertising for that election (Chaples, 1985).

Finally, there are the Senate protestors, a group not discussed in the traditional literature on swinging voters. These voters are usually people with a 'normal' psychologial identification with one of the major parties but who use the Senate ballot to indicate some dissatisfaction with that party.

In recent elections, as the Hawke Government has altered Labor's long-held policies on issues like industrial relations and uranium mining, Labor Party identifiers have used the Nuclear Disarmament Party, the Greens and The Australian Democrats as vehicles for their Senate support while continuing to vote Labor in House elections. Supporters of Call-to-Australia, the Harradine movement in Tasmania and, in earlier elections, the Democratic Labor Party, used their objections to the views of major parties on moral issues in a similar manner. In 1987, many Liberal progressives and civil libertarians voted for the Australian Democrats for the Senate for similar reasons. The Australian Democrats, who were founded on the 'keep-the-bastards honest slogan', have attempted to institutionalise their party as a middle-ground Senate protest party, capitalising on both proportional representation and increasing voter cynicism towards both major parties to provide their party with an institutionalised position in the middle of the Australian electoral process.

Determinants of partisanship in Australia

The literature on Australian voters contains many references to factors that separate the preferences of some groups from others. Ethnic and racial background, place of residence, religion, age and many other factors have been said to separate some groups of voters from others on certain political issues. But few topics in contemporary social science have been the subject of more controversy than the discussion about the relevance of socio-economic class to voter loyalties in Australia.

The two most recognised contemporary scholars of mass political behaviour in Australia have been largely in agreement in arguing that there is a declining relevance of class to both individual voting and to determining the party identification of most voters. As Don Aitkin has written in his second edition (1982):

> No part of the first edition of *Stability and Change in Australian Politics* aroused more criticism than the chapter on class and party. An antagonistic response might have been expected, since the thrust of the argument had been that class was not a very good explanation of Australian partisanship . . .

While Aitkin's later revision of his book suggested some alteration in this picture—(he documents, for example, a 'massive decline in non-manual workers' support for the non-Labor parties')—he still concludes that 'measures of class explain little of the distribution of partisanship.' (Aitkin, 1983: 19–21).

David Kemp has been even more emphatic in maintaining that changes in Australian society have led to a decline in the significance of social class for political life. Kemp believes that:

- Australians show little contemporary evidence of class consciousness. Class labels 'are lightly worn, have no consistent content and are unstable over time'.
- Sixty percent of contemporary Australians subjectively view themselves as 'middle class' while only 37 percent see themselves as 'working class'. (Aitkin's 1979 findings were 56 percent claiming to be middle class and 26 percent working class.)
- Class self-placement of voters is only weakly associated with party choice and accounts for only about 6 percent of the variance in explaining differences in party identification. The occupation of the voter explains about 4 percent of the variation in voting.
- New parties like the Australian Democrats are even less related to the class structure than are the Labor and Liberal Parties. In addition, the major parties have been forced to modify their traditional class appeal because of a high level of materialism amongst Australian manual workers,

> because of 'the absence of issues with a distinctive class impact and the emergence of a society in which only a minority see themselves as working class and which has low class consciousness and where a winning electoral strategy cannot be based on class appeals alone' (Kemp, 1977: 63).

While the arguments of Aitkin and Kemp are grounded on solid empirical evidence, it may well be that the relevance of social class to Australian politics has yet to be resolved. Chris Chamberlain has demonstrated that there may be major differences between the Australian middle class and working class in their political participation and in the way they relate to the political process.

In Chamberlain's carefully designed study (1983, chapter 4), working-class Australians were found to be less likely to accept elections as representative of voters' opinions, were more skeptical about the ability of our politicans to understand the problems of ordinary people and were less trusting of their ability to keep election promises. While 69 percent of upper-middle and 64 percent of middle-class people demonstrated a broad commitment to the Australian political system, only 45 percent of working-class respondents did so in Chamberlain's study

Likewise, in a study of working class voters from the Mt Druitt housing estate in the outer western suburbs of Sydney, I found there were certain kinds of attitudes that Labor and non-Labor voters held in common. Working-class voters of both a Labor and non-Labor persuasion put equal and substantial emphasis on the importance of family life, exhibited equal faith in the law and police, demonstrated equal support for the Australian system of social security benefits and exhibited similar levels of support for their local council (low) and their state government (moderate).

In contrast, however, working class Labor supporters demonstrated substantially lower levels of general political efficacy, weaker trust in the Federal Government and greater support for electing a socialist alternative to government. Moreover, working-class Labor voters were far more likely to believe there was a class bias in government and in Australian society than were working-class Liberal voters (Chaples, 1980: 434–35).

These findings support, at least in part, the argument of David Kemp that 'cultural position' on key philosophical issues is clearly more potent than is class position in influencing partisan orientation. Still, the inability of researchers to successfully determine a voter's class does not mean that class factors should be ignored. Better research will be needed on class and voting before we can say this with more authority.

Gender and voting

According to Aitkin and Bell (1984):

> Of all the changes that have taken place in the Australian electorate in the past 20 years the most profound has been in the political outlook of women. For generations, women were the mainstay of conservative politics in

> Australia. They liked the traditional and the familiar; they liked strong and relatively paternal governments; they were not at all in favour of political and social change in areas such as censorship or immigration or in anything to do with the family. Above all, they were much less likely to vote for the Australian Labor Party.

Yet most of the evidence from the 1980s confirms a growing interest in politics amongst women and a substantial reduction in the gender-gap in voting. While women in the 1960s were about 11 percent less likely to vote Labor than were men, by 1979 that gap was reduced to 7 percent, and by the 1980s to somewhere between 3 and 5 percent. And amongst the younger age groups, the gender gap seems to have disappeared altogether.

Why have women moved away from their traditional non-Labor biases? The most cited hypothesis has to do with women's increased participation in the workforce. As more women became financially independent, their politics have also become more independent of their husbands.

Closely associated with this has been the reduction in the gender gap in formal education in Australia. More women stay at school for longer periods, and more women now go on to tertiary studies. This has contributed to their employability, and it also has helped account for their increased knowledge about politics and their greater collective political skills.

Thirdly, the women's movement itself has provided greater political leadership in the 1970s and 1980s, and that leadership has often been favourably disposed to the position of the Labor Party on key women's issues in preference to their Liberal and National Party opponents.

So important has the independence of women become that in the 1987 federal election suburban women in the age group 24 to 34 were identified by Labor Party research as the single most crucial group of swinging voters. The John Singleton agency invented the Wendy Wood commercials in the 1987 federal election campaign specifically to win support among this group of women. According to Hugh Mackay (1987), 'Women in the early phases of adulthood and motherhood are possibly the most destabilised sub-group of a generally destabilised community'.

While the success of such efforts to target the young women's vote remains a subject of debate, the heightened awareness of a gender dimension in Australian politics cannot be questioned.

Conclusions

The Australian electorate remains a substantial and dynamic puzzle in the late 1980's. Much of the Australian electorate continues to sit on the sidelines while a small group of partisan operatives competes for their attention and support. There is little indication that the combined spectator and apathetic groups of voters will get any more involved in electoral politics in the foreseeable future.

References

Aitkin, D. (1983) 'The Changing Australian Electorate', in H.R. Penniman (ed.) *Australia at the Polls: The National Elections of 1980 and 1983* Sydney: George Allen and Unwin

—— (1982) *Stability and Change in Australian Politics*, 2nd edn, Canberra: ANU Press

Aitkin, D. and Bell, G. (1984) 'Why Women Favour Labor' *The Bulletin* May 22, pp. 38–9

Cameron, R. (1973) 'Swingers: Undecided Mavericks versus Conformist Switchers', in H. Mayer (ed.) *Labor to Power* Sydney: Angus and Robertson

Chaples, E.A. (1980) 'Political Ideas and Party Preferences Among Working Class Australians', in H. Mayer and H. Nelson (eds) *Australian Politics: A Fifth Reader* Melbourne: Longman Cheshire

—— (1985) 'Softly Committed Voters and The 1984 Election', in D. Jaensch and N. Bierbaum (eds) *The Hawke Government: Past, Present, Future* Canberra: Australasian Political Studies Association

Chamberlain, C. (1983) *Class Consciousness in Australia* Syney: George Allen and Unwin

Connell, R.W. (1977) *Ruling Class, Ruling Culture* Cambridge: Cambridge University Press

Kemp, D.A. (1977) 'The Australian Electorate', in H.R. Penniman (ed.) *Australian National Elections of 1977* Canberra: ANU Press

—— (1978) *Society and Electoral Behaviour in Australia* St Lucia: University of Queensland Press

Mackay, Hugh (1987) 'Wendy and the Angry Young Women' *Times-on-Sunday* 12 July, p. 6

Verba, S. and Nie, A.H. (1972) *Participation in America: Political Democracy and Social Equality* New York: Harper and Row

Wilson, P. and Western, J.S. (1973) 'Politics, Participation and Attitudes', in H. Mayer and H. Nelson (eds) *Australian Politics: A Third Reader* Melbourne: Cheshire

Index